GOD'S APPRENTICE

GOD'S APPRENTICE

The autobiography of
Stephen Neill

Edited by
Dr E. M. Jackson

Hodder & Stoughton
LONDON SYDNEY AUCKLAND TORONTO

British Library Cataloguing in Publication Data
Neill, Stephen *1900-1984*
  God's apprentice: an autobiography of Stephen Neill
  1. Social sciences. Statistical methods
  I. Title
  262.12092

ISBN 0-340-54490-2

Published by Hodder & Stoughton, a division of Hodder and Stoughton Ltd, Mill Road, Dunton Green, Sevenoaks, Kent TN13 2YA.
Editorial Office: 47 Bedford Square, London WC1B 3DP.

Photoset by Chippendale Type Ltd., Otley, West Yorkshire.

Printed in Great Britain by Clays Ltd, St. Ives plc

Contents

Foreword

One morning in July 1984 an overseas scholar who had an appointment with Bishop Stephen Neill found him dead, still seated in his chair, with *The Spectator* on his lap. Alone and suddenly the indefatigable reader and writer had stolen away, reading to the end.

The long manuscript of which this book is an abridgement was described by him as 'these somewhat random recollections of grace abounding to the chief of sinners'. Stephen Neill had intended one day, after completing more urgent work, to write a proper autobiography. It is good fortune, nonetheless, to have these recollections, if for no other reason than that they are good reading. A born linguist with a fastidious 'feel' for words, blessed with a tenacious memory full of anecdotes and circumstantial detail, he could lay a spell on any audience. But in fact this book is much more. It holds up a mirror to his times, as well as being a self-portrait (distorted, it may be) by a complex and extraordinary character.

It is disturbing reading – a story of contrasts. There is the pathos of frustrated ambition, the dogging of ill-health, insomnia, psychological imbalance and bouts of depression; but also a childlike enjoyment of praise – 'wave upon wave of applause', he records – and the elation of wielding a formidable intellect and the polyglot gift to hold huge audiences spellbound with lucid expositions in their own languages. There is the boyish friendliness – playing football in bare feet with the Indian lads, or delighted by young people who, when asked what they had come for, said 'We just came' (meaning, we like your company); this, hand-in-hand with a magnifying of episcopal pomp and a gratification with its privileges. There is the fresh and ever-curious mind, but also a reactionary streak, clinging to the incomparable 1662 Prayer Book and making sweeping assertions about the unsurpassability of his favourite writers. An ingratiating charm lives next door to an Irish temper, controlled only with difficulty; the apostolic asceticism is no stranger to a relish for good cuisine. Vanity threatens to spoil one who is conscious of exceptional talents and who knows that he was virtually named for several bishoprics (not to say an archbishopric)

7

and for one of the most illustrious of academic positions; yet, in his heart of hearts, he knows with Bunyan that it is grace abounding and grace alone.

After a conscious commitment to Christ as a boy, Stephen Neill's constant desire was to place his remarkable abilities at the disposal of God. Relinquishing the coveted Fellowship he had won at Trinity College, Cambridge, he plunged into evangelism in South India, using his brilliance and his gift for friendship to get inside the minds and affections alike of simple villagers and sophisticated pandits. India was his first and last love. The premature termination of his ministry there (whatever its real cause or circumstances) was traumatic. Everything else that he did was pushed at him by circumstances – the toilsome years of ecumenical organising and drafting, the Chairs at Hamburg and Nairobi; even the very active last years in Oxford. What perhaps scarcely comes home in this abbreviated story is the astonishing number and the consistently high quality of the books Stephen Neill wrote, and the successful series he initiated and edited of simple World Christian Books in many languages; and all this, regarded by him as merely incidental to his *magnum opus* – alas, left unfinished at his death – the history of Christianity in India.

In these pages readers will find plenty of laughs, as well as moments of difficulty in holding back tears (sometimes because of what may lie between the lines). Sometimes, again, there are passages which illuminate the meeting of East and West, or the birth of the Church of South India, or movements and trends, political and theological. But above all, readers will want to give thanks for the grace of God – grace abounding – and for the extraordinary achievements of this much-tempted, brilliant, enigmatic man.

C. F. D. Moule, CBE, DD, FBA

Editor's Introduction

'If I manage to complete in ten years all that I have in mind to do, I may then perhaps sit down to write my autobiography, and that would be a far more difficult and exacting task than the setting down of these somewhat random recollections of grace abounding to the chief of sinners over a period of rather more than seventy years.'

These words, written in 1973, towards the end of the penultimate chapter of this autobiography of Bishop Stephen Neill, provide the best clue to the nature of this book and to the task which subsequently fell to the editor to perform when it was not revised. Presumably this was because Neill did not finish his three-volume *History of Christianity in India*, apart from the existing books he wanted to revise or re-write. However, 'random' these recollections were not. They were arranged chronologically and thematically, with lengthy historical passages to explain the background to events. Viewed in retrospect, Neill felt he could show the guiding hand of God moving him from one task to another, but whereas sometimes he says he seemed to hear a voice within himself telling him to go somewhere or to do something, this was often preceded or followed by months and years of darkness, ill-health and 'days of small things'.

The second clue comes in the account of his conversion, surely the most important event in Neill's life, when he writes that he will not go into much detail because this autobiography is a record of events, not an *apologia pro vita sua*. Nevertheless, he does go to great lengths to justify his conduct in certain crises in his life. Some of the most significant pages were in the original text of the first chapter, where he described his decades-long struggle against depression, accidie and insomnia, the consequences of mutual laterality (clumsiness due to being neither right- nor left-handed) and an unusual circulatory disorder. Undoubtedly his ill-health was a great handicap to him, and is one of the reasons why he was forced to return from India and was not offered an English diocesan bishopric or a professorship. However, Neill eschews all speculation on what might have been, and concentrates on writing a narrative.

The editing of Neill's manuscript, whether by myself or in the publisher's subsequent redaction, has therefore greatly altered the balance of the book. Unfortunately the accounts of his ceaseless travels, his attendances at conferences, his evangelistic campaigns and general adventures had to be severely cut, but his reflections, comments and opinions have been retained as far as possible. However, this book should still be of interest to the serious student of contemporary church history and mission, as well as providing inspiration both to those who knew Neill personally and to those who did not.

The following general editorial principles were applied throughout. Firstly, there was the need to reduce a typescript of over 1,000 pages to a publishable length, so some anecdotes which were interesting in themselves, but which did not add any insights, either to contemporary history or to our understanding of Neill himself, were removed. Then repetition was ruthlessly dealt with. For example, one anecdote about Bishop Lesslie Newbigin appeared four times without naming him, though he himself related the story in an early work. Obsolete descriptions of forgotten world events have been removed as well. Finally, gratuitous hurt and libel of individuals no longer able to defend themselves have been removed because Neill himself said he did not want to hurt anyone, and this is why he does not identify people of whom he wishes to say something negative. One suspects that such passages were written in the same way in which people write angry letters to the papers late at night and tear them up in the morning. Passages have been removed where there were indications that Neill would have excised them himself. Further, some passages are simply historically inaccurate, and since Neill was himself such a brilliant church historian, it is surely justifiable to change dates and other facts when these are demonstrably wrong. Similarly, names have been checked as carefully as possible. The editor checked the French and German, and is indebted to Professor C. F. D. Moule for correcting the Latin and Greek, and to Bishop Newbigin for the Tamil and Indian place names. Grammar was changed where Neill lapsed into German (and there are reasons for believing that at times he thought in German), but little could be done about persistent grammar patterns due to over-exposure to Greek grammar. Since mistakes are not evident in his other writings, this is presumably something he or another editor removed.

Unfortunately the requirements of editing have sometimes meant that all mention of a subject or person has been lost. For instance, all three accounts of Neill saving someone from drowning have gone, because too many pages were spent setting the scene. His feats climbing mountains and his enjoyment of lavish meals have also gone. So too has the story behind the writing of his classic *A History of the Ecumenical Movement 1517-1948*. Often it was clear where his mind had gone off at a tangent, and by continuing the line of thought without diversion one could produce a shortened Neill narrative. In other places a précis using Neill phrases has been used. The description of how Neill edited other people's books makes this poetic justice. Nothing has been done to this manuscript which he has not himself once done. The original typescript is available for consultation by bona fide scholars in the CMS archives, The Library, the University of Birmingham, UK.

The editor wishes to thank Bishop Lesslie Newbigin for constant help and advice, and the loan of books to check facts; Father Kundu of Calcutta for his recollections and research concerning Archbishop Foss Westcott; Dr van der Bent, former Librarian of the World Council of Churches, for pertinent comments and spelling corrections; and colleagues and friends for their enthusiastic support for the project. Finally, the task was made much easier with the generous help of the staff of the Selly Oak Colleges' Library.

Dr E. M. Jackson
Birmingham

1

Beginnings

It would be hard to imagine any greater contrast than that which existed between my parents – in background, tradition, gifts and temperament. It was characteristic that my father passed on his grey eyes to his daughters, and my mother her brown eyes to her four sons.

My father's father, Henry James Neill, who went out to Australia somewhere about the middle of the nineteenth century, did not do anything so foolish as dig for gold, but struck gold organising a provisioning service for the goldminers. Having married and made a good deal of money, he returned as a comparatively young man to Northern Ireland, and bought the beautiful property of Rockport, at Craigaird, about six miles from Belfast. Rockport, now a well-known preparatory school for boys, has changed remarkably little over the years. There has been a great deal of building all around, but it still has the path down to its own little cove on the Belfast lough, and the same splendid outlook across the lough to the mountains of Antrim. After Grandfather's return to Ireland, the family grew to six sons and six daughters. So large a family demanded an increase in income; accordingly Henry James took over a derelict wine and spirits business, and this, like everything else that he touched, turned to gold under his hands. He must have been a very wealthy man when he died, and he made a wonderful Forsyte will. He seems to have divided his fortune equally among the eleven surviving children, but whereas the boys received their share absolutely, the girls could not touch their capital, and were debarred by the will from leaving anything outside the family. Nevertheless, my invalid Aunt Ethel, who died in 1913, left a life interest in £3,000 each to her faithful companion and two Brett cousins in Belfast, all of whom lived beyond the age of ninety, so that the last dribble from the will of Grandfather, who died in 1894, came to me in 1968.

The picture I have received is that of a typical prosperous middle-class Victorian family. All seem to have lived in considerable awe of their father, who had a capricious and at times violent temper, but all adored their mother, who seems to have incorporated all the virtues of kindness, patience, gentleness and integrity. I imagine that there was a fair amount of Victorian discipline, but not enough to suppress personality, or to prevent the children developing their gifts, and growing into real people with distinct personalities.

There are, in fact, two different kinds of Neills, the cautious and the imprudent. The two eldest sons, Willy, who became a successful lawyer in London, and Harry, who carried on the family business in Madras, Balfour the doctor, Reggie, who was born with only three fingers on his right hand and never succeeded in overcoming this disability, and my father Charlie, all had this streak of imprudence, and while not reckless, managed to get through a great deal of money without having very much to show for it at the end of the day.

It is the aunts, however, who made the most lasting impression on an observant small boy. Aunt Isabel (Ferrar) was my ecclesiastical aunt. When I visited her in later years, she was usually able to produce a bishop for dinner, or at least an archdeacon or a couple of canons. Aunt Julie Crawford must, I think, have had less sense of the value of money than anyone else who has ever lived. She enjoyed ill-health for sixty years, and finally died at the age of eighty-seven, having enriched one generation of doctors after another. There is no doubt whatever that the majority of these illnesses would be called psychosomatic today, a pointer, perhaps, to an element of instability in the family. She died with her accounts so heavily overdrawn that her will could not be executed.

Defects the Neills had in many directions. One accomplishment they had in an almost unsurpassable degree – that of making supremely happy marriages. Some time after Uncle Tom Cartright died, Aunt Janey told me how, as a girl, she had seen him come up the path to Rockport with two of her brothers, and had known immediately that he was the one for her; and then added, 'It was a wonderful forty years,' in the same tone of voice one would use for saying, 'It was a wonderful weekend.' My parents lived together for fifty-two years. Some time after my father died, my mother said to me one day, quite casually, 'Of course, you know, we were really sweethearts right up to the end.' One who has grown up in such an atmosphere of happy and lasting marriages always starts with the assumption that a marriage will be a success, and never fails to experience a slight shock when these high expectations are not fulfilled. Perhaps in later generations we have not quite lived up to the standards of our elders, but on the whole, the same good fortune seems to have followed us, and as far as I can recall, there has been only one divorce in the family in seventy years.

There was not, as far as I can gather, very much religion in my grandfather's home. Naturally Charlie, my father, who was born on 12 November 1868, was baptised in the local parish church, where I preached on the last Sunday before the outbreak of war in 1939. There would be christenings, confirmations and weddings in church, conventional attendance at Mattins every Sunday, and the occasional presence at Holy Communion. Yet my father, a naturally religious person, had from an early age a strong desire to enter the ordained ministry of the Church. At this point the voice of the Victorian father decreed he was to be a doctor, and that was that. Henceforward his education was directed to this end.

My father spoke from time to time of his schooldays, and always with the deepest distaste. Take a very shy and sensitive Irish boy, and fling him across the Irish Channel to the wastes of East Anglia and the rigours of an English public school in the 1870s, and it is hardly likely he will be happy. My father claimed to have been very good at Greek prose, and he certainly developed far more than the average athletic ability, but nothing was done to develop in him intellectual or aesthetic tastes. Whatever he acquired of these came much later and, in the main, as a result of his intensely earnest Christian faith.

Strangely enough, my wealthy grandfather kept his schoolboy sons very short of money; not, I think, deliberately, but simply through a total failure to understand their needs. As soon as they left school, they seem to have had as much money as they wanted. So when my father left school and entered Gonville and Caius College, Cambridge, to begin his medical studies, he passed from a world of suffering to a new life of almost unlimited and intoxicating freedom. It is at this point that the two branches of my family tree begin to converge.

The Monros are a highland clan and have their own tartan. My maternal grandfather, James Monro, was born in Edinburgh into a well-to-do family. From an early age he manifested intellectual gifts of the highest possible order. By the age of eighteen he had passed through the University of Edinburgh, collecting on the way the gold medal in philosophy. In 1857 he came third in the examination for the Indian Civil Service. In view of his youth he was kept back for a year, part of which he spent studying law in Berlin, but in 1858 he set off to govern the British Empire. Before he left Scotland he wrote on the fly-leaf of his Bible the noble words of the prophet Micah, 'to do justice, to love mercy and to walk humbly with thy God'. From these high standards he never declined. Unfortunately an attack of poliomyelitis left him slightly lame in both legs, and for the rest of his life he walked with the support of a stout stick, a very formidable figure in the eyes of small grandsons.

On his first leave in 1862, James Monro was married to Ruth Littlejohn of Aberdeen. Her grandfather was James Bentley, who became Professor of Hebrew and Oriental Languages in Aberdeen in 1797, and who 'came out' in the 'Disruption' of 1843, renouncing his post, as one of the 474 ministers who sacrificed their benefices, manses and churches to follow Thomas Chalmers (d. 1847) into the Free Church of Scotland. A very shy man, he seems never to have exercised an active ministry in the Church, but his deep piety and concern for the well-being of all mankind led him to gather his friends together to pray for the evangelisation of the world. His family claimed a connection with Richard Bentley, of Trinity College, Cambridge, the greatest of all English classical scholars, and 'Bentley' has remained a common family name up until this time.

So, some time in 1862 Ruth Monro arrived in India to begin a companionship of fifty-seven years and to share in all her husband's interests and concerns. She found herself at once the mistress of a somewhat palatial establishment. This was to a certain extent a matter of necessity. In Northern India certain tasks can be performed only by certain castes, and if a servant of the appropriate caste is not retained, the work will simply not be done. In days when there was no running water, no indoor plumbing or sanitation, and daily riding, whether on horseback or in a carriage, was considered essential for one's health, the staff of Europeans in a position of importance was bound to be large.

My grandfather arrived in India at a fortunate moment for anyone engaged in the service of the government of India. That was the year in which Queen Victoria, in a famous proclamation, brought to an end the anachronistic rule of the East India Company, and declared that for the future responsibility for the welfare of the peoples of India would rest with the Crown and Parliament of the United Kingdom. In practice little changed; the men who had served the Company stayed on to serve the Crown and the old cumbrous and bureaucratic system survived, but there was a new spirit. The spirit of the Evangelical Revival had deeply penetrated the Indian administration. The leaders, as men of their own day, looked out on human history from the standpoint of divine providence, and as they considered the strange series of events by which a handful of men from a distant and Western isle had become masters of the destiny of India, could not but conclude that British dominion in India was something more than a mere accident, and must be seen in relation to the fulfilment of a divine plan. The word 'responsibility' occurs with monotonous iteration in the documents of that day – responsibility to bring to India good government, order and education, without undue interference with the habits and customs of the people.

One of the greatest of Indian administrators under the Company had been James Thomason, son of a former curate of Charles Simeon in Cambridge, who had become one of the group of 'pious chaplains' in Calcutta. James Thomason, brought up in England by Simeon, had drunk deeply of the waters of the Evangelical Revival, and carried into the tedious work of the administrator the calm and genial holiness which he had learned from his mentors. He proved not only to be a prince among rulers, but, by his work in the Punjab, to have the rare capacity to train others to rule great provinces. James Monro was to join this tradition of just government.

In 1858 there was plenty for a young servant of the Crown to do in the way of clearing up disorder and setting up the structure of the new India. James Monro set himself to master the flexible Bengali language and to make himself completely at home with the mind of the village people. This was his home. Again and again he would say to missionaries and to others who had ears to hear, 'The life of India is in the villages.' Steadily he climbed the ladder of a successful career while children came to the Monro home. Jessye Bentley, who never married, was followed by Charles George, doctor and parson, a most eloquent, skilful expositor of the Scriptures, Margaret Penelope (my mother, 'Daisy', born 1870), and William Douglas, an excellent but somewhat erratic scholar, who taught for years at Winchester College, then returned to India to investigate the languages of Kashmir and the North-West Frontier, and the problems of Bible translations there. Then disaster struck, just as he was thought to be next in line for the lieutenant-governorship of Bengal. Those were the days of the liberal Viceroy, Lord Ripon, who was convinced that the time had come for Indians to be more closely associated with the work of administration, and that a beginning should be made with local self-government. All District Officers were required to submit a report. Grandfather simply wrote what he knew – that under the Act as proposed, the wealthy landowning families would control the elections and select the candidates, and thus gain a legal basis for the depredations which they had previously carried out illegally. This information was most displeasing to those in high authority, but music in the ears of the planters' lobby. The family tradition is that Grandfather's report was stolen from the Secretariat in Calcutta, printed, and a copy sent to every Member of Parliament. Grandfather was entirely innocent, but felt that he had to resign.

When he returned home, his standing was so high that he was taken into the Criminal Investigation Department at Scotland Yard, where he quickly rose to become Commissioner. These were the days of the Fenian outrages, when the new Lord Lieutenant of Ireland, Lord Frederick Cavendish, was assassinated in broad daylight in Dublin, and it was Grandfather's task to put an end to these proceedings. In after years, an evening of 'Grandpa's stories' was an unfailing source of delight to a circle of awed and entranced grandchildren.

Then in 1890 disaster struck once again. I have never quite understood what occurred. Apparently Grandfather had undertaken to get improved conditions for the men who served under him and for whom he had the greatest admiration (a feeling they reciprocated). This became a political matter, and an attempt was made to bribe him with a KCB to withdraw his opposition to government plans. Once again he felt compelled to resign rather than tarnish his honour. It has been alleged that he 'leaked' information, and therefore had to go, but this is inconceivable in a man of his integrity. I fancy that this was the smear circulated by the government to cover up their own shady actions, and to account for the disappearance of a popular figure.

So there was Grandfather, only fifty-two, and for the second time out of a job, under a cloud, and without any of the recognition which was his due. What should he do? He decided to return to India as a simple missionary, to work in the area he had once governed. Apprised of this bizarre intention, his four children said that they would come, too.

In those years remarkable things were happening in the religious life of Britain, which did not leave the universities untouched. Groups of pious undergraduates had held prayer-meetings before, but now these were systematically organised with a view not only to deepening individual spiritual life, but to evangelising the university and beyond. In 1878 the Cambridge Inter-Collegiate Christian Union came into being, the progenitor of Christian Unions in almost every university under the sun. In 1882 Dwight L. Moody was let loose on Cambridge, and after a highly unpromising start was successful in winning the hearts of his hearers and in leading many of them to a living faith in Christ. The 'Cambridge Seven' – the three Studd brothers who avenged England's reputation at cricket after a series of humiliating defeats by Australia in 1881, and four other athletes, made an incredible impact by touring British universities before fulfilling their vows on conversion to renounce everything and go to China as missionaries. J. E. Studd, visiting Cornell University in the United States, won for Christ an undecided young man named John Raleigh Mott, who was to become one of the chief architects of the modern ecumenical movement.

In those days Mott was primarily an evangelist, working through the YMCA, and the World Student Christian Federation, which he founded in 1895. He was very well read, a clear thinker, and a man of prayer, as much at home with French Catholic mystics as with Protestant works. He lacked the orator's graces, and scorned emotional appeals, but the intense earnestness and conviction with which he spoke lent eloquence to his words. With his refrain, 'Give your hearts to the Lord Jesus, and your lives to his service,' he led hundreds of men and women to the point where they had to make a decision: either to accept Christ unconditionally, or deliberately to lose their own soul. Many went sorrowfully away, others entered with great gladness.

What stirred the students most of all was the slogan Mott adopted as the watchword of the student movement, which he persuaded many church bodies to endorse as well, 'The evangelisation of the world in this generation.' Essentially it meant that this generation (of students in particular) was responsible for world evangelisation; but Mott's appeal was coloured by contemporary eschatology and calculations as to how many missionaries were needed to make sure everyone in the world heard the gospel. The watchword was criticised by the Germans for much the same reasons as they criticised the Social Gospel a generation later, because they thought Mott meant the world could be converted in a generation; and by J. H. Oldham and Frank Lenwood, British students who became missionary leaders, for impracticality; and by S. K. Datta, then an Indian medical student and British student leader, for imperialism. Mott's point was that the whole world was open to the preaching of the Christian gospel as it had never been before and – we know now – as it never would be again. Those were the days in which it was taken for granted that to become a 'foreign missionary' – to go forth into 'heathen darkness', to do and to dare in the name of Christ in the face of the immense powers of the non-Christian world – was the highest vocation that could come to Christian men and women.

When Charlie Monro decided to study medicine at Cambridge, he moved into the centre of this maelstrom of Christian talk and activity. It was not long before he made the acquaintance of his fellow medical student Charlie Neill. My father, who so far had known nothing other than the meaningless repetitions of English public school religion and the sober, unemotional piety of the Church of Ireland, must have been constantly amazed and at times overwhelmed by what he found in Cambridge. However, when a young man thrust the New Testament into his hand, open at the passage which reads: 'I know whom I have believed, and am persuaded that he is able to keep that which I have committed unto him against that day,' and asked, 'Can you say that?', Father thought for a moment and replied, 'Yes, I can.' He dated his conversion from that time and place.

Some time later Daisy Monro announced that she also was going to study medicine. At that date the University was not open to women, so she had to take the hospital course, which gave a fully registrable qualification, and survived into our own day, but has now been abolished. Christians in those days really were Christians. My mother has told me that in four years as a student she never once failed to keep her 'quiet time' of one hour spent in prayer and Bible study before breakfast.

In the hall of our house we always had a picture of the Forth Bridge near Edinburgh, and I had never been able to understand why. Then one day it came out. Somewhere about 1892 Charlie Neill and Daisy Munro went for a long walk together in the direction of the Forth Bridge, and found that they agreed remarkably well together. But both being inordinately shy, neither was able to give the other any hint that their total devotion to Christ was being accompanied by a steadily growing and equally total devotion to one another. If they had not been so shy, I might be several years older than I am.

Thus it came about that when Grandfather announced his intention of starting a medical mission in Lower Bengal, he had three doctors ready to hand, indeed four, since my mother's great friend at college, Mary Simpson (later MacNicol), had been drawn into the party and was also prepared to launch out into the deep. But the plan did not advance to execution as smoothly as might have been expected.

Always a friend of order, Grandfather was not in favour of hairbrained individual adventures, and never had any intention of setting up an independent mission. The only missionary society working in the area of Bengal which he had chosen for the operation was the Church Missionary Society; this Society was therefore notified of his willingness to enter their service; but his plan ran counter to everything that the Society's patrons and administrators had come to believe.

Medical missionary work had been practised in India by both men and women since at least 1793, but the CMS had come to consider it almost as axiomatic that the place for medical missions was in areas, particularly Muslim areas, in which any other kind of approach to the population was almost impossible. For this reason, a few years later, all the Christian medical work which had been started in Tinnevelly, South India, was closed down, as the area was believed to be fully open to the gospel.[1] Consequently, when Grandfather made his offer, the Society vacillated, even though almost all the expenses had been guaranteed, and there would be no burden on the Society. At length Grandfather fixed a deadline, and when it passed without an answer, he withdrew the offer. The authorities in the Society responded by almost going down on their knees, imploring him to withdraw his withdrawal. Grandfather said no. The Society had had ample time to decide. He and his children had prayed and fixed the date beyond which they would not wait. Now there was nothing more to be said.

So back to India Grandfather went, supported by his Indian Civil Service pension of £1,000 a year and the prayers and support of a multitude of friends. While deciding where to settle, and awaiting the arrival of the rest of the team, he took the opportunity to give a number of lectures in English to educated audiences, firmly pointing out the consequences for his hearers if they really took seriously the Arya Samaj cry of 'Back to the Vedas' and had to abandon later Hindu customs of caste, idolatry, etc.[2] Then his choice fell on Ranaghat, a railway junction about fifty miles north of Calcutta. On the borders of the town the buildings of the mission hospital rose, and were given the name Doyabari, the house of mercy.

The missionaries were quite clear about what they wished to accomplish. Everything was to be kept as simple as possible, and as near to the standard of life of the people as was consistent with efficient working. Surgery was to be practised on a large scale, but major operations and difficult cases were to be sent to government hospitals. It was not the intention of this missionary party to immobilise themselves by the erection of massive buildings. It was always the hope that once the work at Doyabari was firmly established, it would be taken over by Indian doctors, who were coming forward in increasing numbers, and that the foreigners would then be free to go forward as pioneers in regions as yet untouched by the gospel. There then arose a difficulty. Medical work was to be of the highest efficiency, but this was to be a Christian and not simply a humanitarian enterprise. There should be no workers who were not at the same time consecrated Christians. Ranaghat was in the Nadia (Nuddea) area where there had been a mass movement into the Church following the floods and famine of 1836–8. Bishop Daniel Wilson of Calcutta had visited the mission and declared it the dawn of a new age in India. But little had come to fruition; the standards of Christian conviction and conduct left a good deal to be desired. Consequently the mission found itself unable to employ a large number of Indian Christians in the less technical jobs, and much was done by Europeans that, apart from this strict demand for spiritual excellence, might have been done by local forces. So my godmother, Rosamund Brown, a lady of independent means, undertook the entire responsibility for the registration of patients, as they crowded in from innumerable villages.[3]

Apart from dealing with those affected by the diseases endemic in a tropical climate, there was a good deal of surgery, and it was not long before my father became well known as an eye-surgeon. During the sometimes long periods of waiting, patients were invited to listen to a simple proclamation of the gospel. In this my grandfather, with his excellent Bengali, took his share with everyone else. One frenzied day, three doctors, with the necessary aides, treated just over 1,200 patients.

By committing himself to this work my father had landed himself in a painful dilemma. He had found in the work satisfaction of a kind that he had never dreamed of. All his instincts as a doctor found here the fullest outreach. He was working in a fellowship of Christians which, not without collisions of temperament, had worked out the principles of a common life of very high quality, and he had found the perfect partner for his life's ideals. He could not imagine himself ever being so happy in any other work. But here was the problem. Supposing he proposed to Daisy Monro and she refused him, it would be far too painful for both to continue in this intimate Christian fellowship: he would have to leave. My mother must have gone through a time of perplexity calculated to

try even the profoundest Christian faith. She had been in love
with Charlie Neill for years. She knew the shyness under which he
laboured, and must often have wondered if he would ever pluck up
courage to speak what in Ireland is so appropriately called 'the hard
word'. Moreover, in the open and busy life in which they shared,
and with the extreme precautions in regard to the relationship
between the sexes, which always have to be observed in India,
it was quite difficult for them ever to find a moment in which to
be alone together.

At last the moment came. One evening the two arrived rather
late at the weekly prayer-meeting, looking a little flushed and
curiously happy. The hard word had been spoken; the proposal
had been made and accepted. After an engagement of six months,
which Victorian propriety, but not Indian sentiment, dictated, the
pair were married on 5 November 1896, in the little mud church
in the compound at Doyabari. Neither had ever looked the way
of any other. They gave to their children the inestimable blessing
of knowing that, when they stood together to be made man and
wife, they came as those who had long since accepted the principle
that their bodies were the temple of the Holy Spirit, and as those
whose total self-giving to one another was simply an extension of
that self-giving of each to Christ that was day by day growing
into perfection.

By entering the Monro circle my father had found himself confronted by a kind of culture previously unknown to him. The Neills
were activists – athletes, artists, entrepreneurs; books played only
a small part in their world. For the Monros, books were a very
important part of their world. However, by diligent reading my
father made up in large measure for the defects of his youth, though
he never attained to an appreciation of poetry. Although a layman
and a doctor, my father was first and foremost a missionary, and was
well aware of the importance of theology for his work. While others
slept, he read, and he built up a theological library of considerable
range and variety. But after the age of fifty he rarely read a book
with which he disagreed, and thus, in my opinion, fell victim to a
certain Evangelical narrowness which may have hindered his later
usefulness. Although almost tone deaf, he managed to acquire
an excellent knowledge of Bengali, and the capacity to speak it
almost like an Indian. Nothing more infuriated a later generation
of Neills than the parents' habit of lapsing into Bengali when
discussing anything that they thought it better that the children
should not know.

Looking back, I realise how much my mother suffered from being contrasted all the time with her gifted elder sister Jessye. Yet she had a very good pair of hands and was an excellent cook. It may be that this sense of having been suppressed had a good deal to do with her adventurous decision to take up a medical career, a path in those days not considered at all suitable for a lady. Perhaps this helps explain her concern in later years that none of her own children should be similarly suppressed. She had had an extremely good general education. She had considerable musical and artistic ability, which in a busy life she had time neither to develop nor to maintain. At the age of about sixty she took to writing pious story books for schoolgirls, excellently worked out and expressed, but conveying a type of piety which is out of fashion now. From her mother she had learned the art of managing a large household with the minimum of fuss. In later years, if two or three children arrived simultaneously and unexpectedly, each accompanied by a friend, there would be no objurgations, but simply a judicious 'Let me see,' while in a few minutes she worked out the sleeping arrangements. She also had, in the highest degree, the useful gift of keeping servants and winning their affection.

Into their partnership each of my parents brought the deep shyness which years and experience did little to alleviate. Of this shyness they passed on a double portion to all their children. Shyness is a strange phenomenon; it strikes without differentiation the incompetent and the highly gifted, the unattractive and the supremely beautiful. When very large men such as Archbishop Garbett or Archbishop Mowll of Sydney are afflicted by it, it gives a painful impression of pomposity, which may utterly betray the anxious and gentle individual within who is trying to find expression. I think that perhaps I have been more successful than my brothers and sisters in becoming to some extent free from this menace, but this I attribute solely to divine grace. If one has learned to be at once and deeply interested in the people one encounters, there is little time to be concerned about oneself. But at any moment the old enemy can come surging in, producing those agonising moments of tongue-tied silence when speech would be desirable, or of clumsy speech when it would be far better to keep silence, and so many other inconveniences unfamiliar to those who have had the good fortune to enter the world with a little more self-confidence.

Children came quickly to the Neill ménage: Marjorie Penelope in 1898; Henry Christopher in 1899; Stephen Charles on the last day of 1900; Gerald Monro in 1902; Eric James in 1904; Isabel Ruth in 1906. There was a final little daughter born in 1909, who did not live, and whom we never saw.

The history of the next few years was entirely determined by the relationship of my parents and India and the work that they had taken up. My father was never one to spare himself. Driven on, perhaps, by some deep inner uncertainty about himself, he found it hard to cease from work. It was not long before the exacting climate began to tell on his health. My mother always maintained that she could not have been accepted for service by any missionary society, and that she got to India only as her father's daughter. She too was constantly ill. So by 1902 or 1903 it was clear that long absence from India must be accepted as a necessity, with no guarantee that return would be possible. No one really quite knew what was the matter with my father, so he was packed off on a long voyage round the world; and then for a time we settled in England.

By this time my father had become convinced that he could best serve the mission if he added ordination to his medical qualifications. So, after a short period of training at what was then called the Clergy Training School, now Westcott House, in Cambridge, where he had as a fellow student Fred Western, later to be my predecessor as Bishop of Tinnevelly, he was ordained deacon and priest by Handley Moule in Durham Cathedral and settled down as curate of Haughton-le-Skerne. It was there that my eyes opened consciously on the world – I have no recollections of India in my childhood – a vision of green fields and of the Skerne flowing tranquilly at the bottom of the garden.

At this time I was thrown exclusively into the company of my elder brother and sister. I have a feeling that, never being in the company of children of my own age, I missed some of the natural stages of growing up, and that the constant effort to keep up with the older ones encouraged an undesirable precocity. I certainly never learned to read, I simply found that I could at some point before my fifth birthday.

The biting air of County Durham did not suit my father, and he was advised to try the more genial climate of Lac Leman. So after staying at a village on the Salève, and then in Glion, where the movements of the lake steamers were a source of endless interest to a group of observant children, we moved to Lausanne, where my school career began. At the little Swiss school, where naturally everything was done in French, I did not, at the age of five, understand much of the proceedings, but it is due to this favourable start that I have never had any difficulty with French pronunciation.

A few months of Swiss air, and my father's health showed marked signs of improvement; at once his mind began to turn to India. The work was increasing, the doctors were all too few. It should be possible for my father and mother to spend nine months in India, avoiding the three hottest months of the year, without great danger to health, and in those days money was sufficiently plentiful for a passage to India not to make too large a hole in the family budget. So off they went, leaving us in the charge of the grandparents and Aunt Jessye, over-anxious and over-conscientious, with a Swiss governess, and four Monro girl cousins, three of them older than myself, for company. This was an arrangement for which, in the opinion of the boys, no good word could be said. Fortunately, my parents came back before any grave harm could result. Then, after making the same experiment again, my parents realised that their children needed them, and that until we were grown up and able to stand on our own, India must be out of the picture. My father was just forty years old, and embarked on a family Odyssey which never really ended until his death. India was in his heart and his blood, and he could never settle down to life in England. It would be unendurably tedious to chronicle all the family moves, though some of them must be recorded in due course. I have often thought that it would have been far better for Father if he had not had money of his own. Then, however much against his will, he would have had to settle down, and could not have followed impulses which at times could hardly be described as rational. He returned to India a number of times, more than once for considerable periods. At last, in 1947, he and my mother returned to live with my missionary sister Isabel at Coonoor, 6,000 feet up in the beautiful Nilgiri Hills, and blessed with an almost ideal climate. Some weeks after his eightieth birthday my father resigned from the chaplaincy of All Saints' Church, Coonoor, though continuing with the simple medical work he carried on for the benefit of the poor people of the neighbourhood. When he died a few months later it was found that, though the churchyard had long since been closed, there was a plot, close to the graves of Frederick Gell, Bishop of Madras from 1860 to 1898, and his sister, which had been reserved for the burial of any chaplain who might die during his time of office. Though my father was no longer in office, the Church Committee decided unanimously that of course Dr Neill must lie in that spot just outside the church on its beautiful hill-top. There had never been such a funeral, when Christians, Hindus and Muslims alike came to do honour to their old friend. When, three years later, my mother died, although we had no claim whatever to such consideration, the Church Committee once again decided unanimously that of course Margaret Penelope must lie by the side of Charles. 'The Lord shall be unto thee an everlasting light.' 'His servants shall serve him and they shall see his face.' On Christmas Day 1970, six days before I began the writing of these recollections, I preached in All Saints' Church, Coonoor. I am glad that my parents have been allowed to rest, in sure and certain hope of a joyful resurrection, in the land which next to their own they loved the most.

But back to the family Odyssey. We returned from Switzerland in 1906, and Father took up work as curate at Liskeard in Cornwall, a charge he took for love; this was my first introduction to a country which I know extremely well and which is very dear to me. Here my father was an immediate success. Before long we had an afternoon service for men only, with a regular attendance of two hundred; nothing like it had ever been known in the parish before. Then some strange stirring of the blood led the wanderer to throw this up and try his luck among his own people in Northern Ireland. So he became curate to Ussher Greer in Lisburn, where it came about that as a child I played with Billy Greer, who was Bishop of Manchester from 1947 to 1969. This episode, however, only lasted a short time. My father may have found that Northern Ireland was very different from what he imagined it to be, or it may have been that my mother could not take the gathering hordes of Neill relations; but I believe the decisive factor was my father's conviction, like his father's, that English schools were better than Irish schools, and that with four sons to educate, it was wiser not to expose them to the constant journeyings back and forth across the Irish Channel, of which he himself had such distressing recollections. In September 1910 we moved to Cheltenham, at the foot of the Cotswold hills, where he was appointed Vicar of St Mark's Church.

Within the limits of the parish stood the Dean Close Memorial School, founded by a group of pious Evangelicals in memory of Francis Close, who ended his days as Dean of Carlisle, but had been for many years the energetic rector of Cheltenham. Not long after his appointment to St Mark's, my father was appointed secretary to the governors of the school. Thus began a connection which, after sixty years, is still green and flourishing. My brother Henry and I are both life governors, my nephew Charlie was for a number of years on the staff, and my great-nephew Peter Anthony attended the school.

We were not, however, immediately consigned to the redbrick school and to the care of its more than formidable headmaster, Dr Flecker. Our education began more gently at Suffolk Hall, a private school owned by a gifted man, Arthur Lancelot Soames, whose father was a Liberal MP. We were day boys, apart from when we had our first experience of boarding life, which at the age of eight I found unpleasant and rather alarming. However, the teaching was exceptionally good. Soames was a fierce man, but he knew how to teach. Under his care we made astonishing progress in Latin and Greek, and were even modern enough to have Nature Study.

I did at that school have experience of the astonishing and irrational cruelty of which small boys can be capable. One day, during some examination or other, I lifted the lid of my desk to see whether my elusive blotting-paper was inside it. As soon as the test was over, some young scoundrel came up to me with the assertion that I had been seen cheating. The cry was taken up by others. Nothing could have been more absurd. I am not one who has ever needed to cheat in examinations, and in any case, there was nothing in my desk that could have given me the smallest help, had I desired it. For two or three weeks the persecution went on, accompanied by dire threats as to what would happen if the matter came to the notice of the headmaster. Soames, who had spotted that something was up, failed to rise to the occasion and to stamp on the absurdity at the very start. I think that this experience did me permanent harm; it made it harder for me than it should have been to put my trust in my fellow men, and undermined my belief in the rationality of my species.

Suffolk Hall was only a temporary resting place. My father had become profoundly convinced of the excellence of the Evangelical tradition as maintained at Dean Close School (we have long since dropped the 'Memorial') and that was to be our destiny, in spite of the sedulous efforts of the Soameses to send us in for scholarships at schools of greater renown. Henry went there one year ahead of me. I entered in January 1912, being then just twelve years old. The school then had about 220 boys of all ages from eight to eighteen. The report I have just received shows that there are now 560 boys and (*horribile dictu*) 43 girls in the school.

It would be impossible to imagine a more unsuitable group of founders than the godly Evangelicals who made the plans for the school in 1885. They built the school far too close to the railway line, they failed to appreciate the need for an endowment, so that the school's overdraft was a recurrent nightmare, and they let the buildings grow up higgledy-piggledy, as though deliberately to cause maximum inconvenience all round. One good thing they did was to appoint as headmaster a young untried man of twenty-seven, William Hermann Flecker.

Flecker was born in 1859, the son of a Baptist pastor of Jewish extraction who had come to England as a refugee from Austria. He was virtually self-educated and raised himself in the world solely by his brilliant intellectual gifts and his inexhaustible capacity for hard work. Failing to win a scholarship to Oxford because of nerves, he read law at Durham and obtained his doctorate with a thesis on Justinian. His special field was mathematics, but he could teach any subject at a moment's notice. His musical abilities were considerable. For thirty-eight years he and his devoted wife worked for sixteen hours a day building up out of nothing a sizeable and flourishing school. Yet for all that, I cannot hold any other opinion than that Flecker was a bad headmaster. I do not think that he ever understood boys, and his nervous rages made him terrifying to the more timid among them. He had high ideals and did his utmost to set them before us, but I think that the great majority of boys left the school with no feeling of affection for the man who had guided their destinies in their formative years.

In one thing Dean Close has been extraordinarily fortunate. It has won and retained the loyalty and devotion of a remarkable series of assistant masters. Abominably treated, underpaid, overworked, ill-lodged and ill-fed, they have stuck it out year after year, in some cases perhaps because once there they found it hard to move, more often, I think, from real concern for the place, for the boys, and for the ideals that it has striven imperfectly to translate into action. The tradition still continues.

The Bishop expressed the wish that my father should live in his parish, so he rented the last house of all, Amberley Lawn, at the corner of Lansdowne Road, that avenue of stately Victorian mansions inhabited by retired colonial governors and bankers with their extensive families. Our house was large, but ill-planned, with a considerable garden to which my father added two acres of paddock, presided over by an immense mulberry tree. Henry and I spent our extra holiday for the coronation of King George V in 1911 reducing the grass to a civilised length with the aid of an aged mowing machine.

We were usually a large party at home, especially after my mother's parents and Aunt Jessye moved in on us from Cluny, our old home on the other side of town. In addition to the six of us and the five grown-ups, there was usually a governess, and constant visitors. It is impossible to estimate what we owed to educated conversation, linked to unity in silence at Father's table. Canon Bollett put me enormously in his debt by discussing at lunch Adolf Deissmann's famous book *Light from the Ancient East*. I at once sought it out in the study, and had opened out before me the strange and fascinating world of the Greek papyri discovered in Egypt.

It would be impossible to imagine any parents more utterly devoted than mine to the welfare, in every aspect, of their children. I can see now the mistakes that they made, but their intentions I cannot judge other than kindly. But my father had one defect which cannot be passed over in total silence – he was capricious. He was far more anxious than we knew – about his work, about Mother's health, about financial problems in the future. He abominated Lloyd George and all his works, and went through a phase of talking constantly about emigrating to British Columbia. He was never more than half-serious, but we children had no means of telling whether he was serious or not. He was a great one for country cottages, and would think nothing of spending £800 on a cottage, usually admirably chosen and fitted up by my mother, but probably quite useless in the following year when we had moved to another part of the country. But if a hapless child had left the electric light on all night, one might have thought that the whole family was teetering on the verge of bankruptcy. Father had brought home from India a liability to paralysing headaches. Having suffered latterly myself from the same complaint, I now realise how intolerable he must sometimes have found the noise of children and the incessant problems they create.

Ours was a Christian household. Religion was present all the time, but I do not think it was obtruded. Of course there were family prayers before breakfast every day. The Bible was known and reverenced from Genesis to Revelation. In such a crowded household, it naturally happened that sometimes I slept on a mattress on the floor of my parents' room. Naturally I was supposed to be asleep when they came up to bed; naturally I was not, and so heard the earnest prayers that were offered every night, in which every child was mentioned by name, and every circumstance of the day and of the morrow was brought under review in the sight of God. It was evident to each one of us that God was the unseen member of the household, and to my parents the most real of all. Yet put a dozen over-intelligent and highly sensitive individuals in a single home, and it is certain that they will have what an American friend of mine once called 'a highly non-monotonous existence'; I have never had the smallest difficulty in believing in the doctrine of original sin.

It was, of course, taken for granted that everyone would be in church on Sunday morning. The service was Mattins, unaltered. We sang all the Psalms, the lessons were long, the prayers were those in the Prayer Book, there was no variety except that the Litany was frequently read. Never having known anything else, and taking it for granted that this was the way things were, we were not seriously bored. In those days Father was rather a good preacher, pleasant and easy to listen to. I remember especially one sermon on joy to which I listened with much pleasure and closed eyes.

The teaching given was strongly Evangelical. My parents had come very much under the influence of the Keswick movement, with its stress on the reality of the Holy Spirit, on practical holiness, as expressed in an extremely high standard of conduct and of self-forgetfulness in service, and on the responsibility resting on every Christian to be a witness for Christ. There was much interest in 'unfulfilled prophecy', and the not very scholarly interpretation of ancient prophecy in the light of the events of the End. All Evangelicals of that period were convinced that the survival of the Jewish people through so many centuries of persecution was of providential ordering, and that God had some great purpose still to be fulfilled through his Jewish people in the time of the End. Brought up to believe that Israel would return to the Holy Land in unbelief, the Balfour Declaration in 1917 came to us not as a bolt from the blue but as the answer to many confident prayers.

Of course the missionary challenge was central. It was taken for granted that the charge to make the gospel known to all the nations was the primary and permanent obligation resting on the Church. The slogan 'The evangelisation of the world in this generation' was still in vogue, and still had a challenge for our growing minds. I do not recall any identification of imperialism with missionary aims. The British Empire was accepted with pride and satisfaction as one of the existing realities in the world, and as the greatest force for civilisation and progress that had ever existed in history. With the Indian Civil Service tradition so strong in the family, the sense of responsibility was immensely strong, as was the certainty that Britain would stand at the Son of God's judgement to account for opportunity given. This emphasis was far stronger than that on the glorification of Britain. Yet perhaps the idea was lurking in the background that it might not be a bad idea for Britain to be glorified, and that the cause of God's kingdom was reasonably safe as long as it was in the hands of his Englishmen, who were never to be regarded quite as other men.

In 1913, what had seemed to be our peaceful and permanently settled existence in Cheltenham came to an abrupt end. Father had been worrying far too much about his work and his family and his finances, and in that year managed to produce a fairly comprehensive breakdown. He felt the need to find a lighter sphere of work; but, never one to put himself forward, he did not tell the Bishop of Gloucester of his trouble until after he had accepted the living of Nutley, on the top of Ashdown Forest in Sussex, a centre of peerless and characteristically English beauty. Here we lived in a much smaller house and with few of the amenities of existence. Every drop of water had to be pumped up by hand from a deep well. There was neither gas nor electricity, so we went to bed every night by candlelight. We made the adaptation with surprisingly little difficulty. My mother was always anxious that every child should have a room of its own. As space forbade, she curtained one of the bedrooms, so that Henry and I could each have our own place, screened from sight, though not from sound, of the other. Father eased the pressure by renting a cottage half-way between the vicarage and the church, where he had a study and we had a room where we could keep our books and other possessions.

Young people of today would doubtless think our life in those days very dull, but we did not find it so. We had our bicycles, and could go further and further afield. In the summer there was tennis at the great houses of which there was a large collection in the neighbourhood. On winter evenings we made our own fun, with many kinds of games, charades and our own plays. One of the advantages of a large family is that it can be in the main self-contained and can enjoy itself without being dependent on the resources of others. It was a great event when a good gramophone was introduced into the house. Records were few but well chosen; I think that it was 'Behold and see' from Handel's *Messiah* which first revealed to me what music can be, and what it can do to a man's heart.

The most profound effect of Nutley upon us was, however, that it led to my beginning six years of that boarding life which I have already described as being to me unpleasant and disagreeable.

By the standards of those days life at Dean Close School was not too bad at all. The sleeping quarters were excellent, each boy having his own cubicle, and so with a certain element of privacy, though there were a number of absurd and pedantic rules about silence in the dormitories. But the food was never as adequate as it should have been. On one or two mornings a week breakfast consisted only of tea so nasty that for years I could not drink it, bread and margarine, and paste made out of the remains of last week's joints – no fit diet to be set before growing boys. The midday dinner was better, but so arranged and planned that the meat was almost always cold before the boys got to it. The school, no doubt, counted on the parents to supplement fairly lavishly the regular rations of the boys. My parents had somewhat modest ideas as to what was needed; our tuck-boxes were not lined on the same scale as those of the sons of wealthy tradesmen, though I have no doubt that we were a good deal better off than the sons of impecunious clergy, on whom to a considerable extent Dean Close relied to fill its classrooms.

As in all public schools there was a certain amount of corporal punishment, but not a great deal and in most cases not very severe. Flecker, in his furious rages, could lay into boys with a vigour in which moderation played no part; but this awful fate, in my recollection, never befell small boys, but only older boys who, with one exception, had known perfectly well the extent of their transgression of school rules, though they may have under-estimated the severity of the punishment if they were caught. The same held true of the punishment of boys by boys. I can recall only three cases of excessive punishment, two wholly inexcusable, the third of an older boy, rather a friend of mine at the time, who had knowingly calculated the risk, and when caught out, accepted really rather severe punishment without resentment, and, as far as I could detect, without a trace of psychological injury. My own rare encounters with the law certainly did me no harm.

There was at the time a good deal more irregular sexual activity than I realised. But I think that what C. S. Lewis has written in *Surprised by Joy* is widely true – that if it is known that a boy has certain principles, and is not likely to budge from them, he is very unlikely to be troubled by the unwelcome attentions of older boys. Far more harm is done in the preparatory schools than is generally recognised; it is the boy who arrives at his public school already corrupted who is in the greatest danger all through his public school years. It is often supposed that boarding schools have a worse record than day schools. I doubt whether this is true. St Paul's, in the main a day school, to which two of my brothers went, was certainly worse than Dean Close was at the worst of times. And yet so much depends upon the boy that it is almost impossible to generalise; Cyril Norwood, headmaster successively of Bristol Grammar School, Marlborough, and Harrow, once told me that he spent five years at Merchant Taylors without even so much as knowing that homosexuality existed.

It is, however, true that we received no instruction whatever on the subject of sex and the part that it plays in human life. In confirmation class Flecker made some guarded references, but closed the subject down with the remark, 'Well, perhaps the less I say about that the better.' On one occasion my mother made an equally guarded attempt to open up the subject; but, seeing that I had not the least idea what she was talking about, let the subject drop. If she had only been a little more explicit, I should have been delighted to acquire some information on this enthralling subject. I have no idea how we were supposed to acquire the information which every boy and girl ought to have at the latest by the age of fourteen. Personally, I later took the initiative myself, and got help from worthy clergymen whose names are unknown to fame, but who have a special shrine in my recollections.

It was at this time that I passed through what was probably the greatest danger that I have encountered in all my years – the danger of contracting out of the world and people and things, and settling to live only in the world of books and of imagination.

All my life I have had to contend with the problem of what is today called 'mixed laterality'. I am neither right-handed nor left-handed. Natural functions, such as cleaning my teeth, or things I taught myself, such as tying a knot or threading a needle, I do left-handedly. Things I was taught, such as writing, I do with my right hand. Consequently I always appeared clumsy, and to my embarrassment had to struggle to do things other boys did naturally.

I think that I might have done better if I had grown up in a smaller and less gifted family. As it was, whatever I might think of doing, there was always someone in the family who could do it better than I. If I attempted to do one of the many things at which I was not good, the attempt was likely to be saluted by derision rather than by encouragement. The result was that I tended more and more to retire into myself and to concentrate on the one thing I could do.

My one gift is that I understand words. Since earliest childhood I have been fascinated by the sight and sound of words, by the patterns in which they can be arranged and by the subtleties of meaning that they can express. Even then I dimly understood the power that lies within the reach of the man who can choose and arrange words exquisitely, either in speech or in writing.

From the age of five I read voraciously, uncritically, and always much too fast, a vice of which I have never managed to cure myself. At this stage it was foreign languages which fascinated, but it was Hebrew which was the obstacle which I valiantly surmounted all by myself. Even in Cheltenham days, lying in bed on Sunday night with that appalling work, A. B. Davidson's *Hebrew Grammar* (unrevised), I suddenly found that the barrier of those strange black marks on the paper had been broken, and that I could read Hebrew words. Later I discovered on my father's shelves a book written in the last century by the Revd Peter Mason in which he expounded the Hebrew language in a series of letters to an English duchess. It may have been old-fashioned, but I would count any student lucky today who should find Mason and Bernard on the dim shelves of some second-hand bookshop. By the time I was fifteen I could read without difficulty the simpler parts of the Old Testament.

Again and again my father sought me out in my cold room, and forced me back into the society of the warmer rooms, and out of that world which was becoming more real to me than the world of my brothers and sisters, but I would stay no longer than I needed in that outer and turbulent world. Another sign of my increasing love of solitude was the habit I formed of going off alone for long days on my bicycle, exploring the countryside, looking at country churches, the architecture of which I was beginning to understand, getting a cheap meal somewhere by the way, and arriving home at sundown, tired, but released.

Two events saved me from this danger and turned my life in another direction.

The first was the simple event of becoming a Christian. This is a book of events, and I am not writing a modern *Confessions of St Augustine*, so I will pass over this happening cursorily, and without profound analysis. In 1914 Dean Close was devastated by an epidemic of mumps, and between forty and fifty of us were condemned to spend ten days of the Easter holidays at school. It was a miserable time. Mumps is a most unpleasant disease. We were wretched at not being able to go home. Half-hearted attempts were made to organise things for us and to keep us busy, but it was a bad time. Then Holy Week came along. On the Tuesday evening, as I was lying in bed, it occurred to me that, if it was true, as I had every reason to believe, that Christ had died for my sins, the rest of my life could not be spent in any other way than in grateful and adoring service of the One who had wrought that inestimable benefit. Even now, I see no way of improving on that discovery. I can recall no emotional accompaniment. All that happened was that I got out of bed and said my prayers, a ceremony which had been neglected for a considerable period. At that time I had heard the word 'conversion' used of Hindus who had become Christians; as far as I knew, I had never heard it used of something that could happen to one brought up in so Christian an atmosphere as I, but, up to that point, so totally unaware of the inner meaning of the gospel. Only after much later reflection did I come to the conclusion, which I have never seen reason to modify, that this extremely unromantic occurrence constituted my conversion.

It is extremely difficult for those who can identify the time and place at which they entered into life to believe that there can be any pattern of Christian life other than that with which they themselves are familiar. Yet it is essential to recognise the infinite variety of ways into the kingdom of God. I have the impression that many people who deny ever feeling 'born again' are singularly lacking in awareness of the heights and depths of the Christian revelation, and of its effects on the human personality.

I did not speak to anyone of what had happened to me; nor do I imagine that my family noticed any great change in me. Neills are rough and recalcitrant material for the operation of grace; they can become saints, but it is a very long and laborious process. Nevertheless I did myself notice certain changes that were gradually taking place.

I found that I now said the General Confession with a good deal of feeling; as before, it was the gigantic sin of ingratitude for which I knew that I had asked and received forgiveness.

My fierce temper, the outward expression of so many inward frustrations, began to come under control; though this was only the beginning of a long process, which perhaps will not be complete at the time of my death.

When I was fourteen, I decided to read a chapter of the Greek New Testament every day. This good habit I kept up until I went to Cambridge, by which time I had read through the New Testament five times, and carried off the Carus prize in my first term.

Far more important than anything else was the fact that I began to be intensely interested in people – as people, three-dimensional entities moving in highly improbable gyrations of their own and not simply as figures in my dreams. I am afraid that at times this interest was tinged with an Evangelical and intrusive inquisitiveness about their spiritual state; I hope that it has become a little more human – and humorous – with the years.

A natural consequence was that I was drawn fully into the religious life of the school. In addition to all the formal events, we had a prayer-meeting of our own on Sunday mornings, and later a short meeting for Bible study on a weekday morning. At times the address was given by a master or by some other visitor; at other times boys themselves were the speakers; this was the stage on which I had my first experiences in the art of proclaiming the Christian gospel. This religious life may have suffered a little from over-intensity, but if there was a weakness it was probably an unawareness of the part that is played in the Christian life by quiet growth; young people have a tendency to think that the kingdom of heaven can be taken by storm, and overlook the truth that the saints of the Lord shall walk and not faint.

The second event that set me free from the threatened introversion was the discovery of natural beauty. I seem to have been slow in the development of this aspect of apprehension. When my father bought The White House, Woody Bay, as our holiday home, we heard wonderful things about the superlative beauty of the setting. We went down to spend part of the Christmas holiday there, and arrived tired and fretful after dark. When I threw up my window next morning and looked out, I was frankly disappointed by what I now regard as one of the most wonderful pieces of landscape in the world. Of course the oak trees were all bare and the colours were grey and wintry; but my lack of response at that stage seems to me significant. The discovery came to me considerably later, when the mayor of the little Cornish town in which we lived at that time took me out on one of his purchasing expeditions. While he was considering fat stock and all its problems, I found myself looking at a line of trees standing in the first faint green of spring. Suddenly the beauty of this infinite variety of greens hit me almost like a physical shock. The years have brought me ever-increasing awareness of the abounding generosity of God in the beauty of natural things. Of course the enjoyment and contemplation of such beauty can be carried out as the diversion of the solitary – but for me this awareness has always been akin to worship and has lifted me out of the narrowness of my own inner being.

It was at this point that the First World War hit us. It may be of interest to record that when we heard late one night that war had been declared, we took it for granted that civil war had broken out in Ireland. It had not occurred to us that the murder of an obscure Austrian Archduke far away could affect the destiny of all of us for ever and a day. We had been brought up to believe that war could exist on the North-West frontier of India, or with the less enlightened peoples of the Sudan, but that it was a disease that Europe had long since put behind it. This indoctrination explains the almost frenetic hatred felt for Germany when the curse of war was let loose upon the world in 1914.

With possible disturbances at home we were all too familiar. No one now regards the Edwardian age as a time of calm before the storm; it was a hectic, unpleasant period, and children could not escape the consequences of the follies of their elders. Those were the days of the violent activities of the suffragettes. The ladies of our household came as near as Victorian ladies could to the use of bad language to express the depths of their disgust and loathing for the antics of 'those females'. The great strikes of 1911 and 1912 left an indelible impression on my mind. They seemed to me, even then, not to be an attempt to right evil conditions, something with which we would have had the greatest sympathy, but to be in fact a declaration of civil war, an attempt to blackmail the public.

It was the misfortune of Ireland, then still united, that the Prime Minister of the day was Mr Asquith, whom I always found singularly unlikeable. I have never been able to understand the esteem in which he was held. His great defect as a statesman was that, like so many liberals, he could not believe there was anything which could not be solved by a good debate in the House of Commons. This was why he failed as a war leader, and why he could not understand the cry of desperate Ulstermen: 'Ulster will fight and Ulster will be right.' Under Asquith tension had been allowed to grow between the two communities to such an extent that for us it was positively a relief that it was a European war which had broken out, and not an Irish one, that we would be shooting at aliens, and not at our own blood brothers.

For all that, the early days of the war were grim. There was first the question of whether we should be in it or not. Historians and polemicists may argue as they will about nearer and more remote causes. I know that it was the moral factor, the deliberate breaking of a promise, that brought an almost fully united England into the war. Up until 1914 nations tended at least to adopt the pose that it was better to keep promises than to break them. Since 1914 the nations, Britain included, seem to feel no obligation to observe any agreement, however solemnly undertaken. But the Germans were the first. It was they who pointed the way to that degeneracy of public morality with which we have lived in the later years of this deplorable century.

The first months of the war hardly affected our school life at all. We were still unconvinced that Kitchener's thesis of a long war was sound. It was not long, however, before casualty lists began to come in, and we found in them the names of boys we had known and who seemed little older than ourselves. When Rupert Lockhead came back from the Dardanelles minus an eye, the war then did not seem so far away. The first sign of change was that all the menservants disappeared into military service, and many things which had been done for us we now had to do for ourselves. Then the younger masters were called up, leaving us to the care of the old and infirm. I suspect that the level of teaching in the lower school deteriorated badly, while discipline disintegrated.

Compulsory rationing was introduced only late in the war, but the school made the disastrous mistake of accepting bread-rationing when it was still voluntary. As a result, over a long period we simply did not get enough to eat, given that we were playing football through the long hard winter. By the time the school authorities realised that four small half-slices of grey bread and a large ration of stodgy boiled rice was not enough, the damage was done. For months I, for one, could not run or play any kind of game. I was lamed by a kind of sciatica, which has never recurred, and which I have little doubt was due to debility caused by malnutrition. What the permanent effect on my health was, I cannot say.

The school's second grave mistake was to make an enormous increase in military training. Almost every boy enrolled in the Officers' Training Corps. We were a patriotic lot, with hardly a dissident voice to question the legitimacy of war or the rightness of this war. To train ourselves as far as possible, under the conditions of adolescence, seemed the most adequate method of demonstrating our patriotism. This would have been bad enough, even had it not been compounded by a yet more disastrous error. Flecker's able son, who was a poet and dramatist, had been fairly seriously wounded in Mesopotamia. His father managed to bring him home and get him appointed to command the OTC in school. This meant that for the rest of the war he had guilty feelings which he tried to suppress by imposing the maximum of military effort on himself and on us. The hours spent on drill grew until as another master, also invalided out of the army, remarked, 'This place isn't a school, it's a depot.' Looking back, I think that it was practically all futile, wasted effort, and that we would have been far better employed in enjoying ourselves in the ways natural to boys in the short time that was left to us.

Yet in spite of all these problems and follies, we managed to lead for the most part a surprisingly normal life. I have often asked myself in later years how it came about that a school which in many ways treated us so badly managed to secure our wholehearted and lifelong devotion. I see now that it was because it supplied the elements of stability and continuity in our lives. Throughout these years my father continued his peripatetic career. It was his practice to take over some derelict parish, work it up almost frenziedly for a couple of years or so, and then feel the urge to move on, probably to some entirely different part of England. The result was that we never had anywhere that we could call home. We had no roots, no opportunity to make permanent friends in any of the places where we lived. But the school was always there.

Except during the very worst days of the war, travel was always possible. The school did rather well in bringing in people of some eminence to speak and preach to us. There were some terrible patriotic speakers who made us shudder, but many were very good. Arthur Burroughs, later Bishop of Ripon, and William Temple, later Archbishop of Canterbury, came to speak to us in connection with the National Mission of Repentance and Hope. The calm and scholarly Bishop of Gloucester, Sumner Gibson, was always a welcome visitor. At my confirmation in 1915, a service full of meaning for one who was already a convinced Christian, the address he gave was on the rather unexpected text: 'We made our prayer unto our God, and set a watch against them day and night, because of them' (Neh. 4:9), but the service he rendered me was to introduce me to Robert Browning. In a prize-giving address he quoted the sixth stanza of *Rabbi ben Ezra*, explaining that he and a friend read the whole poem every Sunday and never failed to find strength and inspiration in it:

> Then, welcome each rebuff
> That turns earth's smoothness rough
> Each sting that bids nor sit nor stand but go!
> Be our joy three parts pain!
> Strive, and hold cheap the strain;
> Learn, nor account the pang; dare, never grudge the throe!

It was not long before I possessed a two-volume edition, which lies before me on the table as I write, and though Browning is fairly rugged going for a boy, I cannot over-estimate what I owe to those hours of wrestling. Browning seems today to be almost forgotten, which perhaps is symptomatic of the astonishing flabbiness of a great deal that passes for Christian faith today.

William Temple once remarked to Bishop Charles Gore that his three great teachers were Plato, Robert Browning and the Apostle John. Gore thought for a moment and then said that, with the first two he agreed, but that for him it was the Apostle Paul: 'When I read St John, I find myself in a country of strange and fascinating landscapes, but one in which I can never feel myself fully at home.' In my earlier years I was on the side of Gore; later I came to be on the side of Temple. When I took the Joint Board's examination in religious education, the set book was the Epistle to the Romans. I said to myself, 'I am going to understand this Epistle, or die in the attempt.' Grappling week after week with the thought of the Apostle, aided by my father's copy of Godet's commentary, the famous Sanday and Headlam and their incomparable paraphrase of the first eight chapters, and Armitage Robinson on Ephesians, I came to a remarkably exact understanding of the meaning of the doctrine of justification by faith, to the later astonishment of my Lutheran friends, who assume that no Anglican can know anything about St Paul.

One other intellectual adventure of these years deserves mention. In 1917 I began German, as an antidote to all the Latin and Greek I had been doing. My father's hostility to this idea was overruled by my grandfather, who, it will be remembered, had studied law in Berlin in 1858. I jumped straight into an advanced class, so my grammatical foundation was always a little shaky, but my teacher, to his eternal credit and my great advantage, gave me lessons on my own to read the first part of Goethe's *Faust*. Direct contact with genius meant enrichment of life for ever and a day.

We were all under stress in the war, none more so than Flecker, who in a momentary fit of absent-mindedness when he was rushing to a meeting in London inadvertently left a department store without paying for the things he wished to purchase, and was charged with shop-lifting. He resigned his post to spare the good name of the school, but my father intervened and persuaded the governors not to accept his resignation. When the case came before the magistrate's court, it was thrown out immediately, and Flecker returned to the kind of reception usually accorded to public school headmasters only in the pages of fiction. When the clamour had died down, Flecker astonishingly said, 'Boys, it says in the Book of Proverbs, "He that marrieth a wife getteth a good thing." The best advice I can give you is to marry a good wife as soon as you can. What I have owed to my wife and daughter during these days I have no words to express.' He must have been very deeply moved to make such an uncharacteristic revelation of his innermost feelings. This all made a very great impression on me, as is shown by the clarity with which I recall the details, even if I cannot claim to have quoted his words verbatim.

I have never quite known why I selected Trinity. Gonville and Caius was the family college. My father and Uncle Charlie had been there, and my brother Henry had won an entrance scholarship there, before going off to military service, and was to be followed by my two other brothers and my nephew Charlie. However, my mother's younger brother had been at Trinity, and a photograph of the Great Gate hung on the wall of our dining room. At the age of twelve I announced, 'That is my college.' Perhaps it was in part the need to be different, and for some reason Caius never attracted me. Whatever the cause, I have never once regretted the result.

I knew that the competition would be fierce, but being at a small, somewhat isolated school in wartime, I had no idea how good I was. I was not behind Henry, who had won his scholarship the year before, but I was entering a world of formidable uncertainty. Owing to the accident of my birthday falling on 31 December, I could neatly fit in the examination before my eighteenth birthday, when, according to the regulations then in force, I would be called up. 1918 had destroyed our hopes of Russian victories, and seen the greatest defeats for the French and British armies since the first days of the war. The casualty lists grew longer and longer. Standing before the Roll of Honour in the chapel, Henry and I were startled to see how many of the names were those of boys with whom we had studied and played and fought not so long before the day of their death. It seemed at the time that there would be no end to all that. Then suddenly Bulgaria asked for an armistice; could this really be the beginning of the end? I know exactly where I was on 11 November 1918 when the sirens sounded and told us it was all over – reading Plato's *Theaetetus* in the big schoolroom. We all went into chapel and sang the *Te Deum*; but I could not sing. The sense of relief and deliverance was too deep. As Siegfried Sassoon put it, 'My heart was shaken with tears and laughter . . . The singing will never be done.'

The day after the armistice I had to go up to London to collect the second prize for an essay competition on the theme 'The British Empire and the Empires of the Past'. The wild revels of the day before had died down a little, but people were still roaming recklessly through the streets. Alone in the Kingsley Hotel, I took out my Greek New Testament and read from 2 Corinthians 10: 'the weapons of our warfare are not carnal, but mighty through God to the pulling down of strongholds . . . bringing into captivity every thought to the obedience of Christ'. This was now clearly our task, but listening to the clamour in the city outside, I wondered whether our new armaments would be found adequate to the task. But now I had to concentrate on the scholarship.

My first sight of Cambridge University on a grey December evening failed to live up to my expectations of splendid magnificence. Being the vacation, the place seemed dead, but I was enormously impressed by the gracious courtesy extended to a gauche and timid schoolboy. I was accommodated in rooms with a slightly uncouth young man, a year younger than myself, who, I was appalled to discover, appeared to have read all the works of the classical authors with which I myself was unacquainted. I need not have worried. This was Arthur Darby Nock, later Fellow of Clare College, and at the age of twenty-eight, Frothingham Professor of the History of Religions at Harvard University. We became friends and remained so until his untimely death, with almost all the books unwritten with which he could have enriched the world of scholarship. In fact we also used to talk of Neill's *Euripides*, the edition to end all editions, which also remains unwritten.

With my invincible capacity for doing the wrong thing at the wrong time, in the middle of that gruelling week I developed a painful sty in my right eye, no doubt in modern parlance an 'anxiety symptom'. I lost a good deal of sleep before I got it lanced. After that I had no more trouble.

So the week came to an end with the long slow journey back to Cheltenham with my father (who, knowing how nervous I would be, had generously accompanied me). There followed an agonising wait for a week, because I really had no idea how well I might have done. On Friday evening, the last night of the school term, the results came. Ellam, my coach, ever considerate, had arranged for a telegram to be sent. He came up and said, 'You've got something, but the telegram doesn't say what.' *The Times* next morning told us that Nock and I had been elected to the two chief entrance scholarships in classics to Trinity College, Cambridge. I celebrated by staging a complete breakdown in health, erupting in eczema, which spread all over my body and affected every area where sweat collects.

This event was not really surprising. For more than a year I had been head prefect, with all the responsibilities for the general running and discipline of the school which that office involves. I was playing all games, and I had allowed myself, unwisely, to become Quartermaster-Sergeant of the OTC. This meant looking after uniforms and supplies and a lot of tedious trivialities. In our spare time we went out to help the local farmers – for this we were paid a small sum, which with wartime inflation was very welcome cash in our pockets. I was organising the rather intensive religious life of the school, and making it a point to speak to every boy in the school and convey to him, I hoped, that the head prefect was interested in his welfare. This was in addition to normal studies, and working for that elusive scholarship. For three years I had been driving myself too hard and sleeping too little, so it was not surprising I reached breaking point physically. It was my luck that it was after the scholarship was won, and not before; but I lost a term, even with the expert care of my doctor mother who nursed me back to health.

At this time I became aware of a problem which though not new had not previously forced itself so clearly on my attention, and which was to become a life-long affliction – difficulty in sleeping. Of course in certain cases worry can interfere with sleep. Like every clergyman I have had nightmares about sermons, and even now sometimes wake in a cold sweat, unable to find in the Prayer Book the service I am meant to be conducting. However, my insomnia appears to have a purely physical cause or causes. It began after a teenage illness and persisted until a course of massage in Geneva made me realise that it was related to circulatory problems, and my body's apparent inability to regulate its temperature properly in certain climatic conditions. Since worrying about not sleeping makes the condition worse, I soon learned to get up and do some work, usually writing or reviewing books. For years altogether I never got a good night's sleep, but my output shows I really was awake, and not imagining it. Nevertheless, natural sleep would have been better for me.

At about the same time I also became aware of another kind of trouble, more serious, though at the time I had no premonition of the way it would determine the major part of my career. It was as though all the lights went out in the world. This could happen suddenly, like a bolt from heaven; or it could start as a grey patch somewhere on the horizon, which would gradually spread until the whole heaven was blotted out by this grey blankness. The experience was accompanied by a total lack of interest in anything; what was most disturbing for a young Christian, the fourth dimension of grace, awareness of the divine, call it what you will, was completely blotted out; prayer became a mere formula, with no sense that it was being addressed to anyone in particular or that there was any possibility of its being heard. As far as I remember, attacks in those distant days never lasted for more than three days at a time, and recovery could vary in the same way as the onset of the trouble. I might be in the depths at one moment, and entirely free the next; or the clouds might slowly and gradually dissipate themselves until the zenith was clear again. I diagnosed this affliction as the malaise which often beset medieval monks, *daemonium meridianum*; later I learned to call it *accidie*. I knew therefore that this darkness had nothing to do with being cut off from God, but it was only in later years that I became fully aware of the extent to which misfortune can fall. Some of the experiences of my first year in India were so excessively painful that by January 1926 the darkness was complete. A year in England helped, but this time of trouble did not really clear itself up until 1933.

The years 1933–43 were a time of ups and downs, but mainly of ups; there were periods of intense and productive activity. In 1943, when the strains caused by the Second World War were at their worst, the arrow began to turn down again. This time a visit to England did little to arrest the advance of darkness, and by January 1946 it was again complete. This was the longest and worst period of suffering; it lasted just ten years.[4] Then, appropriately, on 25 January 1956, the feast of the Conversion of St Paul, as I was kneeling at the Holy Communion in the Chapel of Trinity College, I received the message that I need no longer carry the burdens of the past, and that the time had come to take up my bed and walk. I can explain this experience only by referring to the tremendous passage in Cantos 20 and 21 of the *Purgatorio* of Dante, in which Statius explains to the two travellers that, when a soul in the process of purification has remained long enough on one of the terraces of the mount of Purgatory, desire and will combine to give that spirit notice that it is now free to rise and move to a higher terrace; and, when this happens, the whole mountain shakes, and the *Gloria in Excelsis* rises from the lips of the imprisoned spirits, charmed that one among them is now set free to take one step further forward on the way to Paradise.

The message that reached me was no illusion. Never, since that day, has the inner darkness been complete. But, when injuries have been so deep, recovery can only be slow and tedious. It was not till 21 December 1965 that I received a further message that my healing had now reached such a point that I could begin to think of living a normal life. This was confirmed by a further word of healing on Christmas Eve 1970, one week before I started on the writing of this book. All this may sound like moonshine to the sceptical reader; I can only reply that almost everyone who has met me during the last five years has said in surprise, 'How well you are looking.'

Naturally, I have from time to time asked myself where I should have been and what I might have done if I had been gifted with better health. But this is a futile and meaningless question. If it had pleased the Lord to give me even slightly better health, I would have been an entirely different person, and the story that follows would have been an entirely different story. At times I have been tempted to wish that there could have been a little less suffering on the way that I have trodden; but I am sure that I have learned some lessons that could not be learned in any other way. In any case, to look across the river and suppose that the grass is greener on the other side is an absurd and futile waste of time.

I may end these preliminary remarks by mentioning that, when I was quite young, I thought that I should be married within a short time. This did not come about, and the occasion seems never to have recurred. I have been extraordinarily fortunate in my women friends, both married and unmarried; they have added enormously to the richness and variety of my experience. But the opportunity never seems to have come again for that total self-commitment which is the pre-condition of a happy marriage. I can find little to say in favour of the unmarried state. The unmarried man tends to become unendurably fussy over small things, self-centred and resentful of any interference with his established routine. On the other hand, it is good for the Church that some of its servants are free from the cares and responsibilities of a family. If I had married, I should have done quite other and probably better things; I certainly should not have done the things I have done, nor been able to set off at short notice for any part of the globe where there was a job to be done.

After this rather lengthy digression, it is time to come back to the point at which we digressed. After the serious illness of 1919, and my slow recovery from it, I simply went back to school for a final term. 1919 was not exactly a propitious time to think of travel abroad. There were no organisations offering young people the opportunity of service and adventure abroad between school and college, as there are today. We simply went on as before, until the time came to go up to university. Nevertheless, in recollection, that seems to have been a halcyon time. The summer days seem to have followed one another in unbroken beauty. The nightmare of endless military drill was ended, the scholarship was won, and there was no need for any further anxiety. It was altogether a most pleasant interlude. In particular, on Ascension Day, Hugh Butcher and I cycled to Oxford across the Cotswolds, with me returning by train from Bourton-on-the-Water and wheeling my bicycle with an unforeseen puncture into school at 10 p.m. with all the oriflammes of heaven out in the western sky.

I have no complaints to make of the education provided for me at that small, cheap and in those days obscure public school. Looking back, though, it does seem to me odd that when I went to Cambridge I had never heard the name of Karl Marx.

2

Apprentice Scholar

For an extremely shy and awkward freshman to enter a college of six hundred undergraduates, only three of whom he had ever met (and with none of the three did he wish to be very closely associated), was a formidable adventure. There were, however, favourable circumstances that made the first steps less appalling than they would otherwise have been.

As a scholar I was entitled to rooms in College throughout my five years of residence. My first rooms were D3 in the Victorian New Court. My recollection is that the October days after the beginning of term were always beautiful and mellow, with countless flowers still in the gardens, the days getting gradually shorter and sharper in the evenings, with the smell of burning leaves. In the mornings I could lie in my bed, when I had a bed, and see the great trees of the lime avenue. This was the first hurdle to be surmounted – in those days the College did not supply furniture. My father, always one to rise to a crisis, came to see me in; when we first entered my rooms, there was nothing in them but a curtain-pole. We hurried to a second-hand furniture shop, and bought the minimum on which a man could live.

My first impression of life in Cambridge was of the extraordinary kindness manifested by everyone. Even the best school is a rather rough institution; here everything was as different as it could be. The dons treated the rawest undergraduate with the utmost courtesy; my tutor, Ernest Harrison, always addressed me as 'Mr' until in the wonderful jumble of college relationships I ceased to address him as 'Mr'. I had come up with highly fictional ideas of the haughty attitude of the third-year man towards the unhappy freshman. I never encountered anything of the kind.

Nor was I conscious then, as I was a quarter of a century later, of a generation gap between those who had seen military service and those who had come up straight from school. All seemed united in the generous desire to make us feel at home. Though we fell into every conceivable mistake, all this seemed to be endured with a tolerant smile as part of the necessary process of acclimatisation.

Although choosing Trinity as my College was one of the very best things that I ever did, I would not recommend Trinity to any boy, unless he was really good at something – it might only be chess or Morris-dancing, but there should be some special skill as a gate of entry into college life. I have known too many average young men come up with excellent intentions, pursue their studies with integrity, spend most of their evenings in their rooms, and go down without ever having experienced the education that comes from a multiplicity of interests and friends. My gate of entry was my position as a classical scholar. Before long I was elected to the Classical Reading Society, which used to meet once a week to read and translate the classics.

The first task, naturally, was to master the art of study under university conditions. This brought me into contact with the three classical lecturers, each a man of great stature in his own right, each a friend to be remembered with honour, but with regret for what he failed to achieve.

Ernest Harrison was a scholar of impeccable taste and accuracy, whose merits have never been adequately recognised, since he suffered more than almost any other man that I have ever known from the Cambridge *aphasia*, and published hardly anything. He was a superb master of the varied arts of writing Latin and Greek, austere in his judgements on the work of his pupils, and he rarely praised anyone. One of the great moments of my life was when he took up a copy of Greek iambics I had written for him, and said briefly, 'These are very good.'

Donald Robertson, later Professor of Greek, suffered like me from the defect of being interested in too many things. He too left less than he should have done as an inheritance to posterity. He was working for years on Pindar, but the definitive text of that great but (to me) rather uncongenial poet, for which we waited so long, never appeared. The best that we have of him is in the admirable text of Apuleius in the Budé series. Apuleius is one of my favourite authors, and one whom I constantly recommend to students of the New Testament in order to help them to understand what kind of a world it was in which the apostles lived. If theological students cannot take a little simple indecency in their stride, they ought not to be theological students.

Francis Cornford wrote most of the great books on Greek philosophy by which he is remembered after my time as his student. Almost the most important thing about Cornford was his wife, Frances (née Darwin), the poetess, who, like other Darwins, had been brought up in the belief that religion is good for some people, but not for Darwins, and had never really encountered Christianity at all. Forced by her children's questions to start reading the New Testament, Frances found she could accept Jesus' teaching about God, and was baptised and confirmed in the Church of England. She remained a faithful and humble believer.

My classical acquaintances were not limited to my own College. At our first interview Harrison said to me, 'You must hear Mr Sheppard of King's as soon as possible.' Sheppard was not unknown to me by name. He was regarded as one of the ablest members of the anti-Christian front in Cambridge, and I was curious to see him. He had an incomparable gift of making Greek literature live for all kinds of audiences. I listened to him with delight, and whatever his surface convictions may have been, detected in him a profoundly religious spirit. With undergraduate incaution I one day told him so; to which he replied very properly, 'When you are a bishop, I will get a certificate from you to that effect.' Here is the certificate. If I do not meet Sheppard in the kingdom of heaven, I shall feel that something has gone seriously wrong with that institution.

Franklin Angus of Trinity Hall left little memorial of himself except in the recollections of his friends. In the course of his lectures on ancient philosophy he read out to us a number of superlative translations of Lucretius, and we extorted from him the admission that they were his own. But these have never been published, and I fear have been for ever lost in the dispersion of his library. He did not like writing. He was an excellent preacher and lecturer. But he paid a heavy price in nervous exhaustion for this excellence. What he really liked to do was to sit surrounded by younger friends and talk and listen endlessly. No beauty to look at, I think he rather fancied himself in the role of the modern Socrates. A life-long Baptist, Franklin once told me that, when he went up to Trinity, one of the first things he had to do was to call upon the chaplain, and was greeted by the remark, 'Ah Mr Angus, I see that you are a Baptist. I understand that the Baptists are dying out.'

All these were great men, but one towered above them all, A. E. Housman, a poet and the greatest Latinist of the century. To attend one of his lectures on Latin poetry was an exhilarating but also a rather daunting experience. I have never quite understood the purpose of university lectures. As long ago as 1811 von Humboldt laid it down that lectures in the University of Berlin should not impart information; but if they do not, what do they do? Three things in my opinion. They can generate enthusiasm for the subject. They can communicate to the student the results of the professor's as yet unpublished researches. They can make available the results of scholarship in languages that the students cannot read for themselves. The first and the second of these Housman could do admirably. He did not attempt the third because he did not believe there were any. The major advantage, however, of listening to the lectures of the really learned, and this is one that does not fade, is the experience of observing great minds grappling with perhaps refractory material. I cannot now remember a single word that Housman said; however, I still have a vivid memory of the way in which he would concentrate all the resources of his massive learning on the elucidation of a single point.

These recollections of great men must not grow to the dimensions of a Who's Who of Cambridge in 1920; but two more names must, I think, be mentioned.

Our Master was the famous physicist Sir Joseph John Thomson, the man who, I think, did more than any other to split the atom, and on whose shoulders, in my opinion, Lord Rutherford climbed up to exceed his fame. J. J. once stopped me in Great Court, and said, 'I hear you are researching on Plotinus.' I was not surprised that he recognised me; we had met on a number of occasions; but I was surprised that he had ever heard of the subject of my research, still more that he had taken the trouble to remember it.

We used to see about the streets a beautiful old man with a flowing beard; I came to know that he had the most appropriate name, Dr Liveing. On the seventy-fifth anniversary of his coming into residence, the University held a meeting in his honour. After the usual speeches of greeting, the old man, then ninety-five years of age, rose to his feet, and spoke for forty-five minutes without a note and in flawless English on the development of the study of chemistry, of which he had himself been professor for forty-seven years, from the time when the entire chemical apparatus of the University was wheeled into the lecture room on a table, up to the present day. It was confidently expected that he would reach his century, but a careless undergraduate on a bicycle knocked him down, and he died three years short of the goal.

My first year was crowded with examinations. First, in cold January, before term started, came the examination for university scholarships, twelve gruelling papers in six days, including, horror upon horror, an original Latin poem. Nock and I both failed to notice that the last paper was at 1 p.m., and not the usual 1.30, and so arrived half an hour late. It made no difference. The paper was so difficult that we had more than ample time to write down all we knew. He walked straight into the top class, with the Waddington scholarship; I came third, with something called the Davies. This was welcome, both as adding to my slender financial resources, and as giving me some much-needed confidence as to my classical ability. When I look at those old papers, I am astonished that I appear once to have known so much.

The next hurdle, in March, was the examination for a Senior Scholarship at Trinity, £100 for five years, a lot of money in those days. This I took fairly confidently, guessing rightly that I could make the grade, but Harrison shook his head sadly over some glaring mistakes I ought not to have made. The third was the first part of the Classical Tripos. I did not find the papers very difficult, and appear to have done reasonably well.

This had the blissful result that during my second year I had no examinations at all, except for university scholarships again, when I rose to the higher level of the Craven. I have in fact singularly few memories of doing any work at Cambridge. My record shows that I must have done a good deal, but I had worked so hard at school that it was only rarely that I had to exert myself really hard at Cambridge. So I amused myself by working for the university prizes in theology. I have always been a convinced, but not a fanatical, Sabbatarian. When I was studying classics, I read theology on Sundays; when I was studying theology, I read detective stories. The Jeremie Septuagint prize (then undivided), involved minute study of two Old Testament books (in my case Deuteronomy and Jeremiah), with constant reference back to the Hebrew and to works by such writers as Philo and Josephus. This exactly suited my combination of philological and theological interests. For the Evans patristic prize the selection could not have been better from my point of view: Cyprian on the unity of the Church, the *Confessions* of Augustine, Athanasius on the Church, and the first Apology of Justin. The theological faculty was a little startled by this sudden incursion into their field by an unknown scholar who carried off two prizes from under the noses of the theologians.

For more than a century religion has played an extremely important part in Cambridge life. In my day the fare was richly varied, and the number of undergraduates who, in one way or another, came under the influence of the Christian religion was very large.

F. R. Tennant, later to be my teacher, had been a scientist by education and profession, and it was with a rigidly empirical mind that he distilled years of patient thought into his *Philosophical Theology*. He was elected lecturer in theology in preference to Kirsopp Lake, whose book *The Earlier Epistles of St Paul* (1911) is still worth reading. The old master, Dr H. M. Butler, had heard rumours that Lake's theological views were unsound; I have always wondered whether he ever discovered what Tennant's views really were.

Hugh Francis Stewart was, when I first knew him, a small, not very distinguished-looking clergyman of about fifty-five. We had suffered under Stewart and Tulley's extracts from French authors at school, but it had never occurred to me I might one day know the editor and his delightful family. Like my Aunt Gennie, he had the gift of growing more beautiful as he grew older; when he was eighty-four his profile had the magnificence of that of an emperor on a Roman coin.

Just to make sure that we were well cared for, the College maintained, in addition to these learned men, two chaplains: John How, later Bishop of Glasgow and Primus of the Scottish Episcopal Church, and Wilfred Ellis, later Provost of Ndola in Zambia. Both of these were somewhat advanced Anglo-Catholics. Father John was a member of the Oratory of the Good Shepherd, a fellowship of priests who take annual vows of celibacy. Some of the brethren were a little startled when he got married, but he explained that for the first time in his life he had met a lady whom he felt he could sit opposite at breakfast for the rest of his life.

I immediately became a regular worshipper at the College Chapel. On the whole I avoided Mattins and sermons. My diet was early Communion and Evensong, at which an anthem was sung. But the official religion of the College Chapel was only the smallest part of Cambridge religion. About sixty years before, the Daily Prayer Meeting had been started by pious undergraduates, and has been carried on without intermission ever since. Out of this grew the Cambridge Inter-Collegiate Christian Union (CICCU), which I have already mentioned in connection with my father's student days and the Monros. In 1910 an unhappy division took place between those Anglicans who maintained an unyielding conservative position, and others who felt that liberal principles also have a place in religion. The latter formed a separate branch of the Student Christian Movement, as the national movement had renamed itself in 1904. It seems to me that the separation was inevitable, but for fifty years I have helplessly watched these two bodies corrupting one another, the excessive liberalism of the SCM driving the Inter-Varsity Fellowship (the national association of the Christian Unions which followed the CICCU example in the 1920s) into a far greater rigidity of doctrine than it possessed in my day, and the intransigence of the IVF making it almost impossible for the SCM to profess clearly any single article of the Christian faith. Instead of provoking one another to love and to good works, the two have tended to create division, bitterness and a weakening of the Christian cause.

I went up to Cambridge determined to take my time and think carefully before joining any organisation, but it was not long before I found myself drawn in by the ardour of the CICCU. That body, then as now, stood for the necessity of personal conversion, the obligation to holiness resting on every believer, and the duty of Christian witness to the ends of the earth. These were things I understood. I enrolled myself in the ranks. It is sometimes supposed that Evangelical religion is individualistic. I can only say that I have never again entered into so warm and loving a fellowship as that which existed in Cambridge in my day.

It was not long before I came to know Carey Francis, a rather older undergraduate. After a few years, Carey gave up his comfortable life as a Fellow of Peterhouse to go out to Kenya and to run first the CMS school at Maseno, and later, for twenty-two years, Alliance High School, by far the most famous boys' school in Kenya. Loved by few, respected by all, criticised by many, Carey set a matchless standard of competence and Christian devotion. When he died, six thousand people came to the funeral, with members of the Cabinet and leaders of the opposition literally fighting one another for the privilege of carrying his body to the grave. When he retired from Alliance, he could not tear himself away from Kenya and his life's work, so he taught at a school in Pumwani, a poorer section of Nairobi, and was blissfully happy. One day after class, he went to sit down in the headmaster's office. Suddenly his head went back, and in a moment he had entered into light.

A very different friend was Ted Thomas of Pembroke. I cannot remember how I met him, but we entered into one of those unshakeable friendships which lasted through 1924, when I was his best man, to the day in 1945 when I sorrowfully assisted at his burial. Ted's sister Cicely, one of my closest friends in student days, married another friend, Willy Holland of India, the middle brother of the famous trio: Henry the great eye surgeon on the North-West Frontier of India, Willy (W.E.S.), and Bertie, Bishop of Wellington and later Dean of Norwich. This friendship has been renewed in a later generation.

In order not to burden the narrative with names, one other only shall be mentioned, Clifford Martin, most loving and guileless of men, who as Bishop of Liverpool was for many years the best pastoral bishop on the bench. As he was leaving Cambridge, Clifford said to me, 'Stephen, keep the liberal spirit alive in the CICCU.' Soon after he went down, this matter was to be put to the test. Some slight modification of established procedure had been proposed, and accepted by the Committee by eighteen votes to three. At that point a doughty warrior, Clarence Foster, a Plymouth Brother, well known for many years from his work for the Children's Special Service Mission, said that the three felt that this was a matter of basic principle, and that, if the motion was put into effect, they would feel it necessary to withdraw from the CICCU and to start a separate organisation, thus producing in Cambridge very much the situation that arose a little later in Oxford through the activities of my old school-fellow Verrier Elwin. It fell to me, of all people, to say at that point that in my opinion the unity of the CICCU was of the greatest importance, and that, though I had not changed my views, I felt that the more liberal motion should be withdrawn. So said, so ordered. The eighteen allowed themselves to be defeated by the three. It is always difficult, looking back, to judge one's actions. I think that I was right at that time and in the circumstances; there is no doubt that this was a minor turning-point in church history.

We four, together with nearly fifty others who were interested in the project of missionary service overseas, formed the Cambridge Missionary Band (1920), in which members pledged themselves to write letters for circulation twice a year, and to contribute to the support of one among the brethren. Thirty-five of us are still alive. I appear to be the only bachelor among them, and the only one still on the Lord's business in foreign parts. Most of the others have children and grandchildren, an astonishing proportion of whom are in active Christian service today. It is only rarely that we are able to meet; when we do, something of the warmth of the old fellowship still remains.

In my third year, to my utter astonishment, I received an invitation to become President of the Cambridge branch of the Student

Christian Movement, a body with which I had never publicly associated myself. Of course I had a great many friends in the Movement. The President when I came up was A. G. Pite, who after some years' service with the Movement, became a much loved headmaster of Weymouth School. He moved on to Cheltenham, and then at an Old Boys' Dinner, suddenly collapsed and died. Another stalwart was the mathematical scholar C. B. Greaves (Tim), who served in both West and East Africa, and wrote the life of Carey Francis. Nevertheless, it was largely a strange world into which I moved out. I think that we had a good year, with much fellowship, and a fairly effective Christian witness to the University on an intellectual level which the CICCU largely disregarded.

What I principally owe to the SCM is friendship. It drew me out of the somewhat narrow, though intimate, circle of the CICCU into a wider Christian world, including my first contacts with continental students. I particularly valued the first acquaintance with Scottish students, with their humour and the robustness (which is not the same as orthodoxy) of their Christian faith. At that time the chairman of the Central Committee was Alec Boyd, an extraordinarily felicitous speaker, who was to become (in 1938) the loved and trusted Principal for many years of that most famous of Christian educational institutions in Asia, the Madras Christian College. He was present when Glasgow University gave me the degree of DD in 1963, being himself a holder of the same degree. Hugh Martin was launching the SCM Press on its notable career as an adventurous Christian publishing house, assisted by Johnny Walker, gentlest of men, whose sons have a special corner in my affections – thus Christian friendship goes on from generation to generation.

I met William Paton, Mission Study Secretary in 1921, before he sailed for India; this was in no small way to affect my career, as shall later be recorded. The Study Secretary was George Cockin (always so known, though his initials were F.A.). I was rather critical of George and his methods, and not very much drawn to him personally. I cannot deny the allegation of a Scottish student at the Swanwick Conference in 1922 – 'There's the man who went to sleep in George's lecture and then asked more questions than anybody else.' In 1923 George came to see me in my rooms at Cambridge, and in the strange electric way in which these things happen, I suddenly realised that we were very great friends. I assisted at his consecration as Bishop of Bristol in 1946, and sat next to him throughout the Lambeth Conference of 1948.

One of the activities in which religious societies in universities indulge is an occasional mission to the University. In 1919 it was felt that 1920 would be the year for a mission; the world was in turmoil, many traditions had been swept away, and thousands of men had come up from the gruelling experiences of the war, as a result of which they rejected a great deal of the past, but they had not yet found anything very positive to put in its place. All the religious bodies in Cambridge, with the exception of the Roman Catholics (and they had no choice, officially), co-operated. Official religion was cautious in its attitude. Its point of view was caustically expressed by F. A. Simpson, who said that the mission would mean that the University would do no work for a week, and would spend the rest of the term recovering.

Great thought was devoted to the choice of missioners. In the end four were invited. Charles Gore was then at the height of his powers. Sixty-six years old, he had recently retired from the see of Oxford, having been the first Bishop of Birmingham, to devote himself to writing and teaching and fostering that movement for ecumenical Christian social action which was allied to the 'Life and Work' movement. He became increasingly critical of younger Anglo-Catholics. He had that mysterious quality which cannot be described by any other word than weight. On occasion he would preach a sermon of extreme simplicity, such as could well have been preached by the most recently ordained curate; but it would come across with all the immense authority of a devout and learned spirit.

Frank Theodore Woods, Bishop of Peterborough, was one of the leaders of the liberal Evangelical school. A stalwart member of the CICCU in its great days before 1910, he had adopted broader views, and had made himself master of the social problems of Christianity in an industrial age. He also was a speaker of exceptional quality. On the strength of old family friendship, I invited him to lunch one day during the mission; in those days I had not realised how shy so large and great a man could be, and this was a rather disastrous occasion.

The CICCU had chosen the Revd Barclay F. Buxton, who had been a missionary in Japan, a man of infinite devotion, and a Bible student of almost painful intensity. I do not think that he was a good choice for that particular moment of history; we were all full of intellectual questionings, and not so likely to be reached by titles such as 'Can I have a clean heart?'

The Free Churchmen had put forward as their speaker Dr A. Herbert Gray. Gray had become well known through his book *Men*,

Women and God, perhaps the first entirely frank and honest treatment of the whole subject of sex from a Christian point of view. The
book went through edition after edition. In an Appendix it included
a straightforward statement, by Gray's medical brother, of what the
sex act actually is. It may seem strange to present-day readers that
in the 1920s this was regarded as revolutionary boldness.

The mission was well planned and well carried out. Every member of the University received a personal letter, signed by the four
missioners, which included the notable phrase, undoubtedly from
the pen of Charles Gore, that we should attend the mission 'as your
conscience rather than as your curiosity' may direct. Attendances
were very large. I have never seen any exact figures; I would
estimate that out of a student population of about 6,000, not less
than 1,600 were out each night, with about 2,000 on the last night.
This means that, reckoning with an average of four attendances per
head, considerably more than half the members of the University
student body had attended at least one meeting.

I do not know who, if anyone, was converted by this mission.
Probably those who organised it, apart from the leaders of the
CICCU, did not wish for or aim at instantaneous conversion, if
there is such a thing. Their desire was rather to set people thinking,
and to let them know that the Christian faith was one of the options
held open by some of the ablest men and women of their generation.
In this I think it was entirely successful. The immediate impact was
less than that of William Temple's mission to Oxford in 1931. But
in the first place it seems likely that there was far more religion in
Cambridge in 1920 than there was in Oxford in 1931; and in the
second, the thrust was extended over a broad front rather than
concentrated in the testimony of one single man.

During these weeks I was for the first time brought into sharp
confrontation with the Anglo-Catholic movement. I had long been
interested in it, though rather from afar, and had many friends
who had committed themselves to that form of Anglicanism. It
is necessary to understand what the movement was like fifty years
ago. Much of the doctrine of the great founders had receded into the
background. There was a good deal of trivial campaigning over
the use of vestments and incense in church, and much misstatement
of facts. The real centre of the storm, however, was the question of
the reservation of the consecrated elements in church after the
conclusion of the celebration of Holy Communion. Frank Weston,
Bishop of Zanzibar, and one of the heroes of the day, was urging
people in no measured terms to 'fight for their tabernacles'. It was

stated that reservation was intended to meet an allegedly urgent need for the Communion of the sick and dying. But there was a good deal of dishonesty in this; most people of that school wanted reservation for the purpose of adoration, both in quasi-liturgical services and in private prayer.

This was the point at which the dividing line came for me. At about 2 a.m. in Wilfred Ellis' room, a friendly clergyman of a rather extreme Anglo-Catholic variety said to me, 'The difference is that you wouldn't go ten minutes round the corner to say your prayers before the reserved sacrament, and I would.' In that moment I knew where I stood. I saw that his position was so utterly contrary to all that I had learned of the doctrine of the Holy Spirit and of the mystery of Christ dwelling in our hearts by faith that, if I lived to be a hundred, it could never in any circumstances whatever occur to me to go ten minutes round the corner to say my prayers before the reserved sacrament.

I learned from my father lessons of intense reverence at the Holy Communion and in the celebration of it. I hope that I have been able to follow his good example. But what we were concerned about was the Real Presence of Christ as the giver in his own Supper, rather than the Real Presence of Christ shut up in the elements which he himself uses to make his presence known. This is a position which I have never seen any necessity in half a century to modify.

One other activity of Cambridge Christians in those days was so unusual that it must be chronicled at some length. This was the Cambridge Missionary Campaign, in which during the Long Vacation a considerable body of men (never in those days women), all of Anglican persuasion, descended upon some city and, with the permission of the bishop, tried to convey to the parishes in sermons and addresses of every kind the urgency and the splendour of the Christian missionary cause throughout the world. This had naturally lapsed during the war, but was resuscitated in 1920. Inevitably my brother Henry and I were drawn into this effort, and found ourselves with nearly fifty others let loose on the Five Towns, up till that time known to me only through the writings of Arnold Bennett.

A campaign of this kind seems to me far healthier than the evangelistic campaigns which have taken its place. An undergraduate aged twenty is in most cases not mature enough to stand the emotional strains of an evangelistic campaign. I have known real harm done to young people subjected to emotional pressures which they were in no way prepared to withstand. In our campaign it was always stressed that there was to be no emotional appeal. Let the

facts speak for themselves. We were told to master one field of
endeavour and to present it in such a way that the immensity of the
Christian opportunity and the generosity of God's response to man's
feeble efforts should come home to the ordinary church member.
We were not to be afraid of failure, but to believe in the upholding
power of God. Naturally emotion cannot be entirely absent from
the presentation of a cause in which one profoundly believes; but
we obeyed instructions and tried to keep it to a minimum.

Our campaigns were dated by the fact, already noted, that they
were made without the intrusion of the female. The CICCU remained obstinately Victorian, except in the CSSM missions on the
beach (where the legend affirmed that CSSM stood for 'Come single,
soon married'). The SCM pioneered freer relationships between
men and women (whence the exegesis according to which SCM
means 'Single Christians Married'). It is also the case that we were an
Anglican team, without any infiltration of nonconformists and other
lower types. On the other hand, in those days of party strife it was
no mean achievement to get Anglicans of every conceivable shade
of opinion working together in unity, and without any intrusion
of party-spirit; to me one of the most memorable experiences of
Christian fellowship that I can recall.

In 1920 the Vicar of Stoke was that hardy Christian H. V. Stuart,
later Dean of Carlisle, who, if report speaks true, as a young man
went down a mine and worked a full shift at the coal-face to show
that it could be done without drinking beer. My very kind hosts
were the Revd G. H. and Mrs Hewitt, whose son is the historian of
the later doings of the Church Missionary Society. The culmination
of the ten days' work was the great final meeting to which people
came in from all the parishes and filled the largest hall in the Five
Towns – I believe that five thousand people were present. The chair
was taken by the greatly loved Bishop Kempthorne of Lichfield, a
man the outward beauty of whose appearance accurately reflected
the inner grace of a devout and consecrated spirit. Five ten-minute
addresses were given by members of the team. I was selected to
speak on the Christian witness to Israel, a subject in which I have
had a life-long interest. A young man feels a little awed by standing
up before so great a multitude; I found to my surprise that, after the
first sentence has been uttered, it is in some ways easier to speak to
the many rather than to the few.

Half-way through the campaign it began to be evident to whom
the eyes of the brethren were turning as the Secretary of the next
year's campaign. It was a job I did not seek, but one that I felt I could

not refuse. This was my first experience of large-scale organisation; I simply could not have done it without the help of A. T. Schofield of Caius, my predecessor. But in the end the Tyneside campaign was reckoned to be as well organised as any that came before or after. To record all the details of preparation would be tedious.

By the time that all the applications from the parishes were in and dealt with, there were a thousand engagements. I placed all the sheets of foolscap together and backed them with casement cloth; this timetable, six foot by three, was a noble monument of diligence and joinery; unfortunately the writing (we had no typewriter in those days) was too faint, and it was found impossible to photograph it. I had to do a good deal of speaking, as well as watching over the central organisation, and patching the cracks which appeared when one or other of the brethren fell sick or was otherwise out of action. Once again the ten days culminated in a tremendous meeting in the largest hall on Tyneside. Bishop Wild, the least emotional of men, had never seen anything like it in his life, and really let himself go for the occasion. The brethren had asked me to give the final address – only ten minutes, and I have no recollection of what I said, but I do know that it was a devoutly thankful *Nunc Dimittis* at the conclusion of an exceptionally strenuous piece of work.

I have written a good deal about Christian activities at Cambridge, but the majority of my friends were not Christians. I well recall one of these friends putting the question point blank to James (later Sir James) Duff: 'James, are you a Christian?' to which James replied, 'No, but I would very much like to be.' This would probably have been true of a large number of my older contemporaries. Those who had been through the war had for the most part rejected Christianity as they had learned it from parents and schoolmasters – it was very hard for my generation to believe that their parents had been right about anything (had they not caused the war?) – and they had not yet found a Christian faith large enough to encompass the horrors of that time. Some, but not all, later came back to the fullness of Christian faith.

The reader may by this time have almost forgotten that any work is done in Cambridge. It is time to return to my third year, and the serious test of Part II of the Classical Tripos. We had to choose two out of five sections to offer for examination. I chose history and philosophy. The special period in Roman history was the reigns of Claudius and Nero, AD 41–65. This was ideal for one planning to go on to read theology. As before, the papers did not seem to me too difficult, though it was clear that I should have worked harder at history. That year, for some unknown reason, we also had to undergo oral examinations, as they do in Oxford, but my examiners in philosophy were Cornford and Angus, close friends by now, who just asked me one or two desultory questions and congratulated me on my skill in choosing all the easiest questions. I thought I had done well enough to get a first class, and this proved to be the case when the results came out. I had also got distinctions in both my sections, though of this I had been far from sure. I believe that Nock and I are the only two men in history to have taken two sections and obtained distinction in both.

I have never regretted the long years spent in the study of Latin and Greek; indeed, life would be bleak for me on that proverbial desert island without the works of Homer, Aeschylus, Plato and Aristophanes. But now, having reached this pinnacle as a classical scholar, I had to decide what I was going to do next.

It was clear that I could stay up for a fourth year, and I very much wanted to do so. Theology was my choice. I only had one year in hand, so I resisted Tennant's attempts to persuade me to work in his field of philosophical theology, which would have taken two years, and opted instead for the special section in New Testament for the Theological Tripos Part II. This was, I am afraid, a lazy decision, as I already knew a great deal about the New Testament; but there were many fields that I still desired to explore, and I felt that the year would not be wasted.

The door to the world of Cambridge theology had been opened to me not by a theologian, but by a fellow classicist, Martin Charlesworth, of Jesus, whom I had got to know through the university scholarship examinations when we had read some of the obscurer parts of Plato together. It was he who acted as a link between me and Alexander Nairne, at that time Dean of Jesus, who had recently helped award me the Carus Greek New Testament prize. An invitation to lunch from Nairne led to a life-long friendship. Nairne taught me to read the Old Testament with love and imagination, but the greatest of all the services he rendered me concerned his love of the Italian language. In my second year he persuaded a group of classical scholars to buy the Italian grammar especially produced for classical scholars by J. E. Flecker, and before long had us reading the *Oxford Book of Italian Verse*. It was not long before we graduated to Dante, and I became a Dante fan, to my good luck one of the subjects set that year for the College Essay Prize. One's early twenties is just the right age at which to read *La Vita Nuova* in Italian. That I got the prize is a matter of very little moment; I hope that my abiding love for Dante may be registered to my credit somewhere in heaven.

Alan England Brooke was the Ely Professor of Divinity. In 1912 he produced the best commentary ever written in any language on the Epistles of St John, but early in life he had committed himself to the gigantic task of the Cambridge Septuagint, and this occupied the greater part of his working hours over many years. Much of great value that we might have had from him never saw the light. He was one of the first scholars in this century to take seriously the idea of the Fourth Gospel as an independent historical source for the life of Jesus Christ.

One other among our theological potentates must be named – Francis Crawford Burkitt. Unlike most theologians he was a layman, and very proud of his lay status. I never knew exactly what he believed, but he was, among other things, churchwarden of an Evangelical church in Cambridge. He gladdened my heart, in a time of liturgical chaos, by writing a pamphlet on the Communion Service of the Church of England, in which he maintained, as I do, that the 1662 English order for Holy Communion is the best eucharistic service in the world. He desired only one change, that after the Prayer of Oblation the word 'or' should read 'and', so that both the Prayer of Oblation and the Prayer of Thanksgiving should be read. It was in this form that the Communion service was celebrated in Trinity Chapel as long as John Burnaby was Dean. This makes the service rather long, especially if the Ten Commandments have been read; but it gives a better theology and a better balance than that of any other eucharistic liturgy in the world. All the modern liturgies strike one accustomed to this grandeur as nice little services for a small congregation on a week-day, but as wholly inadequate to serve as the great liturgical act of worship on a Sunday. The poverty of our liturgical expression matches the impoverishment of our theological thinking since the great creative days of the sixteenth century.

Once it was clear that I was to study theology, I made a decision of capital importance. I made up my mind that I must be able to read German theology, of the importance of which I had become convinced. I had rather let my German go in the years since I had left school, and I knew that I was setting myself a somewhat taxing task. There was nothing for it but to begin again and to hope for the best. I went along to Hoskyns and borrowed a book.

Edwyn Clement Hoskyns was never my teacher, but he was a friend through many years. He had studied in Berlin under Adolf von Harnack, and was a typical liberal of the early twentieth-century vintage, when an encounter with the writings of Karl Barth made him one of the chief supporters of biblical orthodoxy in England. He translated and in places paraphrased Barth's *The Epistle to the Romans*, a task which took him eighteen months of hard labour, and injected into the Cambridge School of Theology a dynamic and polemical orthodoxy very uncongenial to those who had grown up under the liberal tradition. Hoskyns did not like writing, but he loved lecturing and, still more, the stimulus of discussion and debate in small groups. He came nearer than any other man in the history of English theology to creating a school of the type so familiar in Germany, and of which he himself was openly critical. Michael Ramsey, Oliver Tomkins, John Ramsbottom, Charles Smyth and of course Noel Davey, who admirably completed the unfinished commentaries, were all 'Hoskyns boys'; none of these has left any deep mark on theological thinking in the English-speaking world, but Hoskyns is one of the very few English scholars of whom anyone in Germany has ever heard.

The book that I borrowed from Hoskyns was W. Bousset's *Kyrios Christos*, a noble book, but never translated into English. This brought me fully into contact with the *Religionsgeschichtliche Schule* (history of religions school), the tenets of which were already somewhat familiar through the popularising efforts of Kirsopp Lake's *The Earlier Epistles of St Paul*. In the first hour I read two pages. By the end of three months I could read six pages an hour, and from that time on never looked back. I still have the copy of Cassell's *German-English/English-German* dictionary, which I wore out in the process.

During the years that I concentrated on the New Testament in Cambridge, I went to very few lectures, and in the end to none at all. By the time that I had attended a few lectures of a course, I knew the mind and manner of working of the lecturer, and felt that I would not greatly profit from following him further. I considered I was better employed sitting in the corner of my room reading German theology than attending lectures which might have left me impatient rather than edified. Looking back, I am astonished at the books I know myself to have read in that year. I chanced on a copy of Johannes Weiss on 1 Corinthians (the special epistle for the Tripos that year), to me one of the best commentaries ever written. I also learned a great deal from Eduard Meyer's *Ursprung und Anfänge des Christentums* ('Origin and Beginnings of Christianity'). He was not a theologian, but came to the New Testament by way of his researches in ancient history; at times the caution of the historian stood in pleasant contrast to the extravagances of the theologians. I delved deeply into the question of Christianity and the mystery religions, under the guidance of Reitzenstein; I knew a lot about Poimandres and the Hermetic writings. And I read also another memorable work which has never seen the light in English, Wilhelm Wrede on the Messianic secret; I am of the opinion that Wrede got it all wrong, but I have always learned far more from books that I disagree with than from those that command my ready assent. I must confess to one gap in my reading at that time. I knew by name K. L. Schmidt's pioneer book on 'Form-criticism', *Der Rahmen der Geschichte Jesu* ('The Frame of the Life of Jesus'), but I did not read it; and I did not come across the early works of Rudolf Bultmann and Martin Dibelius. One cannot know everything.

All this introduced me to a world of which I had long been dimly aware, but with which I now had to come to terms. I had been well brought up on the classic Cambridge tradition of New Testament scholarship, immensely erudite, cautious and devout. These Germans moved in an atmosphere of speculation and radical criticism, new to me and at first highly disturbing to a young and pious student. I suspect that the tendency of my mind is naturally conservative; but this is the other side of a profound scepticism, which is unwilling to leap at anything new until it has been able to produce fairly solid evidence that it is something more than the bright idea of a scholar who has to say something new and surprising in order to get his doctorate. So my entire theological and religious outlook had to undergo a thorough house-cleaning and resetting.

My parents were to the end of their days fundamentalists, to use a term unknown in those days. Incidentally, my father's library contained the only copy I remember ever having seen of the twelve small volumes entitled *The Fundamentals*, from which the term 'fundamentalism' is derived. I knew that I no longer saw things as my parents saw them, but my views only changed slowly, without any violent explosion, by the patient absorption of new ideas. There was no breach of affection, though there were times of tension, but it has never seemed to me right or good to shock those whose Christian faith is expressed in terms other than those that I can accept.

At school we studied the Synoptic Gospels year after year, until I was weary of them, and for my first three years at Cambridge, I could read only the Gospel according to St John. When one is pulling the Gospel to pieces, it is all too easy to lose sight of the One who is the central figure in the Gospels. Light came to me from a little book by Burkitt, *The Earliest Sources for the Life of Jesus*, and particularly from the phrase 'the strong and mysterious person who walks through the pages of St Mark'. It suddenly dawned on me that it was possible to read the Gospels as the story of a man. I began reading Mark's Gospel with new eyes. I saw it as the most dramatic of all the Gospels, and Jesus as the one who moved among men with the perpetual but never spoken question on his lips, 'Who am I?' This approach is so familiar today that it may be surprising for the reader to learn that it came to me with the force of a revelation. This is the incalculable debt we owe to the liberals: they gave us back the Man.

The area of darkness surrounded the resurrection of Jesus. I had accepted this as truth, and had always understood the Holy Communion as a meeting with a living friend. But, until I read Bousset I had never really studied in detail the New Testament evidences for the resurrection. It is a perplexing story. The various attempts to make all the narratives fit into one another are more ingenious than convincing. Moreover, like most of the men of my generation, I was still a good deal under the influence of the mechanistic view of the universe in which miracles could not and did not happen. A. G. Hogg had written *Redemption from this World* (1922), the pioneer work in setting us free from the prison of naturalism, later popularised by D. S. Cairns in the much more readable book, *The Faith that Rebels*. But we had not at the time grasped Hogg's idea of the plastic universe. I saw that something entirely out of the ordinary must have happened, otherwise the Christian movement would never have come into being. But just what it was that had happened and how it could have happened in this universe I could not clearly see. This darkness of the understanding recurred from time to time, as darkness of the spirit set in for other and entirely different reasons. The light did not become steady until I came to see the resurrection of Jesus not simply as the resuscitation of a single man, but as the rebirth of the entire universe; what the gospel offers is not a new understanding of self in an unchanged world but an invitation to adventure in a world in which all things have become new.

It is often said that the uncertain happenings of history cannot lead to faith. No, but they can destroy it; history is the great destroyer of myths. If it could be shown, as clear historical evidence, that the bones of Jesus of Nazareth had mouldered away in a Palestinian grave like the bones of any other man, I would cease to be a worshipping Christian. I would still regard the Gospels as the best news ever brought to man, and Jesus as our one hope in a wintry sea, his teaching as our guide to the way in which men ought to live, his example as the inspiration to effort and to self-sacrifice. But I could not proclaim a victory which is some eschatological event to be proclaimed in some distant day at the end of time. I could not partake in a Holy Communion which was simply the commemoration of a long-departed friend. I could not pretend that a fortuitous collection of individuals is the body of Christ. As to the 'how', I still maintain a reverent uncertainty; as to the 'that', I can no longer feel any manner of doubt.

I did manage to keep my fourth year fairly free of examinations, but I did sit for a thing called the Crosse Scholarship in Theology, which involved papers in Old Testament, New Testament, church history and Christian doctrine, and for which I was the only candidate. This is the only time in my life that I have sat a test in Hebrew. I may be ignorant of Old Testament criticism, but at that time I knew the contents of the Old Testament text extremely well; I at once identified the rather difficult passage from Jeremiah about 'burying in Tophet till there was no place to bury' (7:30–4), and translated it with gusto, being careful to keep a reasonable distance away from the familiar English translation. Twenty years later I found that the legend still persisted that I knew Hebrew as well as I knew Greek.

The Tripos caused me little difficulty. I had worked hard and knew my stuff. And I have to confess that I am an extremely good examination candidate, a deplorable capacity in which I take no pride at all. I was always able to see exactly the sense of a question, marshal my knowledge quietly and neatly, and write down absolutely everything that I knew on the subject, but give at the same time the impression that I had vast stores of hidden knowledge which could have been drawn upon if only there had been more time to write. This gift is useful for doing well in examinations, but for no other purpose whatever. It is a gift that I value less highly than any other that I may happen to possess.

Having got theology behind me, I had once again to decide what to do next. All my pastors and masters took the view that I must try for a prize fellowship at Trinity. The problem was how I was to keep myself alive for another year at Cambridge. Scholarships were competitive and very hard to get; grants were few and equally hard to get. I knew that my family could not help any more. If I was to stay at Cambridge, it must be by my own efforts and ingenuity.

When we went to Cambridge, my father told us that each quarter we would find £37.10 in our bank account; that was what he could supply, and the rest we must make up for ourselves. I had friends whose fathers doled out money in dribs and drabs and demanded full accounts. I would have hated this, and was extremely grateful to my father for what seemed to me a far better plan; at nineteen one is ready to accept responsibility for one's own affairs. Only once did I have to ask for more. In 1919 prices were still extremely high – they dropped a good deal in the succeeding years – my father had given me less than the minimum amount needed for my rooms, and I had to ask him to supplement; the money was forthcoming, but with less than enthusiasm, and a hint that it was not expected that such a request would be granted again. I received a very severe letter when on one occasion the College sent my bill to him and not to me. With scholarships piling up, I became in time reasonably affluent, and in my third year was able to afford a second-hand motorcycle. But I was always liable to receive one of those letters from the friendly manager of the Midland Bank, which fifty years later still keeps my account, saying 'We hope you will put this account in order at an early date. I hope you are having an enjoyable vacation. Yours sincerely, J. A. C.'

But now all this was at an end. My father had done what he regarded as his duty, and could not have done more at that time had he wished, since my brother Gerald was not one of the fortunate ones who get scholarships, and it had been rightly decided that he should be given as good a start in life as the others. So who would accept the responsibility for feeding me during a fifth year? My studies of the Cambridge Calendar had revealed to me that there was something called the Burney Studentship in the Philosophy of Religion, worth £200 a year. Money was still coming in from one or two scholarships, and, if I could secure the Burney, I should have enough to live on in modest comfort. I applied and was elected.

Trinity College awards three or four prize fellowships a year, mainly on the basis of a dissertation. The competition is fierce. I would have been eligible to sit in my fourth, fifth or sixth year; but I decided to venture all on a single throw, and let the election in my fifth year decide the issue. To produce in ten months a solid dissertation which, to have any chance of success must be of a standard considerably higher than that usually required for the PhD degree, is a formidable task; to this I must now set myself.

The first thing was to find a subject. This is always the hardest part in research; once the subject has been settled and defined, research can go forward merrily, but there may be a longish period of frenzied and frustrated searching, and there is always the risk of discovering at the last moment that the work has been done by someone else. I had long been interested in Neoplatonism, and in the actions and reactions between the Greek and Christian mind in the later days of the Roman Empire. I felt sure that there was something that could be done in this area, and that my knowledge of earlier Greek philosophy would come in useful. Greatly daring, I wrote to W. R. Inge, the Dean of St Paul's, whose Gifford Lectures on Plotinus, though erratic and unreliable in places, are still the best general introduction to the thought of Plotinus and to Neoplatonism generally.

Inge was not known to me personally, but there can hardly have been a Christian in England at that time who did not know him either by speech or writing. The occasional asperity of his utterance, and the epigrammatic character of his style, had won hosts of readers, both for his serious writings and for his journalistic pyrotechnics in the *Evening Standard*; he could fill any church or college chapel in Cambridge, and was indeed a most gifted and attractive preacher. He could be remote and allusive, but the first time I heard him preach, he delivered a sermon of exquisite simplicity on 'Thirst'. Years later I read in the *Guardian* a sermon of matchless excellence on sin, based on the arrogance of King Jehoiakim, who burned in a brazier the scroll of the prophecies of Jeremiah (Jer. 36). Inge directed me away from the details of literary dependence to the far more exciting theme of the thought-world of the Greeks and that of the Christians, the overlap and the contrast between them. My main source for the Greeks was to be Plotinus, and for the Christians the three Cappadocian Fathers, Basil of Caesarea, Gregory of Nyssa and Gregory of Nazianzus. The important thing was to get down to the texts themselves.

It cannot be denied that Plotinus is abominably difficult. Like Aristotle, he can, when he chooses, write superb Greek, but much of what we possess is in the form of lecture notes or memoranda. Moreover, the *Enneads* were arranged by Porphyry, roughly according to subject and without any regard for chronology, so that the development of the thought of Plotinus can only be traced by conjecture. L. P. Larsen, the greatest of all South India missionaries, advised a Swedish friend of mine that he might benefit from looking at Plotinus before he came to India. 'But,' said my friend, 'one look at the text was quite sufficient.' Many others have felt the same. Professor Harder has said somewhere that, when he set to work on his German translation, there were perhaps not more than twenty people in the world who could read and understand Plotinus for themselves. I hope that I was one of the twenty.

In 1924 we had far less help than is available today. In the first place, we now have the greater part of a reliable text, and translations in English, French, German and Italian. At the time I write, a new English translation, perhaps less literary but more reliable, by A. H. Armstrong is appearing. There have been many specialist studies, almost all of which have added something to our knowledge of this most difficult author. For the Cappadocians, we were still almost wholly dependent on Migne's *Patrologia*. The situation was and is very unsatisfactory. In view of the great importance of their contribution to Christian thought, it is surprising that these three great writers have not fared better at the hands of Christian scholars. Gregory of Nyssa has always been a happy hunting ground for young Roman Catholics in search of doctorates – his well-established orthodoxy makes him safe; I gradually acquired quite a collection of these monographs, and they directed me to passages which otherwise I might well have overlooked. But nothing can take the place of patient and careful study of the texts.

In this year, as in all others, I managed to fit in quite a number of activities outside the regular course of my studies. One of these was my presence at the Conference on Politics, Economics and Citizenship (COPEC), which was held at Birmingham in April 1924 under the chairmanship of William Temple, at that time Bishop of Manchester. To this I was commissioned by the diocesan council of the diocese of Ely. The conference itself was very dull; nevertheless, it was a real landmark in ecumenical progress. Preparations had been going on since 1921, with Hugh Martin and Charles Raven, later Regius Professor of Divinity at Cambridge, in the lead, and with the participation of Roman Catholics almost up to the time of the conference – the rupture took place, naturally enough, on the question of contraception. I had been too much preoccupied with my studies to prepare adequately for the conference. However, the twelve volumes of the preparatory papers are still of the greatest possible value to the student who wishes to know what we were thinking about all those years ago, and COPEC 1924 was of great significance as the British preparation for the Universal Conference on Life and Work which was to be held at Stockholm in the following year.

Throughout these months there was an urgent question all the time knocking at the door. Should I become a missionary of the gospel overseas? With my background it was impossible that the question should be evaded. My parents had been missionaries; however, they had been as scrupulous as could be imagined in not trying to force any of their children into their own mould. Indeed, in view of the great possibilities opening out before me in England my father at times seemed positively to argue against my going abroad. Everything within me cried out in favour of Cambridge. The very stones of Trinity are dear to me. I love the academic life, and seem to have a certain capacity both for teaching and for winning the confidence of students. There is never certainty in such things, but it seemed at least highly probable that I might be elected to a fellowship that year. There can never in history have been anything less emotional than my acceptance of the vocation of a missionary. For years I had been convinced that, since Christ died for all men no less than for me, this gospel of Christ must be preached to all men, whether they will hear or whether they will forbear; that this gospel will not be preached unless a sufficient number of those who are young, free and in reasonable health, are prepared to forgo all worldly ambition and accept the call to become Christ's witnesses and stewards in areas where his name has not been proclaimed before, or where the majority of the population still accept the allegories of some other and non-Christian faith. I had discussed the matter with my father the year before, weighing the claims of Cambridge, and what in those days we still called the mission field against one another. He remarked, 'Knowing you as I do, I have very little doubt as to the way in which you will decide.'

He was right. During the course of the year 1924 it became clear to me that my allegiance to Christ was going to cost me many of the things that I held most dear, but that, without total betrayal of that allegiance, there could be no turning back. If no other in the world were to go, still I must go. Like almost all young Christians, I had had some romantic illusions about the work of a missionary. It was my desire, like that of St Paul, not to build on another man's foundations; I pictured myself as a pioneer in some area in which the gospel had never been preached before, a pretty picture for a man who has the utmost difficulty in repairing a puncture or changing the wheel of a car. I imagined my linguistic gifts being used in reducing to writing some languages which no white man had ever learned before, and of which the grammatical structure had for the first time to be discovered. I have often felt that the Lord exercised his sense of humour in arranging for me to go to South India, one of the oldest mission fields in the world,

and to the study of Tamil, a language with which Europeans had
been occupied for four hundred years. But so it came about. The
negotiations which led to the formation of the Church of South
India in 1947 had already begun; I was already deeply committed
to the ecumenical ideal of the union of the Churches. And so South
India it was. Oh *sancta simplicitas*! I hoped that I might be ordained
to the ministry of that united Church.

I do not know at what point exactly the decision was made –
in those days I did not keep a diary. All that I can remember is
that some time between January and April 1924 it became clear to
me that I would not be able to settle down to any work with full
concentration unless I had a timetable to guide me. I decided to
write my dissertation in July and August, and to take September
as a holiday month. The question of the fellowship would be
settled in October, and I would leave for India in November or
December. Actually my ticket was bought in June, before I sat
down to write.

Now that the question of date had been settled, the problem of
ordination had also to be considered. I was by now a passionate
student of theology in almost all its branches. Then, as now, the
thing that I cared about far more deeply than anything else was
that men and women should be brought to know Jesus Christ.
But I was far from convinced that the ordained ministry was the
vocation in which I could best use such gifts I had, and find the
freedom of spirit without which Christian work can all too soon
become a burden and not a joy. My father, himself ordained deacon
at the age of thirty-three, encouraged me to find my own way, to go
slowly, and not to let myself be hurried by the opinions or advice of
my friends. I made up my mind to go to India as a layman, and to
make my final decision in the light of what I found in the 'mission
field'. It seemed sensible, however, to get all the preliminaries out
of the way, so that if I decided to be ordained, my work would not
be interrupted by a period of residence at a theological college. To
that end I enrolled myself as an associate of Westcott House (once
known as the Clergy Training School), where my father had received
his brief training for the ministry twenty-two years before.

One of the best things that happened to me in my first year
at Cambridge was that I made the acquaintance of Bertram Keir
Cunningham, who had been brought in to revive the Clergy Training School. He soon made it a power-house in the life of the Church
of England, and a nursery of bishops. He had a unique gift for
enabling men of the most diverse schools of churchmanship to live

together in amity without tearing one another's eyes out. I took to going to Compline, which he said in the simple little upper room we used before the chapel was built, and which was an experience in itself. Even more impressive to me was the dead silence after the little service had come to an end, a total absorption in adoration and supplication which became part of me, and of which, though much has departed with the passage of years, I hope some part may remain with me till the end. After some time it became almost a regular custom that B.K. would invite me into his room about twice a term for a cup of tea afterwards. So much has been written about B. K. that there is no need for a lengthy panegyric here.

In those months I passed the General Ordination Examination of the Church of England. I had exemption from a good many papers through my Tripos. I forget how many I had to take, but I do remember that I took no special steps to prepare for them. Nevertheless, Kenneth Kirk, later Bishop of Oxford, repented, I hope, of only giving me a pass mark in Christian ethics. The GOE seems to me to be one of the gravest misfortunes that has ever befallen the Church of England. Much of the training for the ministry in that ancient Church seems to me deplorably bad, and I believe that the GOE is somewhere near the heart of the trouble. It is one of those examinations which can be passed without having ever read a single theological book; cheap textbooks and the excellent lecture notes dealt out by many conscientious theological teachers will bring all but the stupidest men up to the point of passing the examination. So it appears many of them have never found it necessary to read any large theological work. One does not go to heaven because one has heard of Schleiermacher, but it is sad that so many Anglican ordinands have never even heard the name of the father of modern theology.

All this time my notes on Plotinus and the Cappadocians were accumulating. When the day came that I had to sort out my thick pile of notes, they fell naturally into five piles, and these made the chapters of my dissertation, though one chapter had three sections. I had said that I would begin to write on 10 July, and this is exactly what I did. I hope that I shall never again have to work as hard as I did in those two months. For the first and last time in my life, my work pursued me into my dreams, and this was a danger signal. I owe much to Geoffrey Eley (now Sir Geoffrey), who saw what was happening and insisted that I sometimes get out and play tennis. Then I fell untimely ill. At school I was always being ill. Most of those illnesses could be easily explained as the result of underfeeding and overwork. At Cambridge the position entirely changed. In five years, I do not think I missed more than two days' work. I had constantly experienced difficulty in getting as much sleep as I needed, and Nock became troubled about the amount of aspirin I was consuming, but that was a chronic trouble, not an actual sickness. And now to fall sick at this extremely inconvenient moment!

The natural explanation is to say that this was psychosomatic, and that overwork and anxiety drove me to my bed. I can find in recollection no ground whatever for supposing this to be the case. I think that I simply fell victim to one of those miscellaneous fevers that wander about the English countryside. I know I was earnestly prayed for in Westcott House Chapel. B. K. came to comfort me, knowing how much the loss of even a few days could mean to my dissertation, but after three days I rose from my bed. A weekend at Southwold with my friends the Hollands, then newly married, set me on my feet again. So back to the treadmill.

The latest date for handing in the dissertation was 31 August. By 28 August I had written all I knew, and had carefully revised my text. There seemed nothing more to be done, so on that day I handed it in to the College office. In less than two months I had written 100,000 words. As far as I remember, allowing for Sundays, and for the period of illness, I had actually had a pen in my hand on only twenty-eight of those days. No one ought to write so much so fast; in later years I have tried, whenever possible, to avoid writing more than a thousand words in a day. The mind grows tired; the exact sequence of thought is easily lost, sentences twist themselves into odd forms. I can write a great deal more in a day, if it is absolutely necessary, but I always say with Naaman, 'The Lord pardon thy servant in this thing' (2 Kings 5:13). It is not surprising that on 28 August 1924 I felt drained of knowledge, of energy, and of everything else that makes life human. I felt that I knew what Angus meant when he told me that, on the day on which he finished the Classical Tripos, there was no sin which he could not have committed.

In my opinion this period of intensive study and writing did me a good deal of harm. To have produced so much so quickly, and in general on a high level of competence, was a tremendous *tour de force*. But scholars do not commit themselves to *tours de force*, that is the work of charlatans. A charlatan is exactly what I felt like when I handed in my dissertation. I had carried out my old examination trick of using every scrap of knowledge that I had acquired, and thus producing a splendid façade behind which there was in reality very little. Perhaps I was unduly hard on myself. Hugh Stewart had told me that the electors looked more for promise than for achievement. I knew perhaps one-fifth of what I ought to have known about Neoplatonism, and one-tenth of what I ought to have known about Cappadocian theology. On the other hand, it would hardly have been possible to do more in the time that I had allowed myself for study and writing. Probably no one at the time in England knew more about the subject than I did, and what I wrote carried with it the weight of the long years in which I had studied Greek philosophy and history. Nevertheless, the experience left me with a profound distrust of what is commonly called research, and a grave disinclination ever to be engaged in it again.

There was one more pious work to be fulfilled before the summer ran out. My father had taken my two younger brothers away from Dean Close, and sent them to St Paul's School in London, a very ill-advised step in my opinion. For many years two Bible classes for boys have existed in the West End of London, one called the Pauline Meeting and the other the Ealing Meeting, run on Evangelical lines, but without the narrowness which spoils so much Evangelical work. Each year the two meetings joined for a boys' camp, held not under canvas, but in a preparatory school rented for the purpose. That year we were a large party at Bilton Grange, near Rugby. Christians have an almost infinite capacity for quarrelling with one another. In all the years that I was associated with the meetings, I cannot remember any dissensions. We appreciated one another's gifts and thanked God for them; we do not seem to have been too much disturbed by one another's failings.

I had to go back to Cambridge for one strange episode – the general examination for candidates for fellowships, twenty-four of us representing a wide range of faculties and disciplines. There were two papers, called 'General Aspects of Literature and History' and 'General Aspects of Philosophy and Science'. There was only one thing certain about this examination: that absolutely anything could be asked. I was told afterwards that my essay on the writing of history had met with the favour of R. Vere Laurence, whose chapter on the Council of Trent in the old Cambridge Modern History is still the best short account of the Council ever written; and this was kind of him, since the burden of my essay was that no such thing as real history can ever be written.

So the date arrived at which the results of the election would be announced. It so happened that there was no place at which

I could conveniently receive a telegram; I therefore decided to go to Cambridge and learn my fate on the spot. If I had failed, I would accept this as confirmation of the guidance I had received to renounce my chance of trying again in the following year and to go straight to India. If I was elected, I would take this as the end and crown of intellectual effort not merely in the five years I had spent at Cambridge, but much further back from the time at which as a boy of nine I had started to learn Greek. As I passed through the Great Gate, the porter, an old friend, said to me, 'I think I have to congratulate you, Sir'; in the shock of relief and thankfulness, my reply was indecorous and need not be recorded here.

It is almost impossible to explain to anyone who does not know Oxford or Cambridge the meaning of election to a fellowship. Long ago groups of learned men agreed to live together as a family – to think together, to eat together, to pray together and to play together – the Fellows' Bowling Green at Trinity is one of the oldest gardens in England – and in course of time admitted young students into the intimacy of the common life. Since the nineteenth century, when fellows received permission to marry, much of the intimate familial character of the common life has disappeared, but much still remains. Once a member of the family, one has entered into a fellowship which can never be dissolved. In bygone days a fellow who did not marry remained a fellow for life, wherever he might be. This system has changed, and I knew that by going to India I would lose my fellowship within a few years. But a past fellow is still in a very real sense a member of the foundation, and retains certain rights and privileges until the end of his days.

The next step was admission to the fellowship in Chapel by the Master, J. J. Thomson. There were four of us, and we well represented the varieties of scholarship in the modern world, the others being respectively a mathematician, a lawyer, and a biochemist. I was myself the first man ever elected to a Trinity prize fellowship on a dissertation on a theological subject. Then followed the fellowship admission dinner, at which it is customary for the Master to make a speech introducing the new fellows to the company. On this occasion J. J., emphasising the absolute impartiality of the election, stated his opinion that, no matter what crimes a man might have committed, if his dissertation was good enough he would be elected to the fellowship. At the reception, A. E. Housman, whom as it happened I had never met, though we had known one another by sight for years, came up to me and remarked, 'If there is any crime which ought absolutely to debar a man from being elected to a fellowship at Trinity, it is that of going to India as a missionary.' This was said with a smile, but I realised that I caused considerable perplexity to my colleagues. Perfect courtesy was shown to practising Christians, but the general view was that they were anachronisms. It was felt to be peculiar that any young man of promise should elect to follow the Christian way, and extraordinary that he should want to go overseas.

I allowed myself a few weeks in Cambridge, partly to settle up a few outstanding matters of business, but also to enjoy for a short time the life on which I was turning my back. As it was my plan to make India my home for the rest of my life, I did not expect ever to see Trinity again. In this I was mistaken, but I did not know this at the time. It was not easy to say goodbye.

It is impossible to set down on paper what I owe to Trinity. I have crossed the Great Court a thousand times and never failed to be uplifted by its beauty, whether on November evenings, when everything was grey, or in the early light of dawn on the rare occasions on which I sat up all night working, or in the blaze of June when the scarlet geraniums round the fountain reflect the heat. Often I have sat in the Fellows' Garden, admiring the tulips, cool and peaceful, growing up amid the long grass, or have watched the light fade out of the sky and heard the last song of the birds as everything faded into stillness. Almost all things in the world have changed since then, but these things remain almost exactly as they were, and are an endless delight to think upon.

Truth is ever more important than beauty. Adoration of the truth I did not need to learn at Cambridge. I had it already from my parents and my earlier teachers. But here it came to me with new variety and new splendour. My elders received me with the astonishing kindness to which I have already referred, endured my awkwardnesses and follies, and introduced me into the austere fellowship of learning. From the best of them I learned endless patience in the pursuit of knowledge without ulterior purpose, temperateness in judgement, willingness to hear the other side, readiness to welcome new truth, and from many of them a broad general charity not too often disturbed by the inevitable asperities and roughnesses of academic life. My Christian faith had become less narrow and less dogmatic; it has survived the experience of encounter with all kinds of men. For all these things I thank God and take courage.

I was to go across France to Marseilles and there pick up the Bibby boat that was to take me to India. Various members of my family came to Victoria station to see me off, but I was travelling alone. As the train moved out of the station, and my brother Henry ran after me to take a last farewell, I must admit to feeling very forlorn and lonely. I took out the beautiful Greek Testament which had been given me for my confirmation (and which I later left in the train in India) and read the first five chapters of the Second Epistle to the Corinthians: 'Not that we are sufficient of ourselves to think any thing as of ourselves; but our sufficiency is of God; who also hath made us able ministers of the new testament; not of the letter, but of the spirit: for the letter killeth, but the spirit giveth life' (2 Cor. 3:5–6).

3

Apprentice Missionary

There was little to commend the *S. S. Warwickshire* of the Bibby line, which now became my temporary home. She was old, slow and cramped; I found myself one of three in a cabin about the size of a billiard table. There were one or two missionaries on board, but the majority of the passengers were fairly rough types returning to Burma as planters, elephant-catchers and heaven knows what else; I did not find much stimulating companionship among them. There being no clergyman on board, religious activity was limited to Mattins read rather gruffly by the captain on Sunday morning. The two advantages of the Bibby boats were that they were all one class, and that they alone among shipping lines on that route, with I think the exception of Hendersons, provided the game of skittles for the delectation of their passengers. The only memorable event on the voyage was the passage of the Suez Canal, with the light of a full moon pouring down on the infinite stillness of the desert, and the majestic progress of the ship seeming hardly to disturb the tranquil waters of the canal.

And then, going down the Red Sea, I fell sick – not sea-sick – I have never been really sea-sick in my life, but one of those mysterious fevers from which I have suffered periodically all my life, and to which I seem to be particularly liable on board ship. There was a doctor on board, but no sick-bay; so, in order to get me out of the overcrowded cabin, he moved me into the crew's hospital, a bare little room in which I could hear all day the crooning song of the lascars, and smell the highly pungent spices which one of the crew seemed to be endlessly grinding for the men's dinner. The fever was obstinate, and I was still shaky when we reached Colombo – not a very good preparation for a life of missionary activity in the East.

There followed nearly a week in Colombo waiting for the small British India vessel that would take me in one night's passage across

79

the waters to Tuticorin, the port town of South-East India. This was a lonely and rather dreary time. I have always enjoyed that short passage across the open sea, though it can on occasion be pretty rough and blowy, and many passengers who have survived the much longer journey from Europe succumb to sea-sickness on this, the last lap. Tuticorin has no harbour, only a roadstead; the descent from the ship into the heaving lighter has to be dextrously timed or accidents may easily occur. Then a hot dull journey across the plains to Tinnevelly Junction, with a change on the way at Maniyacki, nearly thirty miles in one of the excruciatingly uncomfortable Ford eight-seaters, which were beginning to ply on the few metalled roads of the area; three miles in the dark in a bullock-cart, and I was home, in the remote village which was to be my first Indian home. This first day freed me from one anxiety that had for some time been in the back of my mind. I had naturally known a good many Indians in Cambridge and had not liked many of them; how should I find them now that I had come to live among them? I need not have worried; on that first day I found that these were my own people, and it was no idle locution that I had 'come home'. There were ten thousand things to be learned, as there always are in any foreign country, but the immediate feeling in my mind was not that I was a foreigner.

At early dawn my eyes awoke to the splendid panorama of the Western Ghats, which at that point rise abruptly from the plains to about six thousand feet, clothed to their summits in everlasting forest. Away to the left was the nose of Comorin, the great cliff in which the mountains finally break down to the plain, and which from the beginning of time has been a great landmark for sailors making the somewhat perilous voyage round the tip of India. In twenty years I never grew weary of the sight of these mountains. Hidden away among them were glens and valleys of unbelievable beauty; and in the monsoon season the sun used to go down behind them in rivers of molten gold.

Tirunelveli (which the Europeans had debased into Tinnevelly), the southernmost district of India on the coast of Coromandel, was many worlds in one. Where the land could be irrigated it was potentially immensely fertile, though in places exhausted by many years of intensive cultivation and too little reparation in the way of fertilisers. Round Tinnevelly Town the rice fields stretch as far as the eye can see, clothed in the most dazzling of dazzling greens. A northern region is much drier, with black cotton soil that produces excellent crops of cotton in years when the rainfall is adequate. Along the coast and some distance inland is the palmyra forest, where the trees grow so thick that the eye cannot penetrate more than a few hundred yards in any direction. More will be said about the palmyra in another context.

I arrived in the time of the south-east monsoon, when the greater part of the year's rain falls in six weeks or less. The two months which follow are bright, fairly cool, and bracing. Then in March the demon of heat begins to be released and reaches his maximum power in the purgatory of May, when all who can retreat to the hills. June brings the south-west monsoon. This provides parts of Kerala with as much as a hundred inches of rain in three months; but in the rain's shadow it produces only grey skies, tearing winds, an agreeable drizzle, and some sharp bouts of rain. The cooler temperatures are pleasant, but the endless wind, which covers the floors every day with a thin layer of dust and demands that every paper and document be firmly weighted to prevent its flying away into the beyond, becomes wearisome and can be the cause of great irritation. September and October are sticky months, until the north-east monsoon breaks, sometimes almost like the sound of a pistol shot, and so the cycle is complete. The life of all men is determined by this sequence; almost without knowing it, the foreigner becomes adapted to the rhythm, and becomes part of that life of the villages and the fields which has been going on with little change for thousands of years. In my heart of hearts, I am a *pattikkatt'āl*, a dweller in small villages; this India, more than any other India, is my home.

Tinnevelly is one of the oldest fields of Christian activity in India. In 1534 the entire fisher-caste of the Paravas embraced the Roman Catholic faith, more with a view to securing the support of the King of Portugal than from any religious conviction. Eight years later the great Francis Xavier, having heard that these people had been utterly neglected, came down and carried out his wonderful three years' apostleship on the coast. His work has remained. The Roman Catholics have a good deal to show in the interior, but their great strength is on the coast, where the great majority of the hardy fisher-folk carry on with wonderful skill the craft of their ancestors, but some have become traders and accumulated wealth. To walk across the sand-hills, of which Xavier complained, and to find one's way to Ramabhandu, where he spent much of his time and where his grotto is still shown, is a strange experience; one expects to arrive at a fishing village, with just the low poor cabins of the fisher-folk; instead one finds oneself in a city of palaces, with the comfortable dwellings of the merchant-princes, dominated by two gigantic churches, belonging to two different jurisdictions. In the year before I reached India, Mgr Tiburtius Roche sj had been consecrated as the first bishop of the Latin rite in modern times, to care for the diocese of Tuticorin, a strip only ten miles wide, but running the entire length of the coast, from which every European priest, except one or two engaged in education, had been removed.

In 1771 Christian Friedrich Schwartz, greatest of all Protestant missionaries in South India, made his way to Palamcottah, and found there a group of Christian soldiers, and also a Brahman lady named Clorinda, who had embraced the Christian faith but could not be baptised, since she was living as the mistress of a European officer. Nine years later, when he died, she was baptised; Clorinda's church, a small building with no pretence to any architectural elegance, still exists, and is occasionally used for services when the larger church near by is under repair or is being cleaned. The work prospered. Just at the end of the eighteenth century a movement broke out, not far from Cape Comorin, among the hardy Nadars, who make their living by climbing the palmyra trees to extract the sweet juice from which sugar is made. More than five thousand people were baptised by the Lutheran missionaries within a few years, and in spite of long neglect never forgot that they were Christians. Both the Church Missionary Society and the Society for the Propagation of the Gospel entered in, and developed a steady systematic work, as a result of which, when I reached India, the Tinnevelly Church numbered more than a hundred thousand baptised Christians.

The great majority of the Christians belonged to the Nadar community. This remarkable people occupies a peculiar position in the Hindu world. They are not admitted to worship in the Hindu temples, and therefore cannot be regarded as caste Hindus; on the other hand they are not untouchables, and do not belong to that fifth of the population which is excluded from all social privilege. The extremely hard work by which they earn their living gives to many of them a magnificent physique and a hardy aggressive temperament, which when influenced by the grace of Christ leads to great strength of Christian character; when less sanctified, it can produce obstinacy and quarrelsomeness and a state of endemic faction in the villages. Since these folk had for the most part become Christians in groups, they had not had to leave their villages, and so had avoided that dependence on the missionaries which has been the bane of many Churches in India. When the missionaries first encountered them, the Nadars were almost wholly illiterate; they took eagerly to education, and have produced a number of distinguished leaders, including a minister in the first cabinet to be formed in the Madras State after the independence of India had been declared.

To have so great a Church was a wonderful thing. However, it was a real drawback that so large a proportion of the Christians were drawn from a single community. There were Christians of other castes. Indeed, when a colleague and I worked through the list of castes as given in the Census Report, we were able to identify Christians in the twenty or thirty castes which had more than a thousand representatives in the Tinnevelly District. But all these were minority groups, and felt themselves crushed under the Nadar domination. Such divisions do not greatly matter, as long as there is one authority that firmly controls everything from above, and maintains even-handed justice. Let democracy be introduced, and all hell is likely to be let loose.

This was precisely the point which had been reached at the time of my arrival in India; after a long period of strict missionary domination, the Christians of Tinnevelly were to be introduced to the joys and perils of a democratic order.

In 1914 Edward Harry Mansfield Waller, one of the greatest men I have ever known, was asked to become Bishop of Tinnevelly. He had been for a number of years a missionary in South India, and later India Secretary of the Church Missionary Society in London, and so was well acquainted with the situation. He came determined to break up the old missionary organisation and to let the Church be the Church. He laid it down as a condition for his acceptance of the bishopric that he should be chairman of the CMS Council, a position which had always previously been held by a CMS missionary.

Waller's first task was to unify the two great societies, the CMS and the SPG, which divided between them the Anglican work in the area. In early days there had been perfect amity between them, and hardly a noticeable difference in churchmanship; in SPG churches the responses were sung, in CMS churches they were said, and that was about all the difference that existed. But from 1876 onwards a change took place. The SPG began to send out men who had come under the influence of 'Puseyism', some of them representatives of an extreme position both in doctrine and ritual. Some among the CMS missionaries came from the Church of Ireland; almost all of them represented an extreme Evangelical position, utterly loyal to the Church of England as they understood it, but about as far removed as could be imagined from their brethren of the other fellowship just a few miles away. Even the holy Bishop Moore of Travancore, who had worked for twelve years in Tinnevelly, once told me that in all those years he had never once preached in an 'SPG church'. Clearly it was not going to be easy to drive in a single team two so disparate horses.

In one respect, however, Waller was fortunate in the moment of his arrival. On both sides the older generation of missionaries had been almost completely swept away by death or retirement. An earlier experiment in self-government, introduced hastily and without adequate preparation, had led to disastrous results, and had left the missionaries who arrived in India in the late 1880s and early 1890s with a profound distrust of Indian leadership, and a conviction that for a very long time the control of the Church must be in the hands of the foreigner. If any of these had survived, Waller would have had great difficulty in putting his plans into execution. As it was, the few missionaries that there were held moderate views on churchmanship, shared Waller's conviction that the Church must take the place of the mission, and were prepared for every kind of experiment.

Waller was not averse to missionaries, but he saw that the missionary must find his place within the Church. This, and not a distant missionary society, must be the object of his first loyalty, and in its service he must find delight. Intensely shy and sensitive, with considerable powers of clear thought and exposition, and with great capacity for rapid and effective decision, Waller had one great defect; like many shy people with quick and lucid minds, he failed to realise that other people could not always think as rapidly as he, and tended to mistake acquiescence for agreement. He succeeded in pushing through a diocesan constitution, under which the work of the two great missionary societies would be merged and the diocese would really become a diocese; then, at the critical moment, in 1923 he accepted appointment to the more eminent bishopric of Madras, a post which he held with great distinction for eighteen years.

Waller's successor was Norman Tubbs, who had acquired at Cambridge a third class in theology and a swimming blue. He made no claim to intellectual distinction or theological originality; but he had very great power as a popular preacher. He had the gift of making other men's work genuinely his own, and reproducing it on precisely the wavelength that the fairly devout but theologically illiterate layman could immediately understand and appreciate. He had been a missionary in India for sixteen years, and at the time of his appointment to Tinnevelly was Principal of Bishop's College, Calcutta, founded in 1820 and since 1912 an English-medium united (SPG/CMS) college for graduate ordinands. He knew nothing of South India, and Waller, perhaps wisely, had given him very little briefing on the diocese for which he was to care, and left him to find his own way and to make his own mistakes. His first mistake, for which he was hardly at all to blame, was colossal, and from this he was never able to recover.

Waller had immensely under-estimated the suspicion felt in the CMS part of the diocese about his plan of completely merging the two societies in one organisation. Two-thirds of the Christians in that area claimed allegiance to that society locally, but they were scattered and ill-organised, and very inferior in the arts of ecclesiastical diplomacy. The storm-centre was the question whether a cross should or should not be placed on the holy table. This may seem a trivial matter, but those familiar with the history of the Church of Ireland since disestablishment in 1869 will be well aware that the banning of the cross in church had become a symbol of loyalty to truth, and every attempt to introduce it was seen as a conspiracy to destroy the truth. The Irish influence had been strong in Tinnevelly; the Christians of the CMS allegiance were determined not to have in any church anything that could possibly be misinterpreted by the Hindus as idolatrous.

When Bishop Tubbs arrived to take possession of his see, he wisely issued a proclamation that no change in customs and liturgical practice would be permitted in any part of the diocese. Almost immediately he fell from his high resolve. There is on the South Indian Railway a small town named Koilpetta, which is well within the CMS area but to which a number of Christians had come up the line from Tuticorin, which was in the SPG area. The congregation was thus a mixed congregation. When the church was rebuilt, the east wall had in it, above the holy table, a niche which was obviously intended for a cross. The SPG members expressed their desire to present a cross, and asked the new bishop whether this would be acceptable. He very properly consulted his Indian advisers. I do not know what evil spirit of blindness and folly entered into these men; they told the Bishop that no harm would be done, and that he might sanction the installation of the cross. Within twenty-four hours word had gone all over the diocese that the word of the Bishop could not be trusted; he was never able to recover the confidence of his children in the CMS area.

Tubbs was never aware of the strength of this feeling, or of the danger of a schism that might have divided every one of the 450 CMS congregations in the diocese. The feelings had recently been exacerbated by the elections to the new diocesan council. There was a grave danger that, in every village, if one leader decided to stay with the diocese, the other would move out of fellowship with the Church, and carry all his followers into schism. Many of the CMS clergy were sorely tried; finally almost all decided to accept the new regime and to stay where they were, not without many misgivings and anxieties about the future, especially as the future clergy were at that time being trained together in the little Divinity School at Nazareth, one of the most extreme of the SPG stations.

For all that, a schism did take place, the Alvaneri schism. The dissidents had written to the newly formed BCMS in London, hoping that such a strongly Evangelical society would support their cause; to their eternal honour the founders of that society made it plain that they would have nothing to do with schismatic action. The situation was very unwisely handled from above, and this new opportunity for reconciliation was thrown away. Seven thousand of the best Christians, mercifully all in this one limited area, refused to bow the knee to Baal ('to worship the cross', as they expressed it), and came out on their own. They had with them one priest and one deacon. The priest died soon after; they then made the schism irrevocable by ordaining their own ministers, and setting up their own organisation, the Tinnevelly CMS Evangelical Church.

It was a lamentable situation. In many villages the Church was left with a handful of churchmen of less than perfect virtue, while all the devout were in the other camp. A series of lawsuits were decided in favour of the Church, and all the property was handed back to us; but in village after village fine churches decayed without money to maintain them, while across the street the dissident conventicle flourished and the new incumbent's authoritarian attitude exacerbated matters. The 'Sattaya Subhai' still exists, though about half the protesters returned to the fold. Wholly independent and self-supporting, its adherents believe they maintain the only true Christian witness in the area.

It was impossible for me not to be drawn into all these events. I was living just on the edge of the disturbed area, and was all too well aware of the whirlpools of emotion by which I was surrounded. As a very raw recruit, I had no standing in the matter, and there was nothing that I could do about it. I looked on with a wretched feeling of helplessness, observing the astonishing ineptitude with which things were dealt with from above, and the unlovely obstinacy with which the leaders of the schism repelled every effort at conciliation.

It was only by chance that I was drawn so early into these high ecclesiastical politics. My main task was naturally to acquaint myself with the Tamil language. Again and again I have been asked, 'Did you learn an Indian dialect when you were in India?' At this point I invariably explode and reply, 'Do you realise that when your ancestors were dyeing themselves with woad the Tamils were producing great classical literature?' Tamil is in fact one of the two forms of human speech that have been spoken and written for two thousand years, the other being Chinese. There are those who think that Tamil is the hardest of all currently spoken languages to learn. My sister Marjorie, who learned Arabic for two years in Beirut and then came on to Tamil, asserted that without doubt Tamil is the harder of the two. However that may be, learning Tamil is a formidable task.

I arrived on the scene at a particularly bad time. The great tradition of Tamil scholarship among missionaries had practically died out. There were in Tinnevelly only four ordained missionaries; all of them had passed Tamil examinations years before, but not one of them was preaching in Tamil when I came to India. Indian Christians were very discouraging; they said, 'You will never learn our language well, so why waste time trying? We all speak English, so why bother?' It is true that almost all the missionaries were working in institutions in which English was the language of instruction and communication, and hardly needed Tamil. But this was not the way in which I had been brought up. In our family it is taken for granted that wherever you are you learn the language of the people. Brother Henry in Ghana made himself a master of Fanti. My sister Isabel can speak three Indian languages (though she knows well that there are things about her Tamil that I deplore). I made up my mind that I would learn Tamil or die. I nearly did both, but by a narrow margin both I and the Tamil survived.

My first teacher was a young man of high caste with only eight years' education, and whose English was wholly inadequate to any explanation in English of what we were doing together. In those days there were no language schools, such as were later introduced; we wrestled with our teacher, and we wrestled with Pope's *Tamil Manual*. G. U. Pope, who died in 1910, was a splendid Tamil scholar, and everything is to be found in his manual, if you know where to look for it, but it does not always answer the kind of questions that the beginner is likely to ask. So my teacher and I read and read, until I began to be able to ask him questions in Tamil.

My teacher used to come twice a day, from 7.30 to 9 a.m. and from 3 to 4.30 p.m. I grew so weary of him that at times I used to pray that he might forget to come. He very rarely did. He was not expensive; he cost about sixpence an hour. And I had one great reward for our long and weary lessons together – his Tamil was that of a cultured Vellala – these are the great land-holding caste of South India, and, far more than the Brahmans, the guardians of a pure Tamil culture. From him I learned to speak Tamil as she really is spoke. Time was to come when Indians would say that, if they had been sitting behind a pillar in church when I was preaching, they would not have known it was not an Indian who was speaking. This was politeness rather than truth, but it cheered me a good deal that it could be said.

It must not be supposed that I was dependent on one teacher only. I was talking all the time to all kinds of people, and learning from them all. One I remember with particular affection. Arivatam ('blessing') was a garden boy aged about twenty-five, a born Christian, who had had only four years of education in the village school, but whose history was a little unusual. He had about as much, or as little, religion as is common among village boys in any country, when one day during the monsoon he fell into a flooded river, and was being whirled away to his death. In his distress he vowed that, if he was delivered, he would give himself wholly to God. At the crucial moment he saw above him the branch of a tree; he grasped it, and the branch held; with great difficulty he drew himself out of the surging waters and on to the bank ('to climb the bank' is one of the classic Hindu expressions for 'to be saved', to escape from the ocean of rebirth into this world of suffering and frustration). A great many young men who have made such a vow forget it as soon as they are safe; not so Arivatam, who from that day became a changed man. He used to come and see me in the evenings after his day's work was done, carrying his Tamil Bible under his arm; as I turned over the leaves, I was astonished to find on almost every page verses marked that he had either found for himself and noted as memorable, or that he had heard quoted in sermons. Again and again I was amazed at the aptness and profundity with which this simple village boy could speak of the deep mysteries of the Christian faith. What he spoke was not the exquisite and cultured Tamil of my high-caste teacher; but Christian Tamil, that dialect full of specifically Christian terms, largely derived from the Sanskrit, which is calculated to perplex and offend the purist in Tamil speech. (Lesslie Newbigin, who knew Tamil very well, affirmed that the well-known saying, 'Christ Jesus came into the world to save sinners,' had become in the Tamil Bible, 'Christ Jesus came into the world to protect rascals' – welcome tidings to some among the hearers of the message, but not exactly what the Apostle Paul intended to convey!) But this, too, was part of the Tamil that I had to learn. I was always grateful for Arivatam's help.

Only many years later did I hear the end of this story. I was in the city of Ipoh in Western Malaysia, in which the Indian congregation is largely made up of Tamil people, helping in a Bible-reading and study campaign inaugurated by the Bishop of Singapore. In one of my addresses I had, without mentioning names, told the story of Arivatam as an example of what the Holy Spirit can do in the way of enlightening the understanding of a simple Christian who has had none of the advantages of higher or theological education. After the service several people came up to me and said, 'We knew the man of whom you have been speaking. He came here to Malaysia, was ordained to the ministry of the Methodist Church, and died a few years ago.' I had not been mistaken in my estimate of his character and capacity.

When I had reached the point of being able to express myself with some freedom in Tamil, it was decided that I should travel across the district, and spend some time in one of the old classic stations of the CMS, where Bishop Sargent had lived for a number of years, but where the old bungalow had not been occupied for a great many years. Travel in those days was not as easy as it sounds. Abominably uncomfortable eight-seater buses ran along the few main roads which radiated from the centre of the district Palamcottah. But to tack across these routes from west to east was as difficult as it still is to get from Harrow to Rotherhithe across the north of London. One could either go on foot, with a coolie to carry one's worldly goods, or, if the distance was too great, one could take a bullock, and advance in stately fashion at the maximum speed of two and a half miles per hour. Such travel is the nearest thing I have ever known to eternity – it seemed to go on without beginning and without end, in a vacuum in which time seemed to have stood still. In point of fact, the bullock-cart was far less uncomfortable than might be supposed. One usually journeyed by night, to save the bulls from the burning heat of the day. A mattress would be spread the length of the cart; the bells on the bulls' necks would make a kind of lullaby – I have slept better in a bullock-cart than I often do in a luxurious bed with the latest in spring mattresses.

So the long night passed, and in the early light of dawn I found myself at Suviseshapuram, the village of the good news. It was the SPG tradition, derived from the old Lutheran missionaries, to give their stations Bible names – Nazareth, Bethlehem, and so on. The CMS chose good Sanskrit terms to denote different aspects of the gospel. I used from time to time to preach a sermon based on these names. One started naturally at Suviseshapuram, the village of the gospel. Crossing the sand-hills one came to Kudeshapuram, the village of grace, and then by a right wheel to Megnanapuram, the village of true wisdom; then westwards to Anandapuram, the village of great joy, and then with another right wheel to Pragasapuram, the village of radiance: 'Arise, shine, for the glory of the Lord is risen upon thee.'

In the very early days, when persecution was a harsh reality for Christian converts, the missionaries obtained from a benign government large tracts of land, and settled dispossessed Christians upon them. This seemed an ideal solution. The large Gothic church in the midst, the missionary's bungalow, the pastor's house, the schools for girls and boys under the superintendence of the missionary and his wife – what more could be wished? Yet few, if any, of these missionary settlements really prospered. The people who came together in them had no roots, and roots are more important than anything else to village people. History has shown that far better results were attained when the Christians were a strong enough group to maintain themselves in their own village, to stand against the threat of persecution and against all the disintegrating influences of a non-Christian society. Just the necessity of fighting for their own existence seemed to create in these Christians a strength which was often lacking in those who had an easier time of it in the mission village.

Suviseshapuram is just on the edge of the palmyra forest, where the trees stand in hundreds of thousands on the strip between the coast and the more highly cultivated areas inland. The palmyra is not a beautiful tree; it has, in fact, been compared a little unkindly to a gigantic shaving-brush; but there is no part of it which cannot be used by man. The tall straight trunks make excellent pillars for a house or a church; the broad leaves are used for thatching; the fruit can be eaten, though it lacks taste, and the roots produce a kind of tapioca; but what makes it immensely profitable is the sweet juice which rises in astonishing quantities and can be tapped where the spatter of the leaves shoots out from the trunk. This juice very rapidly ferments and makes a kind of sweet and not unpleasant beer. Except for certain licensed trees, the climber is supposed to put lime into his pots, and this will hold up the fermentation for twenty-four hours, during which the juice can be boiled down to make the coarse sugar which is widely used throughout South India. Bishop Azariah's grandfather, who never became a Christian, was a merchant who used teams of donkeys to carry the local jaggery as far afield as Madras.

Drinking was supposed to be controlled by the Excise Department, but in point of fact enormous quantities of toddy were drunk, legally and illegally, all over the place. Drunk on an empty stomach, this drink goes very quickly to the head. Quarrels would easily break out in the toddy-shop, and, since every palmyra-climber necessarily carries an exceedingly sharp knife to make the incisions in the spike, all too often a momentary quarrel would end in a fatal stabbing. It is not surprising that the great majority of missionaries found it advisable for the sake of their work to be teetotallers.

Why does the Tinnevelly Church have its main Sunday service at midday all through the hottest part of the year? This is the kind of question which sociologists love to ask, and to which they are skilled in finding the most fancy answers. The answer is as simple as could be. When the sap is really rising, the trees need to be climbed three times a day, and failure to carry out this duty, Sundays and week-days alike, is as harmful to them as it is to fail to milk the cows. So when many of these Nadars became Christians, there was a real problem to be faced – how were they to get to church on Sundays? The missionaries wisely left it to the people to decide themselves; they agreed that they would miss out the midday climb on Sundays, and so the service came to be held at that for them practical but otherwise unsuitable time. The young men would come back from the first climb about nine in the morning, bathe and have a good solid meal; and then come to church just ready to be lapped in the folds of irresistible slumber. I don't think I have ever managed to keep a whole Tamil congregation awake through a whole sermon at that ungodly time.

I soon came to be absorbed into the life of this Christian village. A century before, the pioneer Carl Rhenius had laid it down that in every village where there was a teacher and a school, the bell was to ring out every evening for shortened Evensong; this good custom is still maintained in seven hundred villages, and a surprising number of people obey the summons of the bell. The service could have been more edifying. The Psalms were read much too quickly. There was a short exposition of the lesson, but all too often this was mere edification with no attempt to make plain to simple people what the words of the gospel really meant. But at Suviseshapuram in those days they had the splendid custom of singing at the end of the service a paraphrase of Psalm 133 by the great Christian poet Vedanayer Sastryar, whose name appears in the first church register of the year 1780: 'The Lord that made heaven and earth give thee blessing out of Sion.' It grieves me that, in the days when Vedanayer Sastryar was no longer in fashion, this admirable custom was given up. I never read or sing that Psalm but I am back in that pseudo-Gothic church with its blunt square tower that stands so unexpectedly on the flat and burning plains of India.

Another excellent custom was that the Sunday evening prayer-meeting was held out of doors, except on the rare Sunday evenings when it rained. In earlier times, as in England until the lighting of churches by gas came in, it had been impossible to light more than a very small part of the larger churches. So the custom had grown up of saying Evensong at 4 p.m., while it was still light, and then holding this prayer-meeting in the street, under the starry sky, and perhaps just one lantern on the table behind which the officiant stood. It was accounted a blessing to have the prayer-meeting held in front of your house, and many requests were received to be allowed to have that privilege. Naturally the service was of the very simplest nonconformist type – lyrics which everyone knew by heart and could sing to Indian tunes, rather long extempore prayers, and an address often given by a layman. This was the best-attended service in the week; some would come in the darkness who otherwise would never be seen in church – to me it was always very moving, dimly to discern white-clad forms half-way along the street in either direction. In Suviseshapuram, at the end of the service it was the custom to march across to the long-uninhabited bungalow and sing aloud a magnificent hymn of praise to Christ the Redeemer.

Naturally I did not find it difficult to make friends with the boys and young men of the village. Only a few were in school. The majority had had just the four years of schooling which were customary at the time, and, with the practice they got in church, could read Tamil well, but their knowledge of the world was naturally very limited. Most of them were palmyra-climbers, but a good many of them had plantain groves, or small plots for garden cultivation, both of which required endless irrigation. The bulls go up and down the ramp, drawing the precious water from the wells, and then the stream has to be guided through the criss-cross of little channels until the whole is watered. To save the bulls or the buffaloes from the burning sun, a great deal of the work has to be done before the sun is too high in the heavens, or towards nightfall. A hard life, but life was not all labour for them; they had a passion for football, and naturally expected me to play with them. The dry bed of the tank served very well as a playground, though strangely far from the green fields of Cambridge. But the boys, themselves playing barefoot, were frightened of my shoes, and I soon found that it would be well to play barefoot myself. This is less painful than might be supposed, though some of the pebbles lying on the tank floor were too sharp for comfort.

All this time I was working hard at my Tamil, for the most part without a teacher, and not with wholehearted encouragement. One day the local pastor found me reading a Tamil work, probably one of the excellent prose summaries of Tamil legend put out by a scholar in Jaffna. He took me severely to task: 'Why do you waste your time on all that Hindu rubbish? All you need is a good knowledge of the Tamil Bible; from that you will be preaching and on that you should concentrate.' The Union Version of 1869 was indeed a remarkable achievement, and I read it constantly; but it had not occurred to the excellent pastor that I had come to India as a missionary to the non-Christians, and that a good knowledge of Hindu Tamil was essential for the work that I hoped to do. However, here I was among Christians and my first task was to communicate with them. Greatly daring, I preached my first sermon in church exactly nine months after my arrival in the country; in the good old days, when discipline was discipline, missionaries were not allowed to preach until they had completed two years of Tamil study. My text was Galatians 5:22, and I kept going for twenty minutes; my hearers had no difficulty in understanding, but I think that it might have been better for me if I had waited a little longer before launching out on pulpit oratory.

It was there that I wrote my letter of resignation. Most good missionaries write at least one letter of resignation some time during their first year, but in the majority of cases the letter is never sent. During that first year, fellow Christians had brought into my life such darkness and suffering that it took me many years to recover from the injuries, and the scars are still there. I had so totally taken India as my home and my second country that it never even occurred to me to leave it permanently. But I thought that for the time being I might be better out of things – I would take advantage of my fellowship, which still had three years to run, learn Sanskrit for a couple of years, and then come back to start again, better equipped for the work of witness among high-caste Hindus. The letter was written. I went across to the church and took my Sunday Bible class for the boys and young men. It happened that my parents were staying in Suviseshapuram and knew something of my troubles. My mother said to me, 'Are you quite sure that you are right to go? These young men love and trust you; you can understand them, and they can understand you. They have given you their complete confidence. Are you sure that it would be right to leave them?' The letter went to its proper destination, the waste-paper basket, and was never repeated. Those rough village boys will never know what they did for me in a moment of crisis.

Another crisis very nearly put an end to my service in India. Three miles from Suviseshapuram lies the village of Ittamoti, where a number of Christians had started a high school entirely by their own efforts. They had secured government recognition, and the grant that goes with it. They were eager that I should take over the responsibility for running the school. There was much that was attractive in the proposal. This was a genuinely Indian enterprise; a large proportion of the boys were Hindus; the nearest high school was far enough away for it to be likely that this school would thrive and prosper. The buildings were deplorable, and the staff not on the highest level of efficiency. In the end the balance turned the other way; but Ittamoti was destined to play quite a part in my affairs.

One day I went over to play hockey with the boys and endured quite a sharp whack on the very point of my shin-bone, what the Tamils most appropriately call 'the horse's nose'. Being used to such things I took no notice of it and walked the three miles home. I could not have done anything worse. Before long the leg began to swell and my temperature to go up; it was clear that I had periostitis, inflammation of the membrane which surrounds the bone, a troublesome and at times dangerous complaint. The textbooks say that the remedy is to keep the limb perfectly still, and to cut right through to the bone. My doctor father was horrified at the idea of having to operate on his son under the most primitive conditions; it is always difficult for a doctor to operate on one of his own children, but when the only possible operating table is the dining table – no, he decidedly thought, better not. Fortunately the blow had cut the leg pretty deeply and some pus was finding its way out, but the situation was less than promising. It was decreed that I must make the long journey to the Nilgiri Hills and stay with Miss Hopwood till I got better.

It was a bad journey in those days – one of the rickety buses to Palamcottah, the centre of the district, and a long wait in a missionary's bungalow; the Trivandrum Express, which in those days managed to race along at an average speed of twenty miles an hour; a change and a long wait at Trichinopoly; another change and wait at Erode at three o'clock in the morning, and then at last Mettupalayam at the foot of the mountains, where Spencer's restaurant supplied an English breakfast that compensated for the sorrows of the night. At last the mountain railway, a remarkable feat of engineering, deeper and deeper into the green mountains, until it seemed as though one must come out on the other side; and then finally there was Ooty station, 7,200 feet above the sea, and the anxious figure of Miss Hopwood, darting from one third-class carriage to another, never supposing for a moment that a missionary would be so extravagant as to travel first class. I never did again on that railway.

Edith Hopwood, a notable and wealthy woman, had spent a good part of her earlier years in Germany, and had acquired an undying passion for the operas of Wagner. Some time in her twenties, in circumstances of which I have never known anything, she underwent a massive Evangelical conversion which changed the whole course of her life. When the CMS decided to open up work among the Muslim women in the hills, Miss Hopwood was found and accepted the call, and came with her mother to live in the mountain city which was to be her home for just fifty years. It was her custom to open her beautiful home to missionaries of many loyalties and many societies; but it was somehow curious that some people loved going to Farley because it was so cheap, and others would have loved to go there but it really was more than they could possibly afford. There you have Edith Hopwood in a nutshell – utterly devoted to the cause of Christ, kind and affectionate and stuffed to the finger-tips with unshakeable and ineradicable prejudices. Like many elderly women, she had a penchant for young men; I was fortunate in enjoying her favour; but undoubtedly her favourite was Malcolm Muggeridge. It is not known to all the admirers of that deft and versatile writer, whom I had known at Cambridge, that he spent three of his early years as a missionary in India. Even then his Christian faith was somewhat patchy, but three holy women decided that they would pray for Malcolm every day until he entered into the full light of the gospel. Ultimately their prayers were not in vain.

So much has been written about Ooty, then in its glory and now in its decline, that not much need be written about it here. During all my years in India it played a large part in my life, and when my sister Isabel came to work with Miss Hopwood, naturally it came to be a place of annual pilgrimage. Farley stands well above the town and has a glorious view across the surprisingly English downs to the striking peak of Mukarta, a view now largely ruined by the Indian government's policy of eucalyptus plantation.

It now being October, and the cooler season, the house was almost empty of guests. In fact the only others were the Revd Jesse Brand and his wife, and thus I had my first introduction to the Strict Baptists. They are rather stern, intensely upright, even puritanical, but with a simple devotion to Jesus Christ which has never failed to win my heart. And they know exactly where they stand. When I knew Jesse better, I once said to him, 'Suppose I come to visit you with an Indian convert who has been brought to Christ by my ministry, and baptised by me by immersion on confession of faith. You will admit him to the Lord's Supper, but you will not admit me. Do you think that that is reasonable?' 'Well, no,' he said, 'but we have our rules.' This I can understand and respect.

Jesse Brand was a splendid specimen of the type 'nonconformist missionary'. Without much educational background, he had educated himself, and had acquired a considerable command of Tamil. He had come to Ooty to recover from an attack of virulent malaria, caught in the unhealthy Koli hills, where he was engaged in pioneer work among hill people, who till he came had never heard a word of the gospel. He, alas, died four years later; but he left behind him a son, Paul, who is now world famous for his original work on leprosy. Jesse had a remarkable wife. At the age of ninety, Mrs Brand was still perambulating the hills of the Salem district, spurred on by an unappeasable desire to preach the gospel.

More important still was my meeting with Miss Ling, of whom I had long known, and whose work as the apostle of the Todas had greatly appealed to me. Catherine Ling had come to India in 1881 at the age of twenty, without any of that preliminary training which would be thought necessary for a would-be missionary today. Like me, Lingy could not bear the atmosphere of the average mission compound in respectable Palamcottah. She decided to go and live in Tinnevelly Town, the great Hindu centre, and persuaded an older missionary to go and live with her. Fortified by this companionship, she found and rented a house. Before long, as was to be expected in those days before the development of tropical medicine, the older missionary died of cholera. The missionary society of Tinnevelly heaved a sigh of relief when a woman missionary was needed for the Nilgiri Hills, and Miss Ling was sent far away into the mountain mists.

The main work of the mission was educational; but before long Lingy found her interest attracted and held by that remarkable hill people the Todas, who lived scattered in their *munds*, never more than three houses together, all over the hills, but always above the level of 7,000 feet. This ancient and purely pastoral people have a language of their own, and customs entirely different from those of any other people. They sit on the tops of the hills, watching their buffaloes graze and feeling themselves to be enormously superior to any other human creatures.

When Europeans first encountered them, there were perhaps a thousand Todas. However, once syphilis was introduced, it ran through the whole people with lightning rapidity; the number of babies born and surviving was not sufficient to keep the tribe alive. The Todas took to drink; when they could not get anything else, the purveying of alcohol to them being strictly forbidden by the government, they would drink methylated spirits, with disastrous results. It was at this point that Miss Ling came on the scene.

The first convert, Kishken, later the Toda catechist, was baptised in 1903. Then one after another, at long intervals, came a number of young men. Grave problems arose as these young men were baptised. How were they to live, and how were they to adapt themselves to the Christian society around them? They discussed the matter among themselves and arrived at three fateful decisions. They would not live in *munds*, the picturesque bee-hive huts with the only door less than a yard square. They said that the moral atmosphere in a *mund* is so frightful that there was nothing for a Christian to do but to make a complete break with the past. In their natural state the Todas never shave, and so have the dignity of Abraham, Isaac and Jacob, who were also the masters of flocks and herds. I have never quite understood why, but the Toda Christians decided that they would not grow beards. And they would not wear the Toda blanket, except on ceremonial occasions. The reason for this was obvious – no mortal man can possibly do a stroke of work when wearing Toda dress, and these young men knew that they would have to work for their living. These decisions made my friends much less picturesque and much less gladdening to the eyes of tourists; but these were their decisions, freely taken, and not imposed upon them by any foreign fiat; and after all, if we give our converts their spiritual freedom, we must not be affronted if the use they make of it is sometimes other than we wish.

When Miss Ling first took me out to visit the boys, things were very much in their beginnings. A bungalow was being built in the neighbourhood of the land she had obtained for them for cultivation, to which she and her companion Miss Daniels would retire when she passed over into younger hands the great work of the schools. A church was to be built a little higher up on the hillside. But our first meeting was in the potato store, where I once again discoursed on the fruit of the Spirit to the best of my limited ability – all the Toda Christians know Tamil, and use it in their church services, though they still speak their own language among themselves. At length the church was finished and my sister Isabel and I were present at the opening, as was Phoebe Groves, one of those splendid uncompromising missionary women who get tougher as they grow older. 'Hum, All Saints Church,' she said with a sniff. 'Much better call it All Sinners.' 'No,' said Bishop Waller, who had come to do the dedication. 'Paul addresses the Corinthians as saints, and look at all the things they did. It shall certainly be All Saints.'

At last my leg had healed, and there was no just impediment to my returning to the other world of the plains. But on the way there was another and touching duty to be performed.

In a village about ten miles east of Palamcottah, a fearful crime had been committed. Many of the men of the village had been sentenced to imprisonment, and were then serving long terms in Trichinopoly jail. There they were faithfully visited by Mr Jacobs, an Anglo-Indian who had been long in the service of the postal department, and was then living in retirement, one of those inconspicuous people whom the Lord is sometimes pleased to use for conspicuous purposes. Under his loving ministry, a number of these men had been converted, and had been baptised and confirmed in prison by Bishop Waller. Their one concern thereafter was that their wives and children should be taught and should share in the benefits that had come to them. I was to stop and visit them on my way home, and to report to the bishop.

There is a chapel in the jail, shared by Protestants and Roman Catholics. Thither Mr Jacobs guided me, and about thirty prisoners were assembled awaiting me, of whom perhaps a dozen were from the village. We held a short service, and I talked to them in my now rather fluent Tamil, to the considerable surprise of Mr Jacobs. Bishop Waller knew a good deal of Tamil, but had never mastered the art of preaching in it. Then we talked of all their affairs; I promised to visit the village, and to make sure that their desire for the teaching of their families was being attended to.

Then a good many years later I went as a priest to lay the foundation-stone of the church they were planning to build. It takes a long time in India for poor people to build a church. I think that ten years had passed before I was able to go as bishop and dedicate the church that had been completed with so much prayer and labour. In my congregation were some of those who had heard me eighteen years before in Trichinopoly jail.

The life to which I was now to be introduced was very different from anything that I had previously experienced. I am by nature a village-dweller, and had no special wish to come and live in a town, especially such a town as Palamcottah, bristling as it was with missionary institutions. In fact it was a hive of mission activity. Half-way to Tinnevelly Town was a large high school, mainly for Hindu boys, and a small college department, up to the intermediate level, which had been presided over for the record period of forty-seven years by H. F. Schaffter, the son of one of the early Swiss missionaries in the area. Close to the cathedral was another large high school, mainly for Christian boys, a teachers' training school with the attached model school, and just over the wall, a school for girls ruled with a rod of iron by Mrs Ardill, who had arrived in India as a bride in 1891, and lived in or near Palamcottah for sixty years. At the other end of the town was the Sarah Tucker College, in which girls could study from the kindergarten up to the BA, another boys' school, the first school for the blind in South India, splendidly run by a blind missionary, W. G. Speight, whom I later had the pleasure of appointing a canon of the cathedral, and the first school for the deaf, also a model of efficiency. I was to live with G. T. Selwyn, and to help in the high school and the training school.

Selwyn was a remarkable man and a far better missionary than I ever had it in me to become. Shy, awkward, not intellectually gifted, a hesitating preacher, if he had stayed in England he would probably have ended up as the much-respected vicar of a country town. In India he grew in stature through the carrying of an immense weight of responsibility, and ended up as my successor in the bishopric of Tinnevelly. As a young man, he had changed single-handed the relationship between missionaries and Indian Christians. This had become fixed, formal, and at times positively unfriendly. Selwyn made himself an Indian to the Indians. Living the far side of Tinnevelly Town, in charge of the catechists' training school, he had taken into his house a remarkable group of high-caste converts, with whom he lived as an elder brother, sharing their lives, eating all meals with them, not to the advantage of his health, and completely adopting Indian ways. Everyone was welcome at any time at his table; the barrier between Indian and foreigner was completely broken down. The one drawback in this great achievement was that Selwyn had so far Indianised himself as to lose that slight distance which gives the missionary an objectivity such as the Indian Christian finds it hard to attain to. He was not always wise in the choice of his friends, and, under their influence, the quality of his judgements did not always match the greatness of his heart. But to live with such a man was an education in itself.

One difference soon impressed itself deeply on my mind. Most of the mission high schools for girls had the services of three missionary women, unmarried and highly trained teachers. In my time not one boys' school in the Madras State had the wholetime service of a man missionary; those who gave part of their time to this service were for the most part business administrators rather than expert teachers. The one aim of the school tended to be to drive the boys through a rather unimaginative syllabus which would lead to the Secondary Schools' Leaving Certificate; learning copious notes by heart was the rule, and there was hardly any attempt to teach the boys to think. Forty-four years later I was to hear, in the city of Ipoh in Malaysia, a remarkably vivid description of my teaching methods from one of my old pupils, some of whom became life-long friends: if any boy gave a silly answer, I used to write the word 'think' on the blackboard in large letters; it was not long before it was unnecessary to write more than the letter 't' – the message got across.

Much as I appreciated all that I was gaining from life in Palamcottah, this was not really what I wanted to do at that time; my wish was to be out in the villages, where I would be talking Tamil day and night, and have contact with Hindus more than with Christians. My wish was understood, and it was arranged that I should become head of the band of evangelists, who toured from place to place to make the gospel known in areas where no Christians lived. But before I changed my occupation, there was to be one short period of exceptionally valuable training. Dr Stanley Jones came to Palamcottah to conduct a mission to non-Christians; he expressed willingness to have me as his helper for a month.

Jones was then about forty years old, and at the height of his powers. He was doing something that at that time no one else was doing in India. Many lecturers of distinction have gone out for one cool weather season, toured around and delivered their message, and gone home. Jones had made this his life-work. Every year he would prepare with the utmost care five lectures and a few sermons. Then for nine months he would be on the road, visiting in turn all the greater cities of India, Burma and Ceylon. His fame as a lecturer had travelled everywhere. Indians love eloquence, and wherever he went he could count on an audience of three to five hundred educated Hindus and Muslims, who would listen quietly and with respect to a message in which Christian truth was fairly and temperately expressed. (Too temperately for some conservative missionaries, who alleged that Jones watered down the gospel; I do not think that this was fair – he claimed that his task was to make his hearers think, and not to press them to immediate conversion.)

The success of Stanley Jones' method owed much to the influence of that ambiguous and ambivalent man Mahatma Gandhi, who made no secret of his devotion to Jesus Christ, and of his high regard for the Gospels. He did indeed tell a large audience of missionaries in Calcutta in 1925, just a year before I joined Dr Jones, that the deepest source of inspiration for his life he found not in the Gospels, but in the Bhagavad Gita. But he urged young Hindus to read the Gospels for themselves, and to find out what the teaching of Jesus really was. For the first time in the modern period, therefore, Hindu India was ready to listen to the voice of Jesus Christ.

There is, however, another side to this picture. Mr Gandhi made it quite clear that he never had been, and never intended to be, anything but a Hindu. He told his admirers that they could get from the Gospels everything that he had got, without prejudice to their faith and to their standing as Hindus. Conversion was anathema to him, as disobedience to God; if God has caused you to be born as a Hindu, that is where it is your duty to stay; any thought of abandoning the religion of your birth must be dismissed as no more than wilful arrogance. We had interesting evidence of this in Bangalore. At one of the meetings the chairman, a Hindu lawyer, got up and delivered his closing remarks as follows: 'As Dr Jones was speaking, I was deeply moved by all that he told us he had found in Jesus Christ, and I found myself powerfully attracted. But, during the answering of the questions, I had time to sit quietly and think; and I saw that everything that Dr Jones has found in Jesus Christ, I myself have found in my dear, dear Lord Krishna.'

My task was to follow Dr Jones round and to do everything that he did not want to do himself. As regards the English work, this did not include any major address and was limited mostly to answering questions. But I found myself with more than enough Tamil work to do. I preached in a Tamil church in Colombo, and I spoke at

Port Pedro in Ceylon, and at the large convention in Jaffna – in fear and trembling, as the people of Jaffna think that they are the only people in the world who can speak good Tamil. I also spoke in Madurai at the annual convention of the American Madurai Mission – with unexpected effectiveness; to emphasise a point, I brought my hand down sharply on the top slat of the desk in front of me; this immediately separated itself from the rest of the desk and fell with a crash to the floor. The audience was deeply impressed by the fervour of my faith, if not by the eloquence of my Tamil.

After lecturing at the Bangalore summer school, held every year in the United Theological College there, I returned to Tinnevelly, having gained some experience of conditions in the larger towns and cities. It was indeed of vital importance for me that I should observe the rising tide of nationalism among the educated classes and meet some of the leaders of the Church who were beginning to increase as the missionaries steadily decreased. Now I had to get on with my new job as head of what used to be called the Itinerancy. Here one needs to know the history of that work.

In 1845, Thomas Gajetan Ragland, Fellow of Corpus Christi College, left Cambridge in the service of the Church Missionary Society in India. In his visits to Tinnevelly, as the Society's Secretary in Madras, he had been struck by the sad contrast between the south and the north of the district. In the south, mission stations were to be found every few miles, and there were flourishing and stable congregations. A large Indian ministry was rapidly coming into being through the ordination of the best and most experienced of the village catechists. In the north, there were a number of small and scattered congregations dating back to the 1820s and 30s, mostly made up of very poor and illiterate people. In an area containing more than a thousand towns and villages, there was not a single missionary, and only one or two Indian priests. Ragland became convinced that the solution to this disparity lay in the development of a band of evangelists, pledged to constant itineration and to the broadcast sowing of the seed of the gospel, until in one or other part of this large field signs of a coming harvest were to be seen. The evangelists would live in tents, always an exacting form of life in that climate, and would be constantly on the move; but they would have a home to which periodically to return, and in which to spend the rainy weather, as itineration during that period is almost impossible in that land of black cotton soil.

Ragland was a mathematician, and the precision of his mind is reflected in the plans which he drew up. Every one of the thousand villages was to be visited at least once every year. This could be done if the slender strength of the band was divided into two. A careful record was to be kept of all visits; a note was to be made of all signs of encouragement, and of every place where more concentrated work might prove profitable. Every attempt was to be made to press home the message by personal conversation, and to render its effect permanent by the sale of literature. Ragland, who was slightly deaf, never became a fluent Tamil speaker; but he rightly saw that in this, as in every form of missionary work, success would depend in the main on the Indian helpers, to whose further training the most minute attention was to be directed.

For a few years all went well. And then disaster struck. Two of the young missionaries died in Ragland's arms at Panarajendapalli. Not long after, in 1858, Ragland himself died at Sachiapuram, the mission station outside the fiercely Hindu town of Sirchari; his grave is to me one of the holiest places in the world. However, the Itinerancy was not allowed to die out. It became the custom that young missionaries, after being allowed out of the nursery at the end of two years' service, would spend the remaining three years of their first period in India in itinerant work, as the ideal means of becoming really fluent in Tamil, and getting to know the country and the people. But as time passed and missionaries became fewer, this no longer held. The work was left in the hands of a missionary whom no one quite knew what to do with, and who continued valiantly in this exhausting work till he was more than seventy years old. Moreover, instead of keeping to Ragland's careful and systematic methods, the Itinerancy had been allowed to wander at random all over the area, and to spend a considerable part of its time in South Tinnevelly, where the work of preaching the gospel to the non-Christians ought to have been the sole responsibility of the local churches. The missionaries, unwisely, had tried to make the Itinerancy a preserve of high-caste Christians, on the theory that they would have more ready access to caste villages than Christians on a lower level of acceptability. But many of these men, especially the recent converts, had little in the way of culture, and only a limited knowledge of the religion which they had abandoned. Preaching ceaselessly from their very limited stores of knowledge, and with few opportunities of renewal, they tended to become drained of all vitality and to lose what little effectiveness they had ever had. It was thus to a somewhat rickety organisation that I was now to devote the service of my talents.

I found my team encamped in a rented house in the small town of Ambasamusham, not far from the foot of the mountains. All the lands along the mountain foot were splendidly fertile. Not far away was the great spinning mill of Messrs Harvey and Sons, at that time, I believe, the largest mill in the world, regularly fed by the excellent cotton from the black cotton soil areas further north. This added further prosperity to the region.

The routine of our camping life was exacting. Early prayers were held six days in the week at 4.45 a.m., and by 5 a.m. we were off to our first preaching, in a village perhaps two to three miles from the centre; we started this early in order to catch the people on their way to their work in the fields. One of our number could play the fiddle, and we had two singing boys, who had quite a good repertoire of Indian songs, and sang lustily to gather the people together. Having done our best with this first audience, we would make our way to another village, looking especially for a street of weavers or craftsmen, who did not go out to the fields. We were usually home soon after 8 a.m. A bath and breakfast followed, and then some quiet hours of thought and study. At 12 o'clock the evangelists came in for instruction and midday prayers; like the village teachers, they were supposed to take an annual examination, and the lessons I gave them were supposed to help them in their preparation. At 5 p.m. we would sally out again and carry on our preaching, till the early fall of night, nine degrees from the equator, brought us home, tired and ready for bed not later than 9 p.m. On Wednesdays, there was no evening preaching, but the men came in for a devotional session, preceded by a missionary litany, written in rather high Tamil and printed on execrable paper, which I was expected to conduct; sweat flowed in rivers as I wrestled with this dreadful document. And it was not always easy to find helpful topics to be dealt with in my still very limited Tamil.

This was a healthy mode of existence, and many of the earlier missionaries had thriven on it. I was greatly hindered by my chronic difficulty in sleeping. I usually slept a little in the afternoon, but not enough to make up for the shortness of the nights. Only rarely did I manage to stand up to the full twenty days of our camping time, and I always returned to headquarters very weary. At the end of the first month I was dining alone with an Indian convert friend, Selwyn being out. I heard the clock strike, and said, 'That's 9 o'clock, I'm going to bed.' Only next morning did I learn that it had really been 8 o'clock; for once I had tumbled into bed and slept for ten hours without waking.

Sundays normally brought a visit to the local church; we generally camped in or near a village where there was a fellowship of Christians. It usually fell to my lot, as leader of the group, to preach; I now realise that almost all my sermons must have been far above the heads of my hearers; it takes time for the foreigner to forget his abstract way of thinking and to realise the limitations of his hearers' range of experience. Nothing is more deadly in a sermon than the illustration which does not illustrate.

I was very ill-satisfied with a great deal of what we were doing; but it must be remembered that I was not yet twenty-six years old, very new to the work, and it did not seem to be my place to issue instructions to men twenty years older than myself. At one point, however, I did soon feel it incumbent on me to make a protest. Among the streets we visited for preaching were, naturally, many inhabited by the outcastes. I noted that in these areas my colleagues would dwell on nothing but the material advantages which might accrue from accepting the Christian faith: 'Become Christians, and the mission will build you a school and protect you from your oppressors. Mr X belongs to your community and started life in a village just like this; he became a Christian and now he is in government service and earning Rs.300 a month.' I did not say anything directly; but one Wednesday afternoon I went through the New Testament book by book, showing, in the famous words of Lord Bacon, that 'prosperity is the blessing of the Old Testament, and adversity of the New'. Every new group of Christians in India with which I have had to do has had to face sooner or later a period of hostility, and even persecution, at the hands of non-Christian neighbours; not to warn our hearers of this possibility seemed to me the gravest treachery to the gospel. The one among my colleagues who more than the others had become an intimate friend, told me that there had been a great deal of discussion among the men, but that in the end they had come to the conclusion that my view was correct and biblical.

It was at this time that Selwyn and the bishop put their heads together, and decided to communicate to me their strong feeling that I ought to be ordained. I cannot say that at this time I felt any overpowering inner vocation to the ordained ministry. I was totally committed to the service of the Indian Church; if that Church, through its constituted leaders, told me that I could serve it more usefully as a clergyman than as a layman, it seemed to me that I must pay most careful attention to this advice. I pondered, prayed, and agreed. I have never regretted the decision. The service took place in Tamil in what was later my cathedral; as the only candidate, I had to read the Gospel in Tamil, something of an ordeal before a large and rather critical congregation. My old friend Willy Holland came over from Travancore to preach the sermon, on the very appropriate text, Mark 3:14 – 'And he appointed twelve, that they might be with him, and that he might send them forth to preach.' After the service, old Rao Sahib M. Ariminathan, the priest-in-charge of the cathedral, said to me, 'I have coveted your gifts for the Tinnevelly Church.' I realised that up till that time, knowing of my continuing connection with Cambridge, my Indian friends had regarded me as a visitor; now they felt that I really belonged.

During all this time there had been much debate at Trinity as to the terms on which prize fellowships should be held. It had been decided that the period should be reduced from six years to four, and rules regarding residence had been made a good deal stiffer than in previous years. My fellowship would run out in October 1928. Would it be a good idea to go back to England and take advantage of it for a further year's residence in Cambridge? I was much divided in mind; India had become my home, and I was reluctant to break my service. On the other hand, I had had a rough time of acclimatisation, having gone down nine times with unexplained and not very severe fevers; it seemed only sensible to recognise that I was much exhausted, and that I should take the opportunity to get a fresh start. I would not be wasting my time in Cambridge; I would give myself to the study of Sanskrit, and of that background of classical Hinduism, a knowledge of which I felt increasingly to be necessary for my work. So it was decided.

Before I left, I was to be introduced to two further interesting aspects of the life of the Tinnevelly Church.

The first was a great harvest festival. It takes an effort of the imagination to realise the isolation of a small Christian congregation of perhaps fifty people in a village of six hundred Hindus, cared for by a perhaps not very well-educated catechist, and receiving a visit from the local pastor perhaps once in two months. The CMS missionaries, having sympathetically realised this, planned that the annual harvest festival should be held for a whole region, and that all the Christians should be invited to come into the central station of the district. These were such noisy occasions that as a young man I detested them; as I grew deeper into the life of the Church, I realised the immense value to the more isolated Christians of seeing themselves as part of something big, of apprehending something of what it means to belong to the one body of Christ.

My first harvest festival was at Nullur, where ordinarily 3,000 people would gather for three nights and two days. The two days of the festival were crowded with engagements. Each day started at 5 a.m. with a somewhat vociferous prayer meeting. There would be special meetings for men, and for women and children; usually some adult baptisms; a great celebration of Holy Communion; a meeting of the Indian Missionary Society, which had been founded in 1903 by V. S. Azariah and pioneered in the diocese of Dornakal, of which he was consecrated first bishop in 1912; and perhaps some lantern slides – we had not in those days risen to film strips. But of course the central event was the great ingathering service at midday on the second day, held in a *pandal* (a kind of awning made of poles decorated with banana leaves and matting), since no building could hold even half of the people who crowded in. Preaching at this service was a real ordeal. There would be a ceaseless hubbub from the temporary street of shops which had risen like an exhalation from the earth; calves and sheep and goats, later to be presented as offerings, would be tethered all round the *pandal*; children running here and there would add to the din. In those days we did not run to electricity and amplifiers; it was a case of shouting at the top of one's voice and hoping that some among the hearers would hear and remember something. I well remember how on a later occasion, also at Nullur, every time that I made an impressive pause in my sermon, a cock would crow loudly in assent; I ended completely exhausted, having been torn asunder between a hysterical desire to laugh and the absolute necessity of getting on with my sermon.

The bringing of the offerings which followed the sermon was really impressive. Splendid young men would stride up lightly carrying heavy sacks of rice; old women with just a handful of chillies from their garden, children with a bunch of plantains, many bringing coins; the whole would take about three-quarters of an hour.

Then one had to go round and bless all the livestock, which fortunately was not going to be offered up in sacrifice, though it looked rather like it. And then at last one was free to call it a day and to steal away to the coolness but not to the quiet of the bungalow; the auctioning of the offerings in kind would go on far into the evening. And so at last the people would go, having seen many old friends, heard a plethora of words, and perhaps caught a glimpse of that strange and wonderful mystery, the body of Christ upon earth. In my later years I loved attending harvest festivals – but I tried, if I could, to spend the night a good many miles away.

The other activity to be recorded was our annual camp for schoolboys. Long ago, when the regiment was at Palamcottah, they had used Courtallam, at the very foot of the mountains, as a sanatorium and had built there an immense bungalow, which had later been acquired by the Church. It is a ravishing place. The views over the flashing green of the paddy-fields and the encircling arms of the hills are delightful. The days would be spent, as in all schoolboy camps, in Bible study in the mornings, games, bathing, expeditions, and then the main meeting in the evening, when we tried to make the Christian faith a living thing to boys whose experience of it had so far been little more than conventional. There was one special rock where I used to go to prepare my talks – with infinite labour, as everything had to be in Tamil for the sake of the younger boys. I think we always spoke too long, but Indians are used to long speeches, and manifest at least a patience greater than that of their counterparts in England.

Almost every year there would be some boys ready to be baptised. This was a great event. The baptism took place, of course, by immersion, in an exquisite rock pool, with a great rock above it on which the other boys could sit and take part in the service. One year a great friend of mine, a splendid athlete, had at last decided to be baptised. As Selwyn put him under the first time, 'in the name of the Father', he lost his footing, struggled to the surface, only to be ruthlessly plunged under again 'in the name of the Son'; and by the time he had completed the third immersion in the name of the Holy Spirit, he struggled to the shore very thoroughly baptised inside and out.

Before I left for England, I spent some days in the strongly Hindu town of Sankaranayanarkoil. I was helping the local pastor at the Holy Communion; when he uncovered the vessels, I found myself looking at the pelican, the sign of Corpus Christi College, engraved on the side of the chalice; I knew at once where I was; I had read that Ragland had left the four silver cups that he had won as mathematical prizes at Cambridge, to be used as chalices in the churches of his beloved North Tinnevelly. So here he was once again, this brooding presence of a saint, challenging the Church to take up once again the work that he had left unfinished.

Much could be recorded of the year that I now spent in Cambridge, but little that is relevant to this story.

The India to which I returned was a different India. My friend Willy Holland, after serving for some years as Principal of the CMS College in Kottayam, on the far side of the mountains from where I had lived, had left that job to join in a new adventure on which some friends of his had launched themselves. This is the area of the very ancient Church of the Thomas Christians. Holland's young friends belonged to a number of the sections into which that ancient Church has become divided. They had decided to found a Christian College, to serve as a means of bringing these separated and often warring sections into closer fellowship, and also to serve the northern part of the Travancore State, in which Christian educational enterprise was far weaker than in the South. The Alwaye Christian College was born. Holland found himself extremely happy in this situation; Christian fellowship was deep and real, and he found himself for the first time in his many years in India working with Indian Christians who treated him as an equal and accepted him as a friend. But he had suddenly found himself faced with a difficult problem of conscience. The CMS had asked him to become Principal of St John's College, Agra, and he was inclined to accept, but he had just arranged for two young Oxford men to join him at Alwaye as short-term missionaries. He did not feel that he could leave Alwaye unless someone could be found to take his place and to introduce the new recruits to the College and to their job. So he asked me whether I would take his place.

I have always felt it my duty to consider carefully every offer of this kind that has ever come my way. So I considered Alwaye; but I was aware of a strong instinctive dislike of the idea of going there. I could by now speak Tamil fluently and the Tamil country had become my home. I had been at Alwaye for the baptism of my god-daughter, Mary Holland, and her twin brother Michael, and had not found it attractive. The humid climate and the endless green of that country which gets a hundred inches of rain in a year pleased me less than the harsher colours of the landscape the other side of the mountains.

It occurred to me, however, that a break had come in my activities in Tinnevelly. There was no job urgently awaiting my arrival, and nothing would be put seriously out of gear if I delayed my return by a year. I did not for a moment think that Willy Holland would accept my offer to go to Alwaye for a year; he had wanted someone much more permanent to take his place. But, when I broached the idea to him, he nearly hit the ceiling in his delight, and averred that this would solve all his problems. It was to these new surroundings and to this entirely new type of work that I was now to betake myself.

My first task was to get to know the two young Oxford men. They were remarkably different. One had done remarkably well in classics and came out with a really distinguished degree. But he was withdrawn and very hard to get to know. He was a good teacher, and I think was much respected by the students. Always a somewhat advanced Anglo-Catholic, he not long afterwards joined the Church of Rome, whether under my influence or by reaction against it, it is not for me to say. The other was extrovert and outgoing, with a great gift for developing good relations with the students and making real friends among them. He always says that I was the first person ever to help him to understand what Christianity really is. Certainly when he came to India he had very little understanding of it; but I think that he very much exaggerates the part which I played in helping him to a clearer and firmer Christian faith.

I was never happy with the teaching side of the work. The Indian tradition is that of endless learning by heart, and even at Alwaye the students had little idea of the difference between a trained and an untrained mind. With the junior classes it was possible to do something; but as examinations came near, the College was a dismal scene of students walking up and down, all day and most of the night, memorising their lecture notes. They were much addicted to horrid little books of notes on the prescribed texts, full of inaccuracies and well calculated to strangle at birth a student's appreciation of the beauties of the English language. In the degree class, what they really wanted was simply the dictation of answers to every conceivable examination question, and summaries of novels by Meredith and Hardy that they would never read. I did my best to help them, but it was often sorely against my conscience.

One thing that struck me very early in my stay at Alwaye – it was taken for granted that no Hindu or Muslim student would ever be converted. In the early days of Christian colleges in India, conversions had taken place in fair numbers. Then the barriers between the religions hardened, and a change of allegiance became practically unknown. This was more true in Kerala than in perhaps any other part of India; the 'Syrian' Christians had become almost identifiable as a caste – and in India to change your caste is something that you simply cannot do. There was, however, very considerable Christian activity, and among the students there were some who were obviously marked out for future leadership in the Churches. The Anglicans were by far the best disciplined, the Mar Thomas the most charming, the Jacobites the most difficult; these last I felt were always a little on the defensive, knowing that their Church had had more difficulty than the others in entering into the modern world. With our many non-Christian students we had good relations of friendship and co-operation, but this never seemed to develop into any interest in the gospel.

I felt that there were too few practical outlets for the Christian feelings of the students, and that we ought to try some experiments in social service. We started evening classes for the many boys about the compound, with games and some Christian instruction thrown in. One of the pillars of this work was an admirable student, T. B. Benjamin, son of an admirable father, Archdeacon Benjamin of Kottayam. After ordination, T.B. went to work among depressed-class people, and with great heroism set himself to learn to live on the same level of poverty as they. This experiment could not last very long. At the time of writing, T.B. is Bishop of North Kerala.

One of the problems of Kerala is that people do not live in villages, but in isolated houses scattered all over the countryside. The College was surrounded by a dense but almost invisible population, their little huts being almost entirely hidden by the foliage of the trees by which they were overshadowed. It was clear that most of them belonged to the depressed classes and were living on the border-line of extreme poverty. There was no evidence that any of them were Christians, and almost all were illiterate. I decided that the only thing to be done was to visit every house within a mile of the College, give it a number, and enter it on a plan, find out all that we could about the inhabitants, and then consider what we could do to help them. We had no surveying instruments; but a compass and our own two feet supplied the basic information; a number of students understood what we were about and entered eagerly into the game. It took time, but gradually the bits and pieces began to coalesce and a remarkably workmanlike plan began to emerge. The inhabitants were extremely suspicious, thinking that this was some police ploy to harass them; later investigation showed that in a large number of cases they had given an imaginary name instead of the real name of the owner. It was clear that the first need was the provision of elementary medical aid, malnutrition being one of the main causes of the various ailments from which they suffered. A dispensary came into being and started operations, if I remember rightly, with three drugs – aspirin, iodex and magnesium sulphate – and after all, with these three one can tackle a great many of the ills from which the human body can suffer. This stage did not last long; when Eileen Crowle arrived, and brought with her the experience on the North-West frontier of a highly trained and more than competent nurse, our amateur beginnings disappeared into the limbo of forgotten things. The dispensary soon attained a

high level of efficiency, and provided a much-valued service to all
the people on this side of the river.

One of my problems at Alwaye was that of language. I dislike
very much being in a place where I cannot at least make myself
understood in the language of the common people. So with the help
of a student I launched out on the study of Malayalam, the language
of Kerala. Malayalam and Tamil are much alike, but accent and
intonation are so different that, as with Spanish and Italian, it is
almost impossible to speak both of them well. Tamils unkindly say
that Malayalam is bad Tamil spoken through the nose; Malayalis
respond by saying that theirs is the best and purest form of the
language. But even the Malayalis must admit that their language
has no ancient and classical literature as has Tamil. The Brahman
influence has been very strong, and in consequence the adulteration
of the Dravidian base with Sanskrit has gone much further than in
Tamil, and has affected not only vocabulary but even grammatical
construction. I got to the point at which I could speak fairly fluently,
and could read intelligibly, but I never got to the point at which I
could preach without an interpreter.

The limited knowledge that I had acquired proved useful to me,
as such knowledge always does. I used from time to time to go over
to the Anglican church on the other side of the river, and was there
brought into touch with the life of the Church outside the College.
I took a confirmation class for students, which, by special request
of his father, a schoolboy, K. John, was permitted to join. Our
paths did not cross again for forty years; in 1968 I encountered my
former pupil as the Chairman of the Chamber of Commerce of the
city of Madras.

This is noted not just as passing reminiscence, but as a first
indication of something that has been of great importance in the
life of both Church and State in India. For centuries the Thomas
Christians of Kerala, descended from migrants from Iran and Syria,
had lived isolated in their narrow strip of country between the
mountains and the sea. The rest of India hardly knew them, and
they had never shown any concern for the evangelisation of India,
but now increase of population and educated unemployment began
to drive them far and wide in search of profitable employment.
They are an intelligent people, and when Western education was
offered to them, they took to it with avidity. Literacy is higher
among them than perhaps in any other community except the
very small community of the Parsis. Very early marriage, more
common in the north of their area than in the south, had kept the

girls back; but, as more and more girls found their way to school, they began to show themselves at least the equal of boys. As all the available posts in Kerala began to be filled up, they began to cast their eyes on wider pastures; their quick intelligence, courteous manners and general reliability made them widely acceptable. In part the migration was planned; the Mar Thoma Church especially began to feel a sense of missionary responsibility, outside as well as within the borders of Kerala. The justification for colleges such as Alwaye is that, though it may make few converts at home, it is preparing a Christian élite of men and women to carry the gospel far and wide in their daily avocations.

One of my excursions from Alwaye was naturally to the Maramon Convention for the deepening of spiritual life. This was organised more or less on the lines of the Keswick Convention in England; but everything in India takes on a specifically Indian guise. The convention is held in a dry river bed, and the meetings take place in a vast *pandal*. When the congregation disperses after a session, it looks as though all the umbrellas in the world had come on pilgrimage to Maramon, the faithful carrying them as protection against the rays of the sun, which in that hot season can be very fierce indeed. The central figure in the convention was always Bishop Abraham Mar Thoma, the junior Metropolitan of the Mar Thoma Church. My greatest reward for attending the convention and speaking at it was the opportunity of becoming acquainted with this remarkable man.

Abraham had grown up in the Malabar Church. I never learned the circumstances in which he came over from the unreformed to the reformed section of the Church. But it is clear that at some point he had experienced a deep Evangelical conversion. He had come under the influence of Thomas Walker of Tinnevelly, who, at first suspicious of 'Keswick teaching', had come to embrace fervently the Keswick doctrine of the 'second blessing' and the sanctification of the believer. In due course Abraham was sent to Wycliffe College, Toronto, then in the heyday of its Evangelical career, and came back, not theologically well-equipped, but well-balanced, shrewd, and with an understanding of the world outside India. He was one of the two Indians I have ever known who had some understanding of the way in which the Western mind works; the other was, of course, Bishop Azariah. At the age of thirty-two Abraham was called to the episcopate. This meant that he could never marry, since the Mar Thoma Church has kept the ancient Eastern Orthodox custom, by which parish priests are married, and bishops are celibates.

Abraham accepted this as part of his total acceptance of the yoke of Christ, and as a necessary qualification for the service of Christ in the particular vocation to which he had been called.

Bishop Abraham was, in quite simple terms, the most Christlike man I have ever known. No doubt this impression was a little heightened by his almost Syrian colour, and the flowing robes which he always wore, but the real likeness came from within and not from any outward trappings. Abraham was a man of supreme simplicity. When very young he had learned to trust in the promises of God and to expect that they would be fulfilled. If he had a problem, he would think nothing of spending all night on his knees; when dawn came, he would have the answer to his problem. Yet there was nothing sentimental about his piety. If emotion tended to get out of hand at the convention, Abraham was always there to bring it under control by a word or a glance. And he had at all times a gay and sparkling sense of humour. His people regarded him, and not without good cause, with almost superstitious reverence.

This is by far the largest crowd I have ever addressed. Even in those days it was reckoned that 30,000 people would be present at the larger meetings; today attendance is reckoned at over 100,000. They seemed to stretch far away into the distance, and it seemed almost impossible to make any kind of contact with them. The difficulty was increased in that very few of the speakers knew Malayalam, and so had to make their contact through interpreters, and this I have always found excessively difficult.

The time was coming at which a serious decision had to be made. My colleagues were anxious for me to make Alwaye my permanent home. I think that they had found me in some ways difficult as a colleague, but they felt that I had certain intellectual gifts that outweighed my manifest imperfections. They asked me to join the fellowship, to which only Willy Holland among foreigners had ever belonged, and to accept permanent appointment to the staff. I took this offer very seriously. Yet I was fairly sure in which way the decision would finally go. I never felt really at home in Kerala; the Tamil country and my friends the other side of the mountains were always drawing me; I felt that teaching English to somewhat unwilling students could not be my vocation for life. If there had been any great urgency of need, I would have stayed, but the CMS had already found an admirable candidate, Brian Crowle, who had seen service as a short-term missionary on the North-West frontier. When he arrived at Alwaye with his admirable wife Eileen, they at once took the students to their hearts, made a home for them, set in motion many Christian enterprises, by their quiet example maintained the highest possible level of Christian spirituality, and conferred innumerable benefits on the life of the College. I think that the greatest service I ever rendered Alwaye College was in leaving it.

So I crossed the mountains again to my earlier haunts, to find a much changed situation. Norman Tubbs, married and with four children, found it impossible to exist on the salary provided for the Bishop of Tinnevelly. There was just so much for the bishop: for example, if he wanted a chaplain or a car, he must pay for them out of his own pocket. Moreover, a much-loved child had died in Palamcottah. So when the opportunity came to leave Tinnevelly for Rangoon, Tubbs was grateful, and had no hesitation in accepting the call. Frederick Western was chosen as his successor.

It would be impossible to imagine a greater contrast than that between Tubbs and Western. The only thing that they had in common was that both had been at Cambridge. Western was the son of a London lawyer, a man of the most perfect integrity and a rather austere High Church layman. When he died, he left instructions that nothing was to be engraved on his tombstone but his name, the dates of his birth and death, and the single line from the *Dies Irae, Mihi quoque spem dedisti*, 'To me too thou hast given hope.' Western had been at the Cambridge Clergy Training School at the same time as my father, and at that time had seemed very uncertain both of his faith and of his vocation. He made his way to India, and for a time was associated with Sadhu Sundar Singh and the American, Samuel Stokes, in a kind of brotherhood. I had met him once in Cambridge and thought him the dullest speaker I had ever heard. Ugly, awkward, unbelievably shy and withdrawn, it seemed most unlikely that he would ever become an excellent bishop; but this was the miracle that came about.

Western was in fact an exceedingly able man. He was an excellent man of business, and very soon had the diocese in splendid shape from the administrative point of view. He had read mathematics at Cambridge, and had inherited a great deal of his father's legal skill and sagacity. He was a tremendous reader, often in strange and out of the way directions, and at times revealed a pleasing and wholly unexpected streak of humour. The more I got to know him, the more I appreciated his gifts. When I was able to share with him some of the troubles I had with insomnia and depression, he came nearer than any man before or after to understanding what was amiss and how I could be helped.

I owe it to him that for the second time I was headed off from leaving India.

I came back to the diocese at a crucial moment. The supply of Indian clergy had fallen unduly low, and there had been a good deal of dissatisfaction with the methods and standards of training. Now the whole system was to be reorganised. It was laid down that all candidates must be either university graduates or matriculates with two years' training as teachers. Before entering the seminary for their three years of theological study, they were to spend two years as probationers, one year as village catechists under the care of an experienced priest, and one year as evangelists engaged in the direct preaching of the gospel to non-Christians. The first set of probationers were to take the place of the old Itinerancy. I was to take charge of these eleven men for a year. I was allowed to select as our centre Sachiapuram, the home of Thomas Ragland, and the place in which he had died.

So I settled into the bungalow, from which the greater part of the furniture had disappeared, and gathered around me my team of helpers. We soon established a routine. We met every morning at 6.30 in the church, and spent an hour there. Morning Prayer was said, replaced once a week by a celebration of the Holy Communion; the rest of the hour the men were free to read, or pray or meditate as the Spirit moved them. I gave a number of lectures, far too theoretical as I now think, but I was as new to the trade as they were, and had to learn by making mistakes. On Wednesday afternoon we met for a prayer-meeting; and here I think we had some success in learning how a Christian group can learn to pray together intelligently and without weariness. Gradually the penny dropped. My method was to let prayer flow for a quarter of an hour, and then to pause for the singing of a verse or two of a hymn; and then to go on for another quarter of an hour. On one occasion we found that we were able to continue for an hour and a quarter, without the stream of prayer running dry, and without any sense of weariness.

During the ten days in each month which we were to spend in headquarters, we had various outlets for work. On Sunday mornings I would provide a celebration of the Holy Communion with a sermon, attended by all the probationers, and by teachers and others who liked to come. Then I would send the men out into the surrounding Hindu villages to collect the children and hold a sort of Sunday School. In one such interval, with the approval of the local Indian 'Rural Dean', as we would call him in England,

I called in a number of younger teachers from the mission schools over quite a large area, for Bible teaching and for training in the pastoral work which they were expected to carry on in addition to their work in the schools. Again, looking back, I realise that I enormously over-estimated both their knowledge and their capacity for absorbing knowledge; what I learned from my mistakes was to prove of great value later on. Then, following up what I had learned with Stanley Jones, I would give lectures to educated Hindus and Muslims in the towns. Of course I never had anything like the number that he was able to assemble; but I have had quiet and respectful audiences of anything from thirty up to a hundred. I used to take immense trouble preparing these lectures; I cannot say that I have evidence of anyone having been converted through them, but I never felt that the effort was wasted, since by this method we were making at least a temporary contact with that class in India which more than any other it is difficult to reach with the gospel.

The greater part of our time was to be spent camping – basing ourselves generally on the few and scattered Christian congregations that were to be found in the area. I usually cycled out to our intended place of camping, talking to people by the way-side and trying to get to know the area and its needs. I used to ask whether they knew anything of the Christian gospel; in quite a number of places the reply was, 'Yes, years ago Christians used to come round here, and talk to us; they were very good people, and used to give us very good advice, to do good and not to do evil; but for a good many years we have not seen them.' This indicated that for a considerable period the area had been much neglected, and that Christian activity had diminished rather than increased.

Then the blow fell. We had hardly got our routine established, and settled into regular ways of work, when a meeting of the North Church Council was held at Sachiapuram. The bishop called me aside and said, 'I am afraid you will have to go to Nazareth.' The little theological school, which for some years had been training only catechists, was now to be reopened for the training of ordinands. Looking round our scanty missionary staff, the bishop had concluded that I was the one who had the necessary qualifications, and ought to be called to this work. He knew my concern for the north, and my interest in direct evangelistic work, and therefore understood the sacrifice involved. But, knowing him, I knew that he would have pondered the matter deeply, and that his decision would probably be the wisest in the circumstances.

This is what had always happened. As soon as any attempt had been made to get active work going again in the north, the south would exercise its pull, and in general the pull of the south would prevail. I had no wish at all to exchange the way I was living for the far more comfortable conditions of the south. It had been my aim to sink myself deeper and deeper into the Tamil language, and into a knowledge and understanding of Hinduism and the Hindu way of life, and so to qualify myself to be an effective witness for Christ to the educated and high-caste Hindu; I had no wish to become a missionary to Christians. Least of all did I wish to settle down in an old mission-station where, as in Nazareth, the gospel had been proclaimed for more than a hundred years and where everyone was at least in name a Christian.

On the other hand, though always an adventurer at heart, I have always believed that the voice of the Church is a voice to which the Christian must listen with the most careful attention, though he is not pledged in all circumstances to obey it. If the Church thought that the training of the ordained ministry was the task which at the moment I was best qualified to carry out, probably I ought to set that considered opinion above my own desires. The manner of life I had adopted was very exhausting; with my always rather precarious health, it was not likely that I would be able to carry on in that manner for a long period; the bishop certainly thought that it would be better for me to have a more settled kind of existence. The aim of the missionary must be to multiply himself; if I could put into the hearts and minds of half a dozen Indian Christians something of the vision that seemed to have been given me, I should probably be doing a better job than if I tried to carry out the work myself. So the decision was made. I did suggest that the work of training for the ministry could better be carried on in an area less fully Christianised than that of Nazareth and its surroundings. But this was turned down by the Church Committees. The seminary, they said – quite untruly, as history will show – has always been at Nazareth; at Nazareth it must always be.

So the days of apprenticeship and adventure were to come to an end. I was now to be absorbed into the conventional pattern of missionary work, and into the traditional and well-established order of the life of the South Indian Church.

4

Apprentice Theologian

The history of Nazareth goes back to 1796, when the land was granted to serve as a refuge for Christians who for one reason or another had had to leave their villages. When I came to live there, it was a large village of about 2,000 inhabitants, all of them Christians, and with rather a high level of prosperity. It had a station on the branch line running from Tinnevelly Town to the sea-coast at the famous pilgrim centre of Tinnechemalur, where the gigantic temple had been forty-six years in the rebuilding and was still unfinished. Nazareth stands just on the edge of the *teri*, a strange region of sand-hills, which stretch for miles along the coast a few miles from the sea. The term sand-hills is a misnomer. During the south-west monsoon, when little rain falls, the tearing raging winds pick up from the mountain slopes a heavy burden of richly fertile soil; as these off-shore winds meet the sea breeze, which springs up almost every day about midday, they are wont to drop a considerable part of their burden, and over many centuries these hills of rich red earth have built up to a height of rather more than 200 feet at the highest point. In long walks through the *teri*, uninhabited save for large numbers of wild cattle that have strayed away from civilisation, I was at length able to identify the highest point, and from it to look down in all directions on an area in which there were Christians and a church in almost every village. When water can be got to it, this red soil is admirable for cultivation. All round the *teri* foot, where the underground streams come near the surface, there are many oases of brilliant fertility. The higher areas bear nothing but scrub and desert plants.

Nazareth has always been the centre of many mission activities, with an exceptionally large population of mission employees. There was a high school and training school for girls run by two, and sometimes three, missionary women of total dedication and rather unusual intellectual capacity. There was a middle school for boys, shortly to be raised to the level of a high school. There was the largest mission hospital in the diocese, competently run by a man and wife who were both doctors. There was an industrial school, run by a gifted missionary, the Revd A. P. Randle, whose wife, a well-qualified teacher before the marriage, became the manager of the boys' school. There was a large church, under the care of an Indian graduate priest who was so Westernised he kept his shoes on during services, whereas I, with my passion for total identification with the Church I served, followed the Indian custom and very rarely entered a church without leaving my sandals at the door.

Sandwiched on a narrow strip of ground between the hospital and the industrial school, was the seminary over which I was to preside – a two-storeyed building with a classroom below and a chapel above, a shabby side room, which could be used in case of need as a second classroom, and a street of ten small houses, in which one member of staff and the students were to dwell. One look at this set-up, and I reckoned that, if the seminary was ever to become anything but an inferior institution, little respected and little regarded, we would have to move.

The seminary had been closed for some months, and for some years had not been training ordinands. The first thing was to work out a syllabus and plan of action. Looking back I cannot imagine how I could be so foolish. I had served a fairly long apprenticeship in India, but the syllabus I produced was purely Western; I had, indeed, included in it a study of the religions of India, but this was the only concession to reality in a syllabus which could well have been produced by someone who had never set foot outside England. Yet the bishop had approved it, and to this syllabus we were tied, until gradually common sense prevailed, and we began to ask ourselves what the students really needed to know in order to fulfil their ministry under the conditions of an Indian Church.

Next I had to get to know my colleagues. I made the great mistake of allowing the diocese to impose upon me the two men who had been instructing catechists before my arrival. One was already past the retiring age. He had been a boy of thirteen when the patriarchal missionary Marjoselius came to Nazareth in 1876, had survived and suffered all through those long years of tyranny, and represented a formal and correct tradition of High Church Anglicanism. Blameless and upright in character, he represented a tradition of theological training which belonged to an already distant past. His younger colleague was a fiery nationalist, temperamental and over-sensitive, and I think acutely aware that he had been thrust into a position for which his gifts and his knowledge were grossly inadequate. We worked together for the most part peacefully, but we never reached that intimacy and mutual confidence which I had enjoyed with so many Indian clergymen in earlier days.

Then I had to make acquaintance with my students in a new capacity. We had been together at Sachiapuram, but now we were to be much more officially related in a seminary, where they and I were both far more self-conscious than we had been in the simpler atmosphere of the north. Almost at once I became aware of a number of intellectual blocks, which were to defeat nearly all my efforts to teach theology as I believe that it needs to be taught. What they wanted was to be able in three years to take down from dictation enough sermon notes to last them for the rest of their natural lives. When they realised that this was not in the programme, they hoped to be given clear and simple answers to any theological questions that could be asked, to learn their lecture notes by heart, to regurgitate these as examination answers, and so to pass with flying colours. When I explained to them that a student who exactly reproduced his lecture notes as an answer could not hope for a mark higher than 45 per cent, they felt that they were being very badly treated. Any effort to think was far beyond the older among them. We were gratified when an external examiner from the diocese of Madras remarked, 'These students may get everything wrong, but at least they have been taught to think.' The best that I could do was to make the rule that, if lectures had been given in English, examinations would be in Tamil, and, if lectures had been in Tamil, examinations would be in English. This at least prevented the sheer reproduction of notes; but it was regarded by the students as a very mean trick.

Of one problem I was well aware long before I got anywhere near Nazareth – that of helping students to cross the bridge from a pre-critical to a critical attitude towards theology. I knew that all our students would be dyed-in-the-wool fundamentalists, not because they had thought anything out, but because they had never been told anything else, and because a greatly revered generation of missionaries had held and defended a ruthlessly conservative position long after this had been abandoned in the greater part of the thinking Christian world. I had a great deal of sympathy with this point of view, for the Bible was regarded as the deliverance from the darkness of heathenism, as the light on the wayfarer's path, and as the absolutely reliable source of knowledge on every conceivable subject. How could one replace this view by another without doing irreparable harm in the process?

One European colleague who worked with me for a short period held the view that the men had got to learn critical views sooner or later, and that the best method was to fling them in at the deep end, and straight away. I have seen the same method used in the United States of America, and it seems to me that it invariably produces one of three possible results. It may bring about grave crises of faith; it is easy within a year to break down the simple faith with which a student has come to college, and then only two years are left in which to rebuild that which has been destroyed; there is no guarantee that this will be successfully accomplished. The student may say to himself, 'I will learn what they teach here, because I have to pass my examinations, but I will not believe a word of what they say,' and so leave college with exactly the same uncritical and uncriticised faith as he had when he entered. Or the student may embrace with avidity the results of critical investigation without any understanding at all of the nature of those investigations, and may later do grave harm by flaunting these new convictions before congregations entirely unprepared to receive them.

I was determined that such disasters should not follow upon my work in Nazareth. I was determined from the start that theoretical and practical training were to be held closely together. From time to time we used to close down teaching and go out for a week's camping and preaching to non-Christians. And we agreed to take as our special responsibility the work in the neighbouring parish of Puttayanmaneri, where 1,300 Christians lived in six villages. Students were assigned to the various villages, and were to work on Sundays and Wednesday afternoons under the direction of the pastor and in fellowship with the resident teacher-catechists. It soon became clear that this was an impossible arrangement, and I found myself pastor of the parish as well as warden of the seminary. At that time it was most unusual for a foreigner to find himself in sole charge of an Indian parish; but I can never be too thankful for the two years' experience in which I learned a great many things about the life of the Indian Church which otherwise I would never have known.

Almost all our Christians were of four or five generations' standing. There was a good deal of formal piety, but, as it seemed to me, an extensive lack of any direct experience of what the gospel was all about, and a total lack of interest in the non-Christian world and in the conversion of the Hindus. It was our task to attempt to bring back some life into this formally correct but generally lifeless mass. One of the first results of our work was that, without any special stress on the Holy Communion in our teaching and preaching, the number of acts of Communion doubled itself within a year. Each of the larger villages had a celebration once a month, but two of the churches had a weekly celebration on a weekday, and these I usually took myself. The communicants seemed to feel that something was happening, though they might have been hard put to it to express in words just what they supposed it to be.

At an early stage I found myself engaged in a wholly unexpected field of pastoral activity. The headteacher in our main village was a young man of quite exceptional ability and devotion. One day he told me quietly that a number of couples in the village had never been married and were technically living in sin; could anything be done about it? When we began to look into the situation, we found that in a number of cases there had been no deliberate and planned flouting of the law of the Church; men and women, usually elderly, had begun to live together, and had then been ashamed to come forward and ask for the blessing of the Church; one or two of the women concerned were Hindus but were now willing to be baptised. Some had been too poor to find even the Rs.4 required as a wedding fee, and in some cases considerably strained the law of the Church. I consulted the bishop, who took a very generous view of the situation; he agreed that all those living in irregular ways must be regarded as having excommunicated themselves; but that the lifting of the excommunication and the preparations for Christian marriage could go forward together. Banns had to be called, but under the Indian Christian Marriage Act banns can be called on saints' days; this made it possible to shorten the period, and to avoid publicity which must be painful to those whose real state had been unknown to almost all their fellow Christians. Within a few months we were able to restore to Christian fellowship fourteen persons who had long lived on the margin of the Church. I learned a never-forgotten lesson as to the need for intimate and detailed pastoral care. This was an old, well-established and well-cared-for congregation; I wondered how many hundreds of similar cases were to be found scattered in various parts of the diocese.

My next activity was as a church builder. Just outside the large village of Pillaigenturam was the *cheri*, the separate hamlet inhabited by members of a 'scheduled caste', more commonly called outcastes, a number of whom were Christians.[1] By the side of the irrigation tank stood a half-built church. We had two admirable methods of securing help. The SPCK was prepared to supply the last 10 per cent of the cost of building a church, if the other 90 per cent had been raised locally. There was in South India a Christian doctor who was making a great deal of money through the sale of patent medicines; I never discovered whether these medicines were good for the healing of disease, but there could be no doubt as to their money-making properties. Having a sense of Christian responsibility for the use of his money, the good doctor put the roofs on to an astonishingly large number of village churches; let the request be made in the right way, and the consignment of tiles would follow in an amazingly short time. I felt that the people only needed a little friendly stimulation, and that within a very short time we would get the job done. My sister gave the east window-frame; it had wooden shutters but no glass; I gave the altar and communion rails, with a very pleasing pattern of the instruments of the passion, chosen by myself and worked out by the industrial school. It was not long before I was able to call the bishop for the dedication of a neat little church, thirty-two feet long, and capable of seating a hundred people, sitting on the floor as we always do in Tinnevelly.

At the other end of the parish, another village had a church of sun-dried brick and thatch, which they wished to replace with a pukka building. When I consulted the circle chairman about this, he replied, 'The people have been talking for years about rebuilding their church; but they will never do it.' 'Ho,' said I, thinking otherwise. Though it was a poor village, there were some exceptionally nice people there; and I felt, rightly as it proved, that, again with a little gentle stimulation, they would settle down and get the job done. No sooner said than done. Their first action was to pull down the old church and to build a quite satisfactory school with the materials that were found to be usable. Then the new church began to rise from the ground. During the dry season, when there was not much work in the fields, the entire village would turn out to share in the work. Skilled, paid labour was used only for the arch-work above the doors and windows, and for the setting of the roof; everything else was done by the people themselves. This was a sight to gladden sore eyes. Everyone had a job and knew what the job was. The small boys were carrying stones from the pile of 'broken stone' already prepared. The women were drawing water from the well. The young men were treading out the mortar; the girls were carrying the mortar on their heads to the older men who were standing by the walls, and carrying on the work of masons with inborn skill. And so the work went forward with a will, and once again it was my pleasure to call the bishop to the dedication, to carry out the ceremony with triple circumambulation and all the necessary doings.

My final service to my parish was to be as a miracle-worker. One year in July the people of Thailapuram came to me, and said, 'Our well is dry; there is no prospect of its filling up again until the rains come in October. What are we to do?' I went with them, and saw the women of the village standing in a queue, each woman allowed to fill just one water-pot from the trickle that was oozing into the bottom of the well, and that was to suffice for cooking and washing for a day. I knew something of the make-up of our country; I knew that there were many underground streams, carrying the water from the mountains to the sea; I thought that this well might be over one of the underground streams, and that by boring we might touch this hidden supply of water. My suggestion was adopted. The boring apparatus was of the most primitive kind – a sort of harpoon on a rope; the men of the village took it in relays six at a time to draw the harpoon and then let it fall again into the hole which gradually grew deeper – slow, hard and tedious work. Six days passed, and still not a drop of water in the well. They had come to a hard stratum of rock, on which their harpoon seemed to make hardly any impression at all; discouraged, they went on simply in the strength of my faith. The next morning they came to me with shining faces, and said, 'There is water in our well to the height of two men.' From that day to this the water has never failed; when everything all round is burned up and bare, there is always a strip of green round the bishop's well. They came to me again and said, 'For three hundred years our fathers have suffered in this place from lack of water; the water was there all the time and we never knew it.' This has served me many a time as a sermon illustration; the grace of God is there all the time, but we fail to touch it because we do not go deep enough to the place in which it is to be found.

We worked in those days. At Christmas and Easter all the four main villages wanted to celebrate Holy Communion. It had become the custom, in our parish, as in many others, for the parish priest to go on all through the night, moving from place to place, celebrating four times and preaching four sermons. I saw no reason to change this good custom. It meant leaving home at about 11.15, and starting the first celebration at Pillaiyarmanai at 11.30. Sometimes I had a deacon to help me, but more often I was alone. It was specially delightful at Easter to be bicycling along under the paschal moon, with the palmyra trees whispering in the light breeze and creating the strange illusion that it was raining. Each church would be most beautifully decorated with long streamers of white, red and pink oleander, and illuminated with so many candles drinking up the

oxygen that at times I had to put some of them out in order
to keep on my feet in small and ill-ventilated sanctuaries. The
congregations never knew exactly at what time the priest would
arrive, so they would be all assembled waiting in church, passing
the time singing lyrics, though on one occasion I was a little
overcome to find them at 2 a.m. on Christmas morning engaged
with true Anglican enthusiasm in saying the Athanasian Creed.
By the time that I reached the fourth village, it would be getting
light. I would finally arrive home at about 7.30 a.m., dead tired,
having administered to about 350 communicants. A quick bath,
then breakfast, and at last blessedly to bed, with nothing more to
do until possibly baptisms at 4 p.m.

One of our chief concerns was to make contacts for the students
with the wider concerns of the life of the Church and of the student
world. In India, as in the United States, the Student Christian
Movement had started life as the 'Student Y', the students' branch
of the YMCA. I had been at the notable meeting at Purnamuller in
1928, at which the SCM came into separate existence, and, under its
vigorous General Secretary, Augustine Ralla Ram, began to spread
and to flourish. Soon after my coming to Nazareth, I was asked to
take the main series of addresses at the Madras Presidency Camp
to be held at Tranquebar, and to bring some students. This was,
both for me and for them, an opportunity not to be missed.

I always enjoyed these camps, and the opportunities they provided of meeting students and teachers from other colleges, some
of whom became intimate friends. Far more exciting was the Quad-
rennial Conference to be held at Rangoon, at which a thousand
students from all over India, Burma and Ceylon were expected.
It was planned that 350 of us would go from Madras to Rangoon,
deck passage on a BI boat. There was just room for me to set up
my camp-bed on the deck; at night the ship looked as though it was
tenanted entirely by the sheeted dead. Mercifully we had mill-pond
weather all the way. As one fellow passenger remarked to me, 'If
there had been any wind, this ship would have been a *shambles*.' The
possible consequences of a storm are too horrible to be imagined.

The conference proved to be enjoyable and in a number of ways
amusing. On the voyage I had become very friendly with a group
of students from Kerala, all of them rip-roaring nationalists and
supporters of Mahatma Gandhi. When I met them in Rangoon, they
were all wearing smartly cut suits of Western style. I mocked them,
saying, 'Is this your nationalism?' Next time I saw them they were
looking much nicer in their graceful Indian dress; whereupon they

seized me and said, 'Now you have got to wear it too.' I said, 'I am perfectly happy wearing Indian dress, but I haven't brought any; if you supply it I shall be delighted to wear it.' No sooner said than done; but there was only one difficulty; I had no sandals with me, and I very much object to wearing English shoes with Indian dress; so there was nothing for it but to go about barefoot. I learned later that this earned me an enormous and entirely undeserved reputation for holiness: 'This young *sannyasi* missionary, who has adopted our ways and even goes about barefoot.' I was thoroughly enjoying myself and was not sensible of any discomfort. While I was in this guise, a student from Ceylon took a photograph of me sitting at the foot of a tree cross-legged, and, appropriately, looking as much like the Buddha as possible.

In one respect this conference had a marked effect on my fortunes. I knew that the Anglican Church in Burma used eucharistic vestments. I have never worn them, and, with my Church of Ireland background, had always been very reluctant to wear them. What was I to do in this strange land? I pondered the question on the boat; and suddenly realised that what I might wear in church was now a matter of supreme indifference to me. The proclamation of Christ in word and sacrament was so infinitely more important than anything else that frills and trimmings fell into their proper perspective. If my wearing these vestments would anywhere commend my ministry, I would be prepared to wear nothing else till the end of time. I was due to celebrate at midnight on Christmas night in the chapel of the Holy Cross, the small Anglican theological college in Rangoon; the kind and devoted missionary in charge, Fr Farrard, kindly showed me how to get on the unfamiliar garments, and the step was taken. I still regard the eucharistic vestments as a singularly unhandy set of garments, and why anyone should wish to wear a maniple I have never been able to conceive. But I had found a new freedom. I made the change without any thought of possible personal advantage to myself. I learned afterwards that my willingness to accept something that was not entirely agreeable to myself had had the effect of conciliating a good deal of Indian opinion which had previously been hostile to me.

On the return journey we were once again blessed with perfect calm. I had announced a watch-night service, and a considerable number of students managed to rouse themselves from sleep to join in worship. I had managed to persuade a distinguished Indian woman, Mrs Mona Hensman, to give an address. Then, at what I judged to be three minutes to midnight, I called for silent prayer.

We sat in stillness, as the ship moved silently forward over the peaceful sea, under a golden full moon. My watch was exactly right; after precisely three minutes eight bells were given, and the new year was born. This was one of those golden moments, not to be forgotten as long as life shall last.

During these days stirring events were taking place in India, and it was impossible to remain unaffected by the rising tide of nationalism. Since nationalism as represented by Mahatma Gandhi and Pandit Jawaharlal Nehru triumphed, there has been a tendency in retrospect to simplify the story, and to suppose that this was the only kind of nationalism which had any chance of success. This was very far from being the case. When I reached India, the prominent people were the Indian liberals, moderates, Gladstonian liberals to a man, deeply devoted to the idea of the Commonwealth, prepared to co-operate with the British authorities in India. Some of these men, among them Sir Mirza Ismail, a Muslim who for many years was Prime Minister of the Hindu State of Mysore, had acquired wide experience of administration. They were by no means anxious to hasten on the day of independence. Only gradually did it become clear that the appeal of these men was too intellectual, and that their movement could never become a popular movement. It was Gandhi who succeeded in turning himself into a legend in his own lifetime, and in swaying the hearts of the masses as probably no other man in the history of India has succeeded in swaying them. From about 1926 his influence was steadily on the increase, and in the end the independence of India was to be achieved by revolution and not by gradual progress.

For the most part Indian Christians had been indifferent to politics; they came from the underprivileged classes, which had little or no instruction in Indian culture, and had been accustomed to servitude rather than to participation. British rule had meant to them a marvellous emancipation. Justice was not easy to secure; but there was at least a chance that before a British magistrate the poor man would not be overwhelmed by the bribery indulged in by the rich. Even to the outcaste there was now offered the possibility of education, and of employment in the police, in the armed forces and in other branches controlled by the government. People on this level had no desire other than that the British Raj should continue to the end of time. What they feared above all was the restitution of the rule of the Brahmans which from time immemorial they had experienced as unscrupulous, oppressive and corrupt. Until about 1926 there seems to have been little difference between the simple

Christians in the villages and the educated Christians in the towns; to the latter also British control had meant a world of opportunity and advancement, and they had little desire for a revolutionary change in the situation. About the year 1926 a change began to be manifest; the more forward-looking Christians began to be aware of the great changes that were in the air, and to realise that they had better begin to plan for their own future in a world of revolutionary change.

The missionary force, though never ceasing to maintain its general cohesion and mutual loyalty, was deeply divided. At one extreme, women missionaries living in the villages were almost solidly opposed to the national movement. It has to be remembered that, long before the Congress party obtained any measure of control on a provincial or national level, it had succeeded in securing a majority in local and district boards and in municipal councils. In almost every case it had shown itself selfish, corrupt and incompetent. These women, horrified by the increase in corruption and in the oppression of the poor which they saw on every hand, desired nothing less than the success of Mr Gandhi and his legions. At the other extreme, some missionaries such as Dr Forrester-Paton, of the famous Paton and Baldwin knitting wool company in Scotland, and of the Christa Kula Ashram at Tirupattur, and the American Mr Keithahn, came out unashamedly on the side of Gandhi and his non-violence, and believed that therein was to be found the salvation of India. My friend Willy Holland, while maintaining in public a detached attitude, told me that Gandhi, by his concern for integrity and for the real welfare of the poor, had impressed him more than almost any other man whom he had ever met. Between these two extremes of unconditional support and outright opposition was to be found every line of the intervening spectrum.

I found it exceedingly difficult to make up my mind. Like every missionary of my acquaintance, I regarded myself as pledged to work for India's political maturity and independence. But I was far from certain as to how this could best come about. I never met Mr Gandhi, but I found it impossible to overcome a deep distaste for him and for all his methods. Before I ever came to India I had read the horrifying story of Chaudri Chaudra, where an Indian crowd had stormed a police station, poured kerosene on twenty-two policemen, set the station alight and burned the unfortunate men to death. In the trial of Mr Gandhi which inevitably followed, the statement of Mr Gandhi and the judgement of Mr C. N. Broomfield, the judge in the case, a temperate man, urbane and dignified in the extreme, sum up the entire tragedy of the Indian freedom movement and the impossibility that either side should understand the other. Mr Gandhi spoke only in justification of himself, and accepted no responsibility for the violence which had followed on his teaching. Mr Broomfield said, 'I do not forget that you have consistently preached against violence and that you have on many occasions, as I am willing to believe, done much to prevent violence. But having regard to the nature of your political teaching and the nature of many of those to whom it was addressed, how you could have continued to believe that violence would not be the inevitable consequence, it passes my capacity to understand.' This was my perpetual perplexity. On every occasion, up till 1947, in which Mr Gandhi set in motion a campaign of non-violent non-co-operation, the result was outbreaks of violence all over the place; the dead did not come to life again when Mr Gandhi dissociated himself from the violence which his campaign had let loose.

The height of the crisis was reached on 23 March 1931. A young fanatic named Bhagat Singh had thrown a bomb into the meeting-place of the Assembly and had later committed a dastardly political murder. The gentle Viceroy, Lord Irwin, at that time deeply engaged in his famous negotiations with Mahatma Gandhi, had deeply considered all the circumstances, and had decided that Bhagat Singh could not be reprieved.

Many people hold that no circumstances can ever justify the infliction of the death penalty. But, in 1931, as the law of India then stood, for murder deliberately carried out, and where there were no extenuating circumstances, there was no penalty other than death. I felt at the time, and still feel, that there was no option open to the Viceroy to act otherwise than he did. Mr Gandhi was placed in something of a dilemma. He had condemned violence; yet he knew that the vast majority of his younger followers were on the side of Bhagat Singh. In his periodical *Young India* he wrote rebuking violence, but warmly commending the spirit of patriotism evinced by Bhagat Singh; in the minds of his readers the shadow of the condemnation was entirely lost in the brilliance of the commendation. A few days later almost all the boys in our schools were wearing Bhagat Singh medals in their button holes. In our Courtallum Camp that year George Azariah, son of Bishop Azariah, spoke movingly on the choice that had been set before the people of Israel, Barabbas or Jesus Christ.

In a situation of this kind the younger supporters of 'the revolution' invariably demanded that the Church should line itself up behind the forces of revolution. In view of the many ambiguities in Gandhi's methods and his defence of them, many of us felt that this was not the way in which political freedom could best come to India and were therefore unable to enrol ourselves in the ranks of his supporters. This led to much painful misunderstanding with our Indian friends. Even those who believed themselves to understand the way in which the Western mind works would tell us that, probably without our own knowledge, we were crypto-imperialists, and that we really believed in the innate inferiority of the Indian man. It was inconceivable to them that a foreigner could at the same time believe fervently in democracy and political progress and retain his right to be critical of the man who had succeeded in making himself the idol of large sections of the Indian people. This was an unpleasant time at which to be at work in India; and, the deeper one's affection for the Indian people, the more unpleasant it was certain to become.

I still believe that on the whole British rule in India was beneficial. But at the time I was sternly, and at times harshly, critical of the details of administration.

When I had been three years at the seminary, I became due for leave in England. It was high time. I had been five years in India, overworking all the time, and was completely exhausted. I spent the long vacation at Cambridge very enjoyably. Then I was asked to take the annual mission to undergraduates of the Oxford Inter-Collegiate Christian Union in October. My doctor strongly advised against it; so I went to Oxford to consult Christopher Chavasse, Master of St Peter's Hall, and later Bishop of Rochester. I had not been more than two minutes in his study when he said, 'Would you like to come here for six months?' I asked for a day or two to consider; then, there being nothing against it, I agreed to go, and thereby let myself in for six of the happiest months of my life, partly because of all the congenial Evangelical spirits in Oxford at that time.

Of the mission in St Aldate's I will record nothing except that it brought me, quite unexpectedly and for the first time in my life, the experience of being completely without fear in the pulpit. It had never before been my good fortune to experience this miracle. And now, on the third night of the mission, I entered into this new and unknown dimension, as I spoke of the mystery of the forgiveness of God and reconciliation with him. This was a permanent deliverance. I will not say that I have never again fallen into the abyss of uncertainty and anxiety, but only once in later years has my throat gone dry with panic; this, not surprisingly, was at the first session of the Lambeth Conference of 1948, when I was unexpectedly called upon to address their assembled lordships.

All this time my heart was really in India. Various offers of work in England, some of them highly flattering, had come along, but there had never been a moment's doubt that I must return to where I belonged. I was impatient to get back. It was high time. I had left rather precise instructions as to how things were to be carried on in my absence, but these had been disregarded in many particulars, in no case I think to the advantage of the work. The seminary was in a bad way, and the task of getting it on its feet again was long and laborious.

A considerable effort of imagination is needed to picture what a small seminary was like in those days. We had a library of perhaps a thousand books, including some rather surprising and valuable items, such as a complete set of the Parker Society's publications presented to Dr G. U. Pope's Institution at Sangrapuram in 1847; but many of the books belonged to a different theological epoch and were quite unusable; in the end, judging that a considerable number might be more harmful than profitable to those who might use them, I dug a large hole in the ground and buried them out of sight. We had little money with which to buy new books; in that isolation it was difficult to know what to buy, and there was always the difficult choice between books that the students might be able to use, and books that teachers really needed for the preparation of their lectures. For fifteen years I received a personal allowance of £20 a year from the Warren Trust for the purchase of books, and this grant was invaluable in enabling me to build up a considerable library of really indispensable books, including many of the most important theological works of reference.

I had usually to hand over to my Indian colleagues what appeared to be the easier subjects. But a subject which on the surface appears to be easy, such as the life of Christ, may in reality be among the most difficult; I was not always well satisfied with the way in which these subjects were being taught. For the rest I had to fill in myself. In such a situation one does not teach what one knows, one teaches what has to be taught. At different times in India I have taught Old Testament, New Testament, Christian Doctrine, Church History, Pastoralia, Religions of India, and Greek. The result is that there is no area in theology of which I know very much, but none of which I am wholly ignorant. This has its advantages; theology, like medicine, requires its general practitioners, and I have never greatly regretted this gruelling discipline, though it seems to have rendered me incapable of the minute and detailed research which I admire so much when it is carried out by others.

At times I was spending thirteen periods a week in class. In addition, I was responsible for the training of the probationers who were out in the field as catechists or evangelists. Throughout all this time I was without any adequate secretarial help, and had to keep the accounts and do all the correspondence of the seminary myself.

It might have been thought that this was enough to keep anyone busy; but, as it came about, I was just on the edge of a change which almost overnight transformed me from a private into a public figure.

It was now nearly ten years since I had come to India. I had never travelled further than Madras; and I had concentrated so closely on my own work, that though I was now known to a number of people through my writings, and still had many friends in England, to the greater part of the Christian world, even in India, I was an unknown man. But now my bishop decided that I had gifts that should be more widely used in the service of the Church, and arranged for me to be elected as an alternative representative of the diocese of Tinnevelly to the General Council of the Church of India, Burma and Ceylon.

Until 1930 that Church had been legally a part of the Church of England. It had no power to change a single word of the Prayer Book. New dioceses had been created by what can only be called a series of subterfuges. Until 1930 Tinnevelly was not really a diocese at all – it was simply an area cast off from the diocese of Madras by consensual compact; this meant among other things that we suffered the deprivation of not being able to have an archdeacon of our own.

By a series of dextrous negotiations all this was changed in the years leading up to 1930, when the Church of India emerged at last as an independent Anglican Province, managing its own affairs, linked closely to all the other Anglican Churches in the world, but not in any way dependent on any of them. The success of these negotiations was largely due to the skill and persistence of the great Metropolitan and Bishop of Calcutta, Foss Westcott. When well into his sixties, he came deeply under the influence of the Oxford Group movement; to him, as to many other shy and withdrawn men, this came as a wonderful liberation of the spirit. He moved with dignity in any assembly, and held the respect of a succession of viceroys. Above all, he had unparalleled gifts as a chairman.

The General Council of the Church of India, Burma and Ceylon, is one of the very best assemblies in which I have ever sat. Owing to the size of the country, it could meet only once in three years; but when it did meet, it attended strictly to business. Membership was only 130; owing to the practice of electing alternates to both clerical and lay delegates, attendance was always high, and there was no nonsense about absence when sessions were in progress. We were there to work, and we worked. When, for the first time, I looked in on the Church Assembly of the Church of England, I was appalled at the contrast. There one saw an array of empty benches, delegates lounging about in the corridor, and a general feeling of apathy and boredom. I will not attempt to say why this contrast should exist, but, as my acquaintance with other Anglican Churches has grown, so has grown my admiration of the Church of India. In churchmanship we stretched from the highest to the lowest; yet I can remember no occasion when any spirit of party acrimony entered into our proceedings; our task of making the kingdom of Christ known in India was far too absorbing for us to be distracted by such trivialities.

One way in which the skill of Westcott as chairman was shown was in the variation of the tempo and the intensity of business. If there had been a taxing discussion on some rather technical point, or on some matter on which there was deep division of opinion (for such divisions can exist entirely without acrimony), he would switch to entirely non-controversial items such as fixing the date of the next meeting, or a vote of congratulation to some member of the Church who had been singled out for distinction in Church or State. This helped very much to keep us from getting overtired by our work (and Calcutta can begin to get hot by the end of January when our meetings were generally held); it also meant that no one ever knew when an item in which he was particularly interested might come up for discussion, and this certainly helped in the discouragement of truancy, which may have been one of the Metropolitan's motives for adopting this method of conducting business.

In this august assembly I made my début as a freshman in January 1935.[2] I knew six of the fourteen bishops, and had a number of friends among clergy and lay delegates, but for the most part it was an unknown land. Yet, almost before I knew where I was, I was betrayed into notoriety by my fatal flair for drafting. Consequently I was unanimously elected clerical secretary of the Council. It had become the tradition that a bishop was secretary of the Episcopal

Synod-related bodies, and that a priest was in fact responsible for the minutes of the General Council.

This new work brought me closely into touch with the episcopal secretary, Bishop Saunders of Lucknow, a master of business methods. From him I learned invaluable lessons in the art of minute-keeping. He taught me how all-important it is to get every resolution in writing from the hand of the proposer during the session; if that is done, reducing the many slips of paper to order is a tedious but not impossible task; if the proposer has fled away to the jungles of Upper Burma without leaving his brain-child in writing, endless delays and frustrations are likely to occur, and the minutes may not reflect accurately what passed. Our minutes were brief and to the point and did not incorporate lengthy reports of endless discussion. These, however, were all recorded. Miss G. I. Mather, of the diocese of Lucknow, was and is an incomparable stenographer; she used to get down a fairly full précis of the speeches, and type them out the same evening, so that all could be filed in the Metropolitan's office along with the more official papers of the Council. I have long been associated with Miss Mather, who typed the manuscripts of many of my books with fidelity and intelligence, and to whom I am indebted for deciphering and typing these memoirs.

As clerical secretary of the Council I was also secretary of the Standing Committee, which met more frequently and did most of the business. I would attend the Episcopal Synod as an assessor, that body working under the rule that it must be attended by an equal number of presbyters, and *four* laymen – presumably to prevent their lordships from talking more than their usual ration of nonsense. And if, as sometimes happened, the Episcopal Synod met together with the Standing Committee, I would be on hand as secretary. As soon as I became bishop I was promoted to be episcopal secretary. This meant that for nearly ten years I was continuously at the heart of things; little passed in the affairs of the Church that did not at one time or another come under my notice.

More important than any other subject which came before us was the question of church union in South India. The Metropolitan secured my appointment as one of the Anglican delegates to the Joint Committee on Church Union in South India, which had been in session off and on since 1919. This, too, became one of my major preoccupations for nearly ten years.

The first draft of the Scheme for Union for South India had seen the light in 1929. It was the result of ten years of patient thought and planning; and, when it appeared, it was supposed that not many years need pass before the Union became an accomplished fact. History was to show that this optimism rested on no solid foundation. Church union looks very nice when it is a distant prospect. As it approaches, people begin to count the cost and to find that union demands sacrifices that they are not prepared to make. Now each Church expressed reservations. Fifteen years of further effort were needed to wear down opposition, and to make possible the acceptance, by almost all, of the seventh edition of the scheme.

The Anglicans would have preferred that unification should be accompanied by some form of recommissioning of the ministry. When it became clear that the non-Anglicans would in no circumstances accept any form of recommissioning that would be satisfactory to the Anglicans, it was agreed that the best solution would be that we should commit all our Churches and their ministries to God in their separation, and ask him to give them back to us unified and with all the power and validity that their ministries would need for their exercise in a united Church. But what would this mean for Anglicans? Would it mean that an Anglican congregation might find itself committed to the care of a former Congregationalist who had never received episcopal ordination? To ease these sensitive consciences, the Committee had agreed in 1928 to insert the following 'conscience clause':

> They therefore pledge themselves and fully trust each other that in the united church no arrangement with regard to churches, congregations or ministers will knowingly be made, either generally or in particular cases, which would offend the conscientious convictions of any persons directly concerned, or which would hinder the development of complete unity within the church or imperil its subsequent progress towards union with other churches.

In 1932, as a result of controversy surrounding the implications of the clause, it was found necessary to rephrase the clause in a considerably longer form, the form in which it is now included unalterably in the documents of the Church of South India. The crucial phrases are: 'Neither forms of worship or ritual, nor a ministry, to which they have not been accustomed or to which they conscientiously object, will be imposed upon any congregation.' Did this mean that, during the thirty years' period allowed for the completion of unification, no ministers of the Church who had not received episcopal ordination would ever minister in an Anglican church? It was clear that this was the view taken by the Metropolitan himself, and by other bishops who leaned to the High Church persuasion, and that only on that understanding had they been able to commend the scheme to the authorities of the Church of England. We had to explain to them that this was not at all what was meant; no unwelcome ministry would be *imposed* by authority on any Anglican congregation, but there was nothing to prevent any Anglican group from inviting a former non-Anglican to minister in their church temporarily or on a more permanent commission, if they desired to do so. This came as a considerable shock to those who had interpreted the conscience clause otherwise, and, as the correct interpretation became known more widely, we lost a good deal of support for the Scheme in Anglican circles. However, if we had not made it clear that this departure from strict Anglican principles would be accepted, we would have been unable to make any progress whatever in our discussions with the representatives of other Churches.

To be admitted to so venerable a conclave cannot but be a solemn and moving experience. When in February 1935 I walked into the first meeting of the thirteenth session of the Joint Committee, the room seemed to be filled with those who could appropriately be addressed as 'Fathers and brethren'. The chairman was the Revd H. Gulliford, who had already served the Methodist Mission in Mysore for sixty years. He was later replaced by another Methodist stalwart, C. H. Minchen, an excellent Tamil scholar whose whole life had been given to South India. Looking round the room, it was difficult not to be amused by the portrait constantly drawn of us as 'good and worthy men, no doubt, but with little knowledge of theology, who were gravely misleading the simple Indian Christians'. Of the six Anglican bishops most closely associated with the work of the committee, two were triple firsts from Cambridge, one was a double first, and one had obtained a first class in the old Classical Tripos before it was divided. Among 'the simple Indian Christians' was A. J. Appasamy, later Bishop of Coimbatore, who was an Oxford D.Phil. in his own right.

The question that was to recur again and again, though it was not always expressed in quite so trenchant a form, was simply this: 'We have given way to the Anglicans on the point of episcopacy; at what point have they given way to us?' There was a strong feeling that the Anglicans had gained everything and given away nothing, and that, whatever might be said to the contrary, in thirty years'

time the Church of South India would be in reality an Anglican
Church. It is hard to explain to a citizen outside the Commonwealth
what it means to belong to the Commonwealth. It is even harder to
explain to a non-Anglican what the Anglican Communion means
to an Anglican with a living sense of this world-wide reality. For
the sake of union with our brethren in South India, we were
prepared to lose our membership in that great fellowship. We
had accepted the fact that we should be outside it. This had not
been clear to many Anglicans, who with the triumphalism that
is perhaps characteristic of Anglicans had blandly assumed that,
once the wandering children had come home, the Church of South
India would be simply another Anglican Province. At the Lambeth
Conference of 1930 Henry Waller had to explain very clearly to the
assembled bishops that this would not be so, and that the Church
of South India would be as independent of the Church of England
as the Church of Sweden or the Church of Finland. Some of the
bishops were aghast that any Anglicans should wish to leave the
old familiar shores of earth and take off into outer space. Others
were greatly relieved; after all, it does not matter very much what
mischief the children get up to, provided that it is clear that it is
not in our own back yard that they are getting up to mischief. This
was the sacrifice that we were prepared to make; of the South Indian
bishops on the committee, not one expected ever again to attend a
Lambeth Conference.

This sacrifice we were prepared to make; the gravity of it was
mitigated by the assurance that Anglicans who went into the Church
of South India would be able at once and unhindered to resume
their Anglican status on returning to more backward parts of the
world where union had not been attained. But all the time some
of our friends in the other Churches were trying to manoeuvre
us into such wide departure from the Anglican tradition as would
make impossible any further communion, corporate or personal,
with the Anglican Communion outside South India. This we were
not prepared to consider; much as we longed to be completely at
one with our brethren in one single Church, we did not feel that
that local unity should be purchased by breaking up an already
existing and world-wide fellowship. Thus it seemed to some of
our friends that we were all the time saying different and contra-
dictory things.

Intercommunion before union became a burning issue. It had
become traditional at meetings of the Joint Committee for the
Anglicans to hold services of Holy Communion, and, making use

of a liberty which was widely practised in India and recognised by the authorities of the Church, to invite the non-Anglicans to be present and to share in the sacrament. The time came when these non-Anglicans decided, as they had every right to do, that they would hold their own services of Holy Communion, and would invite the Anglicans to partake. The proposal had, of course, to be referred to the Episcopal Synod; officially elected representatives of a Church cannot follow their own individual discretion, but must be sure that they are acting according to the mind of the Church. The matter was debated on a high level of theological integrity and earnestness; in the end the Synod came down very cautiously on the rightness of permitting exceptions to the traditional Anglican rule that intercommunion should follow rather than precede the establishment. Some Anglicans hold that intercommunion before union is one of the best possible ways of leading on to the desired fullness of union; they have never produced any evidence in favour of the view that union is promoted by such methods, but this is a view which is sincerely and honestly held. From my personal knowledge of Bishop Azariah, as well as from remarks of his that have been recorded in print, I judge that he was a supporter of this position. Others held that intercommunion is the expression of a unity in faith and order, and that to practise it in advance of that unity is an attempt, to put it crudely, to force the hand of the Holy Spirit. Yet others are prepared to recognise that, though rules are rules, and ought not to be lightly set on one side, there are occasions on which the higher rule of charity must take precedence over any written rule, and the Church must be free to set aside traditions by which it has ordinarily felt itself to be bound. There was never any breach of fellowship within the Anglican delegation; to this day I have no idea who did and who did not receive Communion at the celebration carried out according to the Free Church order. But we were well aware that we were being observed by others. I did myself attend that celebration. To me it was not a time of blessing; I did not feel that I had been brought nearer to my brethren of the other traditions, and I was aware all the time of the bitter discord that we were sowing throughout the whole Anglican Communion. I still feel that a grave mistake was made. If the Free Church brethren had been willing to wait, it would have done them great honour. If they had felt that unilateral participation was impossible and that they must for the time being withdraw from our Communion, we would have regretted it, but would have felt that that was a decision which they were fully justified in making.

The consequence of the decision and of our actions could have been foreseen. The Anglo-Catholic wing of the Anglican Communion throughout the world almost unanimously withdrew its support for the Plan of Union. Many who up till that time had been favourable, though with many reservations, felt that they could go no further. Much of the clamour was virulent, unprincipled and irrational. The Christian has to learn to expect such things and to disregard them, if he is certain that what he is doing is right. In this matter, I felt and feel that the wounding of consciences and the straining of loyalties was unnecessary and harmful, and that we would have been brought sooner and more peacefully to the haven where we would be, if we had been prepared to follow together a different way. I know well that this is not the popular opinion; but these pages would be valueless if I did not set out in them frankly the inner side of my experiences. To abstain from receiving Communion together is painful; but it is honest as reminding us that division is a harsh reality, which cannot be evaded. Intercommunion is pleasant, but it can be dangerous, since it can so easily lead us to overlook and evade precisely those things that must not be overlooked or evaded, and may encourage us to imagine that we are nearer to unity than we really are. Looking back over nearly forty years, I am unchanged in my opinion that a grave mistake was made in 1932, and that the union discussions never recovered the tone and quality that they had in earlier years.

Having rather reluctantly accepted episcopacy, some of our friends in the following years did their utmost to make it clear that episcopacy is not really very harmful, since a bishop is no more than a presbyter to whom one or two extra functions have been committed by the will of the Church. But that is not the view of episcopacy generally held in the Anglican world. Believing passionately as I do in the priestly character of the whole Church, and agreeing with Martin Luther that baptism makes us priests and ordination makes us ministers, I still think that the Church has gained greatly by the division of labour and the concentration of certain responsibilities in a small number of hands.

There was much in Anglican episcopacy, as they had seen it, to which our Free Church friends took grave exception. Until 1930 some of the bishops had been appointed directly from England, and it seemed at times as though the offer of an Indian see came as a consolation prize to those who were not quite good enough to rise to the height of an English diocese. Some of the bishops had large incomes and lived in a splendour that contrasted painfully

with the penury of most of the Free Church missionaries.[3] The
term 'my lord' grated in the ears of those descended from a long
line of Puritan ancestors. On all these points we were in entire
agreement with them, but old prejudices die hard. In the end, we
only won them by taking them round and trying to show them on
the spot what we tried to be and do. As they came to realise that,
in our view, the bishop is the servant of all, and that what he is
called to is primarily a spiritual ministry, they came to the point
of being willing to say that, though they still believed their fathers
had been right in rejecting the debased episcopacy of the late middle
ages, they had now become convinced that episcopacy as a gift of
Christ to his Church was expedient for the Church of South India
in the twentieth century. It was Harry Waller who put the word
into the Scheme for Union for South India. When I criticised it, as
suggesting that the office of bishop was being accepted on grounds
of mere expediency, he floored me by quoting the Gospel according
to St John, 'it is expedient for you that I go away'. I still think,
however, that the use of that word in that particular context was
not expedient.

One thing was especially dear to the heart of our Congregational
brethren. They wanted to extort from the Anglicans a clear and
unmistakable declaration of the full equality and validity of all
ministries. But that is exactly what many of the Anglican delegates
could not give. We were gladly willing to admit the spiritual effectiveness of these other ministries; this did not alter our conviction
that the ancestors of our friends had made a grave mistake when they
rejected episcopacy – especially where, as in Scotland, they could
so easily have retained it. This our friends could not understand.
To them the spiritual effectiveness was all that mattered; any
suggestion of regularity and anomaly they regarded simply as a
residue of legalism from which the Anglican consciousness had
not been purged; what more natural than that they should do their
utmost to effect the purgation?[4]

We were anxious to go as far as we could. We could not honestly
accept the parity of ministries, in the sense in which our Free
Church colleagues understood the term; but we were anxious to
express, in the clearest possible terms, our sense that God had
blessed and acknowledged these other ministries, and through them
had brought into being great Churches, which by their fruits showed
that they were true parts of the living body of Christ. So it came
about that one day our chairman, C. H. Monahan, proposed that
we should include in our statement a famous Methodist phrase,

that God had looked on all our ministries 'with undistinguishing regard'. This is an expression to be found in a great Arminian hymn of Charles Wesley, in which he decisively rejected the Calvinist view that only some are destined to be saved, and affirmed the principle that Christ in very truth has died for all. It is a fine and resounding phrase; and yet I feel that there was something of sentimentality in the incorporation of it in that moment into a serious theological document. By this stage of the repeated revision of the Scheme of Union, every change was going to be scrutinised by anxious, and sometimes hostile, eyes in every part of the world, some looking for still further betrayals of the truth by Anglican delegates, others searching for signs of yet further craven yielding to the Anglicans on the part of those who ought to have been valiant for truth against them.

Here again my reputation as a draftsman pursued me. The drafting of the day's results was one of the most difficult tasks that I have ever undertaken. Discussions roamed far and free, in part because the chairmanship was not always as decisive as it might have been, in part wisely, since it was essential that all points of view should be expressed, and that no impression should be given of an attempt to curtail discussion or to give more favour to one group than to another. In consequence, whereas in the General Council one usually ended the day's work with a neat pile of agreed resolutions, here one was presented with a rag-bag of shreds and patches; it was often difficult to make out what had been agreed, and to bring any sort of coherence out of a miscellany of thoughts and suggestions. The sessions were long, and in the humid climate of Madras exhausting, even when tempers had not been roused by the handling of some particularly delicate issue. Between 11 p.m. and 1 a.m. one is not at one's brightest, and I can see now that much of the drafting was carelessly done. The Scheme as a whole lacks elegance and is far too long. It could have been greatly improved if someone had had the time, and had been authorised to put the whole thing together, eliminating repetitions and producing a certain uniformity of style.

For ten years far too much of my time was spent away from Tinnevelly, and in committees and conferences; this seems to be an inevitable consequence of being called to any position of leadership in the Church. But now it was time to go home, and to find myself involved in the strangest fiasco of my career. In spite of our mutual provocations and frustrations we were all sure that union was coming very soon, perhaps within two or three years; to that we were committed and we were determined to see it come about. We were agreed that, as far as possible, we would act together as though we were one, and so prepare the way for the fuller and more corporate unity to which we were pledged. One of the points at which it seemed wise to begin was common theological training.

At that time India was spattered with a number of small denominational seminaries, where a small staff of overworked teachers would instruct ten or a dozen students in the ways of righteousness. We at Nazareth usually had about a dozen students and three teachers; Pasumalai of the American Congregational mission had two teachers and a rather smaller body of students; Vellore of the American Dutch Reformed Mission had half a dozen with, if I remember rightly, one full-time teacher. Such methods are ruinously expensive. For theological teaching to be successful, the teacher-student ratio should be rather higher than in other disciplines, but for half a dozen teachers to be instructing at most less than thirty students obviously involved a criminal squandering of the resources of the Lord's people. We decided to amalgamate our seminary with that of the Americans.

Madurai, the largest city in South India after Madras, is the great home of Tamil culture. The four towers of the immense temple brood in somewhat sinister fashion over the whole countryside. Here Robert de Nobili arrived in 1606, to carry out his noble experiment of turning himself into a casteless *sannyasi* in order to win the Brahmans. Here the Americans had built up over a century a very considerable work. There was a great hospital and several churches. At Pasumalai, just outside Madurai, American bungalows, great palaces of stone, rose one above the other up the hill. There was a boys' high school and a girls' school, a training school for teachers, an industrial school, a printing press, and, tucked away in a corner, the little theological seminary presided over by the formidable Dr Banninga.

Banninga, as his name implies, was of Friesian stock, and came from a family which maintained in full the simple Calvinistic piety of the Dutch Reformed Church, but Banninga had moved far from the home of his ancestors, had adopted liberal views, and the almost completely non-ecclesiastical approach of the American Madurai Mission. Rather surprisingly, he had become an ardent supporter of the Scheme and of church union, and, had union come in 1937 or 1938, he would certainly have been one of the first bishops of the new Church. By reason of his long and close association with Bishop Western and other Anglicans, it seemed natural that he should take the initiative on the plan for bringing the two seminaries together into one.

A special joint committee was appointed, and held several sessions. Pasumalai had far better buildings and equipment, and it was almost inevitable that we should decide that that was where the new seminary must be located. Then Banninga, who was old enough to be my father, said with touching humility that, if the seminary was to be at Pasumalai, it was clear that the principal must be an Anglican, and that he would therefore renounce in my favour his obvious claims to the post. So said, so ordered. I found myself offered the post of principal of the new united seminary, and, being accustomed to doing what I was told, signified my acceptance of the offer, but with a heavy heart. To move to Nazareth was bad enough; to move to Pasumalai would be ten times worse. With my predilection for the simplest forms of living, I could not see myself occupying one of the vast stone palaces. I find it hard to breathe in one of these centres where one missionary institution is piled on top of another. I did not like the American ethos of the place, and I did not know how I would get on with the prevailing liberalism. But the decision had been made, and so I went home to prepare myself for another upheaval.

And then, as is so often the case in India, the utterly unexpected happened. When the Bishop brought our proposals to the Executive Committee of the Diocese, they were met with a stone wall of silence. At that time anti-union sentiment was rising rather high in the High Church part of the diocese. Our orthodox clergy had been considerably upset by rumours, and more than rumours, of grave unorthodoxy in the American Church; they were far from sure that the sacramental traditions of Anglicanism would be maintained in such an atmosphere. One speaker after another voiced doubts and anxieties. In the face of such opposition it was clear that the plan would have to be abandoned; there was nothing for it but to go to the Americans with our tails between our legs and tell them that we had over-estimated the desire for unity in the diocese of Tinnevelly. By going too fast Bishop Waller had produced a schism; by going too fast Bishop Western had produced a fiasco. I think that I can claim to be the only man living who has been principal of a seminary thirty years before it actually came into existence, under a remarkable Principal, Dr Samuel Amirtham.

Once back at Nazareth, I made up my mind that we had simply got to move the seminary. For five years we had endured our imprisonment between the hospital and the industrial school, and this could go on no longer. Move, yes; but where? So the long discussions and controversies had to begin all over again. Various other sites were looked at; but the power of the pressure group at that time was very great: the seminary has always been at Nazareth; at Nazareth it must remain. We were told that land in great quantity was available in the *teri*, on the edge of the sand-hills, less than a mile from the village, and that the people of Nazareth would gladly sell the land at cut-rates for the privilege of keeping the seminary. Water could almost certainly be found.

Water was naturally the primary consideration. We bought a few acres at a reasonable price, and then brought in a water-diviner, a pious man, who walked around our land, knelt down and prayed, and then said, 'This is the place; you will find water.' A well was dug; water was found in sufficient quantity, so the question of our future home was settled. Then followed the business of acquiring land, thirty acres in all. The first appearance of the site was not pleasing – dry red earth, with some few thorn-trees and desert plants, and the inevitable palmyras; but what I had seen in vision, since the great majority of our students were married men, was a seminary in the form of an ideal Indian village, with the chapel in the centre, and classrooms and streets grouped about it.

I was determined to move as soon as we could. So the first thing was to build a temporary chapel and classrooms; this was accomplished at a cost of £120. The buildings were thatched, with pillars and wide open spaces, provided with sheet tin shutters which could be lowered in the brief season of the heavy rains, or when the monsoon wind was filling everything with grit. These two buildings proved remarkably attractive and durable. Before long the chapel acquired the feel of a real place of worship.

The next necessity was a house for myself. I planned a nice house, with a very large verandah, on which in that genial climate a great part of the life of a family could be lived, and above it a sleeping terrace. I had hardly moved in, when the SPG sent us out a married colleague, A. Michael Hollis. To everyone's surprise I moved out of my own house into a much smaller house built for an Indian member of staff. But there I had all that I needed, with three small rooms, a courtyard in Indian style, and my kitchen on the far side of the courtyard. In none of our houses was there running water, or any indoor plumbing or sanitation. Every drop of water had to be drawn from a well by hand, and a bathroom still meant a small room with a tin tub into which a servant would periodically pour hot water. The absence of electricity meant no electric fans, no radio and no refrigerator. One colleague, who had some money of her own, did install a radio, but the replacement of batteries was always difficult and reception was poor. Refrigerators, which pay for themselves in six months in that climate, can be run on paraffin, but we none of us had the money to make the initial expenditure, and the mission did not believe in supplying luxuries.

There were one or two cars in the mission, but these were mostly for people like the diocesan treasurer, who had to make long journeys of inspection to all kinds of places. We travelled third class by train, dusty and tiring but incredibly cheap, and, once we had learned the language, a marvellous way of making contact with all sorts of people. I never once encountered any unfriendliness; the foreigner seemed to be far more an object of interest than of dislike. When I had been twelve years in India, an aunt gave me £50, with which I purchased an aged Hillman from a colleague who was departing on leave. This good friend ran on faith and prayer; an income of £168 does not provide for the running of a car on even the most economical lines, and I was entirely dependent on the gifts of friends. As it is a fixed principle with me never to ask for money, such gifts could not be counted on; but friends were good at understanding and even anticipating my needs, and for the most part the car stayed on the road. My health began incredibly to improve. I now realise that I had been taking far too much out of myself by going about constantly on my bicycle; if I had had the car five years earlier, a great deal of later trouble might have been saved.

Those were distressful years. The economic blizzard, which struck the United States in 1929 and gradually spread to the rest of the world, naturally affected adversely the finance of all the missions; we were not as badly hit as the American missions, but many schemes of development had to be abandoned, and there was little prospect of improvement in any near future. To make matters worse, we ran into a succession of weak monsoons and inadequate rains. My first years in India coincided with a period of slowly but unmistakably rising prosperity. Then the sun-spots turned against us, and, though there was no famine, there were many signs of increasing poverty. My colleague at the industrial school, A. P. Randle, spoke year by year of the increasing number of boys who were coming into the school suffering from malnutrition. The pay of the village teachers fell far into arrears. Boys and girls were withdrawn from school because the parents simply could not afford the fees.

All the time the political horizon was growing darker. We were unaware at the time of all the disasters that Hitler was cooking up for the world. Most men of my generation had pro-German leanings; we were inclined to think the best of Hitler as long as this was possible. He had, after all, done great things for the German people; he had given them work and food and a sense of national self-respect and power. In the first years of the Third Reich almost all German missionaries were on the side of Hitler, though few, I think, had any direct connection with the Nazi party. But gradually the realities of what was happening in Germany came home to us and to our German friends, and even those of us who had been near-pacifists for twenty years had to face the possibility that there might be worse things in the world than war.

It must not be supposed that we spent all our time brooding over our anxieties. For the greater part of the time we were able to go on unhindered with our work, though never with quite the same spontaneity that there had been over ten years earlier.

As houses went up, we moved more and more of our students to the new site, and the temporary chapel became more and more the centre of our life. On Sundays we had an early celebration with sermon for the students, who then went off on their various concerns in the increasingly numerous villages to which they ministered. Later in the morning we had a village service for the wives and children and servants. I very frequently took this myself, and greatly enjoyed this simple pastoral ministry.

Not long after we had made the move, I embarked upon a radical change in our methods of teaching. Since 1883, Anglican theological education in South India had been carried out entirely in English. I was very ill-satisfied with the results. What the students had learned in English they could not express in Tamil; they had not really learned to think theologically and, though they had acquired a good deal of useful information, very little of this, as it seemed to me, found expression in the pastoral work in which they were engaged after they left our care. I decided to make Tamil the medium of instruction. Tamil theological literature being very scanty, naturally most of the books would be in English. My own custom was to expound and discuss the subject in Tamil, and then to dictate a brief summary in English, to make sure that the students had a carefully prepared and accurate statement by which to refresh their memories of the discussion.

This change brought me up against a great deal of opposition from the Indian Church itself. In spite of the national movement,

English still had great prestige as the language of all higher studies. My passionate concern for all things Indian led only to my being suspected of a new imperialism, a desire to depress the clergy, and to lower the standards of theological education. I stuck to my guns, but could never be sure of wholehearted support from my many Indian friends in the older generation.

For eight and a half years theological teaching was my daily and hourly concern. The work was heavy and toilsome, especially as at no time did I have adequate secretarial assistance. But I never allowed myself to become imprisoned in the work, and always found time to occupy myself with other pursuits.

The fate of village teachers and catechists, more than a thousand of them, always lay heavy on my heart. The training they had received as teachers was probably far superior to that given in the nineteenth century; but hardly any of them had received any training at all for the spiritual work that he had to do as a catechist in charge of congregations.

Our first attempt to help these scattered colleagues in their work took the form of the publication of four sermon outlines every month. We planned the sermons in courses, an Old Testament series rubbing shoulders with a practical course on the problems of Christian living in an Indian village. I used to write one outline a month myself, and arranged for the others to be produced by colleagues and sometimes by the students. They were not always very good, but they represented at least an effort to help the teachers both with method and content. The local churches eagerly welcomed the plan; we were able to produce the monthly leaflets very cheaply, and through the local churches they found their way into the hands of just about every teacher in the diocese.

For years I had been so busy being a missionary to Christians that my opportunities for serving as a missionary to the heathen had been few and far between. I was, therefore, particularly glad when I received an invitation from Indian Christians in Tuticorin, our post town, to go and give four addresses to educated non-Christians. I was well known there, since one of my chores had been to relieve the chaplain from time to time and take the English services in the old Dutch church, built in 1700 and handed over to the Anglicans when the Dutch settlement ceased to exist.

The invitation to speak to non-Christians came at a time when the demands of work were particularly heavy. There was nothing for it but to finish my day's work at Tirumaraiyur, drive the thirty-six miles to Tuticorin as it was growing dark, give my address, and drive back through the night to face another long day of teaching. The arrangements had been admirably made. Benches and chairs had been placed in the open air outside the church; by that time of day the whistling sea-breeze of midday had died down, and the nights were cool and fragrant. I could not see my hearers very well, but it was clear that between three and four hundred had come to listen, the great majority of them educated Hindus and Muslims of exactly the kind that we had hoped to attract.

By far the most important of my extra-curricular activities was membership of the Third World Missionary Conference held at the Madras Christian College, Tambaram, eighteen miles south of Madras. The first of these great missionary conferences had been held at Edinburgh in 1910, and it was there, by common reckoning, that the modern ecumenical movement was born. The second took place at Jerusalem in 1928, and is remembered especially for its concern with the problem of secularism in its relationship to the religions of the world. It was not self-evident that any further conference of the same kind would ever be held; such gatherings are enormously expensive, and there is no excuse for holding them unless there is really important business to be done. However, between 1928 and 1935 the world situation had radically changed, with the rise of National Socialism, imperialistic Shintoism and nationalism in the Middle East. Two great sections of the ecumenical movement, Faith and Order, and Life and Work, were to hold conferences in 1937, and it was already clear that the outcome of these conferences would be plans for the formation of a World Council of Churches. The missionary movement, out of which the ecumenical movement had been born, could not be left outside, so the IMC organised a meeting to be held at Hangchow, China, in December 1938.

I was absolutely convinced that it was the will of heaven that I should be a member of the conference. When the list of delegates from the Indian Churches was published, I read down it with confident expectancy and increasing disillusionment. When I got to the bottom of the list, I was pained to realise that my name was not on it. Something had gone gravely wrong with my calculations. Was it conceivable that I had been wrong?

Then the unexpected happened. The good old trade union of the Student Christian Movement did its work, and a letter arrived from William Paton, the organiser of the conference, to ask whether I would attend the conference by special appointment, and serve as chairman of Section VIII, 'On the Training of the Ministry'. The appointment caused considerable surprise. It must be stressed that I was still, after fourteen years as a missionary, an unknown man. Most of the sixteen chairmen of sections were veterans widely known throughout the world. Only two of us, Graaf van Randwyck of Holland and myself, were under forty. But Paton had his reasons. Chairmanship is not an altogether easy art. The chairman of an international assembly must be possessed of great sensitiveness, great patience with those whose own language is not English, firmness with English and American members who try to monopolise the discussion, and a determination to get things done, but without an appearance of undue haste and hustle. The missionary movement had not always been happy in its choice of chairmen, and Paton, knowing me from my SCM days, was confident that I would get things done. As to the other gifts and qualities, he just decided to hope for the best.

The great disappointment was that the venue of the conference had to be changed. Already the invasion of China by Japan, though decorously clothed under other names, was a grievous reality; it was decided that Hangchow was too near the scene of conflict to be suitable for an international conference, and we were informed that we were to meet at Tambaram.

John R. Mott at that time exercised unique authority in the Protestant missionary world. He had laid down two excellent principles – that at least half of each delegation must be made up of nationals of the country represented, and that at least half of the delegates must be under the age of thirty-five. Provision was thus made for continuity, and we were delivered from the tyranny of the hierarchy of old men, reappointing themselves perpetually to attend ecumenical conferences. There was no nonsense about youth delegations, of the kind favoured by the World Council of Churches; once there, we were all equally members with full rights, and I cannot remember any single occasion on which anyone asked who had appointed whom, or whether A or B had or had not the right to vote.

Indeed, this democracy was perhaps the most remarkable feature of the whole Tambaram conference. John R. Mott as chairman, seventy-three years old but still apparently in the possession of undiminished powers, had a head start on everyone else; and the same could perhaps be said of William Paton. Everyone else started out equal, though perhaps some ancients were a little more equal than others. One of the English delegates was Cyril Forster Garbett, at that time Bishop of Winchester. I think that he was a little taken aback by this democratic spirit, so different from what he had encountered in the hierarchically organised Church of England. By the end of the conference, through his dignity, sincerity and power of utterance, he had made himself one of the leading figures in the assembly, but this was a purely personal achievement, which owed nothing to the accident of his being one of the premier bishops of England. Perhaps there was no man in the whole assembly to whom it meant more than to this intensely shy prelate. Garbett had always had the conventional High Church interest in 'missions'. Now the younger Churches suddenly became to him a living reality; something exploded inside him, as he realised in a quite new way 'what God hath wrought'; he went back to England a changed man, with an inner liberation of spirit remarkable in one who was already more than sixty years old.

Paton had been determined that the learning of the theological world should be well represented, and had gathered a remarkable team around him. I remember especially the Quaker H. G. Wood, most modest and charming of men, Henry Pitney Van Dusen, later President of Union Seminary, New York, and one of the few good ecumenical chairmen of our time, and Kenneth Scott Latourette, already well known in missionary circles for his classic, though rather dull, *History of Christian Missions in China*, but not yet the universally acclaimed author of the seven volumes on *The Expansion of Christianity*. The Germans were there in force, as usual a not easily assimilable element in any conference. I recognised my old friend Missionsdirektor Ihmels, and met for the first time Walter Freytag of Hamburg, a meeting which was to have surprising effects on my later history. During the first four days of the conference I sat between Prälat Hartenstein of Würtemberg, President of the Basel Mission, and Gerhard Brennecke, at that time a theological student, later director of the Berlin Missionary Society. We were well aware of the political shadows which were darkening in the West; these made no difference at all to the reality of our fellowship in Christ.

There were a few 'key addresses', all of them good; the one which I think will never be forgotten was that delivered by Dr Paul Harrison of Arabia; in half an hour he gave us the history of the noble American mission in the Persian Gulf – five converts in fifty years – and ended a passionately simple address with the words, 'The Church in Arabia salutes you.'

I spent the first four days in the first Commission, on 'The Message of the Gospel' – presided over by Pitney Van Dusen. First the discussion and then the report, as is the way in all these gatherings. I was on the small committee selected to produce the report. We followed what I think was the worst possible method that could have been adopted. Five of us – Hendrik Kraemer, T. C. Chao of Yenching University, myself, and two others – were asked to produce a statement on the Christian faith; and then, after further discussion, Van Dusen was asked to reduce the five to a single statement, an impossible task. We fell inevitably between two stools – the vain attempt to summarise briefly the Christian faith as it has been traditionally held, and the more hopeful attempt to pick out those aspects of the gospel which needed to be specially stressed in 1938. As such statements go, the final result was not too bad, but, in the statement as accepted by the conference, all that remained of my carefully prepared document were the three words, 'We are bold'. The best thing that I got out of that part of the conference was a friendship, based on deep mutual respect, with T. C. Chao, who was just beginning his remarkable transformation from a rather superficial liberal of the American type to a Christian scholar with a profound apprehension of the Pauline dimensions of the faith. Ten years later we sat side by side on the platform of the first Assembly of the World Council of Churches in Amsterdam.

In the second week I had to assume far heavier responsibilities as chairman of Group VIII on the training of the ministry. This was the largest of the groups, seventy-two strong, and as international as it could be. I followed my usual policy as chairman of letting the discussion be as uninhibited as possible, insisting only that the speeches be kept short, and that certain rules of relevance must be observed. I encouraged the shyer members to speak, and find it gratifying to recall that more than fifty-one members took part vocally in the discussion. All the time I was trying to see what lines of agreement were emerging from an apparently shapeless discussion, and at the last session was able to present to the group a fairly clear idea of the lines on which our report should be drafted. When we had done our work, at my suggestion we stood and said the Lord's Prayer, each in his own language. I reckoned afterwards that the ancient words were said in forty-eight distinct forms of speech. For myself, I was so deeply moved that before the prayer ended my voice was drowned in silence.

For this report we followed a much more practical method. When the general plan had been agreed on, different sections were assigned to various authors; the secretary of the group was Dr Chester Miao of China. Dr H. Cunliffe-Jones, then of Bradford, rendered notable service by his fine sense for words, and his gift for clarity. I wrote a considerable part of the report myself and served as general editor. As finally revised by us, it was presented at a plenary session of the conference and accepted with hardly a modification.

This was much more than a formal report. It was a call to action. It initiated almost everything that has been done in more than thirty years for the improvement of theological training in the Third World. Two notable books, C. W. Ransom's *The Christian Minister in India* and B. Sundkler's *The Christian Ministry in Africa*, grew directly out of it. One of our most fruitful suggestions was that, where united action was desired, but no united Church was in existence, the co-operating bodies should adopt the method of the 'miniature university', with common teaching plant and library, but with separate hostels or colleges, in which each denomination could take such steps as it regarded as desirable to maintain its own distinctive ethos and tradition.

Meeting in this world is always the preliminary to parting, and always will be, until we come to what Paul in one of his miraculous phrases calls 'our gathering together unto him'. So we were sad when the time came to go. But we had all gained certain imperishable things. On the first day, when I entered the great hall, and saw the 450 delegates from sixty-seven countries, the words which came to my lips were, 'This *is* the holy catholic Church.' And, as we shared in the two great celebrations of Holy Communion, one Anglican and one 'Free Church', we felt that barriers were being broken down, and that the vision of one great united Church of Christ was in deed and in fact rising above the horizon.

Tambaram meant for me a rather sudden move from obscurity into a certain prominence in the affairs of the Church. An even greater change had taken place before the conference started; when I went to Tambaram, I was Bishop-elect of Tinnevelly.

Friends had long ago reached the conclusion that one day I would have to become a bishop. I did not agree with this prognostication. Men of strong convictions do not often become bishops, and though there were certain parts of a bishop's job that I thought I might be able to do fairly well, it seemed to me most unlikely that this vocation would ever come to me. But through these years a number of events had taken place that had made it necessary for me to think that I might be wrong.

It started when I was on leave in England in 1933 when an old friend, R. O. Hall, Bishop of Hong Kong, made an informal approach about whether I would consider becoming Bishop in Western China. I declined. After all, I was only thirty-two, and also had to decline Rangoon on the grounds of ill-health. An inner voice led me to refuse Archbishop Lang's offer of Mombasa, even though he did dangle before me the prospect of becoming Archbishop if a province were created out of Kenya, Uganda and Tanganika. I also rebuffed approaches from Nagpur and Travancore because, while there were no compelling reasons why I should go, I felt I should stay in Tinnevelly, with its now decimated missionary force. A delegation even came to see me when the see of Colombo became vacant, and patiently followed me to a harvest festival, but in the event I was glad I refused to allow my name to go forward in what proved to be a very distressing election.

Having almost had three mitres firmly placed upon my head and three others dangled not far from my nose, and having been led, as I believed, by the Holy Spirit, to say no to all of them, I had come to the conclusion that my permanent and predestined state in the Church of Christ was that of presbyter. Then, as so often, the utterly unexpected happened.

Frederick Western was of all bachelors the most completely bachelor. He was nearly sixty years old. So when Rupert Bliss burst in upon me and said, 'The Bishop is engaged to Grace New,' I replied pointedly and succinctly, 'Liar!' But the lie proved to be the truth. The wedding took place in the cathedral. It was plain that the painfully shy, gauche Bishop was intensely, though inarticulately, happy. Then tragedy struck. The Westerns were planning to go on leave in England, and were expecting the arrival of a baby during their leave. They were spending a few days quietly at Courtallum at the mountain foot, when aclampsia set in, and before medical aid could arrive, mother and child were dead.

Frederick preached a most moving sermon in the English church in Palamcottah on the vision of Elisha in 2 Kings 6, and then with amazing courage set himself to continue his work as bishop. But friends intervened and told him that he simply must carry out his plan of going to England, and have time to rest and recover. He could rest, but he did not recover. The doctors diagnosed persistent anaemia which did not yield to treatment; they told him that it was impossible for him to return to India. And so we were faced with the necessity of electing a new Bishop of Tinnevelly.

In these five years it had come home to me that for some reasons I would like to be a bishop; I needed a change of job, having become a little weary of theological teaching on an elementary level; my heart was still in India, but it was not clear where I could go unless upwards into the episcopate. When I heard of Frederick's resignation and looked deep into my own heart, I knew that I would very much like to be Bishop of Tinnevelly. But this was the one diocese in the world to which I was sure that I would never be elected. I had been led to take a fairly strong line on various controversial issues; I knew that I was very unpopular in certain quarters. And, in any case, we had all come to the conclusion that the time had come for the election of an Indian bishop. When Tubbs resigned, Azariah, a Tinnevelly man by birth, had been approached, and wisely said that he would not come, unless the election was unanimous; it was clear that caste-feeling was too strong in the Church to make this possible, and the proposal was dropped. In 1938 Azariah was sixty-three years old, and it was hardly possible that he should consider leaving his great work in Dornakal. There was no other obvious candidate, yet we all hoped that we might have the privilege of serving under an Indian bishop. So for the seventh time I put an imaginary mitre behind my back.

The method of episcopal election adopted by the diocese of Tinnevelly provided that any five members of the diocesan council, clerical or lay, could combine to nominate any bishop or priest of the Anglican Communion as a candidate for election to the vacant bishopric. When the list of persons nominated was printed and circulated, there were fifty signatures under my name. It was clear that Selwyn and I were going to divide the vote, and that there was no Indian candidate who had the confidence of any large section of opinion in the diocese.

Much to the surprise of the diocese, I spent the night before the election at Selwyn's house. We discussed the situation, and agreed that, if invited to accept election, we should not stand down in order to impose upon the diocese an Indian bishop whom it did not particularly want. We further agreed that whichever of us was first offered the bishopric should accept and not stand down in favour of the other. We then prayed together, I think for the only time in our lives – I find it much more difficult to pray extempore in English than in Tamil – and then went to bed. On that one night in my life, I, the notoriously bad sleeper, laid my head on my pillow at 10 p.m., fell instantly asleep, and slept like a child without moving until 6 o'clock the next morning.

Under our excellent system, every member of the diocesan council had four votes, though he was not obliged to use more than one. During the election, the council had to choose two bishops to sit with the Metropolitan and make the final choice. We naturally elected Madras and Dornakal. After the votes had been counted, the bishops would have before them a panel of names of persons, each of whom had received the votes of at least 51 per cent of the electoral body, and was therefore regarded as an acceptable bishop by the majority of those concerned in the election. The bishops could use their discretion, and were entitled to pick any one of the candidates whose names appeared on the panel. So, when all had voted, the votes were checked but not counted, and the voting papers sent off by registered post to the Metropolitan, to await the time when he could summon the other two bishops to meet him. This involved a delay of some weeks, during which all of us were free to get on with our customary jobs.

I knew exactly when the bishops would be able to meet to count the votes. They would all be together in Madras on St Luke's Day, 18 October, for the consecration of the Bishop of Travancore; if there were any missive for me from the Metropolitan, it would arrive on the morning of 21 October. That morning I went across and spent our regulation hour in the chapel; the lesson read was 2 Corinthians 12, 'My grace is sufficient for thee'. 'That', I thought to myself, 'is most helpful, whichever way the result of the election may go.' I returned to my study, and found five or six letters on the table; I riffled through them, noted that there was nothing from the Metropolitan, and felt able to accept this result without the smallest emotional disturbance. But then, as I opened the envelopes one after the other, the third down was from the Metropolitan after all, telling me that my name stood first on the panel, and that he and his fellow bishops had decided to invite me to accept the vacant see.

The decision had, in fact, been made weeks before; my mood was one of simple acquiescence, and of hope that the morning's promise would be fulfilled. The same day my acceptance was written, but could not be posted in Nazareth – it was too certain that any letter addressed to the Bishop of Calcutta would be opened and read in the post office before being dispatched. I had to wait until I could get into Palamcottah and post the letter in a larger post office. Nor could I say anything to anyone; the election could not be announced until it had been confirmed by all the other bishops in the province, and India being the size it is, the answers could not all be in within fifteen days. So I gave my lectures for the day as though nothing had happened, and at 4.30 went across to Evensong; there, by one of those astonishing coincidences that are so much more common in real life than in fiction, the second lesson for the day was Acts 6: 'They chose Stephen'; no one else in the chapel even noticed that there might be a possible coincidence.

When the confirmation had been completed, the Metropolitan signified that he would like the consecration to take place on 6 January 1939, just after the consecration of the great new cathedral at Dornakal, which had been fixed for 6 January, the Feast of the Epiphany. When Azariah went to Dornakal in 1912, it was nothing but a railway junction. His episcopate of twenty-six years, during which the Christian population of his diocese had multiplied itself six or sevenfold, had made the name famous throughout the world; now the seal was to be set on his work by the consecration of a cathedral, which, though not very large, was to be notable by reason of the incorporation into it of various motifs of Indian art and decoration. Many of the Tambaram delegates were still in India, and it was clear that we would have a great display of ecclesiastical pageantry.

By another of those strange and happy chances, my parents were in India at the time, and together with my sister were able to take part in the two great services. At the consecration of the cathedral there were at least 1,500 communicants, and even with eight bishops taking part in the distribution of the elements, it was a long service.

I have very few recollections of my own consecration; as I imagine happens with most people, it passed in a kind of dream. Eleven bishops were present and took part, including a Maori, an African from Sierra Leone, and, at my special request, the Swedish Lutheran Bishop of Tranquebar, Johannes Sandegren. The sermon was preached by Selwyn, excellently translated into Telugu by Anthony Blacker Elliott, a fellow Irishman, who was at the time Assistant Bishop of Dornakal. The chief consecrator was Foss Westcott, by now a tried and valued counsellor; the two presenting bishops were Azariah of Dornakal and Waller of Madras, whose names have so often occurred in these pages, and whom I remember gratefully as two of the greatest men and greatest Christians that I have ever known. My dear R. V. Asirvadam, who was old enough to be my father, having been born in 1871, and whom I had decided to make my chaplain, stood by me throughout the ceremony. At the actual moment of consecration, my only conscious thought was, 'This could not possibly be me'; but the presence of so many friends, and the assurance of their prayers, helped through the moments of dismay at the step I was taking, or that was being taken for me.

Then came the long journey back, with crowds waiting at every stop, after we entered the diocese, with garlands and addresses of welcome. And so in the early evening to the big empty house, in which there had been no time to get my possessions arranged; and once again the intense feeling of loneliness and desolation. But I was not left alone for long; suddenly Robin Woods, now Bishop of Worcester, who had been one of the youngest members of the Tambaram Conference, burst in upon me. He agreed to act as my chaplain at the enthronement the next day, and left me in his debt for life by showing me how to fold episcopal robes, a task he had often carried out for his father, the Bishop of Lichfield. The next day my parents and sister arrived, and we were able to get a little life into the house.

A Bishop of Tinnevelly had never been enthroned. When Western came in 1928, the diocese was still legally a part of the diocese of Madras, and, though the parish church of Palamcottah had long been called the cathedral, it had neither dean nor canons, and its exact status was very far from clear. I felt that the time had come when all this had to be changed. Somewhere I had managed to find an enthronement service, and had translated it into Tamil. When I arrived back from the consecration, the Tamil text was lying on my study table. Against the rubric 'Here the Bishop will preach', the incumbent of the cathedral had written in the note, 'No Bishop of Tinnevelly has ever preached from this pulpit.' The last bishop who had been able to preach in Tamil was the old Assistant Bishop, Edward Sargent, who died in 1889. At that time the church had not yet been provided with a pulpit. All subsequent bishops had preached by interpretation, standing on the chancel step. So, as I preached my first sermon as bishop, trying to share with my people my ideal of the servant church and the servant bishop, I knew that there were many among them who were glad to have a shepherd who could speak to them in their own language. Twelve years before, I had been made deacon in this place; now I had been brought back to become in a special way the servant of the servants of God.

5

Apprentice Bishop

I was Bishop of Tinnevelly, servant and shepherd of a flock of about 125,000 Christians, in an area of about 11,000 square miles, living in 1,453 villages, in 700 of which there were schools and organised congregations and in another 300 of which services were regularly taken.

No one tells you how to be a bishop; you have to find out for yourself, by guess and by God, and there are plenty of people ready to criticise you if you go astray. One of the first adjustments I had to make was that from a very small house with a tiny staff to a fair-sized mansion, which I felt it my duty to keep in good order, and which had therefore to be provided with an adequate staff of servants. I was never a prince bishop, but I had to maintain what in England would appear to be a rather lordly establishment.

My chaplain, R. V. Asirvadam, later to be my archdeacon, lived in a separate house in the compound. It was invaluable to have him so near me, but this meant that I lost a rather useful spare bedroom, and had to have my office in my study, never a good arrangement.

I had an excellent clerk, a bright and devoted Christian. He could take down accurately from dictation at sixty words a minute, type with very few mistakes, and knew something about keeping accounts and filing documents. He was much more a friend than an employee. On one occasion, when I was preparing for a rather long absence, he sat up with me till 3 a.m., in order that I might be able to leave everything in perfect order at my departure.

One of Western's noble benefactions to the diocese was that he left me an almost new Chevrolet; I would have had no means of purchasing a car for myself. I had to have a driver, as my car was really the mission taxi, and, if I had not employed a driver, would have been little use to anyone except myself. I did drive myself, but it is rather an exhausting business in India, and I was often glad to

sit back and let the driver take the wheel. It was essential to have
an absolutely reliable and competent driver. I had one of the boys
admirably trained by Randle at the industrial school; he was a good
driver, a fair mechanic, and completely reliable. He too became
completely one of the family, much more a friend than a servant.

The most picturesque member of the entourage was my office
messenger. When one lives two miles from the cathedral, three
miles from the bank and four miles from the railway-station, and
there is no telephone, a messenger is indispensable. I took on a
charming Hindu boy of the shepherd-caste, bought him a bicycle,
and dressed him up in dark blue shorts, a light blue shirt and a
white turban. He was a striking figure, as he dashed here and
there on my concerns. I have rarely had anyone more delightful to
deal with. He regularly attended servants' prayers conducted every
day by my chaplain, and I think became a sincere and believing
Christian, though he was never baptised.

I had a butler and a cook and a sweeper. The cook had the
Indian servants' inimitable capacity for producing something out
of nothing. I also had of necessity two gardeners. We still had no
running water in the house, so one man had to spend most of his
time in seeing to the needs of the house, whereas the other tried
to make plants grow in a rocky soil under the burning rays of an
ever-present sun.

Indians are a somewhat formal people, so when on duty I was
always clad in a white cassock and pectoral cross. My predecessor
used to work in his shirt-sleeves and receive his visitors thus in-
formally dressed, but I knew that the clergy disliked this, and I
decided from the start to adapt myself to their understanding of
what was proper. If anyone came to see me in camp, that was
another matter; he had to take me as he found me. I also made the
rule that no Indian priest who came to see me would leave without
a time of prayer in the chapel and my blessing.

When I became bishop, I had said to myself that the free-and-easy
relationships that I had so long enjoyed with Indians of all kinds
and classes would now come to an end. I need not have been afraid.
Before long my habits became known, and all sorts of people began
to find their way to my roof, like Nicodemus at night – clergy,
old students, teachers, quite simple people with problems in their
Christian life. But only visitors of the male sex came upstairs.
Women I always received downstairs in my drawing-room with
wide open doors. The reasons for this caution will be self-evident
to those who know India.

I was made particularly happy when, some time later, I was staying at Bishop Caldwell's famous station of Ideyankundi, for the centenary. I was housed in the girls' school, the girls at the time being absent, and at the end of a long day of services and meetings was sitting in a shirt and a pair of shorts, enjoying the cool of the evening, when I heard an ominous cough outside, and looked up to see a group of young men standing just beyond the rays of my lamp. I groaned in spirit, since such a deputation almost always meant a complaint against either the pastor or the teacher. However, I called them in and enquired where they came from. They proved to be a group of quite rough farmhands from a village where I had taken a confirmation not long before. So I enquired about the well-being of the village, whether the rains had been good and the crops were growing well, and whether the young people I had confirmed were behaving themselves. This is common form in India, where you do not come too quickly to the point; but in the end, as they showed no sign of coming to the point, I said to them, 'Would you mind telling me what you have come about?' They looked a little surprised, and said, in an untranslatable Tamil idiom, 'We just came,' which being interpreted in English means, 'No particular reason; we heard that the bishop was somewhere in the neighbourhood; he's an old pal of ours, and we thought that we would like to pass the time of day with him; and we are sure that he would like to pass the time of day with us.' How right they were! I felt that the seal had been set on my ministry, and that my love for the people had been understood and accepted.

Owing to Western's illness, and the delays in getting a new bishop elected, there had been a long gap in episcopal work, and much leeway to be made up in the matter of confirmations. It was the custom that the bishop got round once in three years to each of our thirty-one circles; a number of circles were ready and waiting with candidates in many villages. I had to set to work on a steady round of confirmations, and made a number of discoveries as I went.

The very first confirmation that I took was, as it happened, at Nazareth, where I had lived and worked so long. Frederick had left me, for the time being, a cope made out of a perfectly lovely Benares sari. Before the service I sent a message to the women missionaries, 'Would you like me to wear cope and mitre?' An enthusiastic 'Yes' came back as the answer, so I donned these unfamiliar garments. To me, as I have made plain, such outward trimmings had long since ceased to mean anything one way or the other, but my action had symbolic significance. It made it plain from the start that it was my intention to be the bishop of the whole diocese and not of one part of it only.

My first long tour was in the Megnanapuram circle, the centre of a very large number of Christian villages. In each village I asked the candidates, if they could, to come in to the great church of St Paul for their first Communion. On that Sunday morning the church was packed to bursting-point. I had three Indian colleagues helping me. The glowing silver flagon, with the astonishing inscription, 'Holy Trinity Church, Cambridge; the gift of the Vicar, 1836,' stood in splendour on the holy table. (Did Charles Simeon give it to Daniel Corrie, Bishop of Madras, and once his curate, when he returned to Madras in 1836?) I reconsecrated and reconsecrated again. When at last the long service was over, we entered 540 communicants in the register. But there may in fact have been many more.

During these weeks I made a number of discoveries. I decided that ordinarily I would not confirm more than sixty candidates in one service. I wanted especially the young people to feel that at that one turning-point in their lives they had a rather intimate relationship to their bishop, and when the numbers are large this becomes impossible. The work became in consequence very hard for me; in one year I took 122 confirmation services myself, and confirmed 3,500 candidates, which meant sometimes taking three services in a day. I found that each service demanded a separate spiritual effort. Yet it is no easy task to be always fresh, interested and alert; all too easy to forget that what has become a routine for oneself is for the candidates an event eagerly awaited and never to be repeated. Having started out with the idea of using one carefully prepared address for the whole of a tour, I found that I soon became bored myself with the repetition; the only method, for me, was to have four addresses ready to hand, and to ring the changes on them, trying to prepare a new address once or twice a year.

One of my aims was to try to raise the standard of preparation for confirmation above the level which had become customary. I knew that at Nazareth, that great and ancient congregation, all that happened was that, during the fifteen days before the arrival of the bishop, the young people were herded into church every evening to have the Prayer Book Catechism hammered into their heads by rote, without a single word of explanation, or any indication of the connection between the words and the problems of daily living. In other places perhaps even less was done than this. Inevitably the greater part of the work had to be done by the village teachers, whose ideas as to how the work should be done were sketchy; few of the clergy regarded it as part of their duty to talk to the candidates, still less to pray with them individually and to help them to understand the nature of Christian decision.

It had been Western's custom to catechise the candidates before the service, to ascertain what they knew. I decided to continue this tradition, and not infrequently this time with the candidates took longer than the service itself. On one occasion, try as I would, I could get nothing out of the candidates. As they were very simple people, I thought that they might have difficulty in understanding my Tamil, so I invited the pastor to question them, with exactly the same result. So we turned to the teacher, and asked him to put some simple questions; he failed to get a single answer, and it was clear that no serious preparation of any kind had been carried out. I prayed with them, and promised that I would come back as soon as the pastor could tell me that they were really ready. I went back after nine months, and had an excellent time; the lessons had been learned, and there were signs of real seriousness and devotion.

One of the ordeals that had to be endured was meetings of diocesan committees. These occurred twice a year. Our system was very democratic; there was a committee for everything, with usually a majority of laymen; only on the Education Committee was there any considerable number of missionaries. Some things must remain in the hands of the bishop; but almost the whole of diocesan business had to pass through the diocesan committees, and in most fields the bishop could do nothing until the matter had been considered by the relevant committees. For many of our people membership of an important church committee was the one means by which they could gain influence and a measure of authority; so membership became an object of ambition, and some people were skilled in rigging elections to their own advantage and that of their friends. There was in existence a well-organised pressure group which used to meet before each set of committees to decide what was to be done, and again after the committees were over to devise means for the frustration of any decisions that might have been taken against their wishes. My predecessor, shrewd as he was, did not always know exactly what was going on; having himself a quick and very businesslike mind, he wanted to get on with the business in hand and not to waste time; but this meant that often quick decisions were made, before the slower members of the committee, and those less skilled in the English tongue, had realised what was in the wind. I was determined to change things, but as far as possible without appearing to do so.

The first thing was as far as possible to avoid ever taking a vote. Voting is not the Indian method. Instead, there is discussion until a consensus is reached by everyone expressing their opinion, from the youngest to the oldest. It may take hours, but all go home happy, with no frustrated feelings at having 'lost a vote'. I organised committee meetings on a similar basis, making sure all, even the quieter members, had their say. This meant business sometimes took a terribly long time, but the atmosphere was free of tension, and generally we got our business satisfactorily done.

I had hardly become bishop when I had to face a rather important decision. I had received and accepted an invitation to the Lambeth Conference of 1940, and was therefore committed to a visit to England in that year. But, at the time of my consecration, I had been nearly five years in India without a break; these had been years of intense concentration, and at times of considerable overwork. Would it be wise, if money could be found, to take a short spell of leave in 1939, and then return to England for a rather longer period in 1940?

There was a further reason for my visiting England in 1939. I had been elected Hulsean Lecturer in the University of Cambridge for 1939–40. It was therefore settled that I should give the lectures in the October term of 1939, and Trinity graciously agreed to provide a room so that I could live in college.

I left India on an Italian ship somewhere about 10 July, and inevitably fell sick with one of my troublesome septic throats. I had decided to give myself a few days' holiday in the French Alps before starting work in England. As I travelled up through France, I was aware of gathering clouds and deepening anxieties. And yet I could not bring myself to believe that Europe would once again plunge itself in catastrophe. Twenty-one years is a very short period in human history. Everyone over the age of thirty must have had vivid memories of the First World War; were there not still sufficient sane people about to guard us against the suicidal madness of a few? In any ordinary situation there would have been; we did not then realise that we were dealing with a maniac, who had managed to cast his evil and hypnotic spell on the best-educated and most intelligent people on the face of the earth.

I arrived in England on 4 August, a day of sinister memories for older people. After a few days at a Church Missionary Society summer school at Malvern, I set out on a pilgrimage to visit relations in various parts of Ireland, Scotland and England. This tour was planned to end on 3 September, and beyond that date I could not see at all clearly what I should do. It had long been my habit to pray for guidance about all my movements and activities. But at this time my prayer seemed to be unanswered, and no reasonable plan presented itself. I knew that I wanted to get right away to some place where I could devote myself without interruption to the preparation of my Cambridge lectures; but at no point did I come near decision, and the matter remained open. And all the time the international situation darkened; each day the news was worse. When I heard over the radio the news of Hitler's pact with Stalin, my heart stood still, and I said to myself, 'Have we got to go on fighting the pair of them until the end of this century?'

On Sunday 27 August I preached in the little parish church of Glencraig, in which my father had been baptised in 1868. I then flew from Belfast to Glasgow, the only passenger on an eight seater plane, on a day of brilliant radiance – this is one of the few times in my life that I have really felt like a millionaire! And then across Scotland to stay at Stonehaven with Cousin Maggie Anderson, who was then ninety-five, but still as bright as a new penny, and fully able to appreciate her slice of grouse for dinner.

A day or two later I went on to Aberdeen to see great-aunt Margaret Cook, who was only ninety. As we were drinking a glass of sherry prior to lunch, her son Willy came in from the city and said, 'They're bombing Warsaw.' Even at that far more than eleventh hour, I still entertained an almost crazy idea that somehow the worst could be averted, and that even on the very edge of the precipice Europe would find some way by which to draw back from disaster. As Cousin Maggie parted from me the next day, she remarked, 'Well, I can look back on many wars starting with the Crimean'; but the old lady was never to see peace again; she died the following year.

On Sunday 3 September I was to preach at Hewarth church, near Gateshead, of which my brother Gerald was at that time Vicar. I entered the pulpit at a time at which Neville Chamberlain, the Prime Minister, was actually addressing the House of Commons. What does a man preach about, when he literally does not know whether his country is at war or not? I still think that I chose the most appropriate text in the whole Bible: Psalm 112:7, 'He will not be afraid of any evil tidings, for his heart standeth fast, and believeth in the Lord.' As we came out of church, we heard the first air raid warning of the war, why I have never quite been able to understand; and then the news came over the air – the time of

our ultimatum had expired, and for the second time in my lifetime
we were at war with Germany.

The next day saw me at the travel agents in Haymarket. For a
brief moment I had wondered whether I ought to go to the War
Office and offer my services; but very brief reflection showed me
that there were other young bishops who should be readily available,
and that, as I was the only one who knew Tamil, I should get back as
quickly as possible to my own proper job. Fortunately I was booked
on a Dutch ship, and this increased the likelihood of my being able
to get away without too long delay; but the agent explained that it
was impossible to fix any dates of sailing, and that there was nothing
for me to do but to wait for further information. A quick visit to
Cambridge and a talk with Professor Raven settled the question of
the Hulsean Lectures; these could be put in cold storage until after
the war – we did not then know that the moratorium would last for
nearly eight years.

Then down to Cornwall, where at that time my father was Vicar
of St Keverne, near the Lizard. I had nothing to do but to wait;
but it was pleasant to become my father's curate and to help in the
regular services of the church.

We saw the first convoys sail down the Channel. We read the
news of the destruction of Poland. Otherwise the war did not seem
to come very near to us. And then the great news arrived; a Dutch
ship was sailing on 10 October, and I could begin my tortuous
journey back to India.

The first lap of the journey was on a small Dutch vessel from
Gravesend to Rotterdam. The prudent Dutch, not trusting either
Hitler or Mussolini, had decided that the voyage to India should
be round the Cape, and that their five new ships should be based
on Lisbon to avoid the possible dangers of the English Channel.
So we travelled as far as Lisbon in one of the smaller and older
vessels, and then had a week to wait in Lisbon while the cargo was
transferred.

We were never able to go far afield, as we had been warned that
for security reasons only short notice would be given of the actual
time of sailing, and that we had better be on hand when called for.
But I was able to see Lisbon thoroughly and to visit Estoril and
Sintra, and made myself fairly well acquainted with the beautiful
city of Lisbon, from which Vasco da Gama set forth on the voyage
to India that changed the history of the world.

And so the day of sailing came and we set off on our long journey
round the Cape. This was one of the newest Dutch ships, spruce and

well equipped. With their usual courtesy, the Dutch, having heard that there would be an Anglican bishop on board, had shipped a case containing everything necessary for Anglican Holy Communion. So I was able to have regular services, with rather small numbers, the vast majority of the passengers being Dutch, and to keep my end up with Father Lyons, a delightful Irish Roman Catholic priest from New Zealand, who for the one and only time in his life had been exploring the Roman Catholic world and was returning draped from head to foot with coins and medals and crosses for his eager parishioners.

There were on board a Dutch chaplain and a Dutch missionary. As we and the other passengers did so many things together, I felt that it would be good if once at least we were able to worship together. These were still pre-ecumenical days, and my colleagues were considerably surprised at such a suggestion coming from an Anglican bishop. However, they smiled on the project. We were able to find some hymns which exist both in Dutch and English, and the purser's office agreed to duplicate them for the purposes of the service. We planned a service rather like a club sandwich, a slice of English and a slice of Dutch, so that no one would be kept waiting too long for something in which they could share.

It was at this point that my pestilent habit of falling ill at sea asserted itself. My temperature ran up to 103°F, and on Saturday night I went to bed, almost on the equator, with three blankets and four aspirins in the attempt to get my temperature down in time for the service. I did not sleep much; but these remedies worked, and at dawn the temperature was down to 100·4°F. I thought that this was good enough, and carried on.

Everything went splendidly. The saloon was packed to the doors. The Dutch *dominik* preached what he regarded as a short sermon, and this was just about the same as an Anglican would regard as a long sermon. Then I preached a short sermon. Just at that time that noble Christian woman Queen Wilhelmina had been celebrating the fortieth anniversary of her assumption of royal powers, and had told her people (I cannot quote the exact words) that 'I say now as I said then, that the chief object of my life is that Jesus Christ should be glorified.' Taking this as my starting-point, I told my hearers that in the countries to which they were going, they would all be missionaries, whether they desired it or not, and that they could not be a credit either to their country or to their Church unless they could make their own the words so splendidly spoken by the Queen. The first officer of the ship asserted that nothing in his life had ever impressed him more than this service. The only contretemps was that, having started to say the Apostles' Creed, I confused it hopelessly with the Nicene, and then had the greatest difficulty in finding either of them in my Prayer Book.

Having done my duty, I retired to bed and stayed there for the rest of the voyage. I was still a very sick man when the ship discharged me on the jetty at Colombo. The kind Bishop immediately sent for his doctor, who prescribed M & B, and kept me in bed for the day or two before the British India boat made the one-night crossing to Tuticorin. When I reached India, I was somewhat better, but still very far from well. Few greater misfortunes could be imagined than to arrive in this condition to take up all the extra strains of a diocese at war; it was a long time before I recovered anything like normal health.

I was to be faced at once by a severe and unnecessary shock. I had arranged for three young missionaries to join the staff of the diocese, two for educational work, and one to serve as chaplain to the large Anglo-Indian congregation at Madurai, the great home and centre of Tamil culture. For generations the government of India had treated the railways and the posts and telegraphs as the preserve of the Anglo-Indians, those unhappy children of mixed race, who rarely managed to be entirely at home in either world. A considerable colony had grown up round the railway works at Madurai, the Church of the Divine Patience, consecrated by Bishop Tubbs in 1928. The church had never had a resident priest, being served either from the hill-station of Kodaikanal, or from the large SPG station at Ramnad, about a hundred miles down the railway line. I had decided that the time had now come when this important group should be more adequately cared for. I arrived to find that money I had ear-marked for salaries had been used by my commissary and the diocesan treasurer to make up a threatened deficit in the annual budget of the diocese. I cannot now remember by what devices I was able to find the money; all I know is that the young colleagues arrived and did not starve; and I was left with the impression that on the whole it was a bad idea for bishops to go on leave.

Then I had to turn my attention to all the effects that the war might have on the life of the diocese. It was the entry of Japan into the war that made our situation really serious. The war which had been so distant now was at our very doors. We read of one disaster after another. Singapore first, and then Rangoon; then, within a few weeks, the Japanese were at the gates of India. It was touch and go; if British and Indian troops together had not managed to stage a furious defence in those bleak regions between Burma and India, until the first impulse of the Japanese assault had spent itself, it is hard to say where the British army would have found its next line of defence.

We had to face the prospect of a serious disruption of our work. The Bishops of Singapore and Sarawak were prisoners in Japanese hands. The Bishop of Rangoon, who was recovering in America from a very serious car accident, had not become involved. We had to reckon with the possibility of a rapid Japanese advance, and the collapse of orderly government over very wide areas. I suggested that we should all be allowed to arrange for the consecration of Indian assistant bishops, so that, if we were interned, the Church would still be provided with the fullness of ministry as Anglicans understand it. The other bishops did not share my view of the danger, and no steps were taken. But I still think that my view was the prudent one; and had I had the help of my dear R. V. Asirvadam as assistant bishop, my service in India might have lasted a good deal longer than in the end it did.

The Japanese did not come, but we had every reason to suppose that they would. They had made an assault on Colombo from the air, and had found the defences a good deal stronger than they had expected; but it seemed unlikely that this would be their first and last attempt. In fact there was one very curious scare. A signal was received that a Japanese fleet was sailing straight for Madras. The government, knowing that there were no defence forces in the 400 miles between Madras and Cape Comorin, fell forthwith into a panic. Only many years later did I discover what had really happened. The signal was genuine, but it was part of a hypothetical defence exercise and bore no relation to fact. The Japanese, being otherwise occupied elsewhere, were nowhere near Madras. It is hardly to be expected that mythological speculations of this kind should be mixed up with sober reality. But so it was.

There was a rapid exodus of American missionaries. I was in some remote place in the district when the news of the threatened invasion reached me. I had to decide what to do. I knew very well that, if the Japanese did arrive, there would be very little chance of my being able to continue my ministry; but I concluded that I ought to stand by my flock as long as I could, and so decided to stay. By the time I reached Palamcottah, the scare was over and we knew that the Japanese, for the time being at least, would not be coming. But I was glad that I made what I still regard as the right decision.

The scare had one good effect. It revealed to the authorities the appalling incompetence of the administration, both military and civil, in South India. There was a considerable storm in high places. The Viceroy flew down from New Delhi, and rumour had it that both the Governor and the general in command came very near to losing their jobs. Then, of course, in the best British tradition of shutting the stable door after the horses have gone, the military set to work with fearful energy. About twenty-five miles from Palamcottah a vast airfield was constructed at great expense, and, as the war moved elsewhere, this naturally was never used.

As the war went on, the price of grain naturally began to soar. Harvests had not been good, there was a good deal of hoarding, and government efforts at distribution had been only partly successful. One acquaintance told me that he had seen three railway wagons full of grain on a siding; thinking that these had been forgotten, he reported the matter to Madras, only to receive a rather curt note in reply, to the effect that he was mistaken, and that no such wagons existed. After consultation with various leaders in society, I arranged to start a co-operative store near the cathedral, to purchase grain in large quantities and to sell it at as reasonable a price as we could manage. The operation was not completely successful at the start, but the store still exists, and is regarded as one of the monuments of my episcopate.

As the war continued, the government became more jittery, and unexpected strains and tensions began to appear in the situation. It has to be remembered that India itself was bitterly divided on the issue of the war.

On the one side was the magnificent effort of the raising of an army of nearly three million men. No doubt there were mixed motives at work. Pay was comparatively high. To join the armed forces was a refuge from the constant problem of unemployment. But, when allowance has been made for such inducements, the growth of the army did reflect the view of one large section of Indian opinion – that Hitler was a bad thing and that somehow this must be stopped.

On the other side was the sullen and increasingly malevolent hostility of the Congress. In the early days of the war Mr Gandhi had come out in resolute condemnation of Hitler, but he was overruled by his lieutenants, who ruled that this was simply another imperialist war in which India was in no way interested. Of course, among those who took this view there were wide differences of opinion. Some were prepared to welcome the Japanese as fellow Asians, and to fight side by side with them against the British. Others thought that, once the European powers had bled themselves to death, India would be able to pluck the fruit of freedom without further trouble or effort. But on one point there was agreement – no co-operation with the British government and no support for the war.

One of the consequences of this decision was that, on orders from the headquarters of the Congress, all the Congress ministers in the provinces resigned. This was, in my opinion, a serious misfortune, and a grave disservice to the cause of India. In a number of provinces Congress ministers were doing quite well, and gaining sanity and stability from the experience of administration which previously they had lacked. In Madras we were particularly fortunate in that the Chief Minister was the shrewd and effective Brahman, C. Rajagopalacharier, later to be the first Indian Governor-General of India. This splendid old man, who was, I think, born in 1877, was, though he had never left his own country, the perfect example of the Gladstonian liberal. He was never, I think, entirely at home in the Congress party, though he served it loyally over many years, and in later days showed marked signs of independence. He had far greater understanding of the village people and their way of thinking than the great majority of politicians.

The situation became far more serious in 1942, when on 7 August the Congress launched a plan for civil disobedience on the widest scale, with a view to paralysing the government and the entire war effort of the country – and this with the Japanese at the gates. The confidence of the government was severely shaken, and from that time on there was a tendency to suspect everyone and to put the most sinister interpretation on the most innocent words and actions. The resulting situations could be absurd, but they could also be very unpleasant.

Having been almost a pacifist for twenty years, I had been drawn only very slowly to the conviction that Hitler must be destroyed, and that to fight him was to work for the redemption and not for the destruction of the German people. But I had to search my own conscience often and sternly to detect the possible rising up of vindictive and unchristian feelings towards the enemy. I also felt it necessary to give guidance to our Christian people as to the attitude that they should adopt. With this in view I sent out to the members of our four English-speaking congregations a pastoral letter, in which I stated that, as far as I knew my own heart, my only wish was that Germany should be great and free, as I wished that Great Britain should be great and free, and that Italy should be great and free, as I wished that India should be great and free. A copy of my letter fell into the hands of the Collector, the Indian administrative head of the district. I learned some time later that he had sent one of his subordinates snooping round to ascertain whether I was a subversive person.

One day I had just arrived in Ootacamund for my annual holiday, when a young police officer who was serving as ADC to the Governor, seeing me at the early service in St Stephen's Church, hared up the hill to the house where I was staying, and blurted out, 'Why does the Governor now regard you as Public Enemy Number One?' This was somewhat startling, especially as I had recently been in Madras, and dining as an honoured guest at Government House. I sat the young man down to breakfast, and gradually the story emerged.

One of the Governor's pet projects, quite legitimately, was the raising of a large war fund; less legitimately, one of his favourite methods of raising money was the sale of raffle tickets. Strong pressure was brought to bear on every kind of official and servant of the government to sell these tickets. The limit was reached when one of our women missionaries received the government grant for her school short by Rs.7, and fourteen raffle tickets pinned to the form, without so much as by your leave to anyone. This having been brought to my notice, I sent out a circular to all clergy and other officials of the diocese informing them that the question of purchasing raffle tickets was one which was left to the conscience of every man, but that as a diocese we did not approve of this method of raising money, and therefore no one in the service of the diocese must be involved in the sale of such tickets. The same Indian District Collector wrote in to the Governor that he was doing his best to raise money for the war fund, but that one of the chief obstacles in his way was the Bishop of Tinnevelly. He failed to send me a copy of this communication. The Governor failed to inform me, and to ask for my views. Instead, as I learned with some indignation, he had been blackening my name at his own dining-table in the presence of a number of guests.

Naturally, I immediately asked for an interview, which was granted. The atmosphere was somewhat frigid, but at least relations of courtesy were restored. But, I thought to myself, if this can happen to one in my station, of impeccable ancestry and unblemished reputation, what chance has any Indian, on whose character such an unprincipled assault has been launched, of clearing his name and restoring his reputation?

Worse was to follow. The young chaplain at Madurai was not always prudent in speech, and had antagonised some of the doughty English folk of the old colonial school in his parish. Then one day I received a confidential letter from Sir George Bray, a shy bachelor of the highest principles, the perfect representative of the best traditions of the Indian Civil Service. In this I read with some dismay that it had been reported to the Governor that the chaplain of Madurai had been heard to say in public that he hoped the Indians would soon fight for their freedom and win it. The Governor was gravely displeased, and must insist that I transfer the turbulent priest elsewhere. I replied somewhat tartly that the location of the clergy in my diocese was entirely my affair and not that of the civil power; but that I would look into the matter and report to him. I summoned the chaplain and told him of the report that had reached me. I could see from the expression on his face that he was completely perplexed; he said, 'I am sorry, but I haven't the least idea what they are talking about.' Ten days later, he came to see me again and said, 'It's come back to me; I now see where the rumour came from. I was talking in the club to Mrs X [the wife of an American missionary] and I said, "The Indians talk so much about fighting for their freedom; it might not be a bad idea if they really had to fight for it." Of course what I was talking about was the possibility of a Japanese invasion, and of the Indians really having to fight to defend their freedom.' Clearly Mrs X had repeated this in the presence of the English District Collector, who was a friend of hers and an enemy of the chaplain. He had taken the opportunity, without any verification of the facts and without any reference to the bishop of the diocese, to write in this untrue and damaging report directly to the Governor. I at once wrote in to Sir George with a full explanation of the facts. I added, 'You will realise that, if this information had come to me in any other way than through a most confidential letter from you, it would be my duty to prosecute the government's informer in open court.' I was careful to write 'informer' and not 'informant'. I of course knew perfectly well, and Sir George knew that I knew, who the informer was. I am not sure that I could actually have prosecuted him, but it will be understood that my feelings were strong. It is shameful to have to record that such things could happen under a British government; the stress of the times is a very inadequate excuse for such a total departure from the elementary principles of decency in public life.

In spite of my protests to Sir George, I decided that the young man would be happier if I moved him, so I asked him to join the staff of the theological college which I had brought to life ten years before, and which was now under an Indian Principal, Canon Thomas Sitther. This left me with a vacant chaplaincy, and the problem of filling it; I decided to take the risk of ordaining an old soldier, to whom I could give only the minimum of training. I ventured to ordain a brigadier, or rather a colonel, since after the end of his service in Madras Arthur Empson reverted to his subordinate rank. He had been put in charge of a camp for Italian prisoners of war; and, not feeling that there was any future in that, decided to retire as soon as he was eligible for full pension, and to place himself at my disposal. Arthur was a layman of life-long Anglican loyalties, with a far wider knowledge of theology than that possessed by the majority of laymen. The vacancy at Madurai gave me the opportunity, and I decided to throw my cap over the moon and ordain the colonel. When I announced in the church in Madurai that Colonel Arthur Empson would be coming to serve them, there was consternation in the congregation; they pictured a blood-and-thunder type, rattling a cavalry sabre, and wondered how in the world they would put up with him. Actually, Arthur was a kind and gentle, almost grandfatherly type, who read the *Jungle Books* aloud to the Anglo-Indian children, and made himself greatly beloved in the community. After a number of years of successful service, he returned to England and ended his days as the incumbent of a parish in Herefordshire.

During the first year of the war German and Italian missionaries were able to carry on their work with no very severe restrictions. The government, having perhaps learned something from the handling of the similar problems in the First World War, when the German missionary periodicals reverberated month after month with tales of the hardships inflicted by the cruel British on innocent German missionaries (no German of my acquaintance is aware of what the Germans did to British missionaries in East Africa!), had put the whole affair in the hands of one of those incomparable civil servants whom it is an honour to name, Sir Malcolm Darling of the Punjab. With the invasion of Holland, however, the situation changed, and Germans, missionaries and others alike, were interned. There was a considerable colony of them in Kodaikanal, in the Swedish missionary settlement, where there were good houses and a chapel. If one has to be in captivity, it would be hard to imagine a more agreeable prison.

The rules made by the government were reasonable and free from undesirable harshness. Each missionary family received an allowance; one member of the family was allowed to go to the bazaar once a week to purchase provisions. The daughter of my friend Dr Gäbler was even able to continue studying in the American School, and, to the eternal honour of the British and American children, let it be recorded that she never had any difficulty with any of them. Apparently I made a financial contribution to enable her to carry on with her education, nominally out of diocesan funds, but, as the diocese had no funds to cover an emergency of this kind, actually from my own rather limited resources. I thought nothing of this at the time, and had in fact completely forgotten it; but when I met my old friends fifteen years later in Göttingen, Dr Gäbler was happy to be able to introduce to me the daughter whom I had been privileged in this small way to serve during the years of war.

When the situation had settled down a little, the government decided to allow the Germans to have some visitors, and invited them to make a list of those whom they would specially like to see. I am glad and proud that my name was the first on their list. I was, I must admit, rather surprised, since the Swedish Lutheran Bishop Johannes Sandegren was a good friend of all of them; but the Germans seem to have decided that they would prefer an open enemy to a possibly suspect neutral. It happened that that year, 1942, I spent Christmas in Kodaikanal. The weather was splendid and glowing beyond compare, bright and crisp and sparkling. The Christmas services were moving beyond ordinary; I preached on the text, 'I am the bright and morning star.' Then on the two following days I went to see my German friends.

We started with a short service in the little church, taken by one of the missionaries, and then I preached. It was St Stephen's Day, and I spoke a little along the lines of the St Stephen's Day sermon in T. S. Eliot's *Murder in the Cathedral*. Suffering is an inescapable part of the gospel of Christ. If they were called to suffer through isolation from their beloved work and people, they must not regard it as a *xenon*, a strange thing (1 Pet. 4:12), but as a special form of service to which they were called, and in which the rest of us were not privileged to share. The government insisted that a Brahman sub-inspector of police must be present throughout the whole of my visit, including the Christian service. I hope that he found it edifying! Then a long discussion with the whole group about their situation, and the way in which they were managing to survive their isolation. Finally lunch with the Gäblers. Naturally we did not talk politics, it would have been most improper to do so. But not for a single moment did we find that the folly and wilfulness of man had in any way touched the reality of our fellowship in Christ.

After my visit I wrote a fairly long report to the chief secretary to the government. I mentioned that the missionaries were finding things a little tight financially, and suggested that a review of the allowances might be in order. I got back a rather curt note to the effect that no complaint had been received from the German internees and that the chief secretary was surprised by my suggestion. Naturally the Germans had not made any complaint; they were so grateful for the humane way in which they were being treated by the government that the last thing they wanted was to give any impression of ingratitude. But it was just the fact that prices were rocketing; and I was right in thinking that an allowance which had been inadequate nine months before was now hardly sufficient to meet their daily needs.

Some time after my visit, the government moved these married folks and their children out of the agreeable surroundings of Kodaikanal to Satara, where the accommodation was much inferior and the climate far less bearable, and replaced them by German and Italian Roman Catholic priests, who of course were celibate. This is the kind of thing that governments do, apparently without any awareness of the irreparable harm that they do to their own image by their folly.

The war was always with us, in many ways that were mostly tragic, sometimes wearisome, and occasionally even absurd. Yet, in spite of all, we managed to carry on all the work of the diocese, and to this the greater part of our time and strength had to be given.

As always, much of my concern went to the village teachers, on whom so much of the life of the Church depended, and who on the whole were so ill-rewarded. In the nineteenth century they had been most carefully trained for the spiritual side of their work. As the demands of government for efficiency on the side of secular teaching increased, the emphasis shifted. Catechists' training had entirely died out, and all that the men had to help them was such elementary Bible teaching as they had had in school and in the teachers' training college. The old custom of careful Bible teaching when the teachers came together once a month to receive their pay had been practically abandoned.

As a first step towards getting things in order, I had persuaded my predecessor to accept a ten-year syllabus. This was not entirely satisfactory; it meant that a new teacher joining service might find himself studying Jeremiah and the Epistle to the Hebrews without a clue as to what had come before. But at least there was a plan; and any teacher who had conscientiously followed the ten-year course would, at the end of it, have a fairly thorough knowledge of the essentials of theology.

As soon as I became bishop I launched the Tinnevelly Theological Series – four or five books to be published each year in Tamil, related to the examination subjects, to maintain a competent level of theological scholarship but to present the material in a form not too difficult for unformed minds to grasp. I got some of the younger Indian clergy and missionaries to write. I wrote one book each year myself. By this time I could write good Tamil quite readily; with a little revision by the archdeacon, what I wrote could be put into print, though I would never maintain that it was flawless, or such Tamil as a Tamil author would write.

We did not pay any fees to writers. My office was the publishing office. A little later we bought for the diocese a small printing press. The local churches backed us up well, in most cases ordering a copy of each book for each teacher, and recovering the cost from their salaries. Thus we had no overheads and few unsold copies. We were able to sell the books at derisory prices. So in five years we published 2,500 pages of theology in Tamil, most of it of a respectable standard, a good nucleus for the library of a village teacher. Many of those for whom the books were intended never even opened them and continued with the greatest sang-froid to dodge the examinations, but the more intelligent worked hard, did extremely well, and saw new vistas of theological understanding opening out before them.

Having cut the diocesan magazine free from the incubus of examination notes, I set myself to make of it a real means of communication between the Church and its servants. Each month I wrote a longish letter about my own doings. Every time that I went to the Joint Committee on Church Union, I wrote a long and careful account of all that had happened, and asked clergy and lay teachers to pass this on to the faithful, so that no one could have any excuse for pretending that he had not been warned of the imminence of church union. I also gave news of other parts of the Christian world.

Akin to my work as a publisher were my campaigns as a book-seller. As I went round the diocese, I was distressed to see far too few books in the hands of the worshippers – and nothing could be more boring than Anglican worship if you have neither Bible nor Prayer Book. I decided that the price of books must be brought down. The Tamil Bible was a miracle of cheapness; it sold at about the equivalent of two shillings; but in those days that was three days' wages for a labourer in the villages, and really more than they could afford. I asked the Bible Society if they could give a reduced price for an edition of 5,000 copies, bought cash down. They agreed that they could. The SPG in London produced some money from a fund called the Negus fund. I put a little money into it myself, and persuaded some of my friends to do the same. In the end I was able to bring the price down to fourteen annas, a reduction of about 40 per cent; and, to stimulate sales, I promised a bonus of 10 per cent to each local church which bought more than a hundred copies. I need not have bothered! They all bought more than a hundred copies, our edition of 5,000 went out in a few weeks, and I was left for the time being in a state of near bankruptcy. I wrote again to the Bible Society for another 2,500. These came and went like Balaam's grasshoppers. I demanded more; they wrote back to say, 'Five hundred is the very limit of what we can let you have.' Three thousand was the average of sales of the Tamil Bible for the whole Tamil area; by selling 5,000 in a few months, we produced a famine of Bibles. This was wartime; the stock of paper was in Calcutta, the printing press in Madras, with a thousand miles between them and no means of bringing them together. For about a year a Tamil Bible was not to be had for love or money.

Having been so successful with the Bible, we went on to the shortened Prayer Book (including the Psalms but omitting the Epistles and Gospels, and some of the occasional offices), and the Tamil Lyric Book. Here again, by ordering a very large quantity, 10,000 in each case, we were able considerably to reduce the price, and still to cover all the costs of the operation and to leave a small margin of profit. After this, as I went about the diocese, it was a great satisfaction to me to see so many more books in the hands of the faithful. There was no difficulty about getting the books to the people. All that was needed was that someone should see the possibilities, take the initiative, and exercise a little pressure until the operation had been successfully completed.

The village teachers now had the raw materials of their trade. But I was convinced that far more direct teaching and personal contact were needed, if they were ever to become apostles in their limited but all important spheres. So I hit upon the plan of asking the local churches to spare all the teachers of a particular age group, say twenty-four to thirty, for a four-and-a-half-day conference from Monday evening till Saturday morning; I suggested that, if they could meet half the cost, I would find the funds to cover the other half. This meant a group of between twenty and thirty teachers, all of roughly the same age and facing the same kind of problems in their personal lives and in their work. I arranged for senior clergy to come and do the bulk of the teaching, and I always made a point of being present myself throughout such times of conference. I set aside a brief time to see each teacher personally; often this could not be more than ten minutes for each man, but I knew that it meant much to them that the bishop asked each one about his work and his needs, prayed with each one, and sent each one on his way with a blessing.

A bishop who has his ear to the ground can find almost innumerable ways of serving his people. It would be tedious to record them all; I take one or two examples almost at random.

Debt was the perennial problem of our people. One of my old students came to me with a sad tale from a very old congregation that dated back even before the days of Rhenius. The people were of the scheduled castes and very poor. They had fallen into debt to money-lenders of the robber-caste; the rate of interest was so high that, each year at harvest, the money-lenders would come and carry off almost the entire harvest, and there was nothing for the people to do except to borrow again at the same ruinous rate to keep themselves alive until the next harvest was gathered in. The total amount involved was very small, but, having no way to pay it off, they had fallen victims to a cruel and, as it seemed to them, interminable slavery. The priest-in-charge, one of my old students, came to see me, and said that, if I could somehow raise enough money to buy up the entire debt, he would give me his personal guarantee that the people would repay in instalments in the months after the harvest, provided that we could fix a rate of interest that would not make the repayment too burdensome. I enlisted the help of a few Indian Christian gentlemen of means; the debt was bought up, the payments were made on the nail, and the people were set free from their life-long servitude.

Another old student came to me with a slightly different tale of woe. The people in another old congregation had fallen into such poverty that, although they had cultivable lands, they had no bullocks for ploughing, and were too poor to hire them. If I could advance enough money to enable them to plough and sow, he would guarantee repayment, when the harvest was in. The sum involved was so small that I simply advanced it myself. That year the rains were good, the harvest was plentiful, and once again repayment was made in full and on the date at which it fell due.

With intelligent young clergy like this, who saw that all the needs of their people were their concern, we could, I think, have gone much further in this work of debt redemption and economic rehabilitation. Of course we would not always have been so fortunate in our clients; but one must be prepared for a number of failures to balance the successes. However, I had endless things to do, and this was a plan that I never found time to launch on a major scale.

Committees are heartless creatures, and church committees in my experience are no better than any others. I kept coming across cases of minor injustice, and it became one of my chief concerns to see to it that as far as possible these were put right.

It came to our notice that the local churches were refusing to recognise the pension rights of certain widows of teachers earned in the days before we had a properly organised provident fund. I cannot recall the exact details; as far as I can remember, we felt that the churches were under an honourable obligation to pay, but that these elderly ladies had no legal remedy. The numbers were small and the amounts inconsiderable; but to the potential beneficiaries they might mean the difference between penury and a modest competence. I brought the matter before the Finance Committee of the diocese, and suggested that, as we could not compel the local churches to pay, we should accept the liability ourselves. Every Tinnevelly Tamil is a shrewd financier, and I was not at all sure what the reaction to my proposal would be. But this was one of the many occasions on which, by stating a case in a purely Christian way, I was able to secure a Christian judgement, and the old ladies were given their miniscule pensions from the central funds of the diocese. One old dear of seventy-one, who had been awarded the magnificent sum of Rs.2 a month for life, made a special journey to Palamcottah to present to me her thanks in person. I felt that I had done well.

One day an elderly Brahman turned up on my doorstep. He was a teacher in the very large boys' high school in Tinnevelly Town. His tale was that he was going deaf, and the governing board of the school had given him notice of termination of service. But he was in process of acquiring a deaf-aid, and he was confident that with this help he would be able to manage his classes without difficulty. The minutes of such boards came up to the Education Committee of the diocese for confirmation. Rather hesitantly, I brought before the committee the case of this teacher, and suggested that, while it would be improper to undermine the authority of the board, we would be within our rights in asking the board to reconsider its decision. A little to my surprise, the committee entirely agreed with me. The board was good enough to reconsider, and to agree that the teacher should continue in service for six months, at the end of which time the board would consider whether his claim that his competence was undiminished was justified. This little story reverberated round the entire Hindu community. If a bishop had intervened on behalf of a Christian teacher who was being unjustly treated by a Hindu body, there would have been no occasion for surprise. But who was this bishop who was prepared to take action against a Christian board on behalf of a Hindu teacher, whose rights he felt had been in some measure infringed?

In our educational, medical and social work we were serving the whole community. I felt that the government had been remiss in not recognising the splendid work that some of my colleagues were doing. So when Selwyn completed thirty years of service in India, I wrote in on his behalf, and was very happy to secure for him a silver Kaiser-i-Hind. Selwyn was at that time Principal of St John's College, an institution which had come into existence in 1873 and for seventy years had given only the two years of college education up to the intermediate level. When the diocesan constitution came into force in 1925, the then principal, convinced that an Indian commit-tee could not be trusted to look after so important an institution as a college, had arranged that St John's should not come under the Edu-cation Committee of the diocese but should have its own governing board directly responsible to the diocesan council. The consequence was that the diocese felt no responsibility for the College and took little interest in it. One of the very first things I did on becoming bishop, and with the wholehearted agreement of Selwyn, was to bring the College into line with all the other educational institutions and to put it under the Education Committee. The attitude of the diocese changed overnight; this was now their college, and they would see to it that it prospered. I took advantage of a meeting at which I announced Selwyn's Kaiser-i-Hind to suggest that the time had really come at which the College should go first-grade, and offer the full four-year university course. This proposal met with immediate approval; the money was raised and the College launched on a new and highly successful career.

Then there was Joy-Akkal (Akkal = elder sister). I had first met this remarkable woman at an SCM Swanwick Conference in 1924, when each of us was given three minutes to speak about his work.

In course of time she came to be the closest of all my Indian women friends. In days when there were no colleges for women in India, Joy Solomon's father saw no reason why women should be excluded from higher education, so she was sent to Bishop Heber College, Trichinopoly, the sole girl among five hundred boys. I think I am right in saying that she never had any difficulties with the men students; if this is true, it should be recorded to their honour, as in those days the relationships between the sexes in South India were by no means what a Christian would wish them to be. So Joy emerged with an MA in mathematics, to which she later added a second MA in English, and became a lecturer at the Sarah Tucker College for women. After fifteen years of this work she and her great friend, Miss M. A. Frost, decided that they had done enough teaching for one lifetime, and that they would give the rest of their lives to service among the women of the villages. They would found an ashram, a place of simplicity, of devotion, of fellowship and of loving service. They came to see me, and to ask advice as to where they might settle.

I had once been to Sayamalai, a village where we had a tiny, backward congregation; my chief recollection of the visit is of the large hole in the thatched roof of the school which also served as a church. Sayamalai is in the centre of a large village area dominated by the robber-caste, so much so that the local saying was, 'Half for the robber and half for the pot.' There were very few Christians in the area, and those that there were were on a very low standard of Christian knowledge and achievement. But Sayamalai had produced one educated man, who had gone high in government service; he had built himself a solid stone house in his native village, the one house in which it would be possible for educated women to live in a reasonable measure of comfort. Joy-Akkal and Frostie came and saw, and agreed that this was the place. The Vidivelli Ashram, the Ashram of the Morning Star, had come into being.

Some time later the sisters built a chapel on the roof of their house, with low walls, and open to the breezes on all sides. Celebrating the holy mysteries there in the early morning, one felt perfectly at one with the entire life of the village – here a woman in a courtyard pounding linseed to extract the oil, there a fine upstanding young farmer driving out his bulls for a morning's ploughing; graceful girls coming back from the well, their water-pots delicately balanced on their heads, and all the sounds and scents of an Indian village rising around one – no separation there between life and liturgy. It was always a joy to me to visit the ashram, and to become briefly a part of its multiple service of education, medical care and Christian teaching.

The ashram was able to acquire a school in one of the villages about three miles away. When the school was left for a time without a teacher, Miss Joy Solomon, MA, well over fifty years of age, walked three miles in both directions every day so that there should be no interruption in the work. On my one visit to New Delhi, I told the Viceroy, Lord Linlithgow, a little about the ashram and the devotion of its members. The grave appearance of that high-minded Scots Presbyterian concealed a sensitive spirit and a kindly heart. He was clearly much interested, and said with obvious sincerity, 'Do write me about this; it's just the kind of thing we like to know about.' I did as I was told, and it was not long before Joy-Akkal learned, to her own intense astonishment, that she too was the recipient of a silver Kaiser-i-Hind.

One of the saddest things about younger Churches is that after a time they cease to grow, and apparently cease even to want to grow. We were by this time a large family of 128,000 Christians, but the growth rate was very slow, and in many areas, due mainly to the baptism of Hindu girls who came to be married to Christian men. There was widespread suspicion of converts, many of whom were unsatisfactory and needed much loving care before they were integrated into the life of the Christian community. Certainly in one area leaders were going about, saying, 'Don't make any converts, or they'll increase your assessment' the levy made in each area for the central work of the diocese, and related roughly to the number of Christians in the area. So it was always with special joy that we learned of any movement, and of any group of people moving towards Christian faith.

I came to know of a village, Terivedali, where the entire population of about 250 people was prepared to place itself under Christian instruction. I never quite disentangled the whole story; I know that a murder came into it somewhere. But there was no reason to doubt the sincerity of the people. They were moderately prosperous farmers, and no financial inducement had been held out to them. It has to be recorded with regret that we were unable to send a qualified worker to live in the village and prepare the people for baptism. All we could do was to send a pious man of very little education, a native doctor by trade, to go and live there and to do his best. We paid him a pittance, and the people undertook to help him out with food. A great event in the life of the catechumens was the completion of their own little church, built entirely by their own hands, with low walls to keep out the dogs, palmyra trunks as pillars, and thatched with leaves from their own trees. My guess is that it was about twenty-five feet by twenty, so when all the congregation was assembled, it was pretty close quarters, even with all of them sitting on the floor. How proud they were of it! Then they said, 'We cannot have two houses of God in one village. We must destroy the old idol shrine.' The Hindus shook a warning finger at them, and said, 'Don't you touch that shrine or the spirits will be angry.' But they persisted, broke down the shrine, and brought me the spear and the bell and the little gold ornaments that had been placed round the neck of the god, saying, 'We have no use for these things any more. We thought that you might like to have them.'

And then disaster struck. Without warning their leading man died. There was no question of foul play; it was simply a straight-forward heart attack. But the Hindus said, 'We told you so. We warned you and you would not listen. Now see what has happened.' Our people passed through a time of doubt. Were the Hindus right after all? Were the old gods really more powerful than this new God to whom they had recently given their adherence? I would not have been at all surprised if the whole lot had fallen away from the faith, and gone back to the old ways. Miraculously, they held firm. Deeply perplexed by what had happened, they still said, 'What we have found is good, and we will never go back to the old darkness. We do not know why God has called away our friend, but we think that although he had not the sign [baptism], the Lord will recognise him and that he has gone to a good place.' I cannot recall any greater joy in my years of missionary work than that brought by this triumph of simple faith over adversity.

Then came the day for the great baptism of all who had so long been under preparation. Naturally we fixed it for a date after the beginning of the rainy season, in order to be sure that there would be water in the lake. In India one can usually calculate the arrival of the rains almost to a day. Alas, that year the rains were fifteen days late, and on the day fixed for the baptism, a day that could not be changed, if I was to be there, there was not a drop of water in the lake. We did the best we could. In the little square of the village there were some stone troughs; I had them filled to the brim with water. Then the people came forward in families, from old grannies bowed down by age, down to infants in arms, and I went on all through a long hot afternoon baptising and baptising. When all had come and gone, we counted up and found that 250 people had that day been added to the body of Christ. I have heard since that, through the witness of these simple people, Christian congregations have come into being in two other villages. And now, after more than a quarter of a century, they have a fine, solid church to replace their original simple structure of wooden pillars and thatch.

Early on in my episcopate I made up my mind to visit every place in which Christian worship was regularly held. There were 700 towns and villages in which daily services were held, and where each evening the bell would ring out for Evensong. There were in addition 300 smaller centres, in which a service would be held on Sundays by a visiting teacher, but in which no servant of the diocese was actually resident. Beyond these there were more than 400 villages with just a family or two of Christians, and these I naturally could not include in my itinerary. I knew the diocese very well after fifteen years of work in it, but there was much that I did not know, and it has always been my principle that planning should be based on the fullest and most accurate information that can possibly be attained.

One of the good deeds of my wealthy predecessor had been the provision of funds which made it possible to produce the first set of diocesan maps ever prepared. He paid for the materials, and gave me the money which made it possible for me to employ a clerk for the six or eight months during which the work was going on. On a smaller scale there was a large sheet showing the whole of the Tinnevelly district, with every village in which there were fifty Christians or more. There were four sheets on a large scale, on which were marked in all the villages in which it was known that there were any Christians resident. The boundaries of each parish and 'circle' were also clearly shown. This, I have to admit, was a purely Anglican effort; to complete the work, we ought to have been able to show the work of the other missions, and particularly of the Roman Catholics, who were strong in certain areas. But we simply had not the resources for the collection of the necessary information, and we felt that we had done rather well in completing even the Anglican section of the work. We could now at least see at a glance where we were, and form some estimate of what remained to be done.

There were thirty-one circles or rural deaneries in the diocese. I reckoned that it would take an average of ten days to visit one area; if I could tackle four in a year, I should be through in eight years, and there would be available a record of the diocese and all its work such as had not existed for many years.

The enterprise was undertaken as scientifically as our limited means permitted. I sent out a set of more than eighty visitation questions; where these were carefully answered, I started with the advantage of an outline picture of the area to be visited. I tried to arrange for a visit to all the schools to ascertain what was actually being done in the way of religious education. This, however, ran into difficulties, owing to the unwillingness of the clergy to permit inspection of their schools by the comparatively young and up-to-date inspectors whom I wanted to send into their domains. Each tour was carefully planned in advance, so that nights would usually be spent in the more important centres, whereas shorter halts could be made at smaller villages in the course of the day's travelling. Each visitation ended with a day spent in the company of all the clergy and teachers in the area, to discuss the problems that had arisen in the course of my travels. My aim was that each priest and each teacher should feel himself to be part of a great and living fellowship, of which the bishop's presence was the outward and visible sign, and that the work of each part was of concern to the whole. Most important of all, I wrote up in the evening a careful diary of all that I had seen and heard.

It has always been a matter of great regret to me that I was never able to finish my visitation. I still think that the plan was excellent; but the end of my service in India came before the visitation had been completed; the fragmentary records are all that remain of the enterprise.

All that I have written so far has dealt with my work in the somewhat narrow confines of a single diocese, but it was not possible for me to disengage myself from the demands of the Church on a rather wider scale, nor in fact did I desire to do so. I soon found myself in the full stream of these Christian activities on a national and international scale.

The first of my external activities had begun a little earlier and before I became bishop. I had devoted myself so fully, indeed exclusively, to work among Indians, Christian and non-Christian, that it had never occurred to me that I might have things to say that would be of interest to missionaries and other European Christians. It was, therefore, with some surprise that I received an invitation to give three addresses at the 1937 missionary conference at Kodaikanal, on the general subject of the presentation of the Christian faith in the modern world. It had become almost the rule for the missionaries to spend a month or more in the hills to avoid the burning heat of the plains in April and May. Naturally they used to meet for mutual edification, and for consultation on the innumerable problems that arise from missionary work. There were two types of assemblies; the conventions were rather strictly of the Keswick type, 'for the deepening of the spiritual life'; the conference was more interested in theology, and in practical problems of education and of the life of the Church. It was from the latter of these that my first invitation had come.

Many missionaries, deeply disturbed by the liberal theological approach of the 1920s and 1930s, were asking, 'Have we a gospel to preach?' It seemed that my frank acceptance of critical methods, together with rather conservative conclusions, helped my hearers to answer in the affirmative. To my surprise I found that I was on the map as a speaker on theological subjects to missionary audiences. Almost inevitably I was pursued by the invitation to take the major series of five addresses at the Kodaikanal Conference of 1938.

It had become clear to me that what was wanted by many missionaries, especially by the women, who had not had very much theological training, and who in the course of their service had become aware of the gaps in their preparation, was plain down-to-earth talk about the very basis of our Christian faith. So I decided to treat the first five clauses of the Apostles' Creed. These lectures became a book, *Beliefs*. The next year I was asked again, and took the first section of the Creed. These lectures were the source of the book called *Foundation Beliefs*; this has had an equally long life, being repeatedly reprinted also.

To break into the other tradition, that of the more pietistic conventions, was a far more difficult task; but this too was eventually brought about. I was invited to give the Bible readings, and prepared some informal expositions of the Epistle to the Romans. The resulting book, *The Wrath and the Peace of God*, had the honour of being quoted in the report *Towards the Conversion of England*. From that time on my participation in the convention became a regular annual event, and I never had any complaint that the stricter among my hearers felt that their faith was being undermined.

Naturally, as Bishop of Tinnevelly, and therefore a member of the Standing Committee of the Province, I had to play an even fuller part in the central life and administration of the Church of India, Burma and Ceylon. Records of committees are inevitably tedious, and I do not propose to weary the reader with them. I do wish, however, to place on record my recollections of the spirit of our meetings, and of what can only be called the loving fellowship that existed among the bishops of my time. We knew that we did not agree about everything; there were among us wide differences of temperament and churchmanship, as well as of intellectual ability. But we were able to talk to one another freely, and I can recall no occasion on which there was any trace of acrimony in our discussions. Above all, we were loyal to one another; if we had talked a matter over and decided, then the decision would be accepted and carried out by every member of the Episcopal Synod, and the same spirit of loyalty was transmitted to all the dioceses.

Naturally, I retained my membership of various committees, and in particular of the Joint Committee on Church Union. I have already commented on the years of frustration through which we passed. The man who touched the log and released the jam was not one of the great prelates and leaders whose names have appeared so often in these pages, but the quietest of Methodist missionaries, the Revd T. R. Foulger, at that time Principal of the Meston Training College for teachers in Madras, a man so modest and humble that I cannot remember any other occasion on which his voice was heard in the committee. If anyone doubts the reality of the Holy Spirit, let him consider the strange phenomenon of this man being chosen out of all the rest to make at that moment the speech that changed the history of the Church. As was his nature, he spoke very quietly, and simply told us that we had talked long enough, and that the time had come for action; we must go back to our Churches and tell them now that they must face the challenge and say yes or no to the Scheme that had been so carefully prepared and so long debated. We all knew that we were listening to the voice of God, and that we must obey or perish.

This did not mean any immediate or precipitate action. A long and complex process of voting had to be gone through in all the Churches. Anglicans had to correspond all round the world to find out what would be the attitude of all the other Anglican provinces to us, if we entered into the union. But it was clear that I must summon the Tinnevelly diocesan council to meet in February 1944, and that we must then play our part in the making of the great decision. The intervening year must be spent, not in propaganda on behalf of the Scheme, but in intensified effort to bring home to all sorts of people, clerical and lay, the issues on which a decision would have to be made, and the consequences that would follow on the decision, whichever way it went.

One new task imposed on me by the Church was membership of the National Christian Council of India. The National Missionary Council of 1912 had been replaced in 1922 by the National Christian

Council, one of the rules of which was that at least half the membership must be Indian. Willy Holland, who had been a member of both, once told me that though man for man the Missionary Council had been the abler body, the Christian Council was far more effective, since it was beginning to learn the art of speaking with a genuinely Indian voice. Increasingly the government was coming to recognise that the Christian Council spoke for the non-Roman Churches of India. It was steadily gaining the confidence both of missionary societies and of Indian Churches. It was as a secretary of the Christian Council that Charles Ranson, later General Secretary of the International Missionary Council, began to reveal his great gifts as a thinker, orator and writer.

A meeting of the NCC brought me one of the most touching incidents in my years of service in India. The Council divided into two to draft reports on questions of importance at that time, and I found myself vice-chairman of the section which was to discuss and report on the attitude of the Church in times of political crisis – a thorny subject, if ever there was one. It happened that our chairman had to go away half-way through our work. So, at the next session I suggested that we should elect a new chairman, who ought, of course, to be an Indian. They looked at me in some surprise, and then someone said, 'Why in the world? You are one of us. Just stay where you are,' a sentiment which seemed to be generally approved. It seems always to be my fate to compose important documents in a hurry and directly on to a borrowed and abominable typewriter. This was no exception to the rule. I managed to get the report out on time, and it was accepted almost without a change. We tried to lay down the conditions under which Christians might find it necessary, regretfully and courteously but quite finally, to indicate to a government that the point had been reached at which they could no longer obey its orders. I do not think that it was an epoch-making document – no doubt it reposes somewhere unread among the archives of the NCC; but it was an impressive example of the way in which harmony can be preserved among Christians, even when very divergent points of view contribute to the discussion.

I was also responsible for bringing upon myself the heaviest of all my extra-curricular burdens – participation in the revision of the Tamil Bible.

The first Tamil translation of the New Testament had appeared as long ago as 1714, the first version to be made in any Indian language. This, and the Old Testament which followed upon it, had been revised a number of times. Unfortunately, however, the

Churches had not been able to agree on the use of a single version; most of the Protestant Churches used the Union Version of 1869, whereas the Lutherans continued to use a revision of the version produced by Fabricius in 1744. The Union Version was a solid and conscientious piece of work, but it was made just at the wrong time, before modern texts of the Greek New Testament, based on the most ancient manuscripts, had become available. Moreover, there was much in it, which, although intelligible to Christians through long use, would sound strange to a Hindu ear. There was also a rather clumsy Roman Catholic version, made in the nineteenth century, but this hardly entered into consideration.

Not long before I reached India the decision had been taken to set to work on a new version, in the hope that it might be possible to produce a Bible that would be acceptable to all. The work was put into the hands of Dr L. P. Larsen of the Danish Lutheran Church, an excellent scholar with a wide knowledge of Tamil, both classical and popular. He was to be helped by a well-known Indian Christian pandit. The work went on slowly for a number of years, and then the Bible Society produced a tentative edition of the new Bible for the consideration of the Churches. We took to using this in the services at the Theological College in order to test it out. There was much in it that was excellent. Nevertheless, as time went on, I became more and more dissatisfied with it. The poetical books had been translated into a kind of pseudo-Tamil poetry, keeping some poetical rhythms but not following any recognisable metrical scheme. The result was in many cases a rather rough paraphrase, bearing little relation to what the Hebrew really meant, and losing far more in intelligibility than was gained in beauty of expression. It was clear that again and again the pandit had translated the English version without any regard for the demands of Tamil idiom, and Larsen, being a modest and humble man, had held his peace when his partner assured him that this was perfect Tamil.

Then, in 1938, we were warned that the Bible Society was about to produce the definitive edition. I felt that this could not be allowed to pass without protest, so I wrote a letter to the Bishop of Madras, as President of the Madras branch of the Bible Society, setting out, with examples, my concern as to the inadequacies and imperfections of the proposed version. He shared my letter with the Bishop of Dornakal, who agreed that my points were unanswerable. I was not popular in Bible Society circles, since halting the process of publication cost them £8,000.

It was clear that something had to be done. By this time Larsen had left India and his colleague had retired from active service, so a new start had to be made, and in many ways. A new committee was formed, four Indians and four foreigners, under the chairmanship of the Revd C. H. Monahan, a Methodist, whose whole adult life had been spent in South India, and whose diligence and attention to detail were exemplary. We were given one year in which to complete 'the revision of the revision'. I did not at the time give expression to my view that this was completely illusory. In point of fact more than seven years had passed, and I had left India, before a group of tired men stood round and sang the doxology, having completed the revision of the last verse of the book of the prophet Malachi.

We used to meet four times a year for nine days at a time – and forty days a year out of the time of a busy man is too much, as I was to discover; but I enjoyed the work so much and regarded it as so important that I felt that this was one of the things that could not be cut out of my timetable. This was perhaps the most interesting work that I have ever undertaken; it was certainly also the most exhausting.

We have now reached the year 1943. It was clear that I was becoming seriously overtired. I had been nine years in India with only ten weeks in England. Insomnia was becoming an increasingly harmful plague. It was difficult for me to get a real holiday in India, as work followed me to the hills, and it was almost impossible to refuse all the preaching and speaking engagements that crowded in upon me. So I weighed seriously the possibilities of getting back to England. This was not completely impossible; a few people were getting home. But the passage was dangerous and submarine sinkings were many; on balance it seemed to me wiser not to take the risk. At this point George Barnes, Bishop of Lahore, sprang in with what appeared to be a practical suggestion. Why should I not come to Lahore for the Holy Week and Easter services, and then go on for a long holiday in Kashmir? This seemed an excellent suggestion, though, as will be seen, the results of my accepting it were not as beneficial as we had hoped.

Lahore that year was very kind. Summer temperatures there can be terrible; but in 1943 the hot weather came late, and we enjoyed weather like that of early June in England. This was a part of India that I had never previously visited, and there was a great deal to learn. The hospitality of the Barnes family was delightful. Congregations in the beautiful cathedral were excellent, and there was a feeling of response and appreciation in the air. The addresses I gave during the week were published in a little book, *The Challenge of Jesus Christ*, which some years later had the honour of being used by the BBC in its morning religious programme *Lift Up Your Hearts*.

Then came the journey to Kashmir. When the bus emerges from the tunnel at the top of the Bani Hal Pass, to the whole vale of Kashmir and the Himalayas away to mighty Nanga Parbat, it is surely one of the great moments in any life of travel. Kashmir is, in my opinion, the most beautiful country in the world; but as it has been so often described, I do not propose to say much about its beauties.

I spent a month trekking with Gilbert Hort, a most promising young missionary, a grandson of the great New Testament scholar, who was shortly afterwards taken from us by an untimely death.

After Gilbert and I parted company, I pitched my tent in the open cirque of Aru, about 8,000 feet above sea-level. I had brought a great deal of work with me, and the pure holiday of the trekking period was at an end. I had undertaken to make a thorough revision of the Tamil text of Deuteronomy for the Bible revision committee. I was writing a considerable book in Tamil on the Reformation. I was writing up the addresses I had given in Lahore Cathedral. I was writing my second charge to the clergy of the diocese; this was, as it happened, never delivered, but was published under the title *Ecclesia Anglicana*. My idea of real missionary hardship is to sit outside one's tent, when the day's work is over, watching the alpine glow fade from the snow mountains at the far end of the valley, with in front of one a roaring bonfire built up from stray wood gathered from the adjoining forest, with a cup of tea to one's right hand, a plate of fresh apricots to one's left hand, and an interesting book upon one's knee.

These months were not entirely free from pastoral obligations. A number of missionaries were camping in the Aru cirque, and naturally they looked to me to lead them in regular Sunday worship. We used to meet in the tent of my old friend Miss Birdseye of the Methodist Mission; sometimes there would be as many as twenty communicants on a Sunday morning. Then some of the missionaries asked for an evening of Bible study each week; so eight or ten of us met once a week in my tent for a somewhat intensive study of the Epistle to the Hebrews.

The days were passing, and eventually it was time to turn homewards. But my way did not lie directly back to Tinnevelly. I had decided to pay visits to the South Indian Christians in a number of cantonments along the way who felt lonely in North India, where the language is so different, the food unpalatable, and the prejudice against Christians much greater.

In all I visited eleven cantonments, staying in most cases with the general or brigadier in charge. Quite a large volume could be written on my experiences during that month. I will illustrate by picking out a few episodes which stand out with special clarity in my memory.

At Ambala, a great centre of the Indian Air Force, it had been arranged that I should hold a service in Tamil in the early morning, and a service in English in the evening. But it turned out that many of the Indian airmen had flying duties in the morning, so they were invited to come in the evening instead, and when we entered the church I found that the Indians slightly outnumbered the Europeans. We decided on a sandwich service, with more or less alternating sections in the various languages. So, after the chaplain, Evan Claydon, had read from the Gospel of John in English, I followed by reading the same passage in Tamil. To me the interesting thing was the strained attention with which the British airmen followed my reading; clearly for the first time in their lives it had come home to them that the gospel could mean the same to men of an entirely different race as it did to them, and in a language of which they could not understand a single word.

Then there was the place where we had announced an early morning Communion service, and I arrived expecting to find twenty or thirty pious souls awaiting me quietly in church, to find instead a mob of about three hundred laughing and vociferous sepoys struggling to get in through the narrow door of the garrison church. I ascertained later what had happened. A whisper had gone round the cantonment that some units were not being co-operative in the matter of releasing soldiers to attend any service. This reached the ears of the Senior Station Officer, who did not care in the least about Christian services, but did care a great deal about orders being obeyed. So the telephone wires around the cantonment went red-hot, and the chaos at the church door was the result: every unit had produced every man, boy and dog that it could. Having got them inside, the next thing was to decide what to do with them. I first got them separated out according to language, and found that they spoke eight languages and belonged to ten denominations from Roman Catholic down to Salvation Army. I got them singing in turn – almost every Indian Christian knows by heart a few lyrics in his own tongue – and this made them feel at home. Then we launched out on the Communion service. I read the service in a mixture of Tamil and Malayalam, having been prudent enough to bring my Malayalam Prayer Book with me. I read the Epistle in Malayalam and English, the Gospel in Tamil and Urdu, of which my knowledge is limited to the fragments picked up in Kashmir; I then preached in Tamil, and translated my own sermon into English; the local padre put the English into Punjabi, and we felt that everyone got something.

And so to Nagpur, where I was the grateful guest of the Irish bishop, Archie Hardie, and his doctor wife. On Sunday I was to go out to a cantonment about twelve miles away and preach at both the Tamil and the English service. Early in the morning a gleaming military car arrived. But it soon appeared that the driver had had the minimum of training; rain was teeming down, the road was greasy, and I was absolutely certain that before long we should have an accident. We did not have to wait long. The car slewed right across the road and collided with a tree; the tree kindly fell down, its roots having been weakened by the heavy rain, so the impact was much less than it might have been. I got out of the car shaken but unhurt and exceedingly angry. If I go out to take a service, I take a service. I was wearing one of the exceedingly fetching light purple cassocks in casement cloth to which the Bishop of Travancore and I had taken in imitation of the Syrian bishops. I took off the cassock and stuffed it into my robe-case, put up my umbrella, and stumped off down the road, expecting that before long I would be able to get a lift. But, when it rains in India, everyone just stays in bed. There was little traffic, and most of it consisted of bullock-carts going in the wrong direction. At last I saw a bicycle. I compelled the rider to dismount, and explained my need. Miraculously he spoke English, and was most courteous, but said very firmly that he himself was in a hurry and could not possibly lend his bicycle. 'But,' he said, 'there is a bicycle in that house over there, and I think the owner would be prepared to lend it for a consideration.' I viewed this prospect with some horror, remembering some of the abominations that I had ridden in India in my time. But we sallied out together to the house, at last managed to wake the owner, and found that the bicycle was far better than I had dared to hope. Yes, the owner would be glad to lend it, but how would he ever get it back? I explained that I was only going to the cantonment five miles down the road, and that he could come along any time and reclaim it. Not trusting any sepoy one single inch, he was not prepared to trust the bicycle out of his sight; he must come with me. So I mounted the bicycle and put up my umbrella. He got up on the carrier and also put up his umbrella, and in this strange style we managed to cover the remaining five miles of our journey.

The Tamil service was now well on its way. I was greeted by a horrified sexton; I told him to go and fetch the padre while the congregation sang a hymn, and explained to him my predicament. I said, 'Send to your house for dry clothes, go on with the service, and I will get changed, and then come in and preach my sermon at the end of the service.' So said, so done. Of course what I had expected was that he would produce an Indian *Veshti*, the cloth to which I was perfectly accustomed and which can be worn by any man of any size. Instead, trousers arrived; but fortunately the padre was unusually tall for an Indian, and after three months on the mountains of Kashmir, I was exceptionally slim. So all went well; I preached my Tamil sermon, and took the English service, and then proceeded to the house of the colonel, where I was to have lunch.

He was a good deal taken aback by the scarecrow appearance of the Lord Bishop, and had difficulty in understanding the story of my tribulations. 'But we sent a car for you,' he said plaintively. 'Indeed you did,' I replied, 'and now go and see what's left of it.' At this, with the marvellous hospitality which was typical of the British in India, he went indoors and produced for me an exceedingly smart fawn shooting jacket, which certainly had its origin in Savile Row, and a pair of light grey flannel trousers, which might have been made for me. Thus sportingly attired, I ate an excellent lunch and was conveyed back to Nagpur in a second gleaming car.

I knew from letters that, when I got back to Tinnevelly, I should be called upon to breast a sea of troubles. In point of fact things were a good deal worse than I feared.

The first trouble arose from a bitter quarrel between two clergymen. One had succeeded the other as circle chairman of a certain area, and, on looking into the accounts, found them in a very unsatisfactory state. Unfortunately the newcomer proceeded to accuse his predecessor of defalcation. The incriminated clerk defended himself with passion. And then caste entered into it. The newly appointed circle chairman, an old student of mine and one of my closest friends in India, happened to belong to a minority group, and one to which, for no reason at all, I was supposed to be particularly partial. The other belonged to the majority community. He was a man of considerable ability and strong character. He now began to spread it all over the place that he was being victimised because he belonged to the majority group, and that under my partial rule the minorities felt that they could get away with anything. An unpleasant situation, but it should have been quite easy to sort out the tangles and to get the matter settled.

I handed it over to the chairman of the northern area, an upright but slightly lackadaisical priest from one of the so-called higher communities. He got lost in the mists of swearing and counter-swearing, and never got anywhere near the root of the matter. So just before leaving for Kashmir, I handed it over to the archdeacon, with strict instructions that the problem must be settled, and he had full powers as my commissary to do so. The letters made it plain that he had fumbled, and that the situation was worse than when I had gone away.

There was nothing for it but, immediately on my return, to take the matter into my own hands. I first asked the incriminated brother whether he would go before a diocesan court, a lengthy and cumbrous proceeding, or would accept my decision as final. Reluctant as I was to take the responsibility, I was a good deal relieved at his decision. This is not the kind of thing that a bishop ought to have to deal with himself. But by accepting consecration to the episcopate he has agreed to undertake certain responsibilities, and these cannot be evaded. I went away to the seaside for a weekend, taking with me all the documents in the case, studied them carefully, and wrote a judgement which took forty minutes to read. It was clear to me that the accused had not been corrupt, but that he had been criminally casual. Again and again no proper accounts had been kept; when they had to be shown, he had written in amounts by guesswork, and the entries did not always correspond with one another. He had been high-handed in the extreme, and when asked to explain the discrepancies had tried to carry the matter off with noise and bluster. It was probable that a certain amount of church money had disappeared in the process; but in the resulting chaos it was impossible to say exactly how much. I was in any case sure that the amount was not large enough to do the Church, even in a poor area, any serious or lasting damage.

Having finished this unpleasant and tedious job, I returned to Palamcottah and invited a number of leading people in the diocese, including two distinguished Indian Christian lawyers, to meet with me while I communicated my final decision. I naturally also summoned the person principally concerned; but through the wartime confusion in the posts, he never got my letter and failed to turn up. As I began to read, I could sense that the feeling in the meeting was dead against me – the hostile propaganda had not been without its effect, and I had been condemned in advance. I just went on quietly reading, and included in my evidence some of the letters I had received from the accused in the course of the long dispute. At one point I paused and said, 'I suppose that in the whole history of the Christian Church no bishop has ever received such a letter from a clergyman working under his care.' By the time that I reached the end of the document, opinion had swung right round. My hearers were waiting in the stillness of anxiety to hear what sentence I would impose. I would have been more than justified in suspending the offender for a year from the exercise of the sacred ministry. But it seemed to me that this was one of the cases in which mercy glories over judgement; all that I did was to order that he must repay to the funds of his previous area the small sum of money which was quite unmistakably missing from the accounts, and, in view of his obvious incompetence in matters of business, reduced him from the higher status of circle chairman to that of ordinary pastor of a parish. I could hear the sighs of relief with which this announcement was greeted.

It has to be recorded with regret that the one so judged showed no gratitude for the enormous labour that I had expended on his case, or for the mildness of the sentence imposed. He continued to assert his total innocence, and to claim that he had been the victim of a conspiracy. I am afraid that till the end of my time in India he regarded me as an enemy.

Much worse was to follow. It came to my notice that one of those in whom I ought to have been able to repose the most complete confidence was in fact doing his best to undermine my position in the diocese. This rumour came to me first through Indian friends, but I was not prepared to listen to gossip, of which there is always far too much in the Church, and took no notice of what had been told me. The evidence, however, continued to accumulate, and in the end reached a point at which it could be neither disputed nor denied. This hit me very hard.

Then I began to suffer from an agonising whitlow on the third finger of my right hand. An infection of this kind is not infrequently a sign of exhaustion. As later became clear, my state was worse than I thought; one sign of this is that for this period of my life alone I have difficulty in reconstructing the chronology, and cannot be certain that I am recording events exactly in the order in which they occurred. At times the pain was so great that I could not hold a pen in my right hand and had to sign even important documents with my left. Various doctors tried various remedies without avail. Finally, when in Madras for Bible revision, I went to the hospital and had my fingernail removed.

It was by now clear to me that I simply could not go on as I was. The holiday in Kashmir had been most enjoyable and profitable, but it had not had the desired effect of putting my health back where it needed to be. Some drastic changes must be made. I wanted to stay in India. The cause of Christ in India was my great love, and I could not imagine myself ever being separated from it. It seemed that there were two courses of action open to me. I could continue to serve as a diocesan bishop, cutting all the multifarious engagements that had made my life so full and over-full. This was work that I loved; but I felt that there were many others who could do this work as well as I. The diocese was now in excellent condition. We had weathered amazingly the shocks and strains of war. The number of clergy had increased. I had provided the diocese with an Indian archdeacon and three Indian canons. All the council chairmen, the two secretaries of the diocesan council, and the diocesan treasurer were all Indians. Bishop Azariah, coming down to visit us, said that he found a spirit of hope and confidence such as had been lacking for many years. Surely the time had come for the appointment of an Indian bishop. If I freed myself from the daily routine of a diocese, there was an immense job waiting to be done in such fields as conferences and conventions for missionaries, retreats for clergy, and above all in the development of Christian literature in fields in which it was almost wholly lacking. My books were selling well, and it was clear that there would be a demand for many more of the same kind. More important even than writing myself would be the task of getting others to write the books that were so urgently needed. I thought that perhaps I might settle in Bangalore, where the climate is much less exacting than that of Tinnevelly, help in the teaching at the United Theological College, and use all the rest of my time in these supplementary ministries.

Once again I carefully composed a letter, and placed my resignation in the hands of the Metropolitan. What I received in return was almost a cry of horror. Once again my beautifully lucid letter had been too carefully written. Westcott thought that my intention was to return to England. He therefore begged me not to make any decision in haste, above all to wait until we had been able to meet and talk things over in person. We should in any case be meeting before long at a bishops' meeting. When we met, he explained to me why he had written in terms of such urgency. He was now nearly eighty years old, and the time of his retirement was drawing near. He now revealed to me that it was his desire and hope that I would succeed him. It is strange that I myself had never once considered this possibility. If I did not want to go to Madras, ten times more did I not want to go to Calcutta, to live in a vast stone palace in that vast city, and to be weighed down by the innumerable burdens of provincial administration. And yet, as I weighed up all the factors, I could see that there was quite a strong probability that I would be elected. There is no rule in India that the Metropolitan should be elected from among the diocesan bishops, but a certain convention in that direction had been established. I still wonder whether I was not right, whether I should not have stuck to my own guidance rather than yielded to his. But it was hard to stand out against the wishes of so wise and generous a patriarch. So I put on one side for the time being the thought of resignation.

There was plenty to occupy me in the diocese, above all the preparations for our all-important vote on the question of church union in South India. This meant a carefully organised campaign, not of propaganda but of information, once again to attempt to make sure that everyone in the diocese who would take the trouble to ask, would have full opportunity to find out what it was all about, and to reach an unhurried and impartial judgement as to what the Church should do. And then the diocesan council, about 100 clergy and 150 lay people, was convened to decide the issue.

I had so planned it that we would split the debate between two successive sessions, in order that there should be no sense of haste or pressure. I have made no concealment of my deep love for the Anglican Church in India; the reader will know by now that there have been occasions on which I have found myself lost in admiration for it. This was one of the occasions for admiration. The debate to which I listened would not have disgraced the House of Lords. Speaker after speaker rose and, gravely, temperately, relevantly, and at times eloquently, discussed the pros and cons of our going into the union. I wish that those who had so often written of the poor, simple, innocent Indian Christians being misled by the wicked and unscrupulous missionaries could have been there to hear the account which these same Indian Christians gave of themselves. Nearly all the speakers were Indians, and their speeches were naturally in Tamil. At 5 p.m., after three hours of concentrated debate entirely free from acrimony, I felt that we had had enough of it, and that we should go away to think and pray.

Next morning we were at it again, from 9 a.m. onwards, and the debate continued for another two hours. Then, in the strange way that often happens, we found that we had said all that we wanted to say, and stillness fell. When I asked whether a vote might be taken, there was no dissent. So we voted. Our vote was not unanimous, but *nemine contradicente* since two members did not vote against the Scheme but felt conscientiously that they could not vote for it. So we stood and sang the doxology; the diocese of Tinnevelly was committed for good or ill to finding a new existence in the united Church of South India. It was a great day.

It was also an ill day for me. I had passed an almost sleepless night between the two sessions. This was not from anxiety; from an early point in the discussions it had become clear which way they would go, though I had no idea at the start that the vote would be so overwhelmingly favourable. It was simply the result of tiredness. To chair a great assembly, where everything is done in a foreign language, where there must be throughout the closest and most concentrated attention, is an exacting business. I could not detach myself from the business of the day. Perhaps as a consequence, I lost my temper in public in one of the committees which followed on the diocesan council. This was something that had never happened before, and I was determined that it must never be allowed to happen again. But it is not easy, as tiredness grows, to have everything under control.

The thing that finally convinced me that I could not go on was in itself trivial and would not have mattered much at any other time. I was due to go down to the cathedral two miles away to celebrate at the early Communion at 5.30 a.m. This was a service that I always loved. There would usually be between fifty and sixty communicants, all deeply committed Christians; the stillness of the early morning was most moving and most helpful to worship; the only drawback was that one came back at 6.15 with the feeling of having done a good day's work, when in reality the day was just beginning. On that occasion, not wanting to get the car out so early, I went down on my bicycle, and as I went I counted fourteen trees that had been torn up by their roots by the fierce wind of the night before. When I got to the cathedral, my glasses were not to be found; they must have fallen out of the pocket of my cassock, and were never recovered. The serious thing was that, under wartime conditions, my oculist was unable to get the glasses replaced. I could still read good English print without difficulty. But Tamil, with a number of closely similar letters, is not altogether an easy script to read, especially in the dim and uncertain light provided in the majority of our village churches. I found that the strain of my work had considerably increased; if my sight deteriorated, it would become impossible.

It was at this point that I decided to take drastic action. I wrote again to the Metropolitan, telling him that I was now convinced that I must return to England for an extended period of rest, and asked him, if possible, to secure me a passage as temporary chaplain to troops. I told him something of the darker shadows that were crowding in upon me, of which he already knew something through my refusal of the bishopric of Rangoon just ten years earlier. In my opinion an extended interregnum such as had occurred between Bishop Western's leaving India and my consecration would be harmful to the Church, and therefore it would be better for me to resign and make way for the election of a new bishop. The Metropolitan replied very kindly to the effect that he had secured for me first priority for appointment as temporary chaplain to troops, and that he had come regretfully to share my opinion that it would be wise for me to place my resignation in his hands.

No sooner had this become known in the diocese than the Metropolitan found himself deluged by an avalanche of telegrams, more than a hundred of them, which with hardly an exception said the same thing in a variety of words: that I belonged to the diocese and must in no circumstances be separated from it; if the period of recovery proved to be long, the diocese would be perfectly willing to wait as long as need be for my return.

Considerably impressed by this barrage, the Metropolitan succeeded in getting a place on an RAF plane flying southwards, and came down to judge the situation for himself. He interviewed a number of the leading people in the diocese. With one exception, all supported the evidence of the telegrams; they felt it essential that I should continue to serve the diocese; even if the period of recovery was rather long, with a good commissary and occasional visits by other bishops the diocese could not come to much harm. Naturally I was touched by these expressions of affection and confidence on the part of my fellow Christians, especially in the circumstances of the time; but I decided to keep completely aloof from these discussions. All that mattered was the welfare of the diocese, and no attention need be paid to my personal feelings or wishes. The Metropolitan then met the executive committee. It was agreed that I should go to England as planned, and keep the Metropolitan supplied with information on the medical side. Dr A. J. Appasamy, later Bishop of Coimbatore, would serve as commissary; the Bishop of Madras would come down as needed for confirmations and ordinations. This was a sensible and Christian decision. The diocese settled down to wait with eager expectation for my return.[1]

Early on the morning of my departure I celebrated the Holy Communion in the cathedral, and admitted an old friend, the Revd S. R. Gnanakhan, to a canon's stall. Although the notice had been so short, 170 communicants came to pray and to wish me well. The Metropolitan assisted me in the administration. And then it was time to go.

I was to go to Bombay to await news of my passage, but I could not go direct. In the midst of all these somewhat tense discussions I received a telegram from my sister to say that my old friend Miss Hopwood had died. A number of years previously she had been partially paralysed by a stroke, and the frustration caused to her intensely active disposition had made her difficult for Isabel to nurse. So when I went up to Ootacamund, I found Isabel exhausted. I arranged that she should attend to immediate necessities and clear up the house, and then that she should follow me to Bombay and wait until a passage became available.

I had only about a month to wait, staying in the splendid house of the Bishop of Bombay on Malabar Hill. Then the order came that I was to be on board at short notice. But Bombay emigration had made a mistake. One of the ships in our convoy left in heathen darkness, without a chaplain on board. To my ship, in peacetime a Dutch liner, they simply sent a message to say, 'Expect two padres instead of one,' without any indication of my rank or status. So when I walked on board in my smart episcopal hat, the officer commanding troops, who was a strong churchman and also knew his book of rules, turned to his second-in-command and said, 'My God, I hope that bishop hasn't come to stay!' The reader may not be aware that at that time, if a bishop was travelling as bishop, his equivalent rank was Lieutenant-General in the army, Vice-Admiral in the Navy, and Air Vice-Marshal in the Air Force. And that bishop had come to stay.

I found that the other chaplain was the Welsh canon with whom I had become acquainted at Rawalpindi during my tour of cantonments. We quickly settled down to a routine of services. These, unfortunately, were attended almost exclusively by officers. I was all over the ship, including the military hospital and the hospital for crew which I discovered deep down in the bowels of the ship. I made contact with a small group of pious soldiers, mostly of the Brethren persuasion, who were very glad to have my help as leader in their daily Bible study. I did not want to have too much to do, but these variations from mere routine gave me a good deal of pleasure.

Then one day I was sitting with three brigadiers who shared a cabin – a distinguished Indian civilian who had been drafted into the army in charge of welfare, a medical officer who had attained to the rank of brigadier, and one of the young fighting brigadiers who had earned promotion early. Discussion turned somehow to questions of religion. My answers were to their satisfaction. Then one of them said, 'It is a pity that some of the others can't share in this. These are the kind of questions that a great many of them are asking.' I replied, 'I haven't much strength to spare at present. But if you like to organise a study group, I'll be very happy to lead it.' They got to work, and very soon a group was in existence. By the end of the voyage, nearly a month later, we were meeting every day, in order to get through all the questions, with attendances varying between fifteen and thirty officers. The general spirit was excellent, not over-solemn, and at times light-hearted, but with a clear under-current of serious purpose. Many of these young men had really been through it in Burma, and were feeling a great need for some direction and purpose in life. I do not know whether I have ever carried out a more useful piece of service in my life.

Then the axe fell. We had to trans-ship at Suez. Our new host, the *Tegelberg*, was in peacetime a luxury liner, Dutch again, but had been completely reconditioned for the carrying of troops. Fresh from my floating palace, I found that I was now to share a cabin with five colonels and two majors. One could not wish for more pleasant and genial companions; but I did rather sympathise with the colonel who after two or three days remarked, 'Y'know, padre, this is really worse for us than it is for you.' Of the two young majors I have an especially affectionate remembrance, though I have never seen them again.

We sailed in convoy, and throughout the voyage performed the most graceful evasive manoeuvres. But in reality there was by this time very little danger. Every day we were hearing over the radio news of the progress of the invasion of Normandy. It was clear that the war was won, though we knew well that there still might be a long way to go before the end. So we sailed with little anxiety through the Mediterranean and the Atlantic. The coast of Northern Ireland appeared through the mist, and then we were at Gourock on a grey rainy Scots afternoon. My father was at that time Vicar of Barnwell in Northamptonshire, one of the most beautiful villages

in England, where the Duke of Gloucester has his country home.
To this I must make my way by a somewhat roundabout route.

I had been away from England for almost five years. During that
time we had seen in the picture papers nothing but photographs of
bomb devastation. We knew that there was still an England, but
we had found it impossible to form in our minds any clear picture
of what it might be like. I had hardly realised that trains still ran,
and ran on time – I would not have been surprised if we had been
sent home in cattle-trucks. As we drew out of Glasgow the rain
ceased and a bland September sun came out. We sped through the
beautiful border country, and then on into the Lake District, where
all the farms were standing just as they stood when Domesday Book
was written. I realised that much had been taken, but much still
remained. There was still an England to be lived and died for.

I had to change at Market Harborough some time in the middle
of the night, and then again at Peterborough as dawn was breaking.
So on to the little branch line that ran from Peterborough to
Northampton.

Barnwell station. I carried my suitcase the short distance from the
station to the rectory. A glorious, still, clear September morning.
No one stirring.

It was the eve of the Arnhem landing, and before long the
sky was . . . *

* The unfinished state of this part of the chapter is indicated by a break in
mid sentence. A comment found in the manuscript in another hand sums up
the situation: 'No doubt the sky was alive with aeroplanes. He never completed
this section of the book (quite). How fitting! It represented a chapter of his life
never to be completed.' After this point the manuscript is much less polished,
and considerable editorial revision has been necessary.

6

Apprentice Ecumenist

Living in my father's large stone rectory at Barnwell was pleasant enough. But this was not the purpose for which I had come home from India. I had one duty, and one only – to recover my shattered health and to return as soon as possible to a diocese which still urgently needed my services.

At that time England was not the best possible place for a recovery of health.

It was clear that the end of the war and the victory of the Allies were only a matter of time. But there were still many of the inconveniences, to put it mildly, inevitably consequent on a long period of war. Coming back after nearly five years of absence, one could not but be astonished that all the attacks of the enemy had had so little success in disrupting life in England; it was clear that the British people were very tired, but they were still their own phlegmatic, cheerful selves, with far less vindictiveness, if my observations were correct, than in the First World War, and still with the same impish, slightly sardonic sense of humour that enabled them so successfully to laugh at themselves – an art which has never been learned either by the Americans or by the Germans.

A much greater trial was the cold. After ten years in India with hardly a break, I needed warmth, and this was just the thing that was hard to come by. The winter of 1944–5 was terribly cold. I ordered half a ton of peat, which I happened to see advertised in one of the papers, and this helped in keeping fires in when other fuel was in short supply; but passages and lavatories were entirely unheated. Constant exposure to these temperatures undoubtedly did me a great deal of harm, though at the time one simply took what was going and tried to make as little fuss as possible.

Most serious of all was the failure of the doctors to make the careful physical checks which are usual after a long period of residence in the tropics. There is every excuse for them. A great

205

many doctors were on active service; those at home were gravely
overworked. I never manage to look ill. It was clear that I was
gravely exhausted; but there was no special reason to think that
I was also suffering from physical ailments. It is astonishing that
I was never tested for amoebic dysentery; only ten years later
was it established that I was suffering from amoebiasis, and this
not as a result of any initiative of doctors, but an inspired guess
of Isabel's, confirmed by tests at the Tropical Diseases Hospital,
where I eventually received treatment in 1954, after all those years
of debilitation and exhaustion.

So the months passed, spending a good deal of time at Westcott
House, Cambridge, where my childhood friend Billy Greer was
now installed as Principal, working on my favourite subject, the
history of Christianity in India, helping my father at Barnwell,
and undertaking a small amount of speaking and preaching – it
was obviously wise to avoid anything that could cause mental or
nervous strain. But recovery was very slow, and was not helped by
long spells of insomnia again.

One personal loss added to the mood of depression from which
I was finding it hard to escape. The Bishop of Calcutta had written
to William Temple, by now Archbishop of Canterbury, and I had
received in Bombay an extremely friendly letter from William,
telling me to come and see him as soon as I reached England. I
accordingly wrote, but received word from his secretary that the
Archbishop was suffering from an exceptionally bad attack of gout
and was forced to cancel all interviews. I tried a second time with
like result. Then, one afternoon, the lady who was occupying a flat
in one corner of Barnwell Rectory called down the stairs: 'I think
you would wish to know that the Archbishop of Canterbury has
just died.' My heart stood still. William was only sixty-two, and
still at the height of his powers. He seemed to be the one man in
Christendom who could not be spared. And to me he had been a
most cordial and kindly friend. He had been receiving my regular
circular letters from India, and, as I learned afterwards from Mrs
Temple, had always read them with concentrated interest. More
than any other man in England, he was the one to whom I would
have turned for help and guidance in those difficult days.

The first public occasion I attended after reaching England was
the funeral of William Temple, in Canterbury Cathedral, carried
out with all the beauty and dignity for which that great place of
Christian worship is famous. It was a remarkable gathering of old
friends, long kept apart by the tides of war. We went home with a

great feeling of consolation, after a celebration entirely matching his glorious sense of humour. The next time that I was in Canterbury Cathedral was for the enthronement of Geoffrey Francis Fisher as the ninety-ninth Archbishop of Canterbury.

During all these months medical reports of various kinds were going to India, and I could sense the increasing perplexity in which the venerable Bishop of Calcutta found himself caught up. I knew that he was exceedingly anxious for my return to India, being convinced that the Church of India had need of my gifts. On the other hand, he was being subjected to strong local pressure not to delay any longer, but to provide for the needs of the flock in South India by making provision for my replacement as Bishop of Tinnevelly. I had conscientiously left the decision in his hands. He would listen to other voices, and to their opinion as to what was for the welfare of the Church in India.

I knew exactly when word of his decision would reach me. Once again I was travelling through the Thames valley, one of my favourite areas in beautiful England, this time on a visit to Bishop Whitehead, who had been Waller's predecessor in the bishopric of Madras. As brilliant as his brother A. N. Whitehead, the philosopher, Henry had been one of the great champions of the movement among the 'outcastes' which had brought many thousands of poor and illiterate people into the Church of Christ in India. Now, at ninety-five, he was still perfectly lucid in mind and understanding, though obviously physically frail. Whitehead was fifty years older than I; but I realised that for me, as for him, from now on my ministry to the Church in India must take the form of intercession and not of active participation. It was exactly as I had anticipated. The next day I received a cable from the Metropolitan, telling me that it was his considered judgement that I should not attempt to face again the rigours of the exacting climate of South India, and that I should find my place in the service of Christ in England.

Although I had long foreseen this result, it was not altogether easy to accept. For twenty years I had lived India and breathed India and loved India; I had never had any other idea than that, when the time came, I would lay my bones there, as my parents and elder sister have done. It was not easy to come to terms with the idea that I would once again have to take my place in a Western world from which I had grown away, and in which in many ways I no longer felt at home.

Once it was known that I would not be returning to India, and would therefore be 'on the market', there was no lack of openings and calls to serve in one capacity or another. Many friends made no secret of their desire that I would settle down in Cambridge and make the teaching of theology my main activity for a number of years, but there was no area of Christian theology in which I could regard myself as expert. A man is not likely to be happy in a job, if he is constantly coming short of the minimum requirements of efficiency which his own conscience imposes on him. The unduly flattering opinions of my friends did not avail to overcome the profound inner uncertainty. I decided regretfully that Cambridge was not for me.

While I was in this state of indecision, a letter came from Geneva to ask whether I would consider taking part in the preparations for the first Assembly of the World Council of Churches (in process of formation), which it had now been decided to hold in August 1948. There seemed to be a great deal to be said in favour of acceptance. I had for many years been intensely interested in the movements which had led in 1936 to the decision to form a World Council of Churches. It seemed likely that my long experience in the formation of the Church of South India might be of value. My gift for languages might be of service, though, oddly enough, those who sent me the invitation were entirely unaware of this aspect of my capacities. I consulted the Archbishop of Canterbury. At that time he was still hoping that my health would recover to the point at which I might be able to consider appointment to an English diocese, but agreed that a period of ecumenical service might be an admirable bridge period between an India which was now irrevocably in the past, and service in the Church of England which might lie beyond the immediate horizon. There was one difficulty. It was now April 1946. I had various commitments in England which would make it impossible for me to take up residence in Geneva earlier than June 1947. I wrote to Geneva to explain, and thought that this would mean an immediate withdrawal of the invitation. To my surprise I received the answer that this would make no difference at all, that a great deal of the work could be done just as well in Cambridge as in Switzerland, and that, though not as yet resident at World Council headquarters, I could regard myself as fully committed to the ecumenical cause.

So in August 1946 I found myself taking part in the meetings held at Girton College, Cambridge, at which the Commission of the Churches on International Affairs was brought into being, and the plans were made for the first Assembly to be held at Amsterdam. A number of fragmentary memories come back from that first large ecumenical meeting after the end of the war.

I made an urgent plea that the Assembly should be held in 1949, and not in 1948. All experience shows that three years is the minimum time that has to be allowed for the preparation of an international assembly. I was immediately overruled. The Assembly had been planned for 1941; when people had already been waiting for so long, it was not possible to keep them waiting any longer. I am still sure that I was right. When one compares the volumes written in preparation for the earlier assemblies with the Amsterdam series, an air of amateurishness hangs over the latter. After the long separation of the war, the participants did not know one another. We had to gather helpers from all over the world, and time was too short for us to develop a common understanding of what it was that we were trying to do. Moreover, the whole Anglican world would be absorbed in the preparations for the first Lambeth Conference to be held for eighteen years. As so often, my voice was a lone voice; but it is not always the majority that is right.

We ran at once into the appalling ecumenical problem of the diversity of languages. English, French and German have developed a somewhat similar vocabulary, and it is this in fact that makes translation from one language to the other so exceedingly difficult. The obvious word will hardly ever do, and grave misunderstandings can arise when less than the necessary care is bestowed on thinking out exactly what is meant, and on finding the rendering which will exactly reproduce that meaning. The problem, which still continues, has bedevilled a great deal of ecumenical writing and thinking across the years, and has mutilated the English language by introducing a horrible product, to me almost unreadable, known as ecumenical English, which was already with us in Cambridge.

Many things had to be attended to before I could cross the Channel and take up residence in Geneva; for the first year my participation in ecumenical preparations could be no more than part-time work.

In the first place, I had to give my long-deferred Hulsean Lectures on forgiveness. This was a subject which had long interested me. I had come to the conclusion years before that the flaw in most presentations of the Christian doctrine of the atonement was that they attempted to find a place for law in the world of grace, or alternatively for grace in the world of law, and that this cannot be done without a grave distortion of both the main terms. These two worlds are separate from one another and operate on entirely different principles; that is why, in the New Testament, the passage from one to the other is so constantly expressed in terms of death and resurrection. Forgiveness is not unknown among men, though in its pure form it is a rarity. I felt that much could be gained by an exact analysis of what happens when one man freely forgives another. Doubtless there is much in divine forgiveness that goes beyond the furthest limits of what is possible for men; but, if the doctrine of the incarnation is to be taken seriously, there must be some truth in the *analogia fidei*, which sees in the human at its highest some faint reflection of the divine. So, in my course of lectures, the death of Christ as the reality of divine forgiveness was not brought in until the fifth of six lectures. The first lecture was called 'Life in the kingdom of forgiveness'.

Next came my first crossing of the Atlantic, to attend the Whitby Conference of the International Missionary Council. After a gruelling flight, we arrived in New York eight hours late, in the dark. After my long years in India, I was still not at home in the great cities; and having heard so much of the speed of life and traffic in New York, I landed in a state of considerable apprehension. When I had secured a taxi and settled down for the longish journey into the city, the driver confounded me by asking whether I wanted Broadway in the city or some other. I had no idea that there was any other, and had no idea what to say; however, we opted for the city, and in time the Gothic buildings and impressive tower of Union Theological Seminary rose upon our sight.

It was one thing to find Union Seminary; it was another to get inside. My taxi and I drove all round the building, without finding anything that promised to be an accessible entrance. At length we found a pair of students sitting on the steps eating ice-cream. I approached them politely, and explained that I was looking for the President, Dr H. P. Van Dusen, my friend of Tambaram days, and received the rather daunting reply, 'Well, you won't find him, he's in Yarrage.' A little pressure procured the necessary information, and before long I was sitting down to a much-needed steak in a Mercian restaurant, and beginning to enjoy hospitality as it is so lavishly provided everywhere in America.

Two days later we moved on into Canada for the International Conference. The International Missionary Council was always wise and fortunate in the choice of places for its great conferences. Whitby is a charming small Ontario town rather less than thirty miles from Toronto; there, in a most respectable girls' school belonging to the United Church of Canada, we were installed far from the noises and temptations of the great world. This was a small conference, not more than 170 participants; its doings were overwhelmed by the first great Assembly of the World Council of Churches in the following year, and its importance in the history of the Church has never been fully recognised. This was the first occasion after the end of the Second World War on which Christians from many lands were able to meet and to consider the task of the Christian mission in a changed world. Here, for the first time, the representatives of what we now call the Third World were equal in number to those from the older and more powerful Churches; and here again, to my delight, were the Germans whom I had met briefly at Girton, Cambridge, in 1946, when they were still suffering from severe malnutrition but rejoicing in the ecumenical fellowship that sustained them in the war.

The organisation of the conference was in the skilled hands of Dr C. W. Ranson, formerly of South India, and in 1947 the research and study secretary of the IMC. This is certainly one of the best conferences I have ever attended. The programme was not overloaded. The two Sundays were left, as is right, for rest, worship and fellowship. When it was all at an end, Dr Diffendorfer of the Methodist Church remarked, 'This is the first conference of this kind that we have ever ended up without being completely exhausted.'

It must not be supposed, however, that we did not work hard. I had been given the responsibility for one of the major addresses at the conference. Ranson, who knew me well from South India days, had pushed this through in the face of considerable opposition. I was still to a large extent an unknown man. I had never held an executive position in any of the great missionary societies or international organisations. I had been too busy in India to write much, and too tired since my return from India. But Ranson pressed his point and the choice was made. My theme was 'The Church in a revolutionary world'. We did not know at the time quite how revolutionary the world had become, but we did recognise that the long-established domination of the West had finally come to an end, and that the whole situation of the Church and its mission in the world had to be thought out afresh. In my address I maintained that the Church is always the revolutionary society, and that in so far as it loses this character it ceases to be genuinely the Church; it should, therefore, experience no difficulty in finding itself at home in a revolutionary world. It must, however, always be borne in mind that the Church is called to be wholly identified with the world in its needs but wholly independent of it in its desires. Many recent troubles in the Church have been due to failure to pay proper attention to this principle.

At various points in the conference I had shown some skill in drafting. Now the *disjecta membra* of several discussions were thrown into my hands with the command to reduce them to one coherent statement. The result was the document 'Christian Partnership', which was adopted with few changes by the conference. Our choice of the term 'partnership' has been rather extensively criticised by those who have not taken the trouble to ascertain what we meant by the term. We did not mean the kind of human agreement, which can equally be dissolved by agreement. The phrase was 'partnership in obedience', and the operative part of the phrase is 'in obedience'. All Churches are called to obedience, but not all Churches are called to exactly the same kind of obedience. A tiny Church in a Muslim country may serve as an example and as an inspiration to much larger Churches, but it cannot take upon itself the same tasks as can be undertaken by far larger and stronger Churches in countries which at least in name are Christian. Spiritual equality does not necessarily mean identity of responsibility. We saw the task as one; we hoped to work out at least in outline some guidelines for a harmony of different parts and instruments.

Then a heavier task fell on me. I was asked to draw up a statement which could serve as the main report of the conference, and indicate our general understanding of the new world in which we were called to work and witness. Usually such reports come into being through long and wearisome editorial sessions, and in consequence all too often end up by saying nothing at all. There is much to be said for committing the whole work of drafting to a single individual, who, by divine inspiration, may catch the mind and mood of an assembly and may translate it into intelligible form. I had followed the sessions closely and had a variety of notes and memoranda; nevertheless, I knew that to fuse all the work of two weeks into one synoptic vision would be a formidable task.

It would be hard to imagine less favourable conditions under which to work. I had no typewriter of my own with me, and was set down in front of a machine of venerable aspect and formidable size, the action of which was quite unfamiliar to me. I started work at 9 p.m. As I completed and corrected each sheet, it was snatched from my table and carried off to the duplicating room. An admirable lady, one of the few Anglicans on the staff of the school, brought in alternately coffee and orange juice to sustain my flagging strength. At 1 a.m. I sank thankfully into bed. At 9 a.m. every member of the conference had in his hands a copy of all the eleven sheets. On that day my luck was in. When I finished reading the text aloud, a task which took about fifty minutes, Dr Diffendorfer rose and suggested that by standing vote the report be accepted as the authentic voice of the conference. Naturally a few editorial corrections had to be made; but in the main what stands in the book *Renewal and Advance* is what was written with increasing weariness through the hours of that night.

We have been accused of taking up at Whitby an over-optimistic stance, as though the gravest trials of the Christian mission were already over and a better time would be coming. I do not think that a study of the documents bears out this opinion. We did not issue our call to 'Expectant Evangelism' in any blithe spirit of optimism, but in the conviction that the times of greatest need are also the times in which God gives special grace to his Church, and in which it is needed that courage be matched with opportunity.

No sooner was the Whitby Conference over than I had to cross the Atlantic again to take part in another great international conference, the first postwar assembly of Christian youth held at Oslo in July 1947. If the Whitby Conference was the best I have attended, the Oslo Conference was perhaps the worst. To assemble 1,700 young people from almost every country in the world, at a time at which the whole world was still suffering from the effects of the Second World War, was in itself a notable achievement. But the management of such a conference demands great skill and thoroughness in organisation, and to a large extent these were lacking. Many of the students were put up a long way from the conference centre and grew very tired with the constant coming and going. In such a conference one of the problems is always to persuade the students ever to get to bed; at Oslo the executive of the conference made the grave mistake of allowing all kinds of extra meetings to be held, some of them actually announced to be held at 10 p.m. In consequence practically all the young people were too tired to take anything in on the last three days, and the conference just petered out rather than came to a climax.

There were tense moments. This was precisely the point at which the Dutch government in Indonesia, with incredible folly, declared war on the infant Republic, in the hands of which it was already clear that the destinies of Indonesia were to lie. To have Dutch and Indonesian students together in a single conference was no easy thing. Students from many parts of the world were facing acute political problems – this was just at the beginning of the collapse of colonialism; they tended to be more interested in politics than in the more directly spiritual issues of the conference, or perhaps it would be fairer to say that they tended to identify their engagement in a particular political movement with their commitment to the cause of Christ.

It must not be supposed, however, that the conference was nothing but strains and tensions. We were greatly blessed in the weather, and the long golden days of the northern summer rolled by without a cloud. For me it was a time of meeting many old friends and making new ones. I don't know how many people meeting me since then have said, 'Don't you remember? You gave me a glass of beer at the Scansen!' – the open-air restaurant at which I seem to have spent most of my time.

My own duty in the conference was to preach the sermon at the great Sunday service in the cathedral. It would be hard to imagine a more moving experience for a preacher than to see before him a cathedral packed with this crowd of young people from almost every country upon earth. To my relief interpretation was not provided. Summaries of my sermon had been prepared in English, German and French, and, as I spoke very slowly and clearly, I had the feeling that, on the whole, my hearers were able to follow me. There had been a great deal of loose talk about the sovereignty of Christ, as though that was something that was already there and simply had to be recognised. I took the line that this sovereignty of Christ is the great reality, but a reality that is everywhere denied – in the world, in society, in the Church, and in ourselves. We cannot bring in the kingdom of God; we are called to see to it that the sovereignty of Christ is at least asserted in all these realms; but that means that we must see to it that this sovereignty first becomes the guiding principle in our own lives. When one of the students was heard to say, 'Now at last I know what we are here for,' I felt that something of what I meant to say had got across.

The intensely hot summer of 1947 wore on; September came, and with it the date at which I was to transfer myself to Geneva.

The World Council of Churches (in process of formation) had already been in existence for nine years, and since 1943 it had been directed by one man, Willem Adolf Visser 't Hooft, Wim to his friends. There can be no doubt that the formative committee at Utrecht in 1938 had been rightly guided in the choice of its first General Secretary. I do not think that any other man could have achieved what he did. But even great men have their defects. One weakness of Visser 't Hooft was his inability to form a team of colleagues working happily together as equals. He had worked successfully with men older than himself, such as John R. Mott and J. H. Oldham, but he did not know what it means to be *primus inter pares*. He must be *primus*, and preferred to surround himself with younger men, whose gifts bore no comparison with his own, but who could work effectively under his direction. In consequence, few men of ability stayed long in the service of the World Council. In the second place, Visser 't Hooft was an intellectual and not an administrator. Committee work was wonderful; many of the day-to-day operations of an increasingly large organisation were never attended to at all. So it was into a somewhat chaotic situation that I came; and some of these minor matters of business became my concern.

It is almost incredible that when I moved to Geneva in 1947, as Co-Director of the Study Department, the World Council had no regular system of appointment, did not specify the terms of appointment of those whom it called to its service, and had no salary scale. My salary was fixed, not ungenerously, after my arrival in Geneva. I was much disturbed to find that a German colleague was drawing a salary considerably less than that of colleagues who were doing the same work as he; when the attention of the General Secretary was drawn to this irregularity, his abrupt comment was, 'What has he to complain of? He's a great deal better off here than he would be in Germany.' I gradually got things in this direction put right, and, to my own disadvantage, secured the acceptance of the principle that unmarried members of staff should be paid less than the married.

There was no regular programme of worship. Each Monday morning there was a *culte* on the Reformed pattern, consisting almost entirely of a sermon, taken in turn by various members of the staff. I was soon able to change this. We set up a short period of prayer every day, ten minutes before the beginning of the day's work, devoted mainly to intercession for various aspects of the work. There was no chapel in the old set-up in the *route de Malagnou*, a defect which has been corrected in the vast new premises on the *route de Ferney*. Attendance was small, and we had to meet in an office with the minimum of atmosphere. But at least the tradition of a daily act of worship was established, and has been maintained ever since.

There was very little fellowship among members of the staff. My secretary Dorothy Grose (later Mrs Laurie) and I both spent a rather high proportion of our salaries on entertainment, in an attempt to put this right. I instituted a series of Sunday lunches, at a fairly

cheap restaurant in the city, inviting two or three members of staff
and their wives to join me. Later, when I had a tiny flat in the *route
de Malagnou*, close to headquarters, I used to invite three colleagues
in at a time for a glass of sherry after working hours were over. In six
months I had as my guests all those in senior positions, and quite a
number of those who were doing important but subsidiary jobs.

These things may seem trivial; but they are of the utmost importance if the work of a large institution is to run smoothly and
happily, and if a Christian organisation is to be something different
from an ordinary business corporation. But this was not the work
that I had come to Geneva to do. My hands were soon full with
the preparations for the first Assembly of the Council to be held in
Amsterdam less than a year after my arrival in Geneva.

The main task of these first months was to bring into shape the
second volume of the four-volume series *Man's Disorder and God's
Design*, which was to prepare the way for the Amsterdam Assembly.
Following the precedent set by J. H. Oldham in the preparations
for the Oxford Conference of 1937, the plan was that papers for the
various volumes should be prepared well in advance of the date of
publication, circulated to a considerable number of qualified readers
for comment and criticism, discussed in committee, then redrafted
by the authors before being submitted to the editors for final revision
before being sent off to the press. It was not long before we became
distressingly aware that the period allowed us for preparation was
indeed too short. After the long separation caused by the war and
by the Hitler regime, we really did not know who the best possible
authors would be. There was not time to set up the elaborate process
of co-operative thought and mutual criticism which Joe Oldham had
operated with such marked success. We had to reckon with the usual
delay in getting in material from authors. Some sent in material that
simply could not be used, and in one or two cases had to be replaced
at short notice by other writers. We lived in a whirligig of chaos
and chance.

Then came the problem of adequate translation. Here we came
up against a serious divergence of views as to policy. Visser 't
Hooft, with his extensive knowledge of languages, was able to
read almost all communications and contributions in the language
in which they came in, and never seemed able to understand the
harm done by inadequate or misleading translation. The Director
of the Study Department, Nils Ehrenström, my German colleague
Wolfgang Schweitzer and I found ourselves spending hours and
hours wrestling with the versions that came in from the translation

bureau, in the attempt to make sure that what we published represented fairly accurately what the writer meant, and that it read reasonably well in the language into which it had been translated. At that time the translation bureau was staffed entirely by women who had taken a degree in modern languages, but who were for the most part entirely innocent of any knowledge of theology, and in some cases lacked the background of general knowledge which is indispensable for work in such a bureau. The opportunity of securing as head of the bureau an outstanding scholar, Olive Wyon, one of the few women to hold the degree of Doctor of Divinity, was thrown away by sheer mismanagement. We of the Study Department made repeated pleas that the translation bureau should be staffed by young theological scholars competent in at least two languages, and that it should be headed by a man of wide knowledge and of special experience in the difficult art of translation. Many years were to pass before action was taken.

One other activity of these early ecumenical days deserves mention. With the help of Rockefeller money, the World Council first rented and later purchased the Château de Bossey at Céligny, about sixteen miles along the lake from Geneva, to serve as a centre for lay training. Hendrik Kraemer (of Tambaram fame) was persuaded to accept the position of Head of the Institute, and, in spite of frequent ill-health due to his spell in a concentration camp, gave distinction to all its early proceedings. With him were Henri-Louis Henriod, who had been General Secretary of the earlier Life and Work movement, and the distinguished biblical scholar and teacher, Suzanne de Dietrich, all three of the Reformed or Presbyterian tradition. The ecumenical movement has always, and rightly, been concerned about the part of the laity in the Church; one of the most effective sections of the work of the World Council has been its Department of the Laity. The idea was that lay people would come for a course of four months to prepare them for work and witness in the Church and in the world. The Institute was also to be used for gatherings of lay people of different kinds for interchange of thought and ideas about the particular responsibility of Christians of that group or profession in relation to Christian witness in the world.

The idea was excellent; but common sense was not very evident in the early days. Just after the war, when half of Europe was unemployed, it was fairly easy to get young people to Bossey. As the world settled down to normal working, it became more and more difficult to get lay people of the right kind – if they were professionally employed, their churches were not willing to spare them for so long a time; other young people were not willing to undertake a course which would not lead to any particular qualification. Yet, once launched, ideas seem to continue in existence through their own momentum, long after they have ceased to be valid or relevant.

I well remember attending a meeting of the Bossey Council at which a motion was very nearly passed to the effect that no further courses for theological students should be held at Bossey. Only very gradually did it dawn on those in authority that the whole idea and purpose of the Institute had to be re-thought. One of the best things it has done for a good many years has been the winter semester for theological students in association with the theological faculty of the University of Geneva. It has always proved difficult to find scholars able to spare the time required for staffing these special courses; but hundreds of students have had the opportunity of meeting the Christian Church in other forms and guises in the representatives of other and previously unknown parts of the Christian fellowship.

In the early days these problems were quite unforeseen. I used to enjoy very much going out once or twice a week to exercise my gifts as a teacher, sometimes spending the night and becoming fully a part of the group that was in residence. In those days devotional life played little part in the affairs of the Institute. The beautiful ecumenical chapel, incorporating some of the ancient structures of the Château, had not yet come into being; indeed at that time it was regarded as doubtful whether a chapel could be built to meet the needs and desires of the very different forms of Christian confession that were beginning to come together in the ecumenical movement. It may seem strange today that we were so slow to realise how vital a part must be played in the life of the movement by fellowship in worship, and by the discovery of forms of worship unknown to ourselves which have been the life-blood through the centuries of Christian confessions other than our own.

At last all the chapters of our book were in our hands, and were ready to go to the printer. No sooner had this happy day arrived than I was confronted with an entirely different kind of ecumenical work.

Churches and missions in the West had become aware of the odd fact that, though the Churches in Asia all had close connections with Churches in Europe and America, they had hardly any connection with one another; all were like the spokes of a wheel running in to the hub; there was no connection round the rim of the wheel. It was felt that the time had come when some kind of Asian organisation ought to come into being to promote fellowship and understanding in that part of the Christian world. The World Council and the International Missionary Council agreed in setting up a small conference in Manila to consider the problem and to make proposals. I had discussed the matter with Visser 't Hooft over a cup of coffee at the Oslo Conference, and it was quickly settled that I would not merely go to Manila, but would perambulate the East, selling the idea of the World Council to those Churches which knew nothing of it, and in certain cases were highly suspicious as a result of the propaganda of the already active Carl McIntyre and various anti-ecumenical groups.

Misfortune seemed to rest on that tour from the start. My plane from London was delayed for repairs. Once *en route*, the plane was diverted to Shanghai, where I had to change airlines and pay an additional $291 for a flight to Manila. Even then my troubles were not at an end, for I did not have the requisite exit visa and had to visit the Consulate-General's office in order to obtain an official letter to the effect that I was in a state of emergency. Then I had to obtain a passport photo, which involved yet more lost time and further expense.

When the plane finally touched down at Manila airport, forty-eight hours late, and out of the window I saw the purple stock of Bishop Norman Binsted of the American Episcopal Church, I knew that my troubles were at an end. He had come to meet me and to take me to his home. He also brought me good news: the conference had met on Wednesday morning and had wasted the entire day on questions of protocol. On Thursday they had taken a whole day's holiday in my honour. They were about to begin work at 9 a.m. on Friday, in the hope that I might be with them.

The Manila Conference was small, not more than about twenty of us, among whom Dr J. W. Decker of the International Missionary Council, an excellent colleague, and I, were the only Westerners; but it was seminal and prophetic of many things that have happened in the Christian world since 1948. The first thing I noticed was that, though both Decker and I were acquainted with a number of the Asian delegates, not one of them had ever met any of the others before. This division was the real reason for convening the conference; we wanted to work out some means by which the isolation of these younger Churches from one another could be overcome. The colleagues from these Churches were rather suspicious, wishing to be assured that the formation of some local organisation would not cut them off from direct access to the pure

sources of ecumenism in Geneva and New York. Once assurance
had been given on this subject, they saw the advantages of local
co-operation, and the idea of the East Asia Secretariat was born. By
working all Friday and also on Saturday morning, we got our work
done, and I was entrusted with the task of editing and printing the
minutes. This I did on my return to Shanghai.

The Manila Conference made it plain to me that the plans we
had worked out there were relevant to the whole of ecumenical development. I saw the world as made up of eight regions,
largely but not solely geographical – East Asia, the South Pacific,
Africa south of the Sahara, the Muslim world, the Orthodox world,
Europe, North America, Latin America. My plan was that for each
of these regions there should be a central office, in which not merely
Churches and missions, but also such international organisations as
the World Student Christian Federation and the Bible Societies,
and naturally the great ecumenical bodies, should be represented.
World assemblies should be held only once in ten years; in each
year there should be one very carefully prepared regional assembly;
then one blank year devoted to the co-ordination of the results of
the regional assemblies, and then the great world assembly, which
would be able on the basis of ten years of continuous study to face
intelligently and practically the changing situations in the world and
in the Church.

In Japan, Decker and I had an interview with the shy Emperor,
and with the real power in the land, General Douglas MacArthur.
In later years the General exposed himself to merciless criticism;
at the time I formed a very favourable opinion of him, and of the
great work he had done for the rehabilitation of Japan – a man of
real greatness, but with feet of clay. MacArthur talked at us for a
solid hour – one of those discourses of which, after nearly a quarter
of a century, I could reproduce whole stretches almost exactly in
the words originally spoken. He told us that, when he had been
younger, he had been able to make nothing of the story of the cross
– it seemed to him just base and horrible; but now he felt that he
was beginning to understand – if a man had got hold of the right
idea, you can kill the man but you cannot kill the idea, it will go on
into a life of its own. This is far from saying all that needs to be said
about the deepest mystery of human existence; but I felt that it was
not a bad approach for a layman unequipped with any theological
knowledge. He had much to tell us of the work that he had been
doing: the Japanese have never had it so good; they don't yet know
much about democracy, but they will never want to go back to the

old ways. Only when the General had to stop to relight his pipe did Decker, a much more ruthless interviewer than I, manage to slip in the question which was the whole point of our visit. We wanted to get some Japanese bishops out for the Lambeth Conference that same year, and other church leaders for the Assembly of the World Council of Churches; could this be arranged?

'How many?'

'Three for each.'

'Yes, that can be done.'

So we left the presence rubbing our hands and congratulating ourselves on our luck.

In Korea we saw everyone – the two American generals, the British and the American representative, leaders of all the Korean Churches except the Roman Catholic. The Churches were in a sad state of disunity, bitterly divided by the question who had and who had not collaborated with the Japanese. Of my Anglican friends, the heroic Bishop Cooper survived the terrible march into communist captivity. Father Hunt and the charming Irish sister Mary Clare succumbed. All the Korean Christians without exception said to us, 'Don't you realise that we are the front line? This is where it is going to start.'

And so through China again to Taiwan and Thailand; a few days in Singapore where the heroic Bishop Leonard Wilson chaired a meeting for me in the very YMCA building in the basement of which he had endured his horrible imprisonment under the Japanese, and provided me with the busiest Easter Sunday of my life, starting at 6 a.m. with Mattins and Holy Communion in Tamil, and ending at 10 p.m. with a nice unhurried discussion with the Bishop on the future of the Anglican Communion.

I spent a few days in South India with my parents and sister, followed by an improbable air journey to Karachi with a charming naval officer who turned out to be a grandson of Lord Simon. This led to an unexpected meeting, on board a British submarine in Karachi harbour, with Liaqat Ali Khan, the Prime Minister of Pakistan, destined shortly, like Mahatma Gandhi, to fall victim to an assassin.

When I got back to London, my first duty was to call on Dr Geoffrey Fisher, the Archbishop of Canterbury, to report on all that I had seen and done in Eastern Asia. I had seen a good deal of him over the past two years. He had inherited from William Temple a heavy load of responsibility for relations between the Church of England and the Church of South India, now already in existence.

He was grateful for the first-hand information that I was able to give him on this subject. Part of the enormous literature of that time on the problem of South India is an open letter from him to me, indicating the lines he felt should be followed in defining these relations, and the limits that he thought should be set to recognition by the Church of England of this new and highly experimental body. He had also in part taken over the responsibilities of Temple in relation to the World Council of Churches; he had been several times in Geneva, and was following closely the preparations for the first Assembly. At the suggestion of Bishop Leslie Hunter of Sheffield, the Archbishop had appointed me as his Assistant Bishop for Continental and Ecumenical Affairs; this step was important in that it made me eligible for membership of the Lambeth Conference which was to be held in June and July 1948.

It was clear that, as the one bishop with a full knowledge of everything relating to South India, I should have an exceedingly busy time at the Lambeth Conference. Before that, it was essential that I should have a holiday.

Very shortly after taking up work in Geneva, Miss Grose, my secretary, had noticed that the youth pastor of the Waldensian Church, the ancient Protestant Church of Italy, was preaching in the city, and arranged for him to come to dinner to meet me. Thus began my friendship with Tullio Vinay, a man of superlative simplicity, and one of the best and most lovable Christians I have ever known. Tullio was delighted to find that I could understand his Italian perfectly, and he could understand my English, so that there was no difficulty in communication. He told me of his great plan to draw the small communities out of their isolation by building in the Alps a great youth centre. The name Agape, 'love', had already been chosen for this youth village. Tullio showed me photographs of young Italians working strenuously with their hands, until the first snows fell, and building work became impossible. I was enchanted by his spirit and the amplitude of the project, and by the splendour of the site. I said, 'Next year I will come and help to build it.'

And so it worked out. I wrote to Tullio and said that I would like to come and spend five days. After a few days in Torre Pellice, the Waldensian centre, I was convoyed, by young American Mennonites doing relief work in the valleys, up the long Val Chisone and so to Prali, the highest of the Waldensian villages. I was quite prepared to rough it, but was a little relieved to find that there was a small inn in Prali, bare and simple and perfectly clean, in which I was to be put up.

I was made warmly welcome. But, when after lunch I turned out in shirt and shorts and explained that I had come to work, their astonishment knew no bounds. I learned afterwards that, when my letter arrived suggesting a visit, they laid it down on a table, looked at one another in amazement, and said, 'A bishop! What shall we do with him?' They were relieved to find that even a bishop has two hands, and a modest capacity for work as a navvy. The first job I was given was to work with a young Italian on re-siting the pit for the rope railway, which had been dug at the wrong angle. There I learned from him the pleasant Italian proverb, 'Fare e disfare mantiene il lavero' ('Doing and undoing, that's what keeps trade going').

For a number of years Agape played a very important part in my life; it was a place of tranquil labour and rest, away from the perplexities of ecclesiastical life. Is it just my imagination, or is it true that, if you put your hand on a wall at Agape, you can feel the love with which each stone found its allotted place, as the buildings rose like an exhalation from the slopes of that lovely alpine valley?

The five days came to an end much too soon. But in that short time of work and fun I had become completely integrated with that community of love; so much so that, as the car turned the corner and Prali disappeared from sight, I was startled to find that my eyes were filled with tears. And so, with scarred hands and grateful heart, to London and the Lambeth Conference.

Eighteen years had passed since the Lambeth Conference of 1930; the vast majority of us were new boys, and even Geoffrey Fisher, our President, had never attended a Lambeth Conference before. There were some veterans among us; our doyen was the bearded Jimmy Palmer, formerly of Bombay, the only man in history, I think, who has attended four Lambeth Conferences. For many of us it was a meeting of old friends whom we had not seen for many years. One result was that this was a highly democratic conference; anyone could speak, and everyone would be listened to, but not necessarily with equal attention and enthusiasm. There is no doubt at all in my mind as to the two prelates who made the deepest impression on their assembled brethren. Cyril Garbett, Archbishop of York, spoke rarely, but always with a weight and authority peculiarly his own. E. W. Barnes of Birmingham was anathema to the majority of the bishops, especially to the Anglo-Catholics, by reason of his ultra-liberal views; yet each time he spoke his words had a deeply persuasive power, as the expression of the faith of a profoundly Christian man. Geoffrey Fisher made on the whole an excellent chairman, with at times a little too much of the temper of the headmaster, and a certain tendency to be more deeply engaged in the proceedings than it is wise for a chairman to become.

It soon became evident that South India, and the relations of the Anglican Communion to the Church of South India, would be the main theme of the conference. Inevitably I, as the one bishop who had only recently returned from South India, was in the very forefront of the battle. Propaganda against our cause had been vocal, virulent and unscrupulous. One of the favourite gambits was, naturally, that this whole scheme had been cooked up by foreigners – alternatively regarded as old men in a hurry, or as young men in a hurry – and that the poor simple South Indian Christians had no understanding of the scheme which was being foisted on them. Something had to be done to set at rest some of these unworthy suspicions.

The temperature had soared into the nineties, and for the first time the Lambeth Conference took off its coat to do its work. So I opened my first major speech on South India with the words, 'Rising to speak in this pleasant South Indian temperature . . . ', which of course got me off to a good start. I went on to explain that my Indian diocese had been well brought up on the principles of the good Bishop Butler, whose *Analogy of Religion* had been translated into Tamil and published in monthly parts in the years 1858 and 1859 for the edification of our village workers. Naturally this light upon the poor ignorant Christians in South India brought the house down, and nothing was ever heard of them again. The reader can imagine how I developed my argument. Probability, Bishop Butler taught us, is the law of human life. We could not claim that the South India scheme was perfect; but we had wrestled and prayed over many years, and we had been led to the probable conclusion that this would work, and would bridge divisions which had never been bridged in four centuries. All that we wanted was a fair field and no favour. Let the conference keep an open mind and not be over-hasty to condemn. We in South India (though I could no longer speak as one of them) were prepared to be for some years on trial; we did not wish to force the conscience of anyone in any other part of the Anglican Communion; we did ask that we should be believed when we affirmed that it was our intention to take the full riches of the Anglican tradition into the Church of South India.

I spoke for, I suppose, about half an hour. As I sat down my old friend George Cockin of Bristol turned to me and said, 'That'll take some answering.'

There was a Committee on Union, and a Sub-Committee on South India. Naturally I was a member of both of these. And here I must record something that has never before been put on record, and for which I shall never be given credit in the history of the Church – I found myself acting as protagonist of the Anglo-Catholic cause. In view of my well-known Evangelical sympathies and the share I had taken in the formation of the Church of South India, this may sound paradoxical, and indeed it does require some explanation. Here is the explanation. In the early stages of the debates it had become clear that a majority of the bishops were in favour of immediate recognition of the Church of South India and full communion with it. If to these were added the more cautious who were generally in favour, but not prepared to go all the way, the majority would have been able to sweep away all opposition and to carry all before it.

I was determined that this should not happen. I had many friends in the Anglo-Catholic wing, and was aware of the depth of the anxiety felt by many of them as to the step which they were being invited to take into what seemed to them to be rather 'the improbable' than 'the probable'. Controversy tended to settle on questions of the ministry and of the steps taken to unify the ministry in the new Church. But, as Kenneth Kirk, the Bishop of Oxford, said to me, that was not the central anxiety of these good men; their anxiety was about the Church and its future orthodoxy. 'You tell us that this Church is orthodox today; but we know that India is a syncretistic country, what guarantee can you give us that in thirty years' time that orthodoxy will be maintained? A Church may have the best guaranteed ministry in the world; yet if it has fallen into heresy, that Church will no longer be part of the Catholic Church of Christ.' So it seemed to me essential that the fullest possible expression should be given to this point of view, that there must be no overriding of minority opinion, and that, if it were possible, we must all come together in an agreement that would express the common mind of all.

Lesslie Newbigin, who as Bishop in Madurai had taken over the northern part of my old diocese of Tinnevelly, and has brilliantly described it in his *A South India Diary*, was allowed to address the Committee on Union, and made a deep impression by his youthfulness, the glowing sincerity of his Christian faith, and the modesty of his approach. I think that, if he had been allowed to address the plenary session of the conference, a different tone might have been given to the whole of the remaining debates. But this was not permitted; we had not then so far advanced along the ecumenical path that the idea of a former Presbyterian, now bishop of the Church of South India, addressing the assembled Anglican bishops could be acceptable.

The conference conducted its affairs on the whole in a Christian fashion; but as the days went on, there were signs that deep feelings had been aroused and that tempers had become a little frayed; this manifested itself in a number of peculiar ways. It happened that Kenneth Kirk and I were both on a small committee to draft a perfectly innocuous resolution on recruitment for the ministry. When I read out what we had drafted, the conference rejected it, and sent us back to do the work all over again. I said to Kenneth, 'It is quite obvious that by now anything that I put forward will be turned down by one half of the conference, and anything that you put forward will be turned down by the other half of the conference. Let the Bishop of Burnley propose the resolution.' So the Bishop of Burnley, a charming Suffragan, a man of infinite devoutness who had not spoken once during the conference, read out the slightly revised resolution and it went through like a hot knife through butter. A little later a friend asked me, 'Why in the world did you put up the Bishop of Burnley?', and was highly amused when I explained my guileful strategy.

Hard work had gone on for a considerable time in the Sub-Committee on South India. The time had arrived for the drafting of a report. A small drafting committee was appointed, consisting of Kenneth Kirk and myself, with George Cockin of Bristol to see that Kenneth did not twist me round his little finger. I am not accustomed to being twisted round anyone's little finger, but a committee of three is generally better than a committee of two, and George's calm and temperate wisdom was of great advantage to us. Although a strong supporter of South India, and stronger than I had expected, he had not become labelled in the mind of the conference in the same way as Kenneth and myself.

It was at this point that a momentous decision was taken. It was by now even clearer than it had been that, if a straight vote was taken, the bishops favourable to South India would carry all before them; the conference would probably have gone on record as commending the South India union and the method by which it had been brought about, and as advising the several provinces of the Anglican Communion to enter at once into communion, perhaps even full communion, with the new Church. I was determined that this should not happen. Through my close contacts in the Anglo-Catholic wing, I was well aware of the possibility of actual schism, and the setting up of a separate 'Old Catholic' Church in England. But this was not the argument that really weighed with me. I have never been a believer in the verbal inspiration of a 51 per cent majority; on many subjects it seems to me that a two-thirds or even a three-quarters majority, or virtual unanimity, should be required. It was clear that we could not hope for this at the Lambeth Conference of 1948. We agreed to recommend that there should be no straight vote, but that the report should clearly state the two main opposing views (there were many fine gradations of opinion), and leave decision to a later date, when we might hope that the Holy Spirit would have led us into closer agreement than was possible in the tense atmosphere of the first year of the life of the Church of South India. Our suggestion was warmly accepted by the leaders of the majority group, though with some feelings of disappointment on the part of some of them. But in history the majority has been given no credit for this act of self-abnegation by which we refused to override the consciences of our brethren and agreed to wait for fuller light from the Holy Spirit. It has generally been supposed that the defeat of the majority was due to the intellectual power of the Anglo-Catholic wing, and the effective presentation of their case by such outstanding leaders as Kenneth Kirk and William Wand of London (who, if I remember rightly, did not speak on this issue at all!). But this is not the case; the facts were as I have described them. Though angered at times by the many misrepresentations that have appeared in print, I have never regretted that we were led to take this patient, distinguished and essentially Christian stand.

Then two disastrously unfortunate events occurred.

Geoffrey Fisher decided to take the South India vote rather late on Friday afternoon. Only after the vote had been counted did he realise that out of 325 bishops only 221 were present when the vote was taken. The missing hundred had no business whatever not to be in their places, and had no ground whatever for complaint; but it was most unfortunate that the most important vote of the whole conference should have been taken in anything less than a full house.

Even worse was to follow. One might suppose that bishops of all people would be capable of holding their tongues. But, with 325 of them present, it became clear that even this could not be counted on. One overseas bishop had talked indiscreetly and had revealed the actual voting on that Friday afternoon – 130 in favour of our report, 90 against it. The secret had been leaked to the press, and we were revealed in all the nakedness of our absentees. It was not long before rumours began to go around that the vote did not truly represent the mind of the conference. Dr A. S. Duncan-Jones, at that time Dean of Chichester, went on record in print with the definite statement that it is now known that if all the bishops had been present, the voting would have gone the other way. There is no ground whatsoever for this suspicion. Geoffrey Fisher stated emphatically that, as far as any objective opinion was possible, the vote expressed exactly the proportion of opinion in the assembly. My own feeling is that, if all had been present, the majority would have been larger. But, when it came to the point, I fancy that rather a large number of bishops felt their minds inclining towards caution. Geoffrey Fisher may well have been right. What is certain is that our report was accepted by a substantial majority, and that the general opinion of the Anglican Communion, as represented by its bishops, was favourable to what had been done in South India.

So the long conference came to an end. We began the conference with a bad sermon from Henry Sherrill, Presiding Bishop of the Episcopal Church in America; like so many preachers called to utter in awe-inspiring places such as St Paul's Cathedral or Westminster Abbey, he felt that he had to say all he knew, and it just did not come off. At the end we had a simple but most effective sermon from Cyril Garbett, in which he said that, though the Church might be passing through its dark night, the Lord was the Lord of the darkness as well as of the light. And so we parted, some to go back at once to their dioceses, others to take some holiday, yet others to face the further ordeal of the first General Assembly of the World Council of Churches.

It is hard to assess the value of such great assemblies. Lambeth 1948 yielded to the temptation, common to all ecclesiastical gatherings, of passing resolutions on every subject under heaven, most of them not worth the paper on which they were written. There were far too many reports, most of which there was no time either to digest or to discuss. Yet I for one have no doubt that, given certain modifications in planning and administration, such great conferences have a part to play in the life of the Church. We met one another again. We were able to reaffirm the genius of Anglicanism, and at the same time to set the Anglican Communion moving in a new direction of ecumenical adventure. We had secured at least a modest commendation of the Church of South India. On the whole we felt that our time had not been ill-spent and that we had at least something to show for our labour.

For those of us who were involved with the World Council Assembly at Amsterdam there was to be no holiday. After a few days in Geneva to pick up the bits, we moved to Woudschoten in Holland to make the final preparations for the Assembly. Here I made one of the worst mistakes of my career. Those who were planning the work of the other three sections planned in advance the reports of their sections as a basis for the discussion at the Assembly. From my experience in missionary assemblies I steadily resisted this plan; the report ought to emerge from the actual discussions on the spot, and not be presaged by what could not be other than an irresponsible group of delegates. I had not understood the difference between a commission of delegates of the missionary movement, all deeply committed to a single ideal and in consequence with a great deal in common in advance of their meeting at the Assembly, and an ecumenical commission the members of which had nothing in common except the name Christian, and who had no clear idea of the purpose for which they had come together. I was later to suffer bitterly for this failure to apprehend the realities of the situation by which we were confronted.

The World Council has always been singularly inept or unfortunate in the choice of places for its major meetings. The decision to hold the first Assembly at Amsterdam had been reached on sentimental and not on rational grounds. Visser 't Hooft himself was a Dutchman. The Dutch had played a notable part in the resistance to Hitler and his claims. This was to be recognised by locating the Assembly in their greatest city. Amsterdam is indeed a noble city, the Venice of the north. As it turned out, no worse choice could possibly have been made. A great and bustling capital is in any case no place for the holding of an ecclesiastical assembly, for which peace, remoteness and leisure are indispensable prerequisites. When the decision had been made, it could not have been foreseen that the Assembly would immediately precede the inauguration of Queen Juliana of the Netherlands, following on the unexpected abdication of her mother, that admirable Christian woman, Queen Wilhelmina. This unexpected concatenation turned what had been initially an unwise decision into a disaster. The city was crowded by a mass of visitors. Public transportation had snarled almost to a standstill and it was almost impossible to move from place to place. To get the simplest meal at one of the many restaurants in the city took an hour and a half at least. Instead of limiting participation in the Assembly rigidly to the 500 delegates of the Churches, the World Council had permitted the presence of alternates as well as delegates,

of a considerable number of accredited visitors, and heaven knows
how many who had no accreditation, as well as a mixed multitude of
journalists from all over the world. It is not surprising that all those
deeply concerned in the work of the Assembly were completely
exhausted before it slowly dragged to its close.

The Assembly has so often been described that there is no need
here to do more than to indicate some of the main features of
its work, and to record in slightly more detail my own share in
what was done.

The first events were in their way deeply impressive. For the
first service we met in the great Church of Amsterdam, and it was
deeply moving to see assembled the representatives of the most
varied list of Christian Churches that had ever met together since
the day of Pentecost. I had been asked to marshal the delegates into
their places, and nearly brought the World Council to a sudden and
contentious ending by insisting that a Greek Prelate must walk in
the procession side by side with the representative of the Greek
Evangelical Church, the existence of which he did not recognise
and regarded as an outrage on the integrity of the Orthodox Church
of Greece. And how to marshal the representatives of American
Churches who had never encountered a procession in their lives
and did not know what it was? But in the end we got them all seated,
in all their bizarre incongruity. There were two sermons. Together
on the platform were the veteran John R. Mott, still a magnificent
presence but with obviously failing powers, and D. T. Niles of
Ceylon, looking much younger than his forty years. D.T. had first
come to see me as a very young student of University College,
Colombo, and spent the last twenty years of his life wondering
whether he could break through the rules of Eastern propriety
and address me by my Christian name. Each speaker had been
allotted a certain amount of time, with strict instructions that he
was not to exceed it. There was a moment of anxiety when J.R.M.
deserted his script and began to reminisce about all the promoters of
the ecumenical movement whom he had known and who had gone
ahead of us to their reward; it seemed that he might well go on till
midnight, but mercifully sanity returned and he was not more than
six or seven minutes beyond his time. Then D.T. made an effective
speech, in the dialect of Barthian dialectics, on the exodus of Israel
from Egypt, and our pilgrimage under the guidance of God from the
known to the unknown. The procession had preserved some rags of
dignity; the recession after a moment or two collapsed into chaos,
and I made no further attempt to control it.

There was a moment of real greatness when at the first session the Archbishop of Canterbury declared that the World Council of Churches, no longer in process of formation, had been duly constituted and was now in existence, and called the Assembly to prayer.

When we settled down to work, the disastrous errors in the planning of the Assembly soon became evident. Before acceding to his World Council responsibilities, Visser 't Hooft had been General Secretary of the World Student Christian Federation. The criticism was often made that the World Council was the WSCF grown up, and I must record my opinion that this criticism is largely justified; the planning of a students' conference is something entirely different from the planning of an adult assembly; this is a secret which somehow the World Council has never managed to learn. One sets students to write all manner of reports which it is certain that no one will ever read, as a means of keeping them out of mischief and helping to clear their confused and hesitant minds. This is no way to treat grown-up people; a Christian assembly is lucky if it produces one report which will have some effect on the history of the Church.

The first affliction was having to listen to a long series of speeches introducing the work that had been done in preparation for the Assembly. This is always a mistake. If people have read the report, they do not need any introduction to it; if they have not read it, even an introduction of fifty minutes is no remedy for their culpable negligence The resulting boredom tends to paralyse the Assembly and to make any constructive thought impossible.

The fourth speaker out of five, to each of whom half an hour had been assigned, I found myself charged with the task of introducing to the Assembly the report of the second commission on *The Church's Witness to God's Design*. I had read through my written speech the night before and decided that it was devastatingly dull. I threw it on one side and sat up far into the night, preparing an entirely new speech which, as is my custom, I would have to deliver from short notes and not from a prepared text. My unilateral act of independence was rewarded. The three speeches before mine had reduced the Assembly to a state of coma, and I rose to face my half-hour's ordeal with a good deal of apprehension. However, by making a few well-chosen jokes and speaking freely, and driving home my point, I found myself sitting down to wave upon wave of applause.

It must not be supposed that all was tedious in this first Assembly. It was a notable gathering of the clans, and almost everyone who was anyone in the ecumenical movement was there. It was something of an achievement to have on the same platform Foster Dulles, whom everyone expected to become American Secretary of State that year, and Josef Hromadka, the Czech theologian who had gone further than most others in accepting the communist revolution. Also, Karl Barth, after long hesitation, had decided to be there. This was of importance to him. He had always had a conventional interest in missions. Now, finding representatives of the younger Churches, especially the Indonesians, crowding around him, he found his eyes opened to a dimension in the life of the Church that had previously been wholly unknown to him. Here, after many years, he met again Emil Brunner, but the wounds dating back from the year 1934, in which Barth had launched his savage attack on Brunner under the monosyllabic title *Nein* ('No') were too many and too deep, and I fear that fellowship between these two great men and former allies was never really restored.

The preliminaries over, we had to settle down to the work of our various commissions. And here I began to suffer from my unwisdom in not having a prepared text on which the discussion could be centred. I was faced with a too large and wholly miscellaneous collection of Christians, ranging from Greek prelates to whom the word 'mission' meant nothing other than the aggressive missions of Roman Catholics and Protestants to the detriment of the Orthodox Church of Greece, through a Dutch theologian who wished to expound to us a rigidly Calvinist understanding of the doctrine of the atonement, to conservatives such as Archbishop Mowll of Sydney, who did not want anything very exciting, to Ted Wickham, later Bishop of Middleton, who was not prepared to admit that anything commonly called evangelism was relevant in the modern world.

So at the end of four days I was left with a pile of notes, bearing no relation to one another, and instructed to produce the century's statement of evangelism. I now bitterly regret that I did not neglect the discussion entirely and produce out of my own head an apocalyptic statement on a world in disarray, perishing for lack of the gospel of Christ. But I have always felt that a recorder is a recorder; it is his business, as best he can, to grasp the sense of an assembly, and to find the words in which that sense can be recorded and apprehended. And what is the poor scribe to do when there has been no sense of an assembly? I did my best, without any great success. When my draft was read out to the commission, there was no enthusiasm. After some desultory discussion, I was asked to produce a revision. This met with little more favour. Martin

Niemöller launched a little conspiracy to remove me from the post of secretary and replace me by a creature of his own. This was rightly squashed by the chairman. My own plea, that I had had two shots and had no originality left, was overruled. By this time more than half the commission liked my drafts and all that was done to help me was to ask Hendrik Kraemer to write a section on the disarray of modern man; this he did at such length that his statement, if incorporated in full, would have disrupted the proportion of the report; but he was most unwilling to have it shortened. So at last, partly from sheer exhaustion, a report was agreed to by the commission, read to the Assembly in plenary session, and with some few amendments accepted as the official second report, following on that on Unity and Division in the Church.

Reading the report again after an interval of more than twenty years, I do not find it as bad as was maintained by a number of people at the time. For the second World Council Assembly in 1954, an entirely new commission was appointed to produce the earth-shaking report which was to end all reports on evangelism; they ran into exactly the same difficulties as we; I do not find their report at any single point an improvement on ours. I simply do not think that a short report on evangelism can be written; either there is nothing to say, or a long theological volume needs to be produced – and then it is quite probable that no one would ever read it.

The work of the commission on theological issues was balanced by the work of the committees on the more mundane matters of constitution, rules and orders, and other subsidiary issues. I had been so busy with the work of my commission that I had not been able to do anything about my membership of Committee 1 on Constitution and Rules and Regulations. When at last I was able to attend a session, I found it launched, under the chairmanship of Dr Alfons Koechlin, President of the Basel Mission, on a discussion of the basis of the World Council.

This was a thorny subject. The Council, when in process of formation, had adopted the basis used for a number of years by the Faith and Order movement that, 'The World Council of Churches is a fellowship of Churches which accept our Lord Jesus Christ as God and Saviour.' But this basis is itself something of a mystery. It used a formula identical with that accepted by the Young Men's Christian Association at its first international meeting at Paris in 1855, a definition accepted by the YMCA for clearly polemical reasons and as a protest against the rationalism then spreading in the Christian world, which was anathema to the Evangelical founders of the YMCA.

The basis had come under criticism from various angles. The Orthodox, naturally, would have wished for the whole Nicene Creed, if not the decisions of the seven ecumenical councils, as the foundation for the ecumenical movement. Anglicans would have preferred a statement in which place had been found for the trinitarian doctrine of God. The sharpest criticisms came from the liberal Churches, such as the Remonstrants in Holland, and some sections of the Swiss Protestant Churches; these objected to the words 'God and Saviour' as non-biblical, and as suppressing the true humanity of the life of the incarnate Lord. It seemed at least possible that a radical reconsideration of the basis might be undertaken at Amsterdam 1948.

Koechlin was on the point of indicating the grounds on which such a reconsideration should be recommended to the Assembly. I was gravely disturbed. I knew that a number of conservative Churches had come into the Council only on assurance that the basis really represented the views of the leaders in the ecumenical movement as to the terms of affiliation to it. Any change in the basis would lead to a suspicion that they had been sold a pig in a poke, and perhaps to the withdrawal of some Churches from a Council which they had only just joined. Apparently there had been considerable discussion on the matter behind the scenes, and Koechlin was not acting on his own initiative in putting forward the possibility of revision. I knew nothing of this; so I immediately leapt to my feet and expressed my views in no uncertain terms. No worse moment could possibly be chosen for any proposals for modifying and, in the opinion of many, for weakening the basis: the Council had only just come into existence; any change would inevitably create the impression that it did not really know its own mind, and would produce widespread disturbance in the ranks of those Churches which still looked upon the movement with a good deal of suspicion.

No sooner had I sat down than Dr William Barrow Pugh of the Presbyterian Church in the USA stood up and supported every word that I had said: 'Many of our people are conservative; at this point you want to strengthen their faith in the movement, not to undermine it.' He was followed by a formidable Lutheran controversialist Dr Abel Ross Wentz of the United Lutheran Church in America, speaking in almost identical terms. It was clear that this sudden attack from within the sacred precincts of the World Council itself came to Koechlin as a wholly unexpected shot between wind and water. There was nothing for it; it was quite clear that the sense of the meeting was with me, and that there was a very strong feeling that for the time being at least the basis must be regarded as sacrosanct.

Koechlin duly reported this to the higher authorities. The result was perhaps the most innocuous resolution ever passed by an ecumenical assembly:

(a) That this Assembly of the World Council of Churches affirms its conviction that the basis set forth in the Constitution is adequate for the present purposes of the World Council of Churches;

(b) That any Churches that may desire change in the basis be instructed to present their desires in writing to the Central Committee for study and report to the next Assembly;

(c) That the Central Committee be instructed to keep its study of possible changes within the Christological principle set forth in the present basis.

This was perhaps my most decisive intervention in ecumenical affairs. I did not manage to prevent for ever this undesirable tampering with a short and satisfactory basis, but at least I postponed the evil day for thirteen years. I did not desire any change whatever. The basis had proved itself adequate as an instrument both for inclusion and for exclusion. The policy of the World Council has always been clear and consistent. It deals with Churches and not with individuals; it accepts no responsibility whatever for the eccentric views put forward by this or that member of any of the member Churches. Moreover, it did not desire to make windows into men's souls. If any Church is able conscientiously to say that it holds and teaches the Nicene faith in Jesus Christ as God of God, Light of Light, Very God of Very God, that suffices; no further question should be asked. If any Church cannot honestly make that declaration, it should not press its claim to membership; it will not feel at home in this particular ecumenical fellowship, and will be more effective in its witness outside it. I can find no good word to say for the verbose and confused statement which was adopted as a basis by the Council at New Delhi in 1961.

One enormous chore still remained, namely the drawing up of the Assembly's message to the world. I had been appointed to the committee responsible for this task. Once again we suffered from the haste with which the Assembly had been prepared; we had not had time to grow to a common mind. There was no agreement at all as to what kind of a message we felt that we wanted to launch on the world. Some felt that it would be better not to say anything, or, at most in a few sentences to commit the work of the Council to the Churches and to ask their prayers for future ecumenical work. The Bishop of Chichester wanted a sharp message to prick the consciences of men, and, with that irritating pertinacity which was his worst weakness, tried to press his point. Professor Schlink of Heidelberg, coming from the agony and disarray of postwar Germany, said, 'What they need to be told is that there is a good shepherd, and that he is available to them.' Sir Kenneth Grubb said that the Church had only one message to give to the world, 'Believe on the Lord Jesus Christ and thou shalt be saved.' It seemed that we might be landed in complete deadlock. The committee then at last made its one sensible decision, to commit to one single person the drafting of a message, in which as far as possible all the various threads could be drawn together into a unity. The lot fell most suitably on Dr Kathleen Bliss.

Kathleen sat up half the night and came back with a very short message. She said that it had been a real religious experience, and that she felt that what she had written had been given to her. A small sub-committee consisting of Pierre Maury, Lesslie Newbigin and myself had been appointed to sit with her and to make what revisions seemed advisable. It happened that Kathleen, Lesslie and I were all old South India hands. I remarked that the best test of a document like that is to see whether it bears translation, and proceeded to make a running translation of it into Tamil. It went well. Pierre Maury looked on with interested amusement. We felt that at last we were on the right track, and that something was emerging that could be offered to the Assembly with some hope of acceptance. I am recording here only my own experiences, and so I write no more about the message; I was too busy in the later stages of the Assembly to devote any further time to it, and encountered it again only when it was read aloud in plenary session.

It is a good message, not eminent in classical phraseology, or outstanding for prophetic outreach, but plain, modest and practical. It was the kind of thing that people wanted to hear. 'Here at Amsterdam we have committed ourselves afresh to him, and have covenanted with one another in constituting this World Council of Churches. We intend to stay together.' What could be simpler? What more appropriate to that great moment in church history?

This was no frail human covenant, based on man's short-sightedness and prejudice. It was a part of God's covenant with his Church through Christ Jesus, to which we desired wholly to commit ourselves, and which we believed would be our strength and stay through the taxing years that were to follow. We were not deceived. I have many criticisms to make of the ecumenical movement in its later developments. But for all that, Amsterdam 1948 was a great event. The Roman Catholics took no official part at all. Russia stood suspicious and aloof. Many of the conservative Evangelical groups had been unable to overcome their doubts and fears. The Council was overwhelmingly Western, partly through an obstinately narrow definition of an autonomous Church which excluded some of the largest and most thriving of the Churches in Asia and Africa. But the movement was on the way. It had brought together a larger cross-section of the Church of Christ than had ever before been seen in a single room. The Assembly had talked a good deal of sense, and much less nonsense than is commonly to be heard in such ecclesiastical assemblies. The typical comment was that of a layman who remarked simply, 'Why did they never do it before?'

The World Council existed; it was no longer in process of formation. But an immense amount of detailed organisation had to be carried out if it was to carry out smoothly and efficiently the many tasks that had been laid upon it by the Assembly. We retired to Woudschoten to look at ourselves and to consider what was next to be done.

And here what seemed to be a blessing threatened to cast a shadow of permanent menace over the work of the Council. There was universal agreement that George Bell, Bishop of Chichester, must be the first Chairman of the Central Committee of the Council; through his long connection with the Life and Work movement he was widely known throughout the world. His noble work for German pastors in distress, and his courageous protests against the bombing of German cities during the war, had made him more than acceptable to the Germans and to the other forces on the continent of Europe. He was elected with acclaim. What was not known was that he was one of the worst chairmen in the world.

At our very first meeting at Woudschoten we were to pass through a grim experience of what bad chairmanship can do to a meeting. It happened that just at that moment the Lutheran Bishop Ordass had been imprisoned by the communist government in Hungary. Bishop Eivind Berggrav of Oslo, one of the finest Christians of the century, but also one of the most emotional, came to the meeting in a great state of tension and urged that something must be done. This, if ever there was one, was a case for the appointment of a sub-committee of three to consider the matter and to come to the Central Committee with a carefully thought out proposal. Instead Bell allowed a shapeless discussion to drag on, with no one wishing to seem heartless in the face of affliction, and yet with no sensible motion before the Committee. A large part of a day was lost, and in consequence a number of things of vital importance to the future of the World Council were simply never discussed.

My own case is perhaps illustrative of a great deal that was going on, or was not going on, at that time. It is hardly credible, but during those long days of discussion, no one said to me officially, 'Do you want to go on in the service of the World Council of Churches?' My old friend Pitney Van Dusen of Union Seminary, New York, said to me quietly one day, 'They want you to go on; they feel that your gifts very usefully balance those of Visser 't Hooft.' So I waited for the official approach to be made, but nothing came. I knew that a great deal of bickering was going on about the appointment of Dr Robert Mackie, General Secretary of the Student Movement of Great Britain 1928-38, and Visser 't Hooft's successor as General Secretary of the World Student Christian Federation in Geneva. In my case nothing of the sort took place; all that happened was that, on the last evening of the session, a list of names was read out, from which I learned that I was to be Associate General Secretary with special responsibility for Study and Evangelism. I was not consulted as to the terms of my appointment; the question of salary was not even discussed; I received no letter of appointment and no indication of what it was that I was supposed to do.

Looking back over the years, I think that I would have been wise at that time to say no. I felt a good deal perturbed by the atmosphere of this first post-Assembly meeting, and by the way in which the newly appointed committees were handling things. There was much, however, to be said on the other side. I was wholly committed to the ecumenical cause, as a movement for the unity and renewal of the Church, though far from enamoured of the World Council of Churches as it was beginning to take shape, and I had no clear plans for a career if I returned to England.

I was not the only contributor to feel that the whole atmosphere of the World Council of Churches changed abruptly the very day after the end of the first Assembly. Up to that time we had been a company of gay adventurers, setting our sights on a distant and possibly unattainable goal, and deeply committed to one another in the fellowship of the faith. No one asked who was appointed by whom, or who was paid by whom. There was a pleasant informality in the proceedings, such as prevailed throughout its entire history in the International Missionary Council. Now, in the World Council, everything was changed. It had been regularly constituted, and had fallen into the hands of the great American church administrators. To the credit of the United States, it ought to be placed on record that, although the American Churches were paying by far the greater part of the bills, they never used this as an excuse for drawing the reins of policy into their own hands. But inevitably they came to exercise a great deal of influence on the way in which things were run. The American Churches have developed enormous headquarters, of a kind entirely unknown in the rest of the English-speaking world, in which of necessity everyone is an administrator in one capacity or another. The chief administrators tend to run these institutions exactly as though they were a large business corporation or a bank. There is a President and directors, a small number of policy-makers, with all the rest of the staff taking rank as clerks, cashiers or office-boys. The distinction between colleagues and employees is quite rigid. This was something that I simply had not foreseen. I had come to Geneva as a colleague; I was to make the experiment of serving as an employee, and to find that it was an experiment which simply did not work out. I think that those of us who had lived through the pioneer period would have been wise to resign as soon as the Assembly was over, and to leave the further development in the hands of a younger generation. Those who stayed on too long paid a price for their loyalty. Others, like Keith Bridston and Hans Hermann Wolf, who valued their originality and independence, simply had to get out in order to save their own souls.

7

Professor in Germany

Early in 1962 there came to me one of those religious experiences which have been so rare in my life. The inner voice said almost audibly, 'You must go to Hamburg.' A preliminary note will be required to explain the meaning of this command.

Having kept up my reading in French, German and Italian throughout my time in India, I suddenly found myself pitchforked into the German-speaking world as a preacher and speaker when two delegates to the Oslo Youth Conference of 1947 invited me to speak in Reihem, Basel. This went off all right, but the next experience was so awful that it very nearly cured me for good of any desire to become an orator in German. However, there was no escaping from it, Germany itself had to be faced.

More than a quarter of a century later, it is hard to realise what Germany was actually like at the end of the Second World War. President F. D. Roosevelt had launched the slogan 'unconditional surrender'; but it was hardly necessary for him to do so; collapse had been complete. The devastation was terrible. The RAF bombers had continued their work far beyond the point at which any return was to be expected from it. Driving through these broken towns, we could not help wondering whether even the Germans, with their noted diligence, would ever be able to put them together again. In the countryside, of course, the damage was much less, but here too roads had been left unrepaired, agriculture seemed to have returned to primitive methods, and the people were pale, undernourished and ill-clothed.

One of the places I visited was Hamburg, where British raids had been unusually pitiless. It was bitterly cold weather, and refugees from the eastern zone were there in their thousands, waiting for any chance that might come to settle down in a new way of life.

This visit was important to me for three reasons. First, I made the acquaintance of Brigadier John Dunlop, the military commander of the area, who was responsible for a remarkable ecumenical arrangement with regard to worship in the Anglican church of St Thomas à Becket. Dunlop, a member of the Church of Scotland, thought it was nonsense to have two small English-speaking congregations in one place, and prevailed upon the Anglican authorities to allow the Scots to bring in their own minister once every two months, to preach at Anglican Mattins and thereafter to have the Lord's Supper celebrated according to the use of the Church of Scotland. Second, I had an interview with the Bishop of Hamburg, in the course of which he remarked: 'Our greatest danger is Rudolf Bultmann.' I had heard of Bultmann in Geneva: I did not know then that his work would become one of my major preoccupations for many years, as can be seen from my books. My third Hamburg experience was the renewal of my acquaintance with Walter Freytag. My friendship with him, like so many of my international friendships, had begun at Tambaram in 1938. This remarkable man had a Moravian background, and never quite lost the intense piety of the Brethren. Though not a great scholar, he was widely read, and above all had a delicate and sensitive spirit, with an unusual awareness of what was going on in the Christian world. The consequences of this friendship will become clear as my narrative proceeds.

It is always interesting to know what impression one is making on those whom one meets. A bishop travelling on official business has the equivalent rank of Lieutenant-General, and is therefore well qualified to spread alarm and despondency many miles ahead of his arrival. The grapevine carries information from place to place as to what he likes and dislikes. I learned that one thing that impressed the chaplains was that I always fold my robes myself in the vestry with great care. This is just common sense; if robes have to be packed and unpacked frequently when one is on tour, careful folding in just the right way makes all the difference to one's appearance in church. This is of great importance when one is dealing with the armed forces. I also found that four points were relayed without fail from place to place:

(a) This man dislikes fuss.
(b) This man wants everything just so. He will rehearse every single detail of a confirmation service in the vestry beforehand, with all the chaplains present.
(c) This man likes to know in advance exactly whom he is going to meet, and expects to be given a list of them when he arrives.

(d)   This man is interested in making contact with the German
      Churches. Make sure that the local notables are on parade
      and an interpreter is provided.

This pastoral work among the British led me into some interesting
experiences. One day I was in the headquarters of the Youth Section
of the Religious Affairs branch of the Control Commission, when I
met a German lad who became like a son to me, Wolfgang. Wolfgang
had been in the Hitler Youth, then, at an absurdly young age, in the
navy during the last days of the war. Then he got himself converted
in a rather unusual way. The Control Commission had arranged a
camp for boys. When they arrived, it was found that there were not
enough beds; so the officer in charge arranged that he would sleep
on the floor so that one more boy could have a bed. I imagine that
the officer, who is now ordained in the Church of England, thought
nothing of the matter, but the army being what the army was in
Germany, Wolfgang was completely overwhelmed by the idea that
an officer could give up his bed to a German boy. He said to himself,
'If this is Christianity, this is something that I have got to look into.'
The result was that within a short time he became a convinced and
humble Christian. He was enthralled by my talk about India, and
decided on the spot that he would like to become a missionary.

I did not encourage Wolf, as I now called him, to become
an Anglican. I said that he must first become acquainted with
continental theology and church life at its best, so I sent him to
Basel for two years. But after two years he wrote to me: 'It really
is no use. As a German I was a complete heathen. All my Christian
experiences are Anglican; that is where I feel at home, and that is
where I would like to serve.' So I gave in, and sent him to study at
London College of Divinity (St John's Hall), whose Principal was
Dr Donald Coggan. Dr Coggan also treated Wolf almost as a son,
so that he was in danger of suffering from an excess of fathers, not
having had much to do with his German one, owing to a divorce.
All went well, in due course Wolf was ordained deacon, and married
by the officer who had been the means of his conversion. Wolf had
met Rosemary in the small English congregation in Basel (which I
remembered as consisting mainly of old ladies), and while he was
studying she was working as a secretary in New York. When they
were reunited after four years they had no doubt that they were
meant for each other. In his first parish he found that he had to
fend for himself and find a place in which he and his young wife
could exist on his exiguous salary. After three moves in a year,

under notice to quit with a child on the way, he felt he could take it no longer, and with my approval he wrote to his bishop. I am not generally in favour of young clergymen complaining of the conditions under which they are required to work, but in this case it seemed to me that there were reasonable grounds. It says much for the bishop that he immediately came down to the parish, enquired personally into the situation and then without hesitation offered Wolf the choice between two curacies elsewhere. The one he chose brought him under an excellent priest, now a diocesan bishop.

When it was time for him to take an independent charge an unexpected problem arose. Wolf was a German citizen and had no desire to change his nationality, but Church–State relations made that seem impossible. Then the problem was solved by the one option I thought equally impossible – the German authorities allowed him to hold dual nationality. So the story ended happily for all concerned.

All the work I did for the British in Germany was intensely rewarding, but my real concern was to get in touch with the German people and understand their situation in this formidably difficult postwar period. Staying with generals or in Anglican church houses, I was not really seeing much of Germans, and occasional conversations with German church leaders, hampered by my still very imperfect German, did not carry me much further forward. Funnily enough, it was in Frankfurt, in the American zone, that the first real opportunity came, when I was sent to consecrate a Nissen hut for worship, as the English church had been destroyed in the bombing. Here I stayed in a hotel in the heart of the city and for the first time could feel the tides of German life surrounding me.

This was some time after the currency reform had taken effect. To readers nowadays this term probably means nothing, but at the time it was hailed as one of the great achievements of history. The value of the mark was stabilised almost magically. Almost in a night, Germany was changed from a country without hope to a land of hope, though certainly not yet of glory. This was what I sensed from my hotel window in Frankfurt, even though the devastation in Frankfurt was as terrible as it was elsewhere.

The story of the German miracle has been told so often that there is no need to repeat it here, nor is it part of my personal recollections, except in so far as on each of my visits subsequently I could see visible signs of progress and recovery. No one believed that the Germans could do what they have done, but for this tremendous achievement a certain price had to be paid. Yet if that first postwar

generation had not worked its fingers to the bone, its children and
grandchildren would not have had the wonderful country which
they have inherited today.

Naturally my principal concern was with the German Churches.
How had they come through the war? Here again the history is well
known. When Hitler came to power, the majority of Christians
in Germany, both Protestant and Roman Catholic, were prepared
to welcome him as a heaven-sent leader. His later villainies have
tended to conceal what he did for the German people in the early
days of the Reich. He gave them work and food and hope, and
above all a renewed sense of national dignity after Versailles and
the economic depression. It was not long, however, before doubts
began to arise. The horror of the concentration camps began to
be known, but not by any means by the whole of the population.
Churchmen began to be uneasily aware that Hitler's anti-Semitism
was wholly irreconcilable with any interpretation of the Christian
gospel. Few, though, perceived that his ultimate plan was the
eradication of the Churches as well. All this is shown in J. S.
Conway's excellent study, *The Nazi Persecution of the Churches*,
and in Eberhard Bethge's immense *Dietrich Bonhoeffer*, so there
is no need to go into detail here.

Perhaps one third of the Protestant ministers came to accept
the Aryan myth. A considerably smaller number rallied to the
'Confessing Church', the members of which had seen clearly the
theological dangers in Nazism, and had understood what loyalty to
Christ might cost them. About half carried on in a confused and
unhappy state, believing that loyalty to Hitler and loyalty to Christ
could be reconciled in loyalty to the Fatherland. The boundaries
between the three groups were shifting all the time. On the Roman
Catholic side, some consoled themselves that Hitler was a baptised
Catholic, though this did not stop him attacking the Vatican.
Inevitably, given the different ecclesiastical structures, courageous
opponents of Hitler on the Catholic side, such as Cardinal Faulhaber
of Munich and Count von Galen of Münster, maintained a higher
profile than most of the resisters on the Protestant side.

The skill of government propaganda is shown by their success
in pulling the wool over the eyes of such eminent Anglicans as
Bishop A. C. Headlam, Bishop Bell's protagonist. The argument
ran that the party known as 'German Christians' were rather like
liberal Christians in England, committed to the basic truths of
Christianity, yet aware that the expression of these truths may
vary from age to age, and that the possibility of new sources of

revelation is not to be denied. As for the imprisonment of some Christian leaders, that was because they were political agitators, and were guilty of identifiable political offences against the welfare of the country. Ecumenical church leaders were perplexed as to how best to react.

Then and now, the one German Protestant leader whose name was widely known outside Germany was Martin Niemöller. This former U-boat commander turned pastor had been forthright in his opposition to Hitler, and in consequence had spent eight years in a concentration camp. A friend of Bishop Bell's, he more than any other German at that time had the ear of those in power in Geneva. For all my admiration for the character and courage of the man, I could not feel that his advice was always wise. As one German friend said to me, 'Brother Martin is a *Krisemann*, a man who is at home in a crisis; and, if no crisis exists, he is rather inclined to create one.' At one point I thought that his advice was definitely harmful.

Niemöller was behind the noble Stuttgart Declaration (1945) in which German Protestant leaders defined the guilt of their people, and identified themselves with it. Bitterly criticised by some leading conservatives in Germany, this had smoothed the way for the restoration of fellowship between the German Churches and the rest of the Christian world – not that I myself ever felt any difficulty in the way. In my judgement, far more important than material help, valuable though that was, was the opening of doors and windows for the Germans through spiritual fellowship with those Christians whose religious experience had been different from their own. Links had been created in many directions, but with a good deal of confusion because of the multiplicity of agencies involved. What was to happen as this need diminished and Germany became politically independent again? My proposal was that the World Council of Churches, as the one possible unifying force, should build up a powerful ecumenical centre, with some churchmen of world-wide reputation in charge, to maintain and develop these links. Niemöller told the leaders in Geneva that this would be tantamount to treating Germany as a colonial territory. The idea was dropped. A small centre in Germany was indeed maintained, but the excellent American Episcopal clergyman appointed to run it was not of sufficient stature to make any deep impact on the life of the German Churches as a whole. It was at this point, in my opinion, that the German Churches began to become introspective and to lose the openness which had been such a sign of hope in the years immediately after the war.

Hanns Lilje had for years been associated with the Student Christian Movement, and this had given him an international outlook rare among Germans at that time. Lilje's election as Bishop of Hanover to replace a man deeply compromised by his association with Hitler's government was a sign of the new day. He had been arrested for complicity in the 20 July 1944 bomb plot but was liberated before he reached the place of execution. Though not a great scholar, he was well read. No one could meet him and remain in any doubt as to the clear depth of his faith in Jesus Christ. It was this that made him a kind of chaplain to the German Resistance. For some reason, though, his speeches so impressed me with their fluency and eloquence that what he actually said never made much impact on me.

Otto Dibelius, Church President of the old Prussian Union Church of Berlin-Brandenburg, later known as 'the Bishop of Berlin', was altogether a more ambiguous figure. His cousin, Martin Dibelius, was dismissed from his position as Professor of New Testament at the University of Heidelberg for resisting the 'Aryan clause'. A real old Prussian aristocrat, he was outspoken in his hostility to communism, more so than many of his colleagues; the extremity of their opposition to Nazism had led some of these, in my opinion, to a less than commendable tolerance of Marxism and its works. Dibelius was a great man and a great leader – but most definitely not the kind of person I would ever venture to address by his first name.

So there they were – the sailor, the orator and the aristocrat, the leaders best known to the outside world; what would they make of the German Churches, and what would the latter think of the growing ecumenical movement?

Meanwhile, the problem remained about my fluency in German. How long would I be tied to manuscripts kindly prepared for me by my friends? The crunch came, suddenly and unexpectedly, when I discovered that I had been billed to speak in Erlangen, in a baroque church with a Huguenot heritage, on *Christus über Indien*, and neither of my prepared lectures that I had brought with me would do. I shut myself up for three hours with my inseparable travelling companion, Langenscheidt's dictionary, and then sallied forth with a careful lecture mainly on the formation of the Church of South India as an outstanding ecumenical achievement. Somehow I kept going for fifty minutes and emerged exhausted from the ordeal, but kind things were said to encourage me and everyone seemed to appreciate the effort I had made. After that, I never looked back.

Not very long after that, early in 1956, I was invited to Hamburg again. Naturally I went to call on my old friend Walter Freytag. We had a long conversation, in the course of which he almost felled me to the ground by suggesting that I take his place for six months while he travelled on behalf of the German missionary societies. Such a possibility had never even occurred to me. I could by now talk to a meeting of pastors or students in German with some hope of acceptance, but to deliver formal academic lectures and to undertake even temporarily all the duties of a professorship was a very different matter. Freytag had remarked in the course of our conversation that my German was greatly improved, but I could hardly suppose he was serious. I thought no more of the matter until I received an almost frenzied letter from the Dean of the faculty later in the year. 'Are you coming? We simply must know.' This caused new reflection. I decided that if they wanted me as much as that I ought to go. Against my expectation and my will, I was to become a German professor.

I could not have come under happier auspices. I was lodged in the Mission House on Mittelweg, surely a most suitable dwelling for an Anglican committed to the Anglican *via media*. Professor Freytag had already left, but his family was living in the building and showed me all manner of kindness. His younger son Justus, a sociology postgraduate student, became a great friend. He was my listening post for the student world; we met once a week to drink a glass of beer and to discuss the affairs of the world and the movements of opinion among students. As a foreigner, I owed more than I can say to these frank and relaxed discussions. I also had the use of Professor Freytag's office and the help of his excellent bilingual secretary.

Freytag had gathered around him a quite remarkable group of young men, whom he was grooming for responsibilities in the world of German missions. Horst Bürkle, for example, was to become Professor of Mission at Munich after a spell at Makerere in Uganda. Hans-Jochen Margull, who took his place in Hamburg in 1968, was his 'research assistant', and so assisted me. Jan Hermelink, who showed great promise as a theologian, was occupied with the affairs of the German Mission Council. Dr Viening was to introduce something like a revolution in missionary methods in Togoland. Dr Wagner was writing on the then unknown subject of Christian theology in India. And so on. With all these young men I was associated in varying degrees of intimacy.

The Mission Academy requires a word of explanation. It was among the most original of Freytag's creations. It was intended to

bring together four quite different groups of people: candidates of
the various missionary societies preparing for their future work;
missionaries on leave pursuing further studies; theological students
from the Third World, whose churches wished them to have the
benefit of studying in Europe; and finally young ministers sent
by their churches for six months' study of the missionary and
ecumenical situation with a view to their returning to their parishes
as well-informed advocates of these two great causes. Some of
the missionary candidates had undergone a full theological course
in the seminaries of the various missionary societies, a course
which, though very thorough by English standards, was regarded
in Germany as very inferior to a university course. I was asked
to take a weekly session in New Testament exegesis with this
group, and chose the Epistle to the Hebrews, which is generally
neglected by Lutherans. I found there were almost insuperable
difficulties in working directly from Greek to German, and fear
the students found it boring and unprofitable. More successful
were the 'English evenings' I conducted for those intending to
serve in countries where the official language was English. My
main responsibilities, however, were in the University, where I had
to give a two-hour lecture and hold a seminar of equal duration.
My book *The Unfinished Task* had been completed in English,
but was not yet in German: this supplied me with enough material
for a course of lectures. In the seminar I dealt with the church
union movements in various parts of the world, a subject entirely
unfamiliar to them. About sixteen students enrolled for the latter,
and although there was a certain amount of good-humoured laughter
at my grammar mistakes, all went much better than I had feared.
One might say that a good time was had by all.

One of my first duties was to get to know my colleagues. This
was not difficult, because apart from those whom I knew already
there were two admirable social customs which gave me the greatest
pleasure. The first was the practice of faculty members and some
others to meet once a month in the home of one of the brethren. This
being Germany, a number of glasses of wine were drunk and an immense number of cigars consumed. One of the company would read
a wholly unintelligible paper, and then there would be, for an hour
or more, a wholly unintelligible discussion, then everyone would
go home feeling greatly edified. It was during my second period
in Hamburg that, on one of these evenings, our host received a
telephone call and returned with the horrifying news: Kennedy had
been shot. There was a period of stunned silence; then I said, 'In

such a situation there is only one thing to do. Like simple village Christians, we must turn to God in prayer. Herr Müller-Schwäfe, will you lead us in prayer?' Those who know the atmosphere of German theological gatherings such as this may be surprised to learn that such a session dissolved into a prayer meeting; but it seemed at that moment the right suggestion to make, and I think my colleagues were grateful to me for making it.

The other admirable practice was that once a year the theological faculty invited the entire teaching body of the University to join them at the Haus Rissen on the banks of the Elbe, about ten miles from Hamburg, to spend a day together in discussion of some important themes on the border between different subjects. When Konrad Lorenz was our guest speaker as many as a hundred people joined the outing.

We were not the most distinguished faculty in Germany, but we had a number of interesting members, by far the best known of whom was Helmut Thielicke, the Professor of Social Ethics, now well known because of the publication in English of his sermons. I always felt that he was underrated in Germany. He committed the two unpardonable sins of always being beautifully dressed, and of speaking crisp, fluent, colloquial German, in contrast with the all too often slovenly appearance of the German professor, and the crabbed, clumsy productions which came from the typewriters of many German scholars. He was also a really great preacher. The oldest among us was the church historian Karl Dietrich Schmidt, who had been professor at Kiel University until ejected by the Nazis, and had then spent the following years at the missionary training centre of Hermannsburg, until Freytag brought him to Hamburg after the war. I always attached great importance to his assurance that although he lived close to Belsen concentration camp, he had not the slightest idea of what was really happening there, since he was so transparently truthful a man. He was very kind to me, and his death at the age of sixty-eight was a great loss to us all.

I soon detected a great difference between the older and younger generation among our colleagues. The older men had grown up when French was the second language studied in schools, and none, I think, had studied outside Germany. None spoke English readily. The younger generation was quite different. Bernhard Lohse, younger brother of the bishop, had studied for a year in England, Margull in New York, and they were aware of the problems of translation and equivalent terms. I was much interested to find out what, if anything, my students knew about the world outside Germany. At that time there was great eagerness to get outside the narrow confines of their world. Scholarships offered by bodies such as the WCC were eagerly snapped up, but there was woeful ignorance of anything outside the limits of German theology. Most had heard of C. H. Dodd and Reinhold Niebuhr, one student had read E. C. Hoskyns and F. N. Davey's *The Riddle of the New Testament*, and that was about it.

Naturally the greater part of my time was taken up with my exacting duties in the University, but this did not exclude certain expeditions outside Hamburg. I lectured at both the University of Kiel and the *Kirchliche Hochschule* in Berlin on training for the ministry in the younger Churches, a subject of which my hearers were, for the most part, wholly ignorant, but which they seemed to find interesting. The most interesting visit of all was to East Berlin, to take part in a conference of the missionary wing of the Student Christian Organisation. Here I was delighted to be able to renew and deepen my acquaintance with Professor Joachim Jeremias, for whose scholarship and goodness I had acquired the deepest respect. The main object of the operation, however, was to make contact with these students from the whole of the Russian occupied zone. I found them fresh, lively, open and interested. For a generation no missionaries had been sent from East Germany to other lands, and especially since 1945 information had been reduced to a trickle – the practice of watching West German television had not yet begun. Those who have never lived in a situation in which the government rigidly controls all the media have no idea of the effect of this on general knowledge. So it was quite an experience for the students to meet a man who had been a missionary and had travelled widely, and who spoke intelligible German. I was deeply impressed by their attitude. Some of them were theological students. They were perfectly clear-sighted about the difficulties confronting them as ministers of the gospel in a communist-controlled country. Already there was discrimination against those who were confirmed in church, and it was difficult for middle-class students to get places at university. Yet they had resisted the temptation to emigrate to the West. This, they felt, was where God had called them to work. If staying meant trouble and affliction, God would give them grace to see it through. At all costs the life of the Church must be maintained, until communist rule came to an end, as they were sure it would do, one day. I could only admire their quiet and unostentatious courage.

Some of my young friends had been able to visit relations in the West and had found themselves hardly able to breathe in that atmosphere. They found life in the West unbelievably hierarchic, stiff and pompous; to their minds there was much to commend in the free, less formal and more classless type of society in the East. They were critical of the Churches in the West. 'We know our enemy,' they would say, 'and therefore are on our guard; we know that our only strength comes from the Lord of Hosts. You do not recognise your enemy, and have therefore been lulled to sleep. Although the Churches in the West are technically disestablished, in fact you rely on help from the State, on church taxes, on subsidies from America, on every kind of financial guarantee; so you have failed to see that the god you worship is really mammon, and not the God of the Bible.' There was some truth in this, but already in 1957 it seemed clear to me that if German reunification did take place, it would by no means be a case of long-separated brothers falling on one another's necks and rejoicing; there would be suspicion, recrimination, misunderstanding and an infinity of difficulties to be faced and overcome. It has seemed to me that all through the years, this aspect of the problem has been constantly underplayed in almost everything that has been written in the West, and that the Churches have failed to see where the heart of the problem lies.

So my time in Hamburg came to a close. My German had almost miraculously improved. Above all, I felt that I was beginning to get inside the German mind and to feel at home in a country which has never been as congenial to me as France, Switzerland or Italy. Now I had a number of intimate friends, through whom I could learn many things usually hidden from a foreigner.

A few days before my last lecture, the telephone rang: it was the Dean of the faculty, asking me to accept an honorary degree of Doctor of Theology. This was one of the best moments of my life. The invitation was far more than a formal recognition of certain intellectual achievements. I felt that it was the expression of what can only be called the love that had grown up between me and my colleagues. This was all supposed to be a well-guarded secret, but everyone knew, and there was no surprise when the professors of the faculty, in black gowns faced with purple ruffs and floppy hats, processed in. There was a somewhat lengthy Latin address, and an address by the Dean, describing some of my scholarly work, and the handing over of a parchment, and I was duly installed as *Doctor honoris causa*. I proceeded to deliver my lecture, but prefaced it by saying, 'Up till now I have been a guest in Hamburg. Now I am no longer a guest; here in Hamburg I am at home.' This expressed what I really felt: the faculty had made me so much one of themselves that it was no longer possible to feel a stranger.

So I went back to my quiet life of writing and editing in Geneva, and quickly slipped back into my old routine. Then in October there came the news that Walter Freytag had died suddenly of a heart attack at the age of sixty. It was completely unexpected. He had returned to Hamburg apparently in good shape, having had a mass of interesting experiences, the crown of which had been three weeks in China. Now this good, wise and gentle man was taken from us. In one sense God does not need any of us. One man dies, and another takes his place. But in many cases this is only approximately true. He proved irreplaceable, both in Germany and in the ecumenical movement. If his quiet wisdom had continued, later history might have been very different.

For two years the chair was vacant. It eventually transpired that the theological faculty did, early on, discuss the possibility of asking me to come, but decided 'Bishop Neill is much too deeply involved in the ecumenical movement. We could not expect to detach him from that.' They also thought that there was no precedent for a bishop becoming a professor, so they did nothing. They had great hopes of Jan Hermelink, but he was not yet qualified to be a professor. I did accept an urgent call to help them out in a crisis, and when I went for one month in the early summer of 1961 I found great changes. Margull had gone to Geneva, Bürkle was at the Mission Academy, but had not yet gained any overseas experience, and the others had left for their respective posts. Bishop Heinrich Meyer of Lübeck helped out when he could, as he had served for twenty years in India, but his health was very bad. It was a situation of grave poverty, as contrasted with the promise of great riches which Freytag had built up in the years before his death.

Then destiny struck again. In July 1961 Jan Hermelink was killed while driving to the *Kirchentag*, the famous Protestant lay assembly, which was being held in Berlin. He was thirty-seven years old. I knew what this would mean to the friends in Hamburg who had put great faith in him and were keeping the professorship open for him. What were they to do now? It was at this point that the inner voice told me that I must go to Hamburg. I consulted with Margull, who agreed that he should let the Dean of the Faculty know that I was ready to consider the possibility of returning to Hamburg. The result was immediate – a unanimous request from the theological faculty that I should come and fill the vacant post.

Everything was not as smooth as first appeared. They would have liked me to start in October 1961, but I had commitments already and the earliest date I could take up my duties in Hamburg was May 1962. I thought that my friends would say that they could not wait so long, especially as there were other excellent contenders for the appointment, but they stuck to their original decision, and agreed to wait. So it was decided, and my long connection with Geneva came to an end. I had never supposed for one moment that I would live there for fifteen years, but one thing led to another, and every time I planned to leave Geneva there was some urgent job waiting to be done which only I could do, or there was someone who specially needed my help whom I could not leave in the lurch. What remained of my work, however, such as my editorship of the World Christian Book series, could just as well be done in Hamburg as in Geneva. I had already gradually eased myself out of any official connection with the WCC, although it was still my custom to go into the Centre Oecumenique for tea every day with the staff of the World Council, and in this way I kept in touch. By early 1962 there was nothing to stand in the way of a move.

By this time the University was in the process of moving out of its cramped old quarters into the splendid new buildings which were going up in the Von-Melle-Park. The Philosophentürm was complete, but not yet furnished. As they decorated from the top downwards, we were the first to move in. Naturally we had been assigned the twelfth and thirteenth floors, in order to be as near to heaven as possible. Only the meteorologists were above us. As the Dean showed me my office on the twelfth floor, with a magnificent view over the Alster and far away into the country beyond, he said to me, 'I have served German universities for twenty-five years, but I never imagined that one day they would give us offices *with upholstered furniture*.' So even in Germany things can change.

That evening a little dinner party was held in our new building, at which Professor Schmidt handed me my document of appointment. I had always assumed that, as Freytag's successor, I would be *Ordinarius* for Mission Studies and the Ecumenical Relations of the Churches. In that moment, and not before, I learned that this would not be the case. If I had known this earlier, I would not have accepted the post, but I had left it all to Margull to negotiate my conditions of employment, as it is not my nature to bargain for terms. If I think that a job is to be done, I set myself to do it, regardless of the conditions. I did not know that, under the rules, a man cannot be appointed *Ordinarius* over the age of fifty-eight, since it is reckoned that he should serve for at least ten years to qualify for a full pension. So my position was anomalous. I was given full charge of a department, with the status of a professor, but I was not a member of the inner circle of *Ordinarii*. Professor Schmidt carefully explained to me that this was really a distinction without a difference. I would have all the rights of a professor, including the right to present candidates for doctoral degrees.

Everyone had overlooked the one factor that had weighed most heavily in my willingness to come to Hamburg. I had taken it for granted that much of my time would be given to the Mission Academy, where the number of overseas students had greatly increased. The Tutor would look after academic matters, but I knew how lonely and frustrated the students often felt, separated from their families and possessing limited German, and I wanted to help pastorally. However, the Constitution of the Academy stipulated that the representative of the University on its governing body must be an *Ordinarius*. Consequently I could not replace the Dean, and in fact had no official connection with the Academy whatever. The institution was the responsibility of the German Missionary Council, of which Freytag was the chairman, and it was in this capacity that he had watched lovingly over the Academy since its creation. I never had any difficulty working with Dr Martin Pöchsum, his successor as chairman, and while my friend Bürkle was Tutor, I was able to do a certain amount, but the young men who replaced Freytag's team made it clear that there was no essential connection between the Academy and the University's Department of Mission. Was the objection that I was not a Lutheran? Or did they resent the fact that their preferred candidate was not made professor? Perhaps there was concealed resentment in the mission headquarters at my appointment. In any case, it was made clear that, though these young men would not interfere in my narrow sphere in the University, they were going to see to it that there was no interference by the professor in the affairs of the German Missionary Council.

The position of the *Ordinarius* in a German university is very unlike that prevailing in any British university. It is the professors with this status in each faculty who confer degrees and honorary degrees in the name of the university, rather than the Senate or broader governing body. When a professorship falls vacant, they decide whom to call to fill the vacant place; and once appointed, they have tenure until sixty-eight, all the rights of a civil servant, and can only be moved by fiat of a dictator. So here was I, a professor, but not a member of this sacred conclave. As a result, I knew nothing whatever of what was going on. When a new professor was added to the faculty, I learned of the event through the public press, and in no other way. Realising that this was an impossible situation, my colleagues in part remedied it by arranging that I should be recognised as a full member of the faculty, and therefore entitled to attend its meetings. But I became aware that there were still meetings at which only the *Ordinarii* were present, and from which I was excluded.

The situation in my own department was confused and unsatisfactory. Bishop Heinrich Meyer of Lübeck retained his title of Honorary Professor and came in from time to time to lecture. An old friend, Hans Heinrich Havans, who had served for some years in Geneva, and was pastor of the great Michaelis-Kirche, was also on the list of our lecturers. I had the greatest difficulty in securing any kind of co-ordination between the work that the three of us were undertaking. When, at last, I was able to get the three potentates together, we agreed that Meyer should be responsible for missionary history and problems, Havans for ecumenical affairs, and I for the non-Christian religions in relationship to the Christian gospel. This suited me very well; I still have the elaborate notes which I prepared for these lectures, and they have stood me in very good stead on many subsequent occasions. For my seminars I did not recognise any limitation of theme, provided I could keep clear of the subjects that others had announced.

Professor Freytag's last assistant had been left in charge of the department; it was not at all easy for him to recognise that this was no longer the case, and that authority was now vested in the professor. However, when he secured his doctorate, very creditably, and left to work in radio, the situation eased. My new assistant, Rolf Christiansen, was a young man, gravely hindered in his work by a serious heart condition, but friendly and willing. His view of our relationship came out rather startlingly when one day a visitor came to my office, and I introduced him as 'my dear colleague, Herr Christiansen', to which his immediate reply was, 'I'm not your colleague, I'm your assistant.' This was very far from my view of the situation.

Our students had a considerable range of knowledge in the field of theology, but were astonishingly ignorant of everything else. The course was very hard and exacting. Greek and Hebrew were obligatory, and some knowledge of Latin was also expected. This had caused little difficulty in earlier days, when the majority of students had passed through the classical Gymnasium system, and came to university with an excellent knowledge of Greek, and, in some cases, with at least a rudimentary acquaintance with Hebrew. In addition, many of them came from pious clerical homes, in which they had acquired an extensive knowledge of the Bible; but in our day it was as important as it was in England not to assume any knowledge of the Bible. Most of the students came in with no training whatever in the classical languages, and had to grunt and sweat under the weary task of learning enough Greek and Hebrew to scrape through their examinations. We would, I think, have been willing to make Hebrew optional, but any suggestion of the kind brought forth the thunders of conservative Erlangen; Philip Melanchthon had laid it down in 1530 that all candidates for the ministry must be learned in Greek and Hebrew, and no change could be made in this divinely inspired edict. My suggestion that the first year of language teaching be conducted by competent and trained language teachers, instead of being left to bored assistants who resented the demands made on their time and were ill-equipped for the task, met with much approval, but was never put into effect. It is not surprising that the students did not find much time to consider the wide world and its ways; all the same, I think they could have done more than they did.

Their extensive ignorance came out plainly at the time of ex-aminations. Here again the German system is as different as it is possible to imagine. The traditional system had, by my time in Hamburg, been breached at various points, but a great deal of it still remained. Oral examinations put a tremendous strain on both professors and candidates. The candidate migrates from room to room, in each of which he will find at least two professors and a scribe. With my limited German, I always found this a terrifying experience, but I grew in admiration for my colleagues as I observed how they went to the limits in trying to put the candidate at ease, and to help him get out what he really knew. Of course candidates vary enormously in their self-confidence, and in their capacity to express what they know, but in my experience many lame dogs were helped over stiles.

The candidate was allowed to indicate the area in which he desired to be specially tested. Mission and ecumenism being such a vast subject, I usually agreed to a rather circumscribed area, but would ask one or two general questions to give the student the opportunity of showing to what extent, if any, he was in touch with the wider life of the Christian world. On one occasion we had before us two

with lectures due to start in ten days time there was no time for preparation.

However, dark as the situation was, it was not all dark.

University College was under no obligations to find any financial help for the department; but, perhaps without knowing it, it did actually provide indirectly a good deal of help. In the first place, it assigned me, at a very low rent, a large flat in a big block of university residences less than a mile from the main campus and only half a mile from the Anglican cathedral. This was large enough for me to take over the main bedroom as my study, in order to have a really quiet place in which to work, and still have a spare room in which to entertain guests.

The librarian assumed from the start that we were a department like any other department, and put us on the same terms as everyone else. At that time the British government was allocating considerable amounts as counterpart funds for the building up of libraries. Our allotment was £1,000 a year. We went on gaily ordering whatever we thought we would like, expecting sooner or later to be stopped abruptly. As luck would have it, each year a number of departments failed to order up to the full limit of their allotment, and the librarian proceeded to make a reallocation. Though we spent something like £1,300 a year, we always managed to get away with it. A library is so important that I felt it right to put a good deal of my own money into buying books, and my attention to the delicate art of public relations paid large dividends. Through the German Embassy we received a generous gift of German reference books and English translations of German books. The Indian High Commission came along with all the fifty volumes of the Indian reprint of the Sacred Books of the East I wonder how many copies of that series there are in Africa. So our library grew and expanded, and, though still small, at the end of my time of service contained most of the works that are essential to the teacher of philosophy or theology.

Dr Jacobs came along with an engaging readiness to give a course of lectures on the African tradition in religion. I had determined from the start that this must be included in our curriculum. We were fortunate to find so well qualified a scholar, willing to work for us for a nominal honorarium, and to carry on most effectively until the work was taken over by another American, Dr Malcolm McVeigh, whose experience in Angola and Zaire before he came to Kenya gave him an unusually wide range of knowledge and experience.

A rather odd Englishman who had long taught in Canada, an ecologist who in middle life had developed a passion for philosophy, was willing to teach for one term the elementary course on the problems of philosophy. This was a help but also something of a mixed blessing. We started with thirty-five registered students. A good many of these fell away when they learned that for a start we could offer only one course in philosophy, and that they would also have to take a course in religious studies. Furthermore, our ecologist seems to have terrified a good many students, who were finding philosophy a good deal more difficult than they had expected, and who therefore also withdrew from the fray. We ended up with only eighteen.

Still, there we were. We could offer one course in philosophy, the course on the African tradition, to which I added an introduction to biblical studies, with Greek as an optional subject – a respectable if not an impressive start. But I viewed with apprehension the second half of the year, in which I would have to take over the course on the philosophy of religion, and also the lectures on religion in the modern world which would build on the foundation laid by Dr Jacobs, as well as carrying on with the introduction to the Old Testament. As I was already carrying the whole weight of administration, as well as fighting to get our syllabus through various academic bodies, I felt that I simply could not carry so heavy a load. Then, as so often in these four strange years, salvation came just when it was needed, and from an unexpected quarter. Among our visiting professors of that year was T. Cuyler Young, who had at one time been a missionary in Iran, and had just retired from being head of the Middle Eastern Department at Princeton University. I had got to know this friendly and gracious colleague and his equally gracious wife. It suddenly occurred to me that without any great labour of preparation he would be able to take over from me the elementary Old Testament. No sooner asked than accepted; this welcome relief, continued into the following year, just saved my life.

I found the work on the philosophy of religion, based on the excellent book by Professor H. D. Lewis, interesting but exacting. The problem in teaching African students is that very few of them have any general background beyond what they have learned in school. A student may well come from a pious home in which literally the only book is a copy of the New Testament in an African language; it is quite impossible for him to catch an allusion or to understand a proverbial phrase which will be self-evident to the English student, and everything has to be toilfully explained. This is especially true in a subject like philosophy, which naturally is not taught in schools in Africa, and in which both the vocabulary and the manner of thinking are entirely strange to the student. My long years of experience in India helped me to anticipate the difficulties of the African student. But I realised afresh the harm that has been done by missionary societies in sending out raw missionaries to teach theology without any preparation and any opportunity to study the mind and the background of those whom they will have to teach.

During the course of this first year we put on three sets of public lectures. The first, by Cuyler Young, was on a rather esoteric subject, 'A Profile of Persian Islam'. The audience was naturally restricted, but the lectures were excellent, and served exactly the purpose that I had in mind, of making it plain that we were not, as was all too often suspected, simply a department of Christian propaganda. The second series was considerably more ambitious – 'Religious Communities of Kenya', each lecture to be given by a member of the community concerned. We started off with a splash; Professor John Mbiti drew an audience of 270 for his talk on the African tradition in religion. After that both audience and quality of lectures varied a great deal. We had an excellent and amusing account of the Sikh religion by my friend Mr Taran Singh; several of the lectures were average and no more, two were deplorably poor. Then I put on myself a series of four lectures under the title 'Pioneers of Thought, Part 1', dealing with the great creative period of Hinduism and of early Buddhism. Each time I had an audience of about 100, drawn rather from the Asian community in the city than from the University – we never had much success in interesting our Asian students in religion. But these served my purpose well in making friendly links both with the Kenya-born Asians, and with those who had come from India itself. The Indian High Commissioner, Mr Artan Singh, came to all the four lectures, and at the end made a kindly and gracious speech of thanks.

After the first year we were not able to do as much as I would have liked in this field of University Extension work. As the work in the department itself grew, there simply was not strength or energy left over for these extras.

Fairly early in this year I realised that the climate of Nairobi was not going to be kind to me. In many ways the climate is ideal; temperatures normally run between 44°F and 90°F. However, the summer of 1973 was exceptionally hot. Together with the effect of the altitude (5,400 feet above sea-level), this seemed to raise my pulse rate to such an extent that I became excessively tired. I had to give up any attempt to do serious work in the evenings.

GOD'S APPRENTICE

Sometimes I was even too tired to listen to music. Matters were not improved by the return of my old enemy insomnia. Looking back over four years, it seems that almost all my mistakes – and I did make many mistakes, provoking opposition unnecessarily and alienating some who might have been friends of the department – were made in times of extreme exhaustion, when it is very easy to be provoked, like Moses, the servant of the Lord, to speak unadvisably with my lips.

In our second year, the department really began to take shape. The Roman Catholic Secretariat had found money to provide a member of staff on the philosophy side, and thus to meet our greatest need. We were fortunate in having the services of Dr J. G. Donders, the Dutch White Father, who had studied in Holland, Rome and Scotland, and who proved to be a most excellent colleague, with a pleasing wit, ready access to the students, and an extensive store of knowledge. We were also able to secure as a member of the department, in spite of severe financial problems, a young Kenyan philosopher, Dr Henry Odena, who came to us with degrees from Wayne University in the USA and from Uppsala in Sweden. At the start Dr Odena was not very well qualified, but he grew to the work, and showed considerable originality and enterprise, for instance in founding the Kenya Philosophical Association. In any case, we felt it essential to have a Kenyan member of staff in the sub-department of philosophy. In this second year we had more than thirty registered students, a number of them girls who wished to qualify themselves as teachers of religion in schools. In the annual examinations all our students passed, and our external examiner, Professor John Mbiti from Makerere, was highly complimentary, tending to put our marks up rather than to lower them.

All this time a great deal of discussion had been going on as to what a university in Africa ought to be. We had started as an outpost of the University of London, and the students took the London degrees. This had value as helping us to work towards an internationally recognised standard, but it meant that syllabuses, teachers and methods of teaching were all Western, with hardly any dilution, and this was clearly a situation which could not and ought not to continue.

We were all anxious to see the proportion of Africans, and particularly Kenyan members of staff, increased. The University was highly international, with a strong Scandinavian element, as well as Germans, Indians, Americans, Canadians, Ghanaians, and others, but the Kenyans made up less than a third of the total. To the credit of the University it must be said that there was no attempt whatever to flood the University with undeserving Kenyans.

All this was important. Far more important was the general picture of a university that was forming itself in the minds of men. What is a university, and what is it for? The natural answer would be that a university in Africa must be an African university for Africans. That is a view to which I can subscribe only with grave reservations. A university should be universal in its aims, in its teaching, and in its understanding of the nature of knowledge. I viewed with some apprehension the changes that were taking place in some of our departments. In the revised syllabus of the Department of History the first-year student was limited to two obligatory courses, one on the pre-history of Africa, the other on African pre-colonial history, neither in my opinion of high educational value to a first-year student. In the later years there were a number of options, but almost all slanted in the direction of Africa and of revolution. Much the same was happening in the Department of Literature. The student was to spend a great part of his time studying African literature in English, a field of considerable significance historically and sociologically, but only in rare cases bearing comparison with literature in the other great languages of the world.

As far as we were concerned, we were determined to maintain the international character of our department. What is Christianity if it is not international? Nevertheless, as we looked at our syllabus, it seemed to us that it was far too Western, and that we must take steps to relate it more closely to Africa. On the religious studies side, there was no great problem. We were already teaching the African tradition in religion; we extended this course to cover the whole of the first year under the title of 'Religions of East Africa', and made it compulsory for all students; it was now to include religions of non-African origin – that meant in the main Islam, the religions of Asia, and Christianity – as they have been affected by their East African environment. The History Department, although it teaches Islam in Africa, had refused to include Christianity in Africa in its syllabus; accordingly we brought it into ours, with results of which I shall have more to say later on. As related to philosophy the question was considerably more complex. The African still tends to think in pictures, and Western abstract terms have little meaning for him; he can learn them by heart and use them, but they will still continue to be foreign bodies in his mind. And yet, if philosophy is to be taught at all, it cannot disregard the long centuries of travail through which the West has come to its present understanding of the nature and processes of thought.

We were driven back to ask ourselves the really fundamental question: How does the African think, and is there such a thing as an African philosophy? This depends in part on definitions. If by philosophy we mean an elaborate and systematic pattern of thought, then the answer is clear – the African has no philosophy. But if we take the word in a broader sense of a general pattern of outlook on the world, an understanding of life and its responsibilities, something in the nature of what the Germans call a *Weltanschauung*, though a little more defined and less vague than what that word implies, we may say that the African certainly has a philosophy. The African does not think in abstract terms of being, but of vital force, what a thing does or can do. This vital force can be diminished or augmented. An African is not devoid of ideas of right and wrong; but these are related not to offences against an abstract set of laws, still less to transgressions against the love of a holy God; they are seen as actions which enhance the being of the family, or else rend and damage its carefully woven fabric; if the fabric has been damaged, then steps must be taken to see that it is repaired. This is a world which the European enters with difficulty, but in which the African feels himself to be at home.

Part of our problem is that it is really Europe which has created Africa, just as it was the British who created India. African unity is now a basic part of the creed of every educated African; this tends to make him overlook the vast differences which separate the culture of one African people from another. We had a glaring example on our doorstep. I have referred to the danger we were always in through tribal rivalry in Kenya. The culture of the Kikuyu is largely based on the rite of circumcision, which plays a central part in the initiation of a boy into full tribal responsibility. This has been extended to include female circumcision, a barbarous, brutal and senseless mutilation to which the missionaries tried to put a stop, which I myself heartily wish would one day disappear, but which has become as the ark of the covenant to the Kikuyu – I fancy that the majority of Kikuyu girls, even Christians, are still circumcised, more or less in secret. The neighbouring tribe, the Luo, on the other hand, being Nilotic, have never known circumcision, and regard it with a mixture of dislike and contempt. But such differences ought not to hide from us the fact that there is a real unity, of which the Africans have every right to be proud. It was this that Dr Odena set himself to explore in courses on the African approach to philosophy and African social philosophy.

Naturally the greater part of our time and strength was given to the University, but this was by no means the end of our activities. We have always maintained in the classroom a rigidly academic attitude, all the more necessary because of the watchful suspicion of some of our African colleagues. I know that this attitude was very much appreciated by the students, by no means all of whom were convinced adherents of any form of religious community; after some initial perplexity it caused no trouble with the Churches. I had no intention whatever of compromising my position as a Christian bishop. It was made clear to every member of the department that, when he had fulfilled his obligations to the University, the rest of his time was his own, and he could devote it to any activities, secular or religious, which he regarded as congenial or appropriate.

My first concern was with Christian witness in the University. I never saw an accurate breakdown of the religious affiliations of the students. My guess is that, when the total number of students reached 4,000 there were 3,000 who at least had been baptised as Christians – probably 1,200 as Roman Catholics, the remainder in one or other of our innumerable non-Roman denominations – plus 600 or so Hindus, Sikhs and Muslims, and 400 unclassifiable. So we had a considerable parish on our hands.

The first and most obvious facet of Christian ministry in the University was the students' service held every Sunday morning in St Andrew's Church. This had been started some years previously by the chaplaincy, with thirty students present; it continued to grow in most satisfactory fashion, so much so that on two occasions I found myself preaching to a congregation of more than 400, nearly all of them students, a phenomenon that one would not encounter in a great many universities of the world today. I was greatly honoured in that I was the only minister of the gospel whom the students asked to preach for them every term, and the only one whom they ever asked to preach more than once a term.

Another aspect of Christian life in the University was the Christian Union. This could have been a source of division and discomfort. The Christian Union was closely linked to the African Fellowship of Evangelical Students, and through it to the Inter-Varsity Fellowship. Most of the students came from Churches of a strongly Evangelical and conservative tradition, and were timid of anything strange and unfamiliar. Although we knew that we did not speak quite their language, they did however recognise that in our own way we were believers, and that was all that mattered. So sometimes we went up the hill to Nairobi Chapel to speak at their meetings, and felt quite at home with them.

I had been much grieved by the unfriendly attitude of the Anglican authorities, but with the dissolution of the ungainly province of East Africa and the formation of the new province of Kenya all this faded away. With this breath of fresh air, the Church of the Province began to find that it could use my services in various ways.

The first request was to become Chairman of a Provincial Commission on Training for the Ministry, ordained and lay. Here I found myself confronted with a horrifying picture of confusion brought about by an almost complete lack of planning and foresight. The whole province had only four graduate African clergy, only one of whom was a graduate in both arts and theology, and one of whom had left the service of the Church to become a member of Parliament. At the first meeting at which I took the chair, we found that the two hundred priests in the province engaged in pastoral work had to help them an array of about 1,600 catechists, evangelists, church teachers, what you will, the great majority of whom had not received any training whatsoever, since for years the existing Bible schools had been taken off their proper job of training lay workers to give emergency training for the ordained ministry to men of lower qualifications, who had been told that they would never rise above the status of curates. Such a situation bears no resemblance to anything that has ever been known in England. To add to the confusion there was grave dissatisfaction with the training given at St Paul's College, Limuru, where it was felt that Presbyterian domination made impossible any serious training along Anglican lines; the bishops were complaining that men coming out from St Paul's did not even know how to take a service according to the rules laid down in the Book of Common Prayer.

One of the first decisions of the Commission was that there should be no more training of clergy on this inferior level, and that the Bible schools should be put back to their proper task of providing training, as far as their means permitted, for the sorely tried, underpaid and undertrained village workers. We were prepared to make an exception in favour of men over the age of fifty, in whose case age, so greatly respected in Africa, and long experience, would make up for the lack of academic qualifications. It was a considerable shock to learn that the diocese decided to disregard this recommendation and selected ten men for training at a Bible school, during which time the school would have to suspend its training of lay workers. We were completely helpless; we had been given no executive authority.

Another area in which the Anglican authorities asked my help was in the drawing up of a constitution for the Church of the Province. The history of this was curious and complicated. When the diocese of Mombasa covered the whole of Kenya and was directly dependent on Canterbury, someone had drawn up a constitution for it. When the new dioceses were formed, each took over this old document almost unaltered. Besides these diocesan constitutions, there was a sketchy constitution of the province of East Africa, drawn up in 1960, mainly, I think, by Geoffrey Fisher at the time of the formation of that province, and, in my opinion, reserving far more authority to the Archbishop of Canterbury than was consistent with the rights and dignity of an independent province of the Anglican Communion. Some revision of this constitution had been carried out in preparation for the formation of the province of Kenya in 1970, but this had been carried out in the secretive manner which at that time characterised a great part of the life of the Anglican Church in Kenya. I secured my advance copy only deviously and via Tanzania; I think that most of those who had to vote on it saw it for the first time at the meeting of the Provincial Synod at which the constitution had to be adopted. This was diametrically opposed to my view that all such matters should be exposed to the fullest and frankest discussion by all orders of men in Christ's holy Church; I have never supposed that inspiration is concentrated in episcopal brains and fingers.

After the constitution had been adopted, the dioceses were invited to send in amendments. A Commission was set up, under the chairmanship of the Bishop of Mombasa, to receive these amendments and to report to the Provincial Synod. I was invited to serve on this Commission, I suppose because someone had heard that I had a good deal to do with the constitution of the Church of South India. They little knew what they were doing. They imagined that the Commission would meet perhaps twice to deal with the small number of amendments sent in by the dioceses. I was convinced that the whole constitution would have to be reworked from top to toe. Many sections were entirely missing; others had been cobbled rather than created; in many places the writing was shoddy and at times legally the meaning could not be construed. If the Church of the Province was to have a decent constitution to live under, a great deal of work was going to have to be done.

A good deal of the work of drafting fell upon me. There are few greater satisfactions in life than to present a rather complicated draft and to have it accepted with no more than verbal corrections, and I had a good deal of luck in this way in the course of our work together.

After two years of this manifold and exhausting activity, I was quite ready to take advantage of the short period of leave in the West to which I was entitled, especially as I knew that our academic year was in future to begin in July instead of September, and that in consequence in our third year we should have to do twelve months' work in ten and then start our fourth year without the benefit of a long vacation and without any extended period of rest.

Our third year opened propitiously. With an increasing number of students registering each year, we had now passed the 100 mark, twice as many students as I had expected to have after three years' work. It was clear that the department was beginning to establish itself as a regular part of the life of what was by now the independent University of Nairobi, and the University recognised this fact by extending my contract for another two years.

We felt that the department ought to make some kind of a demonstration of our now fully established status. The opportunity was offered by the delivery of my belated inaugural lecture. We managed really to make something of the affair. We had sent out invitations fairly widely, and about 500 people turned up, many of them students, but a good many from all walks of life in the city. The general opinion seemed to be that in my lecture I had made out a reasonable case for the existence of a department that many of our colleagues in the University still regarded with deep suspicion, and some with positive dislike. The lecture was then followed by a highly successful party, attended by ambassadors, high commissioners, prelates, professors and a multitude of other less distinguished friends.

The Church Missionary Society had generously responded to our need for help by sending to us the Revd Dr Terence Day. Dr Day is himself Indian, and had married a lady who is of pure Indian descent, though her family has for some years been settled in Winnipeg in Canada. It was a great asset to us to have a colleague who had both studied and taught in India, and whose knowledge in the whole range of Asian religions meant that I was no longer alone in a field which we had from the start promised would be included in our curriculum. At one point, however, the hopes aroused in my mind were to be disappointed.

From the very day of my arrival the Asian community in Kenya had been a problem to me. Students in the University strictly practised *apartheid*; there was hardly any coming and going between the African and Asian groups. I more than once asked our most earnest Christian students whether they had a single Asian friend; the answer in every case was no. They all assumed that no Asian ever had been or ever could be converted; in fact students, when they have heard that I had spent many years in India, have asked in astonishment, 'But what were you doing there? Are there any Christians in India?'

To a considerable extent the Asians themselves were to blame for this rigid division. Indian traders had come to East Africa to exploit it. Before long they had almost the whole retail trade of the country in their hands; their aim was to make money, and they saw little reason to take an interest in Africans or to identify themselves with the country which they had come to inhabit. Similarly, the Kenyan government, like most other African governments, made no secret of its view that no one in Africa has any real rights except the born black African.

The Churches had had little success in the presentation of the gospel to the Asian population. There are Indian Christians in Kenya, but the majority of them were Christians when they left India; Indian converts in Kenya are a rare species indeed. The only Christian group which had made any real impact on the Asian community were the Southern Baptists. Before long I had been brought into contact with their work in Parklands, and had been invited to speak at their Sunday evening service. I seemed to be an acceptable speaker because of my intimate knowledge of India, a country to which the Indians present felt themselves to belong, though the majority of them had never seen it.

It had been my hope that Dr and Mrs Day, with their knowledge of India and Indian languages, would be able to make themselves at home in the Asian community, and would make friends beyond the limits that the Americans had reached. I could obviously give only a very small part of my time to making contacts in this direction. With this in mind I had raised money privately to get the Days a car and so make them mobile. But nothing of what I had hoped came about. Dr Day performed his duties in the University admirably and showed himself a highly competent and adaptable teacher. He did very good work for six months as acting Vicar of St Mark's, Westlands, a church which for that period had been left without a priest. But Parklands, where most of the Indians live, remained a closed world to the Days; they had less success even than I in breaking down the barrier which, whether in the University or beyond it, separated Asian from African, and the non-Christian from the Christian world.

It had never been my purpose that the Department of Philosophy and Religious Studies should be encapsulated within the University; I felt that its functions must be conceived in a far less restricted way. In accordance with this view we found ourselves led out into the task of co-ordinating higher religious studies throughout the whole country. This is rather a complicated story, but it must be told in outline here.

The old University of East Africa, now defunct, had brought into being a Council on Higher Studies in Religion, which gradually worked out a Diploma in Theology, which was accepted as a standard of teaching by a number of seminaries, Roman Catholic and others, and a Certificate of Religious Studies, which was intended for laymen who wished to extend their knowledge of their faith, and also for teachers who saw here a way of improving their qualifications – the Certificate was accepted by the Ministry of Education in Kenya as equivalent to our A level. I had for years served as external examiner for the Diploma. I did not altogether like the syllabus, and felt both that the setting of examination questions was unimaginative and that the local examining was amateurish, but undoubtedly the Diploma had helped to raise standards all round, and had therefore served a very useful purpose. When the East African University was dissolved, we pleaded hard that the Council should be kept in existence on a basis that would include all the three territories; no attention was paid to our plea, and we were told rather harshly and abruptly that the Council had been liquidated. What was to happen next?

A number of men were half-way through their Diploma course and were now suspended in the air. Makerere University very properly took emergency action and formed a Makerere Council on Higher Studies in Religion, with representation from all three territories, to run the Diploma and carry on the work of the now defunct Council. The Makerere people felt that their Council should be able to manage everything for the whole of the area covered by the old Council; but this was the point at which we in Nairobi began to ask questions. St Paul's College, Limuru, the only institution in Kenya which prepared students for the Diploma, was quite prepared to accept the Makerere Diploma as the examination for which its students would work. It was, however, by no means clear that anyone in Kenya would be interested in a Makerere Certificate. We could not be sure that the Kenyan Ministry of Education would recognise a Certificate issued by a university over which it had no control. What could we do but form our own Council on Higher Studies in Religion? The Makerere people were not at all happy about this plan, but we did our best to soothe their anxieties by insisting that rivalry was the last thing that we intended, and that we hoped to maintain the fullest co-operation in a situation which we had neither created nor desired.

In Kenya superhuman efforts are needed to get anything done at all; the Council was no exception. We planned generously. The University, the theological teaching institutions, the Churches, including of course the Roman Catholic, and also the non-Christian religious communities were all to be represented. The response all round was encouraging. A constitution was drawn up, but, if the Council was to fulfil the purposes that we had in mind, it must be recognised by the University. Here was our first hurdle. I was successful in persuading the Arts Faculty Board that this was really no new thing, but merely the continuation of something that had long existed, and that they had always recognised. So I got by that one. When the matter came to the Senate, our new Vice-Chancellor said rather chillingly, 'Is anyone interested in this?' But the question came up at the end of a very long and fatiguing meeting, when everyone was too listless to oppose anything; we got our way, perhaps without enthusiastic commendation, but at least without violent onslaughts of opposition, and were entitled to put on our notepaper, 'A Council recognised by the Senate of the University of Nairobi, and reporting to the Arts Faculty Board of the University.'

The Council came into existence, and the first meeting was very well attended. I felt that our first business was to get launched a new Certificate in Religious Studies adapted to Kenyan conditions, but this meant getting the syllabuses through the needle's eye of the University. Both the Arts Faculty Board and the Senate pride themselves on the minimum attention they pay to all the syllabuses to which the University gives its august approval. I have to admit that I am not very good in such meetings. I get bored easily, and sometimes give vent to ill-considered remarks that give offence. I knew that the presentation of our syllabus would be the occasion for a right royal free for all, and prepared myself carefully by long and earnest prayer.

The session followed exactly the course that I had foreseen. The younger African members of the Board, some of them outspoken in their rejection of every kind of religion, felt that this was much too good an occasion to be missed, and that this highly suspect department must not be allowed to get away with anything. For once my Irish temper was completely under control. I think the assailants were surprised to find that my equanimity remained completely unperturbed, and that I was prepared to give calm consideration to every proposal, however provocative the form in which it had been put forward. In the end our syllabus emerged a good deal altered, but, I must admit, in my opinion considerably improved – and above all accepted. Altogether a stimulating and enjoyable evening. When we rose, one of the young colleagues said to me, 'You know, we felt we simply must take this syllabus seriously'; and my good friend Professor Ogot, the Deputy Vice-Chancellor, remarked, 'Now they will all be behind you; they feel that it is their own syllabus.'

Once accepted, the Certificate began to catch on. St Paul's College, Limuru, accepted it as the basis of instruction for their students who could not rise to the Diploma level. The big regional seminary, St Thomas Aquinas, a vast mausoleum erected some years before by the American Dominicans, but now under African direction, also proposed to send in some of its students as candidates. Two tutorial classes got going. By the time that preliminary examinations had been held, and some examination fees paid, we found ourselves in possession of the princely sum of sh.180 with which to start a real bank account in our own name.

All this time the students' service on Sunday was going from strength to strength. One of the many odd jobs on which I found myself engaged was the production and revision of a university liturgy to be used at this service. The *United Liturgy* for East Africa was our basis. My chief colleague in the revision was Robin Funsdon, of the Surveying and Photogrammatory Department of the Faculty of Engineering, a former Baptist turned Anglican. We set ourselves to remove some of the infelicities of language, and as far as lay in our power to make the service more biblical, more theological, more dignified, and at the same time better suited to the needs of our students. One of our innovations was a modern declaration of faith as an alternative to the Nicene Creed. This is a little wordy and fluffy, but I think that on the whole it does what it was intended to do. A theological problem was posed by the desire of the students that 'the ancestors' should be commemorated in the liturgy. Everyone is aware of the immense importance of the ancestors (whom Professor Mbiti insists that we should refer to as 'the living dead') in the life of an African people; but how in the world does one commemorate in the Liturgy of Holy Communion ancestors who were not Christian? Here is my solution:

We bless thee for our ancestors
    who lived under thy providence,
    and through whom our peoples have been kept
    in being unto this day.

This seems to me to be true, and to say what can rightly be said; the students seemed to be entirely satisfied with this formulation.

There was a slight element of comedy in the inauguration of our revised liturgy. The students very rightly felt that they should invite the Archbishop of Kenya to use the liturgy for the first time and to preach at the service, but then the dyed-in-the-wool Protestants sent a special message to ask that Festo and I would turn up in full regalia. They had seen photographs in the papers of bishops doing things and felt that this was the way we ought to look. So Festo and I got ourselves up in cope and mitre, not to spoil a Roman holiday. As he kept losing his place in the unfamiliar world of our new liturgy, it was as well that I was standing by him to see him through.

There seemed to be no end to the chores that we felt it right to undertake in addition to the ever-increasing burdens in the University. But all these extras had to be carried out on top of our work in the University. With all the three years now on our hands, and offering in all eighteen courses of lectures, we were hard-pressed, and all of us, I think, overworked. At one stage I reached the absurd point of being in the classroom eighteen periods a week. Obviously, it is impossible with a load like that to do work really on the university level. I was saved by the lecture notes I had brought with me from Hamburg, and by my general knowledge of various subjects, but to give so many bad and unprepared lectures is a soul-searing experience, which I do not wish ever to repeat. Yet in the end the results were good. This was the first time that we were presenting students who would go on immediately to take the BA degree, a diminished dozen from our original registration. One girl had done so well that we were prepared to keep her on for higher studies; but she had done equally well in her other subject, literature, and decided that should be her first choice. In the lower classes, one or two students were on the borderline, but by use of 'compensation' and other pieces of the wreck, all managed one way or another to get safe to land.

Our fourth year opened propitiously with a further increase in numbers. We were now up to 144, rather well distributed between the three years, but a larger number than we could conveniently manage. The Roman Catholics had helped us once again by sending us the Revd R. C. Fuller, whose name had become very well known in England through his work for the Common Bible. We were also fortunate in securing the services as a volunteer of Hugh Pilkington, who in addition to many other virtues had the supreme virtue of possessing a four-seater aircraft, and loving to use it for others.

During this year I had for the first time the experience of lecturing on Christianity in Africa. It is not an easy subject to teach. Much of the basic research had not at that time been done; again and again I had to say to my students, 'About that I cannot say anything, as no reliable material on it is yet available.' The real difficulty, however, lay elsewhere, and was far more difficult to deal with. The minds of all our students had been deeply influenced and thoroughly conditioned by the anti-missionary myth. This runs roughly as follows: 'African society was practically perfect, until the missionaries came along and ruined everything.' In a slightly more virulent form it runs: 'The most evil thing that has ever existed on the face of the earth has been white colonialism. The missionaries were inescapably part of the colonial system; therefore it was impossible for them to do any good, and in point of fact they did a great deal of harm.' If it is pointed out that the missionaries were in most cases there long before the colonial power came in, and that, as in the case of the Devonshire Declaration, which saved Kenya from the fate of Rhodesia, they were as likely to be found opposing the colonial power as to be supporting it – that could not be so, therefore it was not so. 'The missionaries made no attempt to understand the people among whom they lived.' How then did it come about that the early ethnologists were all missionaries, and that the best book ever written about an African people, *The Life of a South African Tribe*, was the work of a Swiss missionary? 'The missionaries studied the people only the more effectively to subdue them.' May not some credit be given to the missionaries for their work in education? After all, without the foundation that they laid, not a single African student would be in the University of Nairobi today. 'The aim of mission schools was only to make the pupils more abjectly subservient to the ruling power.'

Behind this distortion and misinterpretation of history lies the emotional power of the so-called crisis of identity. The old tribal structure has broken down, and with that has gone that sense of security that existed in a close-knit organisation in which every child knew the place in the structure that had been allotted to it. A great many forces had been working for a long time to break up the old structure – the power of Islam, the slave trade, the spread of trade and commerce, the railway and increased mobility; but in the mythology, all the blame for it is laid on colonialism, and in particular on the missionaries. The natural reaction to this sense of loneliness is an almost wholly imaginary idealisation of the past, and a nostalgic desire to return to the womb of tribal existence. This is impossible. Yet where also is the uprooted African of the present day to go? He finds himself citizen of a large country, in which the tribe no longer provides a safe half-way house between the individual and the larger unit and the nation. Political independence has given few of the blessings that had been promised; exploitation seems still to be of the order of the day, except that the exploiters are now Africans and not Europeans. The only group which seems to have escaped this emotional dismay, and even despair, are the committed Christians; these seem to have found a new equilibrium to replace the old balance of the tribe, and in the fellowship of believers an escape from the loneliness and sense of futility which weighed so heavily on those who had not found a new anchor or a new refuge against the storms of modern life.

It was by no means the case that all my fifteen students in this class were committed Christians. It was clear that, as a white man, I would have to walk very warily. I was determined not to conceal anything that I believed to be the truth or to accommodate myself to what I believe to be the errors of the mythology; but at the same time nothing was to be gained by entering into futile controversy, in which affirmation and denial would clash without resolution.

My method was simply to help them to see that the history was far more complicated than they had been led to suppose. Not one of these students had ever been to Ethiopia; they were hardly aware of the existence of this ancient Church, a very odd Church, perhaps, by Western standards, but one which in extreme isolation and ceaselessly threatened by Muslim aggression had yet managed to maintain itself as an African Church for sixteen centuries. In the course of our studies we came up against such doughty champions of black against white as John Philip in South Africa, the French missionaries who supported the great Moshoeshoe I of Lesotho against the Boers, Bishop Colenso whose transcendent merits as a missionary have been unduly forgotten in the rather squalid controversies in which he became involved, the CMS missionaries who upheld the Khama in his struggles for the independence of Botswana, and thereby earned the undying hatred of Cecil Rhodes. They were excited to make the acquaintance of such remarkable figures as the Prophet Harris of the Ivory Coast, and the prophet Simon Kimbangu, and to discover how much of African Christianity has been genuinely African from the start. I made use of the German system of 'seminars'. Each student was invited in turn to read a paper, on a subject suggested by me, to last about twenty to twenty-five minutes and then to be discussed by the other students. They knew that these would have to be factual and not propagandist, and that they would have to defend their views against challenges both from their teacher and from fellow students. The general level was high, and one or two were exceptional; even on so controversial a subject as polygamy, restraint and impartiality were maintained.

The results of my labours were seen in the examination papers at the end of the year. The students were by now well aware that they would not get good marks for agreeing with the views of their professor, that I would not always agree with them, and that they were not expected always to agree with me. I did not, in fact, agree with everything that they wrote in their papers; but it was notable that only one student was still reproducing uncritically the mythology in which she had been brought up.

This year was for me notable in that it was marked by some adventures in the use of an African language. When I came to Nairobi, I had great hopes of learning enough Swahili to be able to help in services and perhaps to preach simple sermons. Swahili is not a difficult language, though perhaps like all languages difficult to speak beautifully. The pronunciation is straightforward, the vowels are almost pure Italian vowels, and the accent on each word is on the penultimate syllable. I worked twice through the grammar, and was beginning to get a good grasp of the structure of the language. I think that, if I had possessed the strength and self-discipline to work one hour longer each day, a mastery of Swahili would have been one of the good things that would have resulted. But the pressure of other things and weariness got the upper hand; I was not hearing Swahili spoken, and the African Churches showed few signs of being interested in inviting me to take part in Swahili services, so my efforts to learn the language became sporadic and largely ineffectual.

My adventures in this field grew out of two overlapping concerns, the first my intense interest in the Masai people, the second my intense interest in better training for our lay workers in the villages.

It seems that the Masai are at last beginning to turn to Christ. All Masai devoutly believe that, when God made the world, he gave all the cattle to the Masai, and that any possession of such creatures by others is a clear case of robbery. Naturally this highly Marxist view of private property does not commend itself to the neighbours. For many years the Masai were regarded as the main obstacle to the penetration of the interior; but, though they did kill off one or two missionaries in the early days, they were probably not as fierce as legend has represented them to be. But they did present an almost solid wall of resistance to the acceptance of the gospel. We have had a certain number of Masai converts, but they have always been few, and there had never been anything like a racial or tribal movement into the Church. And now at long last the situation seems to be changing.

My interest in this attractive people was much stimulated by two visits to our excellent Masai development centre at Isinya, about thirty miles to the south-west of Nairobi. The centre seems to me to be missionary work just as it ought to be. On my second visit I was to preach in the little church, interpreted – and well interpreted – by a Masai student. In the course of my sermon I asked how many of those present had been baptised within the last year, and about fifteen hands went up. Our visiting professor from America, Martin Scharlemann, and his wife were with us; they were in the seventh heaven, never having taken part in quite such a service before, and never having been quite so near to what is obviously the growing edge of the Church.

With this movement of the Masai towards Christ, the Commission on Theological Training considered carefully the need for training Christian workers to develop the movement among them, and reached the conclusion that a fifth Bible school should be opened to bring the diocese of Nairobi more closely into contact with the new situation. Most residents in Nairobi think that the diocese is coterminous with the city, and are unaware that it includes a vast area stretching half-way to the coast, and that extensive sections of Masai land are within the diocese. A survey of the possibilities indicated that Athi River would be the ideal situation for such a Bible school. Athi River is a growing industrial centre, with the tanning industry and a cement factory already established and other industries looking that way. There is no Anglican Church in Athi River, but services were being held in a school, and applications had been made for a plot of six acres on which to build a church and a parsonage; the site would be large enough to accommodate the wished-for Bible school, if ever that should become a reality. We felt that it would be an encouragement to the people there if priests from Nairobi went down from time to time to give them forms of ministry to which they had become almost strangers.

So one bright Sunday morning I drove myself down, faced with the rather appalling prospect of taking the whole Communion service in Swahili unaided. What I found was much what I expected, but if anything a little worse. The Vicar of Kajiado, which was thirty miles away, might or might not come over in three months to take a Communion service. At other times the services were left in the hands of a young man who was willing, and helped me to get things in order, but who had received no training whatever for the work that he was doing, and whose acquaintance with Bible and Prayer Book seemed to be sketchy. The usual interpreter was away, so the task of translating my very simple sermon was undertaken by an elderly gentleman, who also was more willing than competent; what got across to the hearers I hardly venture to imagine. During my sermon I mentioned that this was the first time I had ever taken a whole service in Swahili and asked the congregation to pray for me; after the service the young teacher said to me, 'You said to us that this was the first time you have taken a service; but I would have thought that you were quite well used to doing it.' This was encouraging.

My second visit was on Easter Day. On this occasion both the usual teacher and the usual interpreter were away, so everything was a little more hit-and-miss than usual. I had to choose fresh hymns and lead the singing! There were about eighty people present, and twenty-seven communicants. I felt that they had appreciated my going; as most of them were Luo, to whom in any case Swahili is a foreign language, they could hardly notice the atrocities I committed in my reading.

I had the sad feeling that the Athi River is typical of Anglican lassitude in the face of great opportunities. Nothing more has been heard of the six acres of land. No one has had the energy to pursue the matter with the government. So the prospect of a resident priest at Athi River has had to be relegated to a distant future, and the plan for a Bible school has become purely eschatological.

Before I came to live in Kenya I warned those concerned that they must develop the site of the Chaplaincy Centre, or they would lose it. University students' residences were growing up all round the site; it was in a zone of development, and could easily become a Naboth's vineyard. If the University took steps to acquire it, and offered us as compensation a house of equal value four miles away, it would not be exactly helpful to the chaplaincy cause. I suggested that we might aim at providing a permanent income, to provide for chaplaincy service in the University when the days of the foreigner came to an end, by building small flats and bed-sitting-rooms for which there was an almost unlimited demand in Nairobi as accommodation for young lecturers, graduate students and others on that level of income. My suggestions were taken seriously, though I was surprised at what had grown out of them. We were to have a six-storey tower containing apartments, a vast auditorium, and heaven knows how many offices and other amenities. When we began to look around for loans to help us build our great Babylon, we found that at current rates all the income from our great building would go in debt repayment, and that our beautiful project had to be condemned as useless if considered as an income-producing investment.

There was nothing for it but to go to the Western Churches, and particularly to the German Churches with their immense wealth and their liking for grandiose projects. Here once again we were held up by the excessively narrow interpretation put by those Churches on the word 'development'. I would have thought that the permanent endowment, by one single down payment, of Christian work in a university would be a chance at which any Church body would jump at sight. But not at all. It took endless letters and visits to persuade them that our plan was something in which they might even be interested. I suggested rather bitterly that we had better establish a small leper colony in one corner of our compound and then they would begin to take notice of us. In the end, in order to bring the project within the limits of what they felt could legitimately fit their understanding of development, we had to change the name to the 'Christian Students' Leadership Centre'. Having lived in Germany, I regard the idea of leadership, *das Führerprinzip*, with abhorrence. In my judgement, no single thing has done as much harm to the Christian cause in the world over the last fifty years as the leadership idea. So I was not altogether happy about the change in our title, but at times one must be prepared to bow down in the house of Rimmon; and this time it did the trick. It became plain that a large sum would become available to us from the German Churches, and a rather small sum from Roman Catholic sources in Germany and in the United States. We thought we were home; we learned to our dismay that we had hardly reached the half-way mark.

The German friends told us that, in matters of this kind, they worked only through National Christian Councils. This seemed a little ridiculous as the NCCK represents only the Protestant Churches of Kenya, and in any case has nothing whatever to do with the University. But we made no objection. If the NCCK had been sensible they would have said, 'For this purpose the Churches' Chaplaincy are our agents; our project secretary is on their Committee, and with this we are quite satisfied.' Instead the General Secretary of the NCCK decided that he must take things into his own hands. He affirmed that we had not kept the Churches in touch with what we were doing. This was the direct contrary of the truth. Not long before, I had convened a meeting of church leaders in my own home to talk over with them all that we were doing in the chaplaincy and to ask them to encourage the respective Churches to feel a deeper sense of responsibility towards the future leaders of the country during their time of training in the University. He said that this was entirely a foreign-run enterprise and that the wishes of the students had not been taken into consideration. This again was untrue; we had had student representation on the Committee from the beginning; when consulted afresh, the students gave warm approval to the plans, and repudiated with scorn one suggestion of the Germans – that we should build grass-huts, or something like it, in the midst of the stately student residences that were growing up all around us. He began to convene meetings of church leaders which had no status whatsoever and to which I, though Chairman of the Churches' Chaplaincy, was not invited. What he had overlooked was that the property was held in trust by the Church Commissioners of Kenya on behalf of the Churches' Chaplaincy, that we were the legal owners of the property, and that meetings of local leaders could go on passing resolutions till all was blue but that nothing whatever could actually happen until the Churches' Chaplaincy had met and passed the executive resolutions without which no alien could so much as set foot upon our property.

This wasteful and time-consuming process cost us nearly two years of delay, and the end was not yet.

Owing to the Roman Catholic participation, a new body of trustees would have to be constituted, with adequate representation of both the NCCK and the Episcopal Conference of Kenya. Months passed, and nothing happened. At last we were able to secure an interview with the lawyers who happened to act on behalf of both parties. The man in charge admitted that, owing to preoccupation with other business affecting the University, he had not been able to give attention to our concerns, but now at last legal documents were available for our consideration. When we read the documents we saw at once that he had been wrongly briefed; the documents as they stood would have constituted the NCCK and KEC not trustees but absolute owners of this now extremely valuable property. We had no intention whatever of surrendering our ownership, nor indeed could we do so without consultation with Christian Aid, which had obtained the property for us in the first place. As soon as the matter was explained to him the lawyer saw the point; extensive changes were made in the original drafts, and we could feel that our position had been adequately safeguarded.

By now more than five calendar years had elapsed since I had first warned the chaplaincy that steps must be taken to guard against expropriation by the University. I was beginning to wonder whether I should live long enough to see even the first sod turned in this project which had been so long and so unnecessarily delayed.

All this time our over-long academic year was grinding slowly to its close, and we were once again faced with the nightmare of the examination period. Our examination system, based on that of the University of London, was unduly cumbrous. It involved setting examination papers before the lectures had been given, and the process was so complex that anything could go wrong. In this fourth year the nightmare was worse than ever. Two of my excellent colleagues had corrected their papers at random and had entered the students' numbers at random instead of serially on their mark sheets; in order to save the time involved in sending the mark sheets back to them, I concluded that the best thing was to retype the whole lot myself. Our external examiner was not in very good health, and papers dribbled back from him, hardly allowing time for the co-ordination of our marks with his. I never thought that we should get the job done in time, but somehow we did, and our marks went in only a few hours late.

Then, at the examiners' meeting, the Sociology Department blandly informed us that fourteen students had failed to take one paper. One of our African colleagues whispered to Dr Donders, 'That is quite impossible; if an African student had failed to write a paper, he would sleep in the corridor that night, in order to be in the office the next morning the moment it opened.' However, we wasted an hour discussing what should be done with the delinquent students. During the course of the meeting the sociologists found all the missing marks – all the students, naturally, had in reality taken the paper.

Then, when the marks of all the faculties were presented to the Senate, I noticed that the marks of our one MA student were missing. I was in error over one or two minor points of regulations, but it had not helped that the Arts' Faculty Office had lost his mark sheets. This requires a little explanation. From the start it had been my intention that students should be able, after their BA, to take a higher course of study leading to the degree of MA, equivalent to a good BD in the West. This young Baptist had had four years in the United States, in a rather obscure university in Texas, and was serving as a tutor in the Baptist Seminary at Arusha in Tanzania. His mission was prepared to send him back to America for higher studies, but he himself elected to come to us instead to concentrate on New Testament studies, and to qualify himself to be an effective seminary teacher. We found him intelligent and willing to study, but dangerously over-confident, never in his life having been confronted with anything like high academic standards. His examination results, while not brilliant, were moderately good, and a short dissertation on the Bible in East Africa, during the preparation for which he had taken the trouble to visit four sets of translators and to discuss their problems, was far better than I had expected. The missing mark sheets were found; the Vice-Chancellor took administrative action, and the young man was able to go forward into the second year.

This was much more important than just the teaching of a single student; it meant the breaking of the sound barrier. For twenty-three years I had been urging that higher theological studies should be made available in Africa. Now the University of Nairobi had accepted the principle, and we had shown that it could be done. Students in our department could take the MA degree; and we were also providing research facilities up to the degrees of MA and PhD. This is what I had come to Africa to do, and after four years of hard work, it seemed that the plans were beginning to work and the visions to be realised.

I had supposed that my term of service in East Africa would come to a conclusion with the end of this fourth academic year. But owing to the change in the start of the academic year from September to July, I found that I should be responsible for guiding the department into its fifth year. No sooner had the year opened, than we found ourselves plunged in a new sea of troubles.

In its desire to increase the number of teachers available to the schools in Kenya, the government had brought pressure to bear on the University to introduce a three-year Bachelor of Education

degree, instead of keeping the much more satisfactory system of re-
taining the B.Ed. as a fourth-year course to follow on the three-year
course for the degree of Bachelor of Arts. A Faculty of Education
was set up in the University, and university status was given to
Kenyatta College twelve miles away. The Faculty of Education
admitted an enormous number of students, many of whom would
not have been admitted in any other faculty; and then turned round
and said that, as it taught only methods and principles of education,
the arts and science faculties would have to do all the teaching for
them in other subjects, without any provision for an increase of
staff. We saw the cloud lowering over us, and tried to decide
what we should do when it should burst. The Dean of the Arts
Faculty asked us to prepare statements as to the maximum number
of students that we could take in each department; we stated that
80 was a suitable number in the first year, but that by stretching our
resources we could manage to take 100. But students had already
been admitted by the University. A home had to be found for them
somewhere. In the end we found ourselves with 205 students in
the first year, and a total of 312 in the department. This was a
horrifying situation. We knew that we should be confronted with
a large number of very poorly equipped students, many of whom
had drifted into the department not from any interest in the subject
but simply because they did not know where else to go. We were
in any case seriously understaffed. We had been able to replace our
lost Muslim colleague with a member of the Ismaili community. The
CMS had kindly sent the Rev M. W. Mathews to take the place of
Dr Day, who had already left for Canada. Professor Scharlemann
was succeeded as Visiting Professor by Professor Waetjer, who came
from California at his own expense to help us out. Dr Mateigh was
prepared to face an enormous first-year class and to do his best
with them. Hugh Pilkington, having just acquired the Pusey and
Ellerton Prize for Hebrew at Oxford, signed on for another year,
and was prepared to teach almost any language under the sun.
We could expect help again from St Paul's College, Limuru, from
September. So we could provide a good variety of lectures, with
a number of optional subjects; but tutorial work, and the kind of
close personal relations with students which we had tried from the
start to cultivate, had now become a sheer impossibility.

During this time we became involved, against our will, in a
controversy – the so-called moratorium on missionaries in the Third
World.[1] The idea put forward, in particular by one of the leaders
of the Presbyterian Church in Kenya, is that these Churches will

never find their identity as long as there are foreigners among
them, and that therefore for at least a time all foreigners should
be withdrawn. Unfortunately the theological issues underlying this
controversy are rarely brought out into the open. There are two
views of the Church, one Christian and one tribal. The Christian
view is that the Church consists of all those who are members of
it, and of all those who are not yet members of it; as William
Temple succinctly put it, 'The Church is the only society in the
world which exists for the benefit of those who are not members
of it.' This was the challenge put to the leaders of the younger
Churches at the Whitby Missionary Conference of 1947: 'What are
your plans for the total evangelisation of your countries?' The tribal
view runs something like this: The Church is something visible and
identifiable, consisting of a known number of people; it used to be
controlled by the missionaries; now we have got rid of the missionaries and want to control everything ourselves; in such a situation the
continuing presence of the foreigners is only a complication and an
embarrassment. At the worst this attitude is not far from the political
concept of 'jobs for the boys'. At best it may spring from a genuine
feeling that a Christian of other races always acts in the presence of
the white man, plays up to him, and fails to be his own true self.
In the majority of cases it seems to be a compound of ambition,
resentment at injuries true or imagined in the past, and uneasiness
in the presence of foreigners who may well be better qualified.

The tribal outlook on the Church seemed to some of us to be
particularly harmful precisely at the time at which we were working.
The number of Christians in Kenya was increasing with what I have
described as alarming rapidity. Doors were open everywhere. The
Kenyan government was faithfully observing its pledge to maintain
religious liberty. The question before us was how the evangelisation
of Kenya could best be completed within a generation, or before the
doors began to close. Or, we may formulate the question in another
way: If all foreign help in money and personnel was withdrawn,
would the Churches collapse? For the Protestant Churches the
answer would certainly be no, though for the Roman Catholic
Church it would be more doubtful, because of its still enormous
dependence on foreign priests and sisters. But if we ask whether
the Church could not only survive and maintain itself, bringing
the claims of the gospel before every Kenyan, the answer is that
it could not. International co-operation will be urgently needed for
a long time in this sphere, no less than in those of national health
and education.

In the department we were not specially affected by the tribal view. A group of young Kenyan philosophers was growing up, on whom we should be able to draw as posts had to be filled. But on the side of religious studies the situation was very different. There was hardly a single Kenyan whom we could even consider for appointment except in the field of Islamics. This was not the fault of the Kenyans but of the missionary-controlled Churches, which through their lack of foresight and their failure to attract promising young men to theological study and the work of the ministry had entirely failed to provide for the time when the foreigner would no longer be available. This was generally recognised. If all foreigners had been withdrawn, the department would have consisted of one young Kenyan philosopher, not very well qualified, who was a non-practising Roman Catholic, and one young lecturer in Islamics, a not very active member of the Ismaili community, who had a PhD from Edinburgh but no deep knowledge of Arabic. The presence of the foreigners might be disliked or even resented; but it was recognised as inevitable and endured, especially in view of the evident determination of the members of the department to Kenyanise as quickly as possible.

The Anglican Church had been through its brief period of anti-foreign feeling, but this seemed to have passed away. The Commission on Theological Training over which I presided had passed an emphatic resolution condemning the tribal view of the Church, asserting that the qualification for service in the Church in Kenya was neither race nor colour but living faith in Christ, and willingness to be identified with the Church of the Province. This was certainly the attitude of the older men. But the poison of tribalism seemed to have spread itself in the middle group, and the passion for Africanisation at all costs to have taken hold, to the detriment of interest in the wider outreach of the Church.

These were in the main problems for the future and for others to deal with. But I had seen enough in Kenya to learn again what I had learned long ago in India, that when colour, racism, anti-foreign prejudice, ambition and intrigue enter in the life of a Church, the cause of Christ is bound to be grievously wounded, and to suffer serious set-backs. It looked as though the next twenty years might be for the Kenyan Churches a period of introversion, of opportunities lost because not observed, and of impoverishment rather than enrichment in the life of the Spirit.

I had little time for the consideration of such problems, since my period of service in Kenya was drawing to a close, and the question of the appointment of my successor pressed hard upon me. I had given the administration more than six months' notice that I would not seek a renewal of my contract when it ran out in September. I had very little feeling of growing old; but at times the grind of daily work in the department was growing wearisome, and in any case at seventy-two a man ought to recognise his age and make way gracefully for a younger man. So the post had been advertised, and I had hoped that everything would be settled before the end of April, when I had to go to Malawi to deliver a Livingstone memorial lecture (the centenary of his death fell on 1 May 1973), and from there to England for a short period of leave.

Rather to my surprise the administration asked me to prepare a shortlist of names from among the applicants, and also to sit on the appointments committee. We had little difficulty in discovering our two most favoured candidates.

Professor John Mbiti is a Kenyan, has a PhD from Cambridge, and has made himself quite a reputation as a writer of books in the African tradition in philosophy and religion. He had served for some years as head of the Department of Religious Studies at Makerere University in Uganda, but it was clear the time had come at which he had felt that he would like to return to his own country. There was no doubt at all in the minds of my colleagues on the committee that he would be their first choice for the professorship.

The name of Dr Donders has appeared from time to time in this record. This able, witty, broadminded Dutch White Father had been for three years in practice the head of the philosophy section of our department. He was unknown to a number of the members of the committee, but did extraordinarily well in the interview. In point of fact Donders did not care in the least whether he was appointed to the professorship or not. Given the choice, I think he would have preferred to remain as teacher and pastor rather than to shoulder the burdens and frustrations that weigh so heavy on a professor and the head of a department. On the other hand, though at the time of his arrival he had no clue as to the way in which a university of the British tradition works, under my care he had come to understand the system completely, and in some ways was better at handling it than I was myself. I was sure that he would do whatever seemed to be right, and that he would not allow personal predilections to stand in the way of duty.

It was decided to offer the post to Professor Mbiti. Then we and he were faced with a wholly unexpected problem. Just before coming to Nairobi for the interview with the committee, he had received from the World Council of Churches an invitation to become Director of the Ecumenical Institute at Bossey near Geneva. It was clear that he was desperately anxious to accept the invitation, both for his own sake and for the sake of his wife who is German Swiss; and this in fact he did.

I do not regret having given the last four years of my fully active life to an African university at a crucial stage of its development. But I have come to the conclusion that I have the wrong kind of memory. I remember and feel as vividly and acutely as though they were happening today all the fears and anxieties, the frustrations and failures, the absurdities and contradictions, the feelings of exasperation and near despair. I do not forget the occasional successes and achievements, the moments of happiness in which it has seemed as though something really had got done that was worthwhile; but these things come to me with far less immediacy and vividness than the others. As a result I tend to take a rather dark view of the past, to question what appears to be achievement, and to wonder whether anything has been done that will stand the test of time or even the censure of my own conscience. Yet these years had not been wholly unproductive. In a university which had been completely secular, a Department of Philosophy and Religious studies had been founded and had taken root. The confidence of the Churches had been won. Students had come in unexpected numbers and had both shown and expressed appreciation of what was being done for them. There has been world-wide interest in what we have tried to do. After I had preached my last sermon at the students' service I received the following letter from the Assistant Secretary of the Worship Committee:

Dear Professor Neill,
    The above committee cannot thank you enough for your constant love and devotion to the welfare of the students. It is evident the Lord has used you most graciously in your ministry to us especially during the two consecutive sermons. Many of those who attended were greatly enlightened on the Lord's Prayer.
    May God bless you exceedingly in all your work.
        Yours in his service,
        Esther Njina.

So perhaps, after all, everything was not in vain.[2]

9

A Last Chapter

When I brought my narrative to a conclusion in the year 1973, I little thought that I should be given another ten years of active and varied life. It seems right that my story should be rounded off by some account of the experiences and lessons that later years have brought.

After leaving Nairobi, I allowed myself a period of travel, without long-term plans, but always with the expectation of returning to England and of making plans for a retirement home.

One valuable experience was that of teaching for six months in the Asian University at Westville, near Durban in Natal, as a substitute for my friend Professor Oosthuizen, who was completing a book. I made a leisurely journey across the Pacific. This gave me an opportunity to see something of the exciting developments in Papua New Guinea and Melanesia, where political emancipation has been accompanied or preceded by a parallel movement for independence in the Churches.

In the end, after crossing America and Canada, I arrived back in England, homeless and under the necessity of finding a new home. Just at that time the Principal of Wycliffe Hall, Jim Hickinbotham, whom I had known since his undergraduate days, wrote to invite me to give the first series of Chavasse Lectures, founded to commemorate the two Bishops Chavasse, the younger of whom I had known well. The theme of the lectures was to have some relationship to the mission of the Christian Church, and this was naturally wholly acceptable to me. I spent six very enjoyable weeks there, and the lectures were well attended. When in the course of a conversation with the Principal I happened to mention my problem of finding a home, he remarked that Oxford was not a bad place in which to retire.

A few weeks later he followed this up by offering me a married students' flat; and so I found myself provided with a home in which

318

I would be surrounded by the young, a situation highly agreeable to me in my apparently unalterable bachelor condition.

My second windfall came to me even more fortuitously. I happened to go to the quinquennial meeting of the Society for the Study of the History of Religions, which was being held that year in the University of Lancaster. This was more for the sake of having a leisurely drink with friends than to hear erudite lectures, but nevertheless, when a lecture was announced on South Indian Hinduism, I went along, together with about thirty others, to be enlightened on the subject. All went well, except for the absence of the lecturer. Having just completed a book on the subject, I ventured to speak on the subject instead, and in consequence met Norvin Hein, Professor of Comparative Religion at Yale University and Divinity School, and rather a notable expert on Hinduism, who was in the audience. Some days later, he wrote to say that he had been able to arrange for me to be appointed as Visiting Fellow of Yale Divinity School, and to have the use of the Day Missions Library, which ranks as one of the best missionary libraries in the world. So for a number of years, Yale Divinity School became part of my life.

During these years I set to work to rediscover the English-speaking world, on both sides of the Atlantic. Wycliffe Hall, for example, was completely different from the college I knew when I spent a term there in 1933. The majority of students then came from Christian homes, and in many cases from clerical homes. They had attended church every Sunday of their lives, had a considerable knowledge of the Bible, and a settled, though perhaps rather conventional, religious faith. By contrast, in 1977 probably about two thirds of the students, as it happened to me, were so-called 'new believers'. Coming from homes in which there was no living religion, they had encountered Christ in their late teens or at college, and almost all would speak without hesitation of their 'conversion', in most cases giving the date and circumstances in which it took place. Almost all professed a definite, and in some cases rather rigid, conservative understanding of the Christian faith. They came in with great zeal, but little understanding or knowledge of the Bible. They had little experience of liturgy, and found the regular daily services in the chapel a burden rather than an inspiration. Now they not only had to change their field of study and experience to theology as an academic discipline, but they had to change their approach from the dogmatic methods of a conservative faith to those of an enquiring, open theology. It has always seemed to me that theological teachers are, in most cases, very bad at building bridges from the one approach to the other in such a way that unnecessary suffering, and in some cases very grave crises of faith, are not involved in the process. Too many students seem to me to end their theological studies in a state of schizophrenia, unwittingly assenting to the truth of the new, but clinging fretfully, if not feverishly, to the old. This was one area in which I felt I might be able to help.

Each year I gave a course in twentieth-century Christianity, took my share in preaching, and in the first term gave a short course on the art of prayer, but I declined to become a member of the official teaching staff. Instead I preferred to describe myself as a 'grandfather in residence', and to befriend the students and help them in any way I could. From the feedback I received from time to time, it would seem that my presence was felt to be of value to the general life of the College.

Similarly, I was trying to find my way about the complex life of the Church of England as a whole. The general atmosphere of gloom and despondency, with theological colleges being closed or amalgamated, the number of ordinations per year being restricted, and parishes being combined, often with little regard to the varying traditions and needs of those thus unwillingly brought together, was undergoing a remarkable change. This was due to one man, Donald Coggan, who from the moment of his appointment as Archbishop of Canterbury set himself to preach for greatness. I have no doubt he will go down in history as a great archbishop. During his five-year tenure of the see he was subjected to an unworthy campaign of denigration and detraction, which obscured the great gifts he brought to the office; his humility concealed from many the quiet tenacity with which he worked. It became possible again to plan for greatness. The number of ordinands started increasing, with Evangelical colleges crammed to the doors. Church attendance was slowly increasing. If there were no grounds for great optimism, there was certainly no place for a base and cringing pessimism.

For one achievement Donald Coggan has received far less credit than he deserved. Single-handed, he saved the Lambeth Conference. The conference is, strictly speaking, a large committee of bishops who have accepted the invitation issued to them by the Archbishop of Canterbury on his sole authority. After the disas- trously ineffective 1968 conference, he decided to change the char- acter of the conference by moving it from London to Canterbury, and making it strictly residential. I had argued for this since 1948, intelligent students, both of whom were clearly going to pass. One was unable to make any comment about the third session of the Second Vatican Council which had just been concluded, the other had not the least idea what I was talking about when I asked him about the integration of the International Missionary Council and the World Council of Churches in 1961. This was a typical example of the restricted field of detailed knowledge of most students.

One of the things that had attracted me in the first place to the theological faculty was that all my colleagues were pastors and preachers. They were not simply ordained ministers of their churches, but they were seriously interested in the spiritual welfare of our students. One sign of this was the University Sermon, which was preached by the professors in rotation on every Sunday during term in one or other of the historic city-centre churches. They were badly attended, since the population had long since moved away from there. I think my colleagues were a little surprised when I let them know that I would like to take my turn too, but there was no difficulty about this, and I became a university preacher.

One of my chief purposes was, of course, to enter into close relationship with my students, and to get to know them personally. This was not altogether easy to achieve, because whatever students say of their professors behind their backs, convention requires a rather formal deference. Usually a close relationship grows up only between the candidate for a doctorate and the professor who guides and directs his studies. I knew that it would be difficult to break out of the pattern, but at least I was determined to do my best.

The first thing, obviously, was to find a home. I was determined to have somewhere where I could entertain my colleagues, for example for one of the monthly meetings, and where I could invite the students. It was by no means easy to find the right place. The income of a professor is limited, and rents in Hamburg are very high. The two rooms sub-let to me by an elderly widow were depressingly 1910 in decor, and in any case I wanted a place of my own. Quite by chance, one Saturday afternoon I wandered past a large block of two-roomed flats under construction. It was exactly what I wanted, and on the Monday morning I secured the last available one. I could not move in for several months, as there was much work still to be done in the building. Even when I did move in, not all my furniture had arrived, and I had to spend the first few nights on a camp-bed, which had the irritating habit of dumping me periodically on the floor. But the flat was mine; and I could hardly have chosen better for all the purposes that I had in view.

Strangely enough, this was the first real home that I had ever had in my life. In Cambridge, I had lived in college rooms. In India I had lived in a succession of furnished mission bungalows. In Geneva, never knowing how long I should be staying there, I had made do with a number of furnished flats. Now I was confronted with four bare walls, a floor and a ceiling that I could do what I liked with. The great secret of a home is not to attempt to do everything at once, but to let it grow up around one as the need arises. I spent a good deal of money on oriental rugs and carpets, which my friends supposed to be heirlooms I had brought back with me from India. I recovered from Trinity College the two rosewood glass-fronted bookshelves which I had had made long before for my episcopal house in India. Gradually the place took shape and became a real home.

It was at this point that I became aware of an appalling loss. One of the things to which I was particularly looking forward was having all my books around me once again. When I left Cambridge in 1947 to go to Geneva, I took only about a quarter of my books with me. The rest my brother Gerald had kindly agreed to store in his large parsonage just outside Gateshead. So a well-known contractor was called in, the books were taken away, and I thought no more of it, imagining that the books were safe and in good care, though I was surprised that the bill was so low, and that when I visited my brother, my books were scattered round the house. I made no comment, though I thought it careless of him to take the books out of their crates. Only when the books arrived in Hamburg did I discover the terrible disaster. Something like six hundred books were missing, and valuable sets of volumes were no longer complete.

Gradually we pieced together the story: the books had never been crated, but simply tied together in bundles with string. The removal man refused to carry them upstairs in the vicarage, and dumped them in the hall. It had been a split load, split between two lorries going in roughly the same direction, and one had never arrived. It was impossible to discover what had happened to the missing load fifteen years previously. The documents had been destroyed, and neither the head office in London nor the branch office in Cambridge was prepared to accept any liability.

So I found myself deprived of a number of valuable and in some cases irreplaceable books, of a considerable amount of crockery and china, and of a number of precious pictures. What is a scholar without his books! Some of the working volumes I naturally replaced, but books have a history and personality of their own. Some had been painfully saved up for; some had come as gifts or prizes. The whole history of a lifetime is recorded on one's shelves. There are losses to which one never becomes reconciled; these aching gaps in my wealth permanently diminished the pleasure I was to take in my new and carefully planned home. I could not look at the shelves without being aware of the books that ought to have been there and were not.

However, life has to go on, whatever the heartaches. I had provided myself with a dwelling in order to entertain, and entertain I would. I ran the flat frankly on principles of slave labour. The younger generation is much criticised, and not altogether without reason, but it is quite astounding how willing young people are to help, and to undertake menial tasks in a good cause. For my house-warming, I invited fourteen people, the largest number that I could conveniently seat around my living room, for a wine and cheese party, a festivity apparently unknown at that time in Hamburg. With three slaves in the kitchen everything went smoothly, perhaps because they consumed the extra two pounds of strawberries I had bought to augment the four pounds of berries my guests feasted on. At any rate, there was not a single strawberry left for me when everyone had gone home. Similarly I employed an international team for spring cleaning in two successive years. Six energetic and willing young friends, British and German, washed and scrubbed and dusted, refreshed by beer and other drinks, and an excellent cold lunch prepared by my own fair hands. We worked from ten in the morning until seven at night, and then we went off to my favourite restaurant to celebrate a day well spent.

Apart from entertaining my colleagues and their wives for convivial evenings of coffee, wine and liquer, and conversation, I tried to get all the students attending my seminars to come in groups of not more than eight, sometimes for a simple meal, sometimes for coffee and conversation only. Groups vary astonishingly in openness and responsiveness. Sometimes conversation would flow freely and easily through two hours and more; on other evenings I would have to do most of the talking myself. What impressed the students most was that we always ended up with prayer – a shortened form of Compline, a short reading from Scripture, and the blessing. Anything in the nature of an inner life has fallen out of the consciousness even of the German theological student to such an extent that this always took them by surprise. Years later, when I was in the Transvaal, I met one of the old students of the Mission Academy, and he told me how much these entirely informal evenings in the house of a professor had meant to the students of his generation.

One of my most interesting evenings was with a group of incipient rebels. We had felt that there ought occasionally to be an act of worship in the rather austere building in which our faculty was housed. Professor Müller-Schwäfe arranged for a brief service to be held once a week in the wide open space from which the upper libraries opened. He, on his day a most excellent preacher, was much interested in the liturgical movement in Germany, and the planning of services, which I took my regular turn in conducting, was organised on rather traditional lines. This left a number of students rather unhappy. Discovering this feeling, I invited a number of them to my flat to talk things over. The 'in' word was 'relevant', meaning the same in German as in English, and they said quite frankly that the *Te Deum*, when sung as we sang it in its beautiful German metrical form, meant nothing to them; they wanted their service to come hot from the ferment of the world around them. I did my best to explain the meaning of liturgy, the stability of timeless forms which link us with the Church in all ages and all places, and into which our immediate needs and intercessions can be inserted. I am not sure that I was successful in convincing them, but it was clear that they were surprised and pleased to find a professor who took their viewpoint seriously. When student unrest became one of our burning problems, this was the cry which was heard again and again from the less revolutionary students: 'No one listens to us, or pays any attention to what we think.'

In point of fact, there was much more sympathy in the faculty for these liturgical revolutionaries than they realised. It was arranged they should regularly lead the service. There was something impressive about their concern; passages would be read from the daily newspapers or from periodicals, drawing attention to areas of human need or injustice. Clearly these young people had learned something from Dietrich Bonhoeffer, and his 'religionless Christianity', which of course does not mean, as is sometimes mistakenly supposed, 'Christianity without religion', in the English sense of the term, but Christianity as concerned not with what we do in Church, but with what happens in the world outside it.

The greater part of my time was spent in the University, or in matters relating to its life, but I soon found myself drawn into other concerns.

First among them was, naturally, the Anglican Church. The congregation could boast continuous existence since 1615, making it the oldest congregation with an uninterrupted history of worship in English. The rights granted to English merchants to hold services according to their own use in their own houses were not intended to form the basis for an English Church open to all, but this is in fact what happened. Frau Müller, a valiant Englishwoman married to a German, had kept an eye on the church throughout the war, and now it was being shared with the Church of Scotland, and the Missions to Seamen. The incumbent, Cyril Sharpe, was chaplain to the Missions to Seamen, who paid most of his salary, and had the lion's share of his time. He had no time for sermon preparation until Sunday morning, with predictable results. Both he and the congregation seemed relieved when I took over a good deal of the preaching, including Remembrance Sunday, when the church was packed, and the memorial sermons for John Kennedy and Winston Churchill. There was one delightful consequence of this. A German lawyer who was an ardent Anglican happened to overhear me saying once that if I were rich, I would like good silver in my house. So instead of presenting me with a cheque for my services every year, some gift of silver would arrive. I have before me as I write a very pleasing pair of silver candlesticks, and a silver jug of very unusual and attractive form, both from the committee of the congregation.

One custom which gave me great pleasure grew up in connection with the English Church. Hamburg is not a place where tourists stay long, but a number of them find their way to the English Church, and one never knows who may be in the congregation. At one time I had several young friends who became skilful in greeting people after the service, finding out if they were in Hamburg to learn German, to work for a multinational organisation, or simply visitors passing through. If they were free, we would carry them off for lunch at an excellent Italian restaurant. Then we would take the tram to my dwelling for coffee and further conversation. On occasion I had to throw the group out at 5 p.m. after a steady flow of conversation, partly but never entirely on religious subjects.

As soon as it became known that I was in Hamburg, invitations began to pour in; whenever possible I tried to accept them. These invitations fell into five classes. There were sermons at ordinary services in church, sometimes but not always with a missionary emphasis. There were parish meetings of the type so familiar in England, attended mainly by elderly women, who would listen courteously to anything that was said, but whose minds had taken on such a fixed pattern that it was unlikely that any new idea could penetrate their heads. There were gatherings of earnest clergy, interested in the ecumenical movement and anxious to learn from the horse's mouth what was actually going on in that world. There were meetings of students, usually but not always organised by the *Studentengemeinde*, the organisation of university chaplaincy work which had stepped into the gap created when Hitler suppressed the Student Christian Movement. Finally, there were the annual festivals of the regional missionary societies. I could reconstruct from my diary a list of all those main engagements, but this would be unendurably tedious for the reader. I will just mention a few of exceptional interest.

One of the pleasantest of these escapes from Hamburg was to a national conference of the Schule Bibelkreis, literally 'The School Bible Circle'. The conference was held at Whit at Duisberg, and was attended by about five hundred young people from all over Western Germany. We listened to several carefully organised sermons and addresses, but it seemed to me that these were terribly heavy pabulum for schoolboys, and that I must try to give them something a little lighter. I had taken immense pains with my address on the theme given to me by the organisers of the conference: 'We can live together.' I started by suggesting that this was a very arrogant affirmation, and developed my theme in the form of a dramatic dialogue between myself and the Apostle Paul (Jews and Gentiles), and myself and Sir Thomas More (his great speech to the Council after his condemnation on a charge of high treason). The sustained applause at the end showed that these young people had never heard anything quite like this before, and that it had caught their fancy (once again curtain call as for a *prima donna*!).

This same organisation, at a regional meeting, gave me one of the most interesting evenings of my life. They had invited older men, who had been members of the Bibelkreis twenty-five years before, in the early days of the Hitler regime. At that time young people were asking their parents most awkward questions: 'What were you doing during the war, Daddy?' As a very large number of the parents had a great deal to hide, they were reduced to giving highly evasive answers, but the young people really wanted to know. History as taught in many schools ended with Bismarck or with the First World War; what happened after that was discreetly shrouded in mystery, perhaps by the orders of the occupying powers, who did not wish to give teachers who were crypto-Nazis, as many of them were, the opportunity of putting dangerous ideas into the minds of the pupils. So here was their opportunity. We saw first a film of the national meeting of the Bibelkreis in 1933 or thereabouts, curiously formal and quasi-military by British standards; and then a propaganda film of the Hitler Youth, perhaps from 1939, showing all the glorious possibilities which membership of the Hitler Youth would offer to a jaded and disillusioned generation. Then followed the questions. They almost all tended in the same direction: 'How was it possible that you did not know what Hitler was really up to?' At last one of the older men broke in: 'Now I am going to ask you a question, and I want you to give an honest answer: If you were subjected today to the same kind of propaganda to which we were subjected at your age, how many of you would refuse to join the Hitler youth?' Out of a hundred boys present, only two put up their hands.

By this time, relations between the Protestant and Roman Catholic Churches were better than they had been at any time since the Reformation; I was one of the many beneficiaries of this improved situation.

I paid two visits to Münster in Westphalia, which had now risen from its ashes and been restored almost to its earlier medieval splendour. The first was strictly Protestant – Reformation Day, the anniversary of Martin Luther's publication of the Ninety-five Theses, a day which is solemnly observed on the Continent, but has never become part of the English religious tradition. My subject was 'Reformation and Ecumenism'. The other occasion was more interesting and significant. Münster is one of the few universities in Germany which has a Roman Catholic as well as a Protestant faculty of theology. These had existed in almost total isolation from each other, and it was only the more open attitude generated by the Second Vatican Council which had brought them into a closer and more friendly relationship. I was invited by the two student Christian bodies together to come and give a discourse on the subject of Anglicanism. There has always been massive ignorance on this subject in Germany. There is as yet no satisfactory book on Anglicanism in German. So it was always a pleasure to me to be asked to lecture on this subject and to attempt to lead a German audience into a sympathetic understanding of a Church which appears to Roman Catholics to be all too Protestant, and to Protestants to be all too Catholic.

Another centre in which I shared in the joint hospitality of Roman Catholics and Protestants was Würzburg. The pastor of the student congregation at that time was a young man called Dieter Voll, who had chosen an unusual subject for his doctoral dissertation, namely, aggressive evangelism by the third generation of Anglo-Catholics.

He twice got me to come for a weekend retreat for the more committed among the Christian students, held at a delightful old house about ten miles from Würzburg. He called also for a joint meeting of the two Christian groups in the University. Here the Protestants were in a small minority, but it was evident that old prejudices were giving way to a new spirit, and a serious attempt at mutual understanding was being developed.

I found I was developing quite a reputation as an interesting speaker. Almost all Germans, when asked to speak on any subject, will sit down and write a formal treatise, going back to basic principles, complicated in expression, and with hardly any lighter element. My habit of speaking directly to my hearers, and of trying to get to the heart of the matter without beating about the bush, appealed to a number of my hearers, and the dramatic approach, being rather unfamiliar, again was found to be a pleasant contrast to the usual German approach.

Perhaps my most important contribution, outside the University, was in the field of the growing sense of missionary responsibility in the German Churches. From the beginning, missionary work in Germany has been the concern of private societies, supported by 'friends of missions', and not of the Churches on an official basis. I think it is true that no German Church, as such, ever sent out a missionary overseas until the twentieth century. The society would select its candidates, train them in its own seminary, ordain them, send them out to their work, care for their dependent children if necessary, and care for them in old age. It may be said that the English missionary societies have followed much the same policy. There are, however, vital differences, one being that even the Church Missionary Society, the most powerful of English missionary societies, has never ordained a missionary; it has recognised that ordination is a function of the Church, and not of any limited or local society. In Germany there were two difficulties. Under the regional system of church organisation, a man was ordained to exercise the Christian ministry strictly within the limits of a certain geographical area, ruled over by a certain prince as bishop. It was quite uncertain whether such a church had legal power to ordain anyone for service outside its geographical limits. Second, the academic conditions for ordination were very rigidly laid down. If missionary candidates had been trained in seminaries and not in universities, they had not fulfilled the necessary conditions. So a situation arose in which missionary ordination was of a different kind from church ordination, and it did not follow that one ordained as a missionary would have any right to preach or minister in his own country when he returned there. One result of this was that German missionaries went overseas with very confused ideas on what structure they should create. They were a mission and not a church; how could they set to work to create a church in a non-Christian world?

It seemed to me that, whereas most British missionary societies were living in the nineteenth century, the German societies were governed by the 'enlightened despotism' of a still earlier era. The *Missionsdirektor* (General Secretary), and his assistant the *Missionsinspektor* (Area Secretary), had certainly far greater power than that exercised even by so great a potentate as the General Secretary of the Church Missionary Society. The separation of mission and Church in the areas of missionary operations was almost complete. It seemed to me that the societies had not even begun to consider the vast range of new problems that had come with the rise of the younger Churches.

While I was in Germany things began rapidly changing. The missionary societies were acquiring a more churchly attitude. They realised the advantage of having missionaries who had completed a full university course, and were therefore qualified for church ordination. Some of the leaders of the missionary enterprise had close connections with the Church themselves. My old friend, Missionsinspektor Ihmels (Leipzig Mission) was a son of the late Bishop of Saxony (and both his son and daughter are full-time church workers). Freytag, though he never held any position in the Church, was a churchman to the core. Slowly the fact that, as a result of the work of the societies, great new Churches were coming into existence in many parts of the world, was beginning to penetrate.

On the other side, the Churches were beginning to realise that a Church which is not missionary is not really a Church. In his book *The Household of God*, which had been translated into German and was widely read, Bishop Lesslie Newbigin stresses this point, and makes it clear that missionary outreach is as much a part of the nature of the true Church as the *reine Lehre*, pure doctrine, on which the Lutherans so much pride themselves. The integration of the World Council with the International Missionary Council had made many churchmen in Germany think deeply as to the relationship between Church and mission. The fact that there were two great ecumenical organisations stressed the separation that had existed between stability and extension in the Christian world. Would too close an association between the Churches and mission kill off the missionary enterprise, as the opponents of integration claimed? Why should not the Churches become missionary? Was not Newbigin right in thinking that a missionary extension is one of the necessary marks of a living Church?

At this juncture, I was asked to address a gathering of German church leaders at Arnoldshain. In my lecture, which was published, and widely read and quoted, I said that, if the German Churches wished to continue to pull their weight in the new integrated ecumenical movement, they should be prepared to increase fourfold, and at once, their contribution in money and personnel to the missionary movement. This was a deliberately provocative statement, but it had its origin in the truth.

The Germans had made a great contribution to missionary thought. Gustav Warneck is generally credited with laying the foundations of modern missiology with his five-volume *Missionslehre* (1892-1903). Despite their limitations, Julius Richter's *History of Protestant Missions* and his other works are an invaluable source of useful and relevant information about almost every aspect of missionary work. The Germans, armed with academic study and practical experience in the field, regarded themselves as the only people who really knew how missionary work should be carried out. They contrasted unfavourably what they believed to be the 'Anglo-Saxon' appeal to the individual with the German *Volksmission*, the appeal to the whole life and soul of a people, as put into practice by such great missionaries as Bruno Gutmann in East Africa and Christian Keysser in New Guinea. They conveniently overlooked the fact that the Anglo-Saxons had been at least as successful as the Germans in bringing into existence in many parts of the world large indigenous Churches deeply rooted in the lives and traditions of those peoples who had been won for Christ.

All this could not conceal the fact that, in terms of personnel and activity, the German contribution to the world mission of the Church was minimal when compared with that of the United States, or even of a comparatively small country like Holland. Yet it was clear that in many parts of the world the Germans were acceptable as a Christian witness, partly because they were not suspected of neo-colonialistic aspirations. Hardly any of the immense wealth of the German Churches was dedicated to any good purpose outside Germany itself.

The period during which I was most closely associated with

Germany was, in fact, one in which a deep sense of responsibility towards the Third World was growing up. There was a deep, though often unexpressed, sense of guilt over the events of the recent past, and a feeling that Germany ought in some way to atone for the misdeeds which were still all too vivid in the memories of older people. As the economic miracle advanced and prosperity returned, the rather unattractive self-pity of the years immediately following the war began to recede, and the more thoughtful among the Germans came to realise that they could not dissociate themselves from what was happening in the rest of the world. This was the great period of decolonisation; as one country after another got rid of its colonial masters, the cry for economic aid went up in tones of greater or less shrillness and stridency. The feeling grew up that as governments increased their overseas aid, the Churches ought to expand their giving to charitable concerns, and I found myself at various times involved in discussions which led, in the course of time, to action. The Churches agreed to make part of their income available for service overseas, and brought into being, among other agencies, the *Arbeitsgemeinschaft*, 'the fellowship in service between mission and church', which was located in Hamburg.

It seems impossible for the Germans ever to do anything unless everything has been meticulously recorded down to the last comma. This has its good side in method and precision; but it makes the process of translating idea into decision astonishingly cumbrous and tedious. The other weakness of the German approach is a tendency to like the grandiose, not to say the gigantic. It has sometimes been said, not altogether without truth, 'If you want a thousand marks, don't go to the Germans; if you ask them for a million you are much more likely to get it.' Here again, there is much to be said for this approach. It ought to be within the capacity of local churches to meet their immediate needs, and to raise small sums for special purposes; the help of the large and wealthy churches should be called on only for great enterprises. This is true, yet short-term planning has not always been balanced by consideration of the long-term consequences of a certain course of action. It may seem wonderful to provide a needy area with an up-to-date and well-equipped hospital, but how is the hospital to be financed from day to day? To provide adequate endowments would involve enormous sums of money, but if that is not done, a struggling Third World church may find itself crippled by the effort to maintain an institution which it is far beyond its means to support adequately. However, when all criticisms have been made, and all human imperfections allowed for, the emergence of the German Churches as benefactors on this great scale is one of the most important things ever to occur in the relationships between the richer and poorer nations. When I look at the accounts of my former diocese of Tinnevelly, and see the amounts that have come in from German aid, I am amazed to recall the pittance of Western aid on the strength of which I was expected to run the diocese thirty years ago. It pleases me to recall that in some very small ways I was privileged to help in this development.

German students are generally regarded as being diligent, docile and dull. In a statement of this kind, there is as much and as little truth as is usually to be found in such generalisations. In point of fact, the German student in the period after 1945 passed rapidly through a series of phases, which can be rather sharply distinguished from one another. In the first years, they lay simply stunned with the shock of the defeated. I felt a great deal of sympathy with my young German friends, who had starved under the Weimar Republic, known a brief period of glory under Hitler, and then been struck down to earth in the greatest military disaster. What astonished me was not that they were neurotic, but that they were as normal as they were. Hungry, emaciated, cold, bereft of books, studying in draughty and perhaps windowless classrooms, taught by professors who had emerged from the cellars, or even the concentration camps, they simply hung on, with admirable courage, hoping for a better day.

Then followed the non-political period, characterised by the slogan, 'Ohne mich' ('Count me out') – meaning, 'You can do what you like, but I am not going to get involved.' Despite the achievements of Adenauer and Ehrhardt in overseeing Germany's rehabilitation and reintegration into the West, the solid worth and intellectual eminence of successive presidents, and the development of the German economic miracle, the young people remained obstinately non-political. This became very evident when the Allies, sorely against their will, decided that they must rearm Germany. Young men were called up and began to roam the streets in uniform, to find to their dismay that their friends passed them by in the streets and that no nice girl wished to be seen talking to a soldier.

Then, overnight, they seemed to become violently political. How could this have come about? One major cause, in my opinion, was simply the existence of Eastern Germany. The West German government tried to pretend that it did not exist, that there was only one Germany, and that if this pretence were kept up long enough, the problem would just get up and walk away. But problems do not solve themselves in this easy way. The rulers of East Germany played their cards well, on the whole. At the start there had been a flood of refugees from East to West, but this diminished, and after the construction of the infamous Berlin wall became hardly so much as a trickle. By no means all East Germans wanted to leave their country, but the authorities realised quite early on that, if they were to survive, they must make East Germany a land of hope for the young. Professors in the universities were well paid and had many privileges. Access to the universities was made easy for young people with working-class backgrounds who would not have even dreamed of a university education under the previous regime. News of the superior conditions for students leaked across the borders. When these students managed to make contact with relatives and friends in the West, they were often unsparing in their criticisms of Western society; they found it antique, ossified, unbelievably hierarchical in its constitution. They might not have political freedom, but they seemed themselves to live in a much freer society, with employment guaranteed, and greater social security.

The reactions in the West were naturally very different. Listening, as so many of them did, to broadcasts from the East, the young people found themselves subjected to a steady stream of vilification. What was West Germany other than a sordid betrayal of the whole idea of Germany, a base conspiracy hatched up between the German politicians and the United States to keep a loaded pistol pointed permanently in the direction of the lands of freedom in the East? Stimulated by this barrage, and sometimes by more penetrating criticism from their cousins and friends, the young in West Germany began to cast an ironic and disillusioned eye on their own institutions. German politics were dull, pretentious, and portentous. West Germany had been readmitted to the society of civilised nations, but only because the United States needed a stalking horse in its relentless Cold War; the Germans were fooling themselves if they supposed that Europe was anything other than expendable in the eyes of the Americans. Society was becoming increasingly cosy and materialistic: was there anything really worth defending in this inbred and self-indulgent society? Might it not be that the time had really come for revolution? So the atmosphere changed.

Naturally the universities present themselves as almost the first target for assault. The old German university had been small and intimate. Now universities were springing up all over the place. In twenty years the number of students at the University of Hamburg reached 18,000. Seminars in the Department of English consisted of 150 students, and could not be anything other than a lecture by the professor. With this extraordinarily rapid development, it was impossible to find a sufficient number of competent teachers. The students complained bitterly about the poor quality of the lectures. Everything had become impersonal. Intimate contact between teachers and taught had always been difficult in a German university. Now it had become impossible. The university was just turning graduates out from an assembly line, like a factory, and, as all these monster institutions were controlled by city or regional governments, in which the controlling voice was that of big business, no improvement was to be expected.

I felt a great deal of sympathy with the grievances of the students, and made no secret of this. For many, accommodation was poor. University life meant little more than coming to lectures, sitting in the library and then going home to a sparse and unsatisfactory evening meal. I would have been prepared for very extensive and even radical reforms. However, the situation was manipulated by a small, fanatical clique of real revolutionaries who gained control of the student movement for a time. They seemed bent on destroying everything, without giving any thought to what should replace the old system. Indoctrinated from abroad, and perhaps internationally organised, they were expert at exploiting the situation. Accustomed to the general docility of German students, the authorities of most universities had no idea at all what to do in this situation which had so suddenly burst upon them.

In our theological faculty, we were in a rather fortunate situation. Numbers were moderate, and we had done more than most other faculties to maintain a personal relationship with our students. Moreover, student representatives had for years been present at faculty meetings; they were free to express their opinion on any matter that concerned student interests, but withdrew when professors settled down to discuss matters which were not really within the competence of students. My recollections are entirely of intelligent, courteous and co-operative students.

Other faculties and groups were not so fortunate. We were spared the violence which broke out in a number of other universities, but the Department of Psychology, in the same building in which my office was situated, was occupied by students. I have never known why this department more than any other was the special object of their venom. If the University had not cut off light, heat and water, they would have held out there indefinitely. However, as far as I can recall, there was no outrage, and no insane damaging of property, such as took place elsewhere. So, when an extensive reconstruction of the university organisation took place after I had left Hamburg, I think we were spared many of the absurdities by which others were afflicted. One colleague in another university told me that there the students had acquired the right to a voice in the election of professors. It had become their habit to send out a questionnaire relating to any possible candidate for a post. Only the fifth question related to his academic competence. The first question was about his political affiliation.

This is the story of my own experiences, and not a history of German universities. I will conclude this section by saying that I got out of the German university situation at just the right moment.

My leaving Hamburg, however, was not something that was planned, but was one of those things that just happen. My original appointment ran out in May 1967, but I had planned to stay until I reached retiring age at the end of 1968. I knew that my colleagues liked having me there, and some of them certainly hoped that I would make Hamburg my permanent home even after retirement. At the tenth anniversary of our faculty, when the then Dean mentioned in his address that 'the ecumenical Bishop' had expressed his willingness to stay longer among us, there was louder applause than at any other point in the address. So, on the personal side there was no difficulty; but administrative complications set in.

Our University had two qualified teachers in the field of missions, both of them protégés of Walter Freytag, both of them excellent friends of mine. Horst Bürkle was helping in the Department of Religion at Makerere College and was very happy in his work. Hans-Jochen Margull, to my infuriation, because he had no overseas experience, had gone to Geneva as Secretary of the Department of Evangelism. Now it is a generally accepted principle in German universities that, if a man has been accepted as a qualified teacher (by writing an advanced piece of original research which is examined by the whole faculty, and giving a trial lecture to obtain the habilitation degree, being then known as a *Privatdozent* or tutor), the university which has accepted him is under an obligation to employ him as a teacher and to find him a salary. So here we were, with one professor and two candidates, both of the latter, for the moment, fortunately abroad and holding salaried positions, but both naturally hoping to return to Germany, and to resume their position on the usual academic ladder. What was to be done?

My colleagues wanted to keep me, and moved heaven and earth to get a second professorship established. If missions and ecumenism are understood as I understand them – as the study of the Christian faith in the Christian and non-Christian worlds since about 1848, with backward glances, of course, to much earlier periods – then two professors would be required to deal with this vast subject. But all their efforts were in vain: the second professorship remained a dream, and did not become a reality.

Margull had in the mean time gone to Japan, where he was very happy, and was obviously learning a great deal. This delighted me; I hold strongly to the view that no man should be appointed to a chair in mission and ecumenism (or as I would prefer to say Christianity in the modern world), until he has had a reasonable period of service in the Third World. So many things can be learned directly that can never be conveyed in books, or by third-party evidence. I was particularly anxious that he should stay the full three years; I did not think that a lot of Geneva nonsense could be knocked out of him in less than that time. Then our hands were forced. Bürkle was appointed to the chair of mission in the newly created Faculty of Protestant Theology at the previously Roman Catholic University of Munich, and word reached us that the conservative University of Erlangen was stretching out its hands in the direction of Margull. It is another tradition of the German universities that a *Privatdozent* should accept appointment as professor in the first university that approaches him. If a formal offer were made by Erlangen, Margull would be almost bound to accept it, and would be lost to us for the foreseeable future. The upshot was that I was kindly told by my colleagues that they had decided to call Margull to the position of *Ordinarius* for Mission and Ecumenism, technically vacant since Walter Freytag's death eight years before. They had arranged for my term of office to be extended by six months in order to give me time to look around; and it was clear that they still hoped it would be possible for me to remain in Hamburg. But my official appointment would end with the calendar year 1967.

This was a considerable shock to me. I could not afford to stop working. Having lived abroad for so long, and having served the Church in so many different fields, it had come about that I was not eligible for a pension, either from the Church or the State, except for a minimal Swiss pension from my World Council days. In order to smooth the way to my appointment in Hamburg, I had waived any claim to the large pension which is the usual reward of a German professor when he retires. Yet a Christian need never be anxious about making decisions. They always seem to be made for him in advance, so that when the time comes to move, he knows exactly the direction to go. Just when I was wondering, in considerable perplexity, where I should go next, and what employment might come my way, there arrived a letter from Nairobi to the effect: 'We are thinking of starting a Department of Religious Studies in the University College here. Could you come for three months, as visiting professor of religions, to give some extracurricular lectures and to draw up the feasibility study which the University requires before such a department can come into existence?' I could, and would; the beginning of my work in Nairobi would coincide exactly with the end of my work in Hamburg.

This decision had various interesting consequences. In November 1967 I was host to one of our professors' evenings in my flat. In the course of the discussion, someone asked me what I intended to do next, and when I told them I happened to mention in passing that I was not claiming a pension from the University of Hamburg. This was news to some of the younger colleagues, who had not been in the faculty at the time of my appointment, and they were disturbed by it. They went and looked up the regulations, and found that anyone who had served the University for five years in an academic position was entitled to a proportionate pension. They brought this to my notice and stressed strongly the fact that they had not made any special representation on my behalf, but I was entitled to it. So I applied, and everything being in order, the pension was granted without demur. The amount is not great, but the German mark is worth something, and my pension is related not to what my salary was in 1967, but to what it would be if I had stayed in service until the present day. This has saved me from all anxiety as to the future. I know that unless some unexpected cataclysm bursts on the world and sweeps everything away, I shall have enough money to live in modest comfort to the end of my days.

So my service in Hamburg ended peacefully. My lawyer friend Hans Bender found it convenient to take over my flat with some of my furniture. I thought that I had made it a pleasant home, but this fades into insignificance in comparison with the real elegance that he has bestowed upon it. He also found a most efficient firm to store my worldly goods while I had no home of my own. Bills were paid. Everything was settled. On the last evening of the year, I sat in solitude in my kitchen, surrounded by torn up letters and documents awaiting removal, toasted my solitude in a glass of German champagne, and meditated on the strange ways of providence that made me a German professor, and now launched me into Africa, a continent which I had often visited, but in which I had never expected to reside.

I look back with great gratitude on my time in Hamburg. Perhaps I have never learned so much in six years. I was received with the utmost friendliness by the Anglican and British communities, and have before me as I write a number of tokens of their kindness. I received endless kindnesses from my colleagues who bestowed on me far more affection than a foreigner might be expected to receive. Many of the students accepted me as a friend, and some have become life-long friends. I do not think that I was specially creative as a professor – I could hardly have been in that situation so full of problems and difficulties; but I had held the fort, had been able to restore the credit of the department, and had been able to hand over the work to the one man among all others whom I would have chosen as my successor. I do not think that I could ever have made Hamburg my permanent home, but I have never regretted spending six years there. It is a matter of gratification to me that my name still appears in the list of the professors of the theological faculty, and, unless the regulations are infamously changed, will continue to do so until the day of my death.

8

Professor in East Africa

As a fitting prologue to my years in Nairobi, my first encounter with Africa came in 1950, when the International Missionary Council asked me to conduct a survey of theological education. For twenty years I had been regarded as something of an authority on theological training in the lands of the developing Churches, and my work at the Tambaram Conference of 1938 had not been forgotten. So when the IMC turned its attention to the idea of a survey of theological training in Africa, it was natural that they should call up the old war-horse. It was agreed that I should be set free for four months to head the survey. I ended up the tour completely exhausted, and a little depressed by what I had learned of theological education in Africa, but immensely enriched by old friendships renewed and new friendships made in the course of my journeyings. I had seen too many small, ill-equipped and under-staffed seminaries, in which tired missionaries, many of whom had no special training for the work, were striving manfully to produce a literate and thoughtful African clergy. It is not surprising that Mr Yorke Allen, who ten years later produced A Seminary Survey, accused the Christian missions of simply not taking seriously the work of theological education. What troubled me most was that all the work I had seen was so unimaginatively Western. In West Africa the work was geared to the London Diploma in Theology. An examination more unsuitable for African students it would be difficult to imagine. It seemed to me that few of the teachers, the majority of whom had failed to learn thoroughly any African language, had ever asked themselves how the African mind works, and how students could be helped to rethink Christian truth in their own way and to make their own discoveries. The result was that the students who had passed through the seminaries tended to be pale copies of their Western teachers, and to have lost much of the joyful spontaneity which is the heritage of the African in almost every part of the continent. The task of the theological teacher is to help the sincere student to come to the Scriptures with his own questions, and not with those of Western man; he needs the help of what Western scholarship can contribute, but he must through it all remain himself if in due time he is to add his own treasures to the wealth of the city of God. I felt at that time that very little had been done in the way of wrestling with the deeper problems of African Christianity and the grave responsibility resting on those who are charged with the task of training those who in their turn will be the teachers of the African Christian.

It was nearly twenty years before I could make East Africa my home and put those ideas into practice. It had never occurred to me that I would actually be called upon to do this, yet looking back, it is easy to see that my decision to come to Nairobi, like my decision to come to Hamburg, had been determined in advance by a number of factors, apart from my experiences conducting the survey. I had been brought back on a number of occasions already. One year I was asked to carry out the official inspection of St Paul's Theological College, Limuru, which on my recommendation had become a joint enterprise of Anglican, Presbyterian and Methodist Churches. On another occasion, I was asked by the Theological Education Fund to help in an Institute for Teachers of Church History which they were planning to hold in Nairobi as part of their programme for helping those already engaged in theological teaching to meet their colleagues from other places and catch up with what was happening in the theological world.

Most of my contacts in East Africa had been with the Churches and the theological institutions. This longer stay enabled me to make close contact with University College, Nairobi, and with the problems of Christian work among students on the university level. Unlike Makerere, which had two official chaplains, University College, Nairobi, was entirely secular in character and made no provision for spiritual ministrations of any kind. With some difficulty, the National Christian Council of Kenya had arranged to appoint a chaplain, the Revd Michael Mansbridge, who had done excellent work in the face of opposition from various quarters. His wife was the Warden of the Woman Students' residence; this gave them a flat near to the students' residences, and an attractive undercroft, open to the air, which could be used for services. Alas, when they went on leave, Mrs Mansbridge's health gave grounds for grave anxiety, and it was impossible for them to return. When it was clear that the Mansbridges would not be able to return, and that it was unlikely that any other chaplain would be appointed, those on the spot devised an ingenious and adequate scheme to carry on the work. They formed a chaplaincy team – part black, part white; part clerical, part lay; part university, part city – to maintain a Christian witness and ministry in the University.

One of the drawbacks to the work, consequent on the secular character of the University, was the lack of a local habitation. During one of my visits I had been shown a house, the property of a Christian member of the teaching staff of the University, who was leaving to become Registrar of the University of Lesotho, and was quite keen that his house should be bought and used for Christian purposes. The purchase price was £6,000. The house itself was not much to write home about – the old style of Nairobi bungalow, solid but without aesthetic charm; but it stood in a fairly extensive and attractive compound, with an immense and ancient (by Nairobi standards) jacaranda tree in the centre. More important than anything else, it stood within a stone's throw of the university residences, which were going up one after the other as the University expanded. A single glance was enough to assure me that this was what the chaplaincy team must have as the centre of its work.

I moved heaven and earth to raise money in Germany towards the purchase price. I saw personally my friend Oberkirchenrat Lohmann, the secretary of the Arbeitsgemeinschaft, the body which united the efforts of Churches and missionary societies in the promotion of attempts to develop the Christian cause in the Third World. He was distinctly interested but dubious as to the prospects of success. One might have thought that the opportunity to consolidate Christian witness in such a university in a developing country with a population of something like ten million people was a prospect that would appeal to any body of Christian men, but here we came up against the unimaginable and inspissated blindness of the Protestant Churches. Given such an opportunity, the Roman Catholics will leap at it, if necessary mortgaging some other building to provide the necessary cash. Protestants will firmly look the other way; and of course the opportunity once lost will never come again. I was almost in despair. The owner of the house was pressing for his money, and was not prepared to keep the option open indefinitely. But sometimes when a man's hand has failed, a woman's hand will unlock the door. Janet Lacey of Christian Aid in London happened to be in Nairobi on some entirely different ploy. She was shown the house, said at once, 'Of course you must have that,' went back to London and browbeat her committee into signing a cheque for

£6,000. They had never done anything of the kind before, and to my knowledge have never done anything similar since; but the cheque was signed, and the house was ours. I say 'ours' since, although at the time I had no idea or expectation of ever becoming a resident of Nairobi, I was by now fully identified with the local Christian forces in this great Christian enterprise.

On a later visit, I was asked to lead, in the Chaplaincy Centre now ours, a Bible study group for graduates, giving them clues as to how they might develop a reasoned programme of Bible study together. It was a highly ecumenical group, and several Roman Catholic priests were present. But it was a lay member of the team, Tom Gorman, a Roman Catholic in the Department of English, who was inspired to say, 'Let's have a Department of Religion, and let's get Bishop Neill to come out and run it.' I do not, of course, know all that went on behind the scenes; but apparently this seed fell on good ground and sprouted, and as a result I received some months later the invitation to come to Nairobi and to make the plans for a Department of Religion. The invitation came just at the right moment. I was ready to leave Hamburg. I wanted to go on working. I was deeply interested in Nairobi, and it had been indicated to me that, if all went well, I might be invited to become the first professor in the new department.

My title was to be Visiting Professor of Religion, and I was to spend three months in Nairobi. The Churches were supposed to have raised a certain sum to pay for my passage and to keep me in being during my stay in Kenya. In point of fact a good deal of this money never reached my hands – I might have taken this as an omen and foreshadowing of many things that were yet to come. It was supposed that a flat would have been provided for me, but this also never became fact. I was saved by Raymond Harries, the Provost of Nairobi, for whom a new house had been built on a rather steep slope above the cathedral, with a basement room which had a separate entrance and was regarded as a guest-room rather than as part of the Provost's House. This looked down towards the cathedral, and over a grassy slope, where to my intense delight the children from the cathedral kindergarten exploded periodically from their confinement to gambol in the shade. Here I was made welcome. The Harries were kindness itself, and invited me to have breakfast with them every day, though they were under no obligation of any kind to the university project.

It soon became clear to me that I was not going to have at all an easy time in working out my plans. There was opposition in the air, and a good deal of it opposition from the very people one might have expected to be enthusiastic for the project.

Makerere University were, not unnaturally, less than delighted by the prospect of a second Department of Religion in East Africa. They had been the first, had done the job, and felt themselves quite capable of continuing to do the job for the whole of East Africa. They had failed to reckon with the growing alienation between the three territories, Uganda, Kenya and Tanzania, and the tendency to split the existing University of East Africa into three universities, one for each of the territories. The government of Kenya made it clear that no student going from Kenya to Uganda to take religious studies would receive government financial aid; this meant simply that no Kenyan student would join the Department of Religious Studies at Makerere.

The Churches were darkly suspicious. Most Churches in Kenya are extremely conservative. It was not difficult to persuade their leaders that a University Department of Religion would be a fountainhead of every kind of heresy. Then, when the names of three persons were put forward as possible professors, if the department came into being, it was found that each one of the three would have been a disaster, lacking entirely the confidence of the Churches, and would have killed off the department before it had even had a chance to be born. It took me a long time, and much careful labour, to dissipate this atmosphere of distrust that had grown up around the possibility of a new department.

It was not long before we became aware that some people in Nairobi were writing in a disparaging way to those bodies in the West to which we might look for financial help. The gist of many of these letters was that the idea of a Department of Religion was a private quirk of John Kamau of the National Christian Council of Kenya and Dr David Barrett of the WCC unit of research, in spite of the fact that they had been officially commissioned by the Council to investigate the matter on its behalf. The impression left on the minds of friends in the West was that such a department was neither needed nor desired in Nairobi.

As far as our continental friends were concerned, I think that what saved us from a good deal of unpleasantness was a visit from my friend Professor H-W. Gensichen of Heidelberg, who was closely connected with the Theological Education Fund. I heard that he was coming as far as Makerere to serve as external examiner for the Department of Religious Studies there. I paid out of my own pocket the air fare from Entebbe to Nairobi in order to enable him to see and hear for himself. What he saw and heard was so different from what he had been told that he carried home a report which went far to correct the distorted image that had been projected by those unfavourable to our plans.

What made me saddest was the total lack of interest in the idea of a Department of Religion in the minds of the authorities of the Anglican Church in Kenya. Behind this lay a long history with a good deal of which I was already acquainted.

When Uganda became a separate province with its own archbishop, the other two territories were lumped together in a province of East Africa. The Archbishop of the new province was fired with the desire to make of St Paul's College, Limuru, a great provincial college, serving all the dioceses in Kenya and Tanzania. This involved problems of churchmanship. Kenya had been from the beginning the preserve of the Evangelical missionary societies. Though large parts of Tanzania were under the care of the Australian Church Missionary Society, other areas had been evangelised by the Anglo-Catholic Universities' Mission to Central Africa. The UMCA bishops naturally said that the basis of theological training for their men had always been the daily Mass, and that they could not consider sending their men to Limuru unless this tradition was maintained. This was reasonable enough. But, instead of obtaining from the council of the now United Theological College permission for the Eucharist to be celebrated daily in the college chapel with the traditional ceremonial (a concession which might not have been more than grudgingly granted), the Archbishop provided the priest sent by the UMCA with a conventicle in his own house, in which he might celebrate the holy mysteries for the group of UMCA students after the manner to which they were accustomed. Years later I was to encounter the intense and still unappeased resentments kindled in the minds of the non-Anglican members of staff by this hole-and-corner arrangement.

As part of the grandiose new arrangements for St Paul's, it was agreed that a number of men should be taken in to study for the London degree of Bachelor of Divinity. This was an impossible burden to lay on a small and not specially well-qualified staff, which was already teaching on two levels – for the Diploma, and for the Certificate in Religious Studies of the University of East Africa. The men had been chosen without careful consideration of their abilities; in due course all three failed and no more was heard of the BD at Limuru.

In this somewhat inflamed atmosphere, the idea of a Department
of Religion was not enthusiastically welcomed. The temperature
dropped a considerable number of degrees when the true nature
of such a department became known to the authorities. It seems
clear that both the Anglican Archbishop of East Africa and the
Roman Catholic Archbishop of Nairobi had the idea that, if such
a department came into being, they would have some influence
on the appointments to the teaching staff. When it was made
clear to them that the University College (as it then was) claimed
total autonomy, and that no one outside would have any influence
whatever, it became much more difficult to persuade them that the
Churches should support the project. The Anglican Archbishop
even declared: 'The Church of the Province of East Africa would
not be interested in a white elephant of a department,' which I took
to be an impertinence coming from a younger man, such as he. So
much, I think, of my troubles should be recorded, as an illustration
of the odd way they do things in the Church of Christ.

The first thing was to get the idea of the Department of Religion
widely known. To this end we arranged that I should give, in the
University College itself, three short courses of six lectures each
on, respectively, the great religions of the world, the history of the
scientific study of religion, and the use and meaning of theological
and religious terms. Nothing of the kind had ever happened in
University College before; and we had no idea whether anyone
would turn up. Attendance far surpassed all expectations; the high
point was reached when 170 hearers turned out for my lecture
on Hinduism, after which a girl thanked me warmly for having
given such a beautiful presentation of her religion. After this it
was difficult to say that there was no interest in Nairobi in the
study of religion.

David Gitari, the secretary of the association of Evangelical
students, and later in the service of the Bible Society of Kenya,
had the bright idea of sending a circular round to the schools in which
a Christian Union was known to exist, to ask which pupils would
like, if they went on to university, to have available a department
such as we were planning. The result was powerfully positive, and
these figures went in as an appendix to my report.

Visits were paid to leaders in the different religious communities
in Kenya, in order to make plain to them that a Department of
Religious Studies was not a concealed form of Christian propaganda,
that a serious attempt would be made to acquaint the students with
all the religious traditions that are to be found in Kenya, and that the

treatment of all subjects would be strictly academic. The welcome accorded to me in every place was friendly; but, as I was to find later, the suspicion of a propagandist aim was one which it is peculiarly difficult to eradicate. On the other hand, I never found any difficulty with the students; they seemed to see no inconsistency between the strictly dispassionate and impartial approach of the classroom on weekdays and the ardent proclamation of Christian truth by the same speaker on Sundays.

So, for good or ill, the work was done, and my feasibility study was sent in to be considered first by the Arts Faculty Board and then by the Academic Board of University College. Good work in preparation had been done by the members of the Joint Committee, and particularly by the two ablest African members of the teaching staff, Dr B. A. Ogot, Professor of History and later Deputy Vice-Chancellor, and Dr S. H. Ominde, Professor of Geography. The plan was for a Department of Philosophy and Religious Studies. Those who did not much like religious studies were prepared to endure them in order to get philosophy in; those who did not care about philosophy were prepared to accept it in order to make sure that religious studies were accepted. And so the proposal went through, and, as far as University College was concerned, the formation of the department was only a matter of time. The supporters of the plan were naturally jubilant, and there was clearly a strong desire among them that the man who had successfully made the plans should also be the first professor. I told my friends that I would not put in an application for the post, but that I would keep myself as far as possible free from other commitments, so that if the appointment was offered to me, I would be in a position to accept it. I warned them, however, that as I was already far beyond the University's retiring age, it was most unlikely that any such offer would be made.

We then settled down to an inordinately long time of waiting, and, although my report had been submitted in February 1968, it was clear that we would not be able to start work in the academic year 1968–9, which would begin in September.

The first difficulty was financial. The budget of University College was planned in quinquennia. As we had missed the quinquennium 1968–73, no support from the University could be expected before the quinquennium 1973–8; but it was agreed that if the religious bodies could raise enough money to support the department for three years, permission could be sought from the Ministry of Education to put the plans into execution without delay.

This meant long negotiations with various bodies. In the end, the Theological Education Fund and the Arbeitsgemeinschaft together promised £11,000; the Catholic Secretariat undertook to double this; the Hindu community agreed to add £10,000; the Gandhi Memorial Fund, raised years before by the Asian community for University purposes, undertook to add 10 per cent to whatever was raised by others. So with promises of support amounting to nearly £35,000, it was possible to approach the ministry with some prospect of success. Permission was secured without exceptional difficulty, and this major obstacle to the establishment of the department was removed.

Again we settled down to a long period of waiting. As months passed and I heard nothing from Nairobi, I began to wonder whether I had been foolish in allowing my name to be further associated with the project. By the time that a year had passed, I had concluded that either they had decided not to create the department at all, or had called someone else to fill the post of professor. Then, when I had abandoned all expectation, and was wondering where I should turn for another appointment, the telegram came.

The telegram from Dr Jacobs, the excellent Mennonite Bishop in Nairobi, was followed by a letter in which he explained that the runner-up for the post of professor had been a Muslim candidate, and that, if I refused the job, this gentleman would certainly be appointed. This really left me no liberty of choice. There is no reason why a Muslim should not be head of a Department of Religious Studies; but in this case, apart from personal considerations, it was certain that such an appointment would kill the department before ever it had come into existence. All the money that had actually been subscribed was Christian money. The confidence of the Churches had been won with considerable difficulty and would immediately be forfeited if an appointment was made which did not meet with their approval. So it became clear to me that, unless there was something in the terms of appointment that was wholly unacceptable, Nairobi must be my destiny for the next few years.

There followed another infuriating delay before the official invitation reached me. After I had signed the document indicating my acceptance and sent it off, there was further endless delay. I could get no word as to the date on which University College wished me to take up the appointment; my various correspondents in Nairobi could give me no accurate information. My plan, naturally, was to spend the first year in preparation, giving a few public lectures to get the department known, collecting books for the library, acquiring a colleague to help me on the side of philosophy, and working out syllabuses for work in consultation with the people on the spot. As I had, under considerable pressure, accepted a number of lecturing engagements in the United States for October, the sensible thing seemed to be to plan my arrival in Nairobi for December, with a view to starting teaching work in the following September. But no word came and no word came. At last I said to my secretary, 'I badly need a holiday. I want to improve my Portuguese, with a view to my researches in Indian church history. I shall go to Portugal for a month.' I went to the travel agents to collect information about hotels and flights – and then of course the inevitable happened.

The very next morning there was an urgent letter from the Dean of the Faculty of Arts to the effect that students were already registering for admission in the Department of Philosophy and Religious Studies, that teaching would begin on 22 September, and that I should be there at the earliest possible date. It was already the middle of August. There was nothing for it but hurriedly to clear up my affairs in England, to cancel a number of engagements, and to book my passage at the earliest possible date. I arrived in Nairobi on 10 September to start my new career.

The world on which I was entering was not a wholly unfamiliar world; but I recognised that it was in many ways a new world, and that I must regard myself as a learner.

Kenya had settled down astonishingly well after the long troubles of 'The Emergency', as the Mau Mau uprising had come to be politely called. Under a sympathetic Governor-General, Malcolm Macdonald, the transition from colonial status to independence had been carried through with very little dislocation. Jomo Kenyatta emerged from long imprisonment as a reconciler. There was to be no immediate retaliation for the past, no savaging of European or Asian interests. All were to work together for the development of what was to be unmistakably and unconditionally an African country; but for a time at least others would be able to play their part in nation-building. Under the surface, however, things were less amicable and peaceful than they appeared. Kenyatta was always a Kikuyu to his fingertips, and could not keep himself out of Kikuyu politics. This remarkable people numbered about two million, a little more than 15 per cent of the population, but dominant in every sphere because of their education and tribal solidarity. Tom Mboya, the Luo leader, was murdered in broad daylight in circumstances which suggested government connivance, to say the least, shortly after my arrival in Kenya. Nevertheless, compared with other African countries, Kenya seemed to be a haven of peace, even if there was deep discontent just beneath the surface.

The Christian situation in the country at the time of my arrival was more than remarkable. The immeasurably slow progress marked by the early and heroic pioneers was a memory of a very distant past. About 1910 the pace of progress began to quicken in many, though not all, regions of the country. There had been set-backs at the time of the famous controversy over female circumcision, and during the emergency; but these were only temporary, and very soon the curve began again to turn steeply upwards. In 1972 it was reckoned that something like half the population was already in some sense Christian, though the numbers actually recorded by the Churches were considerably below this figure. From some areas it was reported that the annual increase of Christian adherents was in the region of 10 per cent per annum; at this rate the Church doubled itself in less than eight years.

As a result of the government policy of allocating certain areas to one mission only, in order to reduce the dangers and the confusions of rivalry, we were faced with the problem of a number of tribal churches, a bad situation in a country where tribalism was at all times a major problem. The Presbyterian Church in East Africa, for instance, was almost exclusively Kikuyu, and seemed bent on making itself the national Church of the Kikuyu people. The Anglican Church in Kenya had been saved from this tribal affiliation by its untidy sprawl right across the country from the ocean to the great lakes; but it was not for that reason free from internal problems.

The head of the Church was Leonard Beecher, Archbishop of East Africa, a man of great gifts who had spent the whole of his active career in East Africa, and had played a great part in the development of both Church and country, rising in the course of years from layman to Archbishop.

Dr Beecher regarded it as his vocation to break up what he called the old prince bishopric. He was so far successful that he called into existence six bishoprics where there had only been one, and with four African bishops out of six. What he did not realise was that he had merely replaced one large prince bishopric by six small prince bishoprics. In the old days every CMS missionary had been absolutely supreme in his own area. As late as 1934 the majority of the missionaries remained unconvinced that any effective diocesan organisation would be a good thing; each wanted uncontrolled freedom to go on his own way. Archbishop Beecher, having never served in any part of the Anglican Communion other than Kenya, had never seen any other system of church order at work, and unconsciously absorbed the complete autocratic traditions of the Church which he had served so long. These traditions he faithfully passed on to the African bishops, who had seen even less than he of the developments of synodical government in other areas outside Kenya. The combination in an African bishop of the worst features of the old CMS missionary, of the naturally autocratic tendencies of a great African chief, and of a concept of episcopacy which seemed to me thoroughly un-Anglican, caused me no small dismay. In the diocese there seemed to be no will other than that of the bishop; in the province the only executive authority appeared to be the bishops' meeting, a body which had no constitutional or legal existence. After my experiences in India of a thoroughly democratic organisation of the Church, and my own belief in a radically constitutional form of episcopacy, I was bound to feel a measure of discomfort in a Church organised on so widely divergent principles.

The University which I had come to serve had started life as a small technical college. After a number of transformations it had emerged as University College, Nairobi, one of the three constituent colleges of the University of East Africa. In 1970 the University of East Africa was dissolved, and University College, Nairobi, became the University of Nairobi. Most unfortunately, when the decision was taken to expand the technical college into something larger, the authorities made the grave mistake of failing to move the college out of the city of Nairobi. It had been located in what at the time seemed an adequately extensive site on what was then the northern fringe of the city; but Nairobi was growing very rapidly, the campus was soon surrounded by streets and buildings, and further expansion became impossible. Once lost, the opportunity to move did not come again, and at the time of my arrival a University College with not more than 2,300 students was already working on four campuses. To these was later added Kenyatta College, the big teachers' training institution twelve miles away, which was suddenly elevated to university status, apparently without any planning or any thought as to the effects of this sudden and ill-judged step in the life of the University as a whole.

So there was no lack of problems in the situation into which I was entering. This I had foreseen. But I had no sooner arrived than I discovered that the situation as far as I was personally concerned was far worse than the worst that I could possibly have imagined.

In the first place, the appointments' committee convened to make an appointment to the professorship had behaved with unbelievable levity and academic impropriety. Having been commissioned to make one appointment, they took it upon themselves, without any authorisation whatever, to make two. In academic circles it is unheard of for a professor to find himself saddled with a colleague about whose appointment he has not even been consulted. In this case there were a number of aggravating features. The gentleman selected was an Arabist. As he had to give six months' notice to the institution in which he was employed, he could not arrive before the middle of the academic year, by which time all the students would be settled in their classes, and he would be unable to attract any students; in point of fact the department would have to pay him for nine months for doing exactly nothing. The committee recommended his appointment in the rank of reader, which meant that he would be drawing a salary of not less than £3,000 a year; the committee which recommended the appointment made no financial provision whatever to cover the salary and allowances of the man that they had recommended. This meant that all the financial arrangements that I had so carefully planned and that had been accepted by the Academic Board collapsed like a house of cards.

To make matters worse, before the gentleman in question arrived, I received information that he was not entitled to the degree to which he had laid claim. I made contact with the university in which he had studied, and found that it was indeed so; he had fulfilled part of the requirements for the MA degree, but his dissertation had not been sent in, and he had left in debt to the university. What was I to do? I decided that it would be better to avoid scandal. The Principal of University College and the Dean of the Arts Faculty agreed with me that I should see to it that the unacquired degree should not be shown against his name on any university document, and that I should do my utmost to help him to complete his dissertation and to acquire the degree to which he had falsely laid claim. So for three years I unhappily carried this secret in my inner consciousness. Then, unexpectedly, I was required to send in a confidential report on the work of my colleague in connection with the renewal of his contract. My recommendation was that the renewal should be only for a year, and that any further renewal should be dependent on his completing the still incompleted work for the degree. The General Purposes Committee, having had similar cases to deal with, took a very serious view of the situation, and after making the proper enquiries, declared my colleague's contract at an end. So he left us, leaving a hole of nearly £10,000 in our finances, with not very much to show for it.

This was only the beginning of my financial worries. It soon became clear that the Hindu community did not intend to pay a penny of the £10,000 for which they had made themselves responsible – apparently their leaders were incensed by the appointment of a former missionary. The Gandhi Memorial Fund did eventually contribute, but only half of what they had originally promised, and only after three years' delay. Then, just to make the situation perfect, I learned that the university authorities, without informing me, had extended the period for which the religious bodies were to undertake financial responsibility from three years to five (actually four, because of the enormous delay in effecting my appointment). By dint of scrupulously careful administration, and by timely help from sources which had been untapped at the time of the formation of the department, we were able to pull through. But, for four years there was not a single day on which I was free from financial anxiety; the Finance Officer of the University made it clear that he would not pay out any money beyond the amount which stood to our credit in the accounts. I could never get from the finance department a clear statement of our position, and I could never be sure at the end of the month whether salaries would be paid. If I had known in advance that one of my principal duties as professor would be to raise money for my own salary, it is hardly likely that I would have accepted the appointment.

Nothing had been arranged in advance of my arrival. No office had been assigned to me. In the end I found myself housed in a kind of cubby-hole, with no telephone and with partitions which did not reach the ceiling. The lady who lectured on archaeology in the History Department told me later on that she had listened with enthralled attention to my historical sessions on the philosophy of religion, every word of which was audible over the partitions. I had no colleague. When I suggested to the acting Registrar that it was a little much to expect a professor to run a double department single-handed, and that if they wanted to make a second appointment, they should of course have chosen a philosopher and not a second man in the field of religions, he blandly replied, 'In view of your distinction in the area of philosophy, we thought that you would be able to manage.' Well, there are parts of Greek and Indian philosophy on which I can lecture standing on my head; but I have not had time to keep myself up to date with modern developments; this is a subject which I have never taught, and

but was always told that the American bishops wanted to be among the bright lights of London. In fact they loved the atmosphere at Canterbury, and indeed all the bishops had time to get to know one another, and what had tended to become a purely business assembly became, to a large extent, a time of quiet waiting upon the will of God.

When I finally decided to settle in England, I was already seventy-five years old. I could not expect to be very deeply involved in church life. However, I offered to serve the diocese of Oxford in any way I could. It gave me great pleasure when Patrick Rodger recognised this, and appointed me assistant bishop in his diocese. The diocese of Oxford is fairly well supplied with bishops, but it did fall to my lot to take a number of confirmations, sometimes in very amusing circumstances and at very short notice.

I am not much interested in party questions, but I was glad to see on my return to England in 1975 that a better relationship was developing between conservative Evangelicals and the more rigid fundamentalists. One sign of this renewed fellowship, after the acrimonious debates of the 1950s, was the rapprochement between the Church Missionary Society and the Bible Churchmen's Missionary Society. The two societies decided to set up a joint committee to work out plans for helping churches and individuals face the new problems of Christian responsibility created by the influx of non-Christians from India, Pakistan and East Africa in recent years. They were fortunate in finding a secretary, Christopher Lamb, who combined missionary experience with a notable talent for organisation and a sympathetic understanding of non-Christian faiths. I felt honoured when I was asked to become chairman of this committee, though I did little more than guide the discussions at meetings.

Oxford was rather an exciting place to be during those years. The four main Evangelical churches, and the central Anglo-Catholic church, were all crowded out on Sunday mornings, with a steady number of adult candidates for baptism and confirmation. There was a spirit of enquiry abroad. One of my occupations was a joint service with Michael Green for theological students who were puzzled about their faith and needed help in being open to new truths while remaining loyal to what they already knew to be true. However, this situation was not reflected in the religious practices of the population as a whole. It was difficult to avoid despondency about the minimal church attendance, ignorance of the Christian faith, and the lack of response to diligent witness. The general standards of decency and compassion towards the under-privileged, especially among young people, made me refuse to call this a heathen land, but how does one conduct effective evangelism? No one has as yet, it seems, discovered the way to emerge from the steadily narrowing Christian ghetto into the de-Christianised world by which we are surrounded.

My discovery of England was paralleled by a similar rediscovery of America as a result of my yearly visits to Yale Divinity School. Yale Divinity School had never suffered from the extremes of student domination, but there were a number of conflicting and not easily reconcilable currents. The women's liberation movement was vocal and strong, sometimes appearing to go to the lengths of denying that men have any rights at all. When a woman student, preaching at one of the regular chapel services, used the word 'I' a hundred times in her address, and the word 'God' not once, I could not find myself edified. There was an occasionally noisy 'gay' caucus, but for the most part I found the students friendly and serious, not by any means all in agreement as to the nature of the Christian ministry, but at least prepared to consider its claims as a possible vocation.

The weekly Eucharist, held on Wednesday evenings, became the focal point of my week of work and worship. In March 1975, on the occasion of the jubilee of my ordination as priest, I had the privilege of celebrating Holy Communion according to the Prayer Book rite of 1662, and talking about my fifty years' service, an occasion of deeply felt oneness in the service of the Lord. Though no relatives of mine could be present, I felt I was among my family.

Yale continued to be the central point of what came to be my annual visits to the United States, but I soon began to find very varied fields of usefulness opened out before me, including a wholly unexpected form of ministry.

About 1960, a new form of conservatism began to manifest itself on the American scene. The result was that some of the large and flourishing conservative seminaries were extremely well furnished with scholars who, while deeply committed Christians, were unable to close their minds to the problems raised by critical methods of approach to the questions of Christian origins and doctrines, and found themselves unable to subscribe honestly to the strict conservatives' cherished formulations, such as the inerrancy or verbal inspiration of the Holy Scriptures, as originally given. How could they reconcile conscience with intellectual integrity? Was there any place where they might look for allies?

I came to know that a number of my books were being widely used in these conservative seminaries. My *History of Christian Missions* had been adopted as the standard textbook on the subject in a great variety of colleges, as was evidenced by statistics of almost unvarying sales through the years. Two books on the New Testament, *The Interpretation of the New Testament*, and its more popular successor, *Jesus Through Many Eyes*, suggested to some readers the possibility of combining a full and frank acceptance of critical methods with a form of Christian faith not wholly alien from their own. My friends had amused themselves in earlier days by drawing up lists of seminaries in which I would never be invited to lecture. The reader can imagine my amusement, as I was able to cross off the list one name after another as I was privileged to find open doors in these debarred seminaries, and a warmth of fellowship which it is moving to remember. It would be tedious to list all these encounters, but one or two examples might be briefly mentioned.

Gordon-Conwell, a very large seminary not far from Boston, was largely concerned with the education of black students. I was invited to lecture, rather intensively, for a month on missions and missionary problems. I had a large class, numbering about 100, and including Michael Ford, the son of the then President Ford. Imagine my surprise when one morning I found an envelope on my desk in the lecture room with enough money to enable me to replace the suitcase that I happened to have told one student had been damaged on my journey there! I had asked the students each to write a paper of not more than 2,000 words, though I knew I had let myself in for extremely heavy work marking them. I declined the help of a 'grader', the assistant who is often provided for this work: I like to be able to read the work myself and write in rude remarks in red ink, as required. It meant, though, that I did not complete the marking until 3 a.m., when my train was due to leave Boston at 6 a.m. I caught my train despite receiving the last paper at 10 p.m., and left exhausted, but with glowing memories of Christian fellowship.

My friendship with Professor Glenn Hinson, who has an interest in liturgy and in the writings of Christian mystics, not perhaps very common among Southern Baptists, provided a link to this great Christian fellowship. These Baptists are generally held to be very conservative, and they do maintain very firm views on the doctrine of believers' baptism, so the invitation to an Anglican bishop was the more astonishing. The warmth of friendship extended to me in their seminaries can hardly be described as less than effusive. When

I went to their seminary at Louisville, Kentucky, on one occasion I became critically ill with a particularly virulent form of influenza. After four days' intensive care in hospital, a married student and his wife looked after me until my strength returned, but when I emerged, I was so weak that I literally had to learn to walk a few steps at a time. Staff and students were marvellous in their care for me, and I was nobly paid for the work I had done and the work I could not do.

My next port of call was the University of the South at Sewanee, but most of the time there I lay in my bed, matchlessly cared for by a kind professor and his wife. I managed to give my four lectures and a sermon sitting down. My enforced inactivity meant I was able to give a great deal of time to thinking out in detail all that I had to say. Never in my life have I experienced greater freedom of utterance, or more strongly the sense of being just on target for that audience.

Naturally, with all these wanderings among the dissenters, I was careful to maintain my contacts with the Episcopal Church, which was at this time preoccupied with two major problems – the ordination of women, and the launching of a new Prayer Book. This is not the place to comment in detail on these two important matters in church history. As is well known, the decision in the former matter led to a schism, not large, but troublesome; the strain on many consciences was considerable, and many of those who decided to remain appear to have done so unconvinced of the value of the ordination of women. In the latter question, the American Church accepted not an Alternative Services Book, but a whole new Prayer Book. Naturally, when so much labour has been expended, there are some good things in the book, even excellent things, but the general effect is one of a toning down of the asperities of the gospel.

The Episcopal Church has always been a class church, and seemed well set to become the ghetto of the upper middle class, mainly composed of prosperous white Anglo-Saxons. Alone among the major Churches, it was actually losing in membership, but there were movements of renewal. Personal acquaintance brought me into contact with the Church of the Redeemer in Houston, Texas, which has become noteworthy both in America and England. Here I found what I regarded as three very important safeguards against the possible dangers of over-emotionalism and the neglect of other elements in the Christian faith. The church had maintained a rather high Anglican liturgical tradition, there was regular Bible teaching, much of it amateurish, but filling a gap which is notable in the life of many Episcopal churches, and there were admirable outlets for community service. In particular they reclaimed a state school demoralised and destroyed by the 'busing' policy, whereby 400 middle-class children had been replaced by 400 under-privileged black inner-city children. Church members took positions as teachers in the school and others ran a remedial reading programme. If that is the charismatic movement, it has my wholehearted approval. It was interesting also to observe the steadily growing influence of John Stott and other British Evangelical leaders on young American Episcopalians, although the Evangelical group within the American Church had lost direction, it seemed.

When I finally retired in 1973, I hoped to be able to look forward to an extended and uninterrupted period of writing. The period has not been as uninterrupted as I had hoped; but writing has been one of the main activities of these years. I am not a lover of controversy, though I have, at various stages of my life, become involved in a number of controversies. Two in particular seemed unavoidable. Shortly after my return to England, a number of scholars joined together to put out in 1977 a collection of essays called *The Myth of God Incarnate*. This title seemed to a number of us to be an outrage. Scholars use the term 'myth' in at least six different ways, but the ordinary man takes the word to mean the expression, sometimes in flowery language, of that which never happened. The book's title, and the authority of the writers, seemed to make plain that the doctrine of the incarnation of God in Jesus Christ, by which the Church had lived for nineteen centuries, was now finally disproved and had to be rejected as unacceptable. This was intolerable. It was felt that at the earliest possible date not an alternative book, but an extended review of *The Myth of God Incarnate* must be made accessible to the public. The five collaborators in this scheme were a Roman Catholic bishop, an Anglo-Catholic professor, a somewhat liberal Cambridge don, an Evangelical rector, and myself as a kind of *revenant* from an antediluvian age.

I had agreed to write two chapters. It was known that Professor Macquarrie of Christ Church, Oxford, had been supplied with advance proofs so that his review of the book in the journal *Theology* might appear simultaneously with its publication. It would help to avoid delay if I could have access to those proofs. So Canon Michael Green hied away to Christ Church in search of the proofs. Professor Macquarrie explained apologetically that, having written his review, he had thrown away the proofs, but they might still be in the dustbin. So the angels looked down on the charming spectacle of the Canon and the Professor grubbing around in the rubbish; not without success, for the proofs were found, somewhat the worse for wear, but still usable. I was able to get to work at once on my chapters, in which I combined some serious thought with what I regarded as a pardonable amount of levity. Hodder & Stoughton performed miracles of expedition, and our review appeared not more than a month after the appearance of the book. Yet what had every appearance of becoming a major controversy on a par with the *Honest to God* debate very soon died down. About equal numbers of the book and the review were sold. Supporters of each side felt that a word in season had been spoken, and that was about it.

I arrived in England when the process of Prayer Book revision was fairly well advanced. I was disturbed to find that this did not consist of a thorough, scholarly and up-to-date revision (such as that which produced the 1928 version, widely used though constitutionally illegal), but of a compilation of experimental services which had been temporarily licensed for use at various points since 1967. These eventually found their home in the Alternative Service Book of 1980, but despite the best efforts of the Bishop of Derby, Cyril Bowles, and of the revision committee, to me and to many other church people, the ASB was theologically unsatisfactory, liturgically inept and stylistically deplorable. One of the worst features of the new book was the Revised Psalter, where dignified poetry seemed to have been deliberately turned into banal and pedestrian prose. I did try hard to like the new Communion rite, but I always came away with a feeling of frustration and impoverishment. What was to be done?

I found myself invited to contribute to a volume edited by David Martin and Peter Mullen, to be called *No Alternative: The Prayer Book Controversy*, in which a number of those dissatisfied with the revision would express their criticisms from a great variety of points of view. I was glad my contribution was intended to be non-controversial, simply a survey of the changes which have actually taken place since 1552 (the second prayer book of Edward VI). There is a superstition that liturgical forms can be preserved unchanged across the centuries, but in fact many changes had taken place, though for the most part unauthorised by any legal or ecclesiastical authority. I thought it important to show this, though I did feel it necessary to object to the seductive influence which Dom Gregory Dix OSB, author of *The Shape of the Liturgy*, apparently exercised in convincing leading members of the liturgical commission, and many others, that what was required was a return to the imaginary liturgical purity of the second century, as exemplified by the *Apostolic Order* of Hippolytus.

No Alternative was met by the usual mixture of praise, neglect and adverse comment. One critic described it as power politics. This seemed to me to be a wholly indefensible example of inattention, misunderstanding and unfairness, but what could be done in the time left before final decisions were taken by those who are concerned to defend the glorious Anglican tradition of liturgical worship?

A small group meeting in Oxford reached some conclusions which seemed to me to be of value. First, a change in liturgy means a change in theology. The Reformers knew this, and by changing the liturgy proclaimed the theology they wanted to proclaim. Having a general theological consensus, they could produce liturgical magnificence. In the confusion of contemporary theologies, we cannot do this. Basic theological agreement is a necessary condition of successful liturgical work. Once we know what theology we want to express, we can find the liturgical structures for it. It is no use carping at the ASB, which will be with us until 2000. Frequent repetition by congregations will reveal the flaws, something which is already happening with regard to the Rite A Eucharist.

Second, criticism is pointless unless an alternative can be found. This demands careful study of the best examples of the English language to be found in contemporary literature. There can be no turning back to the past, but there must be certain qualities of permanence, such as characterise the best English writing, and continuity with the past to enable the participant to share the splendour of the English tradition of liturgy.

These are no more than the cogitations of a sorrowful soul, who is unlikely to live to see what emerges after 2000.

Retirement meant that I was free at last to concentrate on the major task I had set myself, that of writing the history of the Church of Jesus Christ in India. By 1930 I had become aware of the fact that there was no single work of history in existence which did justice to the three great streams of tradition, the most ancient churches of St Thomas (the so-called 'Syrian Orthodox'), the Roman Catholic Church, and the Protestants. Even then I formed the hope that I might one day be able to help remedy this situation.

It was never my intention to write mission history *per se*, which seems to me to be a very dull subject. Even in *A History of Christian Missions*, despite the familiar nomenclature, my aim was to deal with one aspect of God's purpose for the whole of the human race he created. So it was my hope to deal with India as a whole, and with the Christian faith as part of the history of India as a whole. The Christian Church has existed in India for at least fifteen centuries, and Christians form the third largest religious community, after Hindus and Muslims. Christians are found in practically every part of India, though they are concentrated more in some areas than others. Their influence reaches far beyond the limits of recognised Christian communities. I was convinced that Christian history could be understood only as the interaction between the Christian understanding of God and man, and those many systems of philosophy, literature, art and religious experience which are the warp of a fabric whose weft is the long story of political, social and economic change. Attention must be paid to the manifold contacts between East and West, and to the many ways Christians attempted to make themselves at home in Indian society. Above all, the Christian historian must attempt to view events from the non-Christian side, to take account of Hindu and Muslim reactions, and to take seriously claims that it, like Islam, is an alien religion on Indian soil. For this, my experience of India and my ability to read documents in their original language were to prove invaluable. At intervals I had written drafts of chapters, and all the time I had kept reading. At last, in 1974, I felt ready to set to work properly.

The first problem was scale. I had drawn up plans for five volumes, but the current situation in the publishing world was such that three volumes was the most any publisher would be likely to consider. This meant jettisoning much material of value, if not of central importance, and reducing the detail which is often what makes a narrative readable. For the contemporary author, the art of omission ranks high among the arts that he has to practise.

I was extraordinarily fortunate in that I had chosen to retire in Oxford, where the Indian riches of the new Bodleian Library are available, supplemented by occasional forays into the India Office library in London, the archives of the missionary societies in London, and so on. In four years of work the first volume was completed, bringing the narrative up to AD 1707, the year of the death of Aurungzeb, the last of the great Moguls, and the establishment of the first Protestant mission: the Royal Danish Lutheran Mission of Tranquebar. This volume covers the beginnings of the Christian Church in India, with the tradition of St Thomas the Apostle, Thomas of Cana and merchants from Jerusalem and the Persian empire who settled mainly on the west coast, and the bishops sent by the Patriarch of Babylon to succour the Church; the dim medieval period as reported principally by Franciscan travellers; the splendid period of the Jesuit mission to the Court of the Great Moguls, and other sixteenth- and seventeenth-century Roman Catholic work; and finally the pioneering work of Robert de Nobili in Madurai, and the appearance of Protestant traders.

I had some difficulty securing a publisher because of suspicions that such a readable book could not be serious history (however many footnotes and references to original sources there were), but eventually the Cambridge University Press gave me a favourable decision. I have never had occasion to regret my choice of a publisher; it has been a pleasure to work with representatives of this noble firm, who have throughout given evidence of all that publishers ought to be.

Two more years of work enabled me to bring the story up to 1858, the year in which the British government took over direct rule of India from the British East India Company. As the years pass, the story becomes even more complicated with the internationalisation of missions, the slow emergence of genuinely Indian Churches and the crystallisation of non-Christian opposition in identifiable, organised and intensely interesting forms. No two historians will agree in their assessment, which is why one's work always has an air of impermanence. The historian can only try to do his best.

I have never found it possible to be simply an academic. If I have to analyse myself, I seem to find three predominant elements – an eager desire to know, a readiness to communicate, a willingness to share. To put it another way, I seem to find in myself elements of the student, the preacher and the pastor. I am glad to find in myself, in my ninth decade, no diminution in the eager desire to know a great many things. I am not inclined to minute and meticulous research on limited subjects; my eyes tend always to stray to wider fields. Like most Cambridge scholars, I suffer from a grave disinclination to write. I dislike the actual labour of writing, which I usually do by hand. I rarely like what I have written; by the rigid discipline of fixing a deadline, I compel myself to submit what I have written to the indignation of the press, but once it has appeared in print I rarely look at it again. Naturally it pleases me when my books continue to sell, but I always experience a little surprise that anyone should want to read what I write.

In my early days, my excessive shyness made preaching a laborious business. I have always been grateful that in the course of time this hindrance disappeared. Preaching is always hard work, especially for those who have to contend with a natural gift of fluency, but there is a great difference between pleasant tiredness which is the reward of hard work, and the emotional exhaustion in which strength is drained away. Most forms of direct communication I enjoy, such as the seminar method in Germany, and similar methods I used when teaching in India. Nothing gives me greater pleasure than to sit with a group of students, many of whom may be unbelievers, attempting to give fair answers to questions fired off at me from all directions, and not hesitating on occasion to say, 'I do not know.'

The work of a pastor is far too intricate to be written about in detail. It is essential to have a really deep interest in others, and a sincere concern for their well-being. The gift of sympathetic listening is indispensable; and without there being complete confidence that everything is confidential, no progress can be made. Then there is that rare ability, which Jesus seems always to have had, to pierce through the web of reticences and evasions to the very heart of the problem and speak an inspired word which brings illumination and release. My natural impatience made me a very slow learner in this field, but I was greatly pleased to reflect that such pastoral work increased rather than diminished with time.

These three overlapping interests led to a good deal of work in these declining years, but two concerns in particular distracted me from my resolve to stay at home and lead a quiet life. The first was my involvement, in an advisory capacity, in the new province which was formed out of the diocese of Cyprus, Egypt, Iran and Jerusalem, with Bishop Hassan Dehqani-Tafti as the first president Bishop. He was a friend of mine from his student days, and when I accepted, each of the bishops appointed me as commissary in England for his diocese. I found myself invited to sessions of the Central Synod and the Standing Committee, and perhaps proved the value of this arrangement by helping with the drafting of official letters and documents. I also had the privilege of being present at the consecration of Samir Kafiti, the greatly respected secretary of the Central Synod, as coadjutor-bishop in Jerusalem, one of the few peaceful episodes in the troubled history of these dioceses and these lands.

My sister Isabel, after a year of retirement in England, decided to make her home in India. We looked around Coonoor, where she had lived for so long, and were almost in despair of finding somewhere suitable, when there almost fell into our hands two three-roomed apartments at a very reasonable price. So she was able to settle down to a great variety of good works, with her much loved Indian adopted daughter, Anwari, now married and the mother of two thriving little boys. (Incidentally, to conform with Indian law, Anwari is technically the owner of our Indian home.) This seemed to lay on me an obligation, if possible to visit India once in two years, to help keep the family together.

These visits were always pleasant, but it is almost impossible for me to relax and rest in South India. The knowledge of the Tamil language, though I do not speak it as well as I used to, is a key that opens many doors, and I am always glad to be of service, when possible. The welcome given by Tamil people to their friends is always more than an adequate reward.

For many years I kept away from my old haunts in Tirunelveli – the ghosts of departed bishops can be a great nuisance. I did accept an invitation to the centenary, in 1978, of the birth of our first Indian bishop, V. S. Azariah, my friend, in whose cathedral I was consecrated bishop. Tom Garrett, the then Bishop of Tirunelveli, kindly invited me to take a confirmation in the village where I had once baptised 250 people in a single afternoon, and which now, against my will, bears our name, Neillipuram. More important was a visit in 1980 for the second centenary of the diocese – the first church register of what is now the cathedral church bears the date 1780. Everything was beautifully arranged, and I felt that those three days really marked an epoch in the history of the church. I had the privilege of preaching at the main centenary service, at which it was reckoned 5,000 worshippers received Communion. I was immensely impressed by the orderliness of everything, and especially by the devout and reverent demeanour of the women. I took as my text: 'There is a river, the streams whereof shall make glad the city of God' (Ps. 46:4). Our river, the Tamraparni, is sacred, because alone among the rivers of that part of India, it never dries up. Sometimes it is no more than a trickle, but there is always some water flowing. Then, far away in the mountains, the rains fall, the river comes down in flood, and the fields are irrigated to the furthest possible point. The reader will not find it hard to work out the parallel which was in my mind; in two centuries the church has had many bad patches, but it has always been there, and when the rains of new spiritual life have fallen, it has been able to receive what the Lord graciously gives to bring about renewed fertility.

At a later point in the celebrations, we went down to the river, and, at a point where there was sufficient water, we adhered to the correct understanding of the Anglican rubric and baptised 500 people by immersion. The parishes had been saving up their candidates for baptism to bring about this memorable total. The arrangements were not quite well enough made to ensure the solemnity of the occasion, but with twelve of us taking part, the service did not take too long, and this was an event which I think no one present will ever forget.

What is one to say about the Church of South India, the product of so many years of hard labour at an earlier period of these recollections? The first impression, I think, when moving about among the churches, is of their immense stability. Of 99 per cent of the membership of these churches, it is possible to say, with a good deal of certainty, that it is inconceivable that they should ever go back to Hinduism or Islam. It has been said by some Indian historians that Indian churches came into being with the presence of Western imperialistic power, and that with the disappearance thereof, the churches would also disappear. Events have clearly proved the erroneousness of these prophecies; there are Indian churches rooted in the soil and rooted in Christ Jesus as Lord; their continued existence seems as well assured as that of the older and wealthier churches in the West.

In many places, however, the churches seem to have settled down too easily to a state of peaceful coexistence with the non-Christians. The strong evangelistic impulses seem to exist outside the mainline Churches or in the independent Indian missionary societies, such as the National Missionary Society of India, which Azariah founded. Yet when all is said and done, they have survived the transition to independence, political and ecclesiastical, and in hundreds of centres the Word of God is preached week in, week out, and the sacraments are administered. The best among the Indian Christians are fully the equals, spiritually and intellectually, of their opposite numbers elsewhere in Asia or the West. The Church of South India stands as a challenge to the whole of Christendom to do likewise. I do not feel my labours were in vain. When I am in South India, I feel that these are my own people; I do not regret any of the years spent in their service.

In my life, days of routine, even of monotony, are more numerous than those which deserve to be marked with a white stone. In eighty years, I have experienced many rough passages. But these concluding years have been for the most part a peaceful time, with a good deal of time for meditation and developing the inner life. Many people, young as well as old, I have found, feel the need to

talk to an older friend about the many troubles which beset believer
and non-believer in these anxious days. Perhaps increase in age does
bring some wisdom, of which the young feel themselves able to take
advantage without a feeling of humiliation. I find myself enormously
rich in friends – of all ages, in many parts of the world, and of many
different avocations. When they turn up to see me, or write, I am
delighted. If they do not make contact, I spend more time praying
for them. As the years pass, I find less and less need to pray for
myself. All I ask for, really, is courage – to carry out the duty as
long as it is required, not to grow impatient, to work as long as I
can while it is day, for night comes when no man can work – but
after all there is no night time but, as John Donne was tireless in
insisting, only the unchanging radiance of an everlasting day.

Notes

1 BEGINNINGS

1   What conditions in Tinnevelly were really like in this period can be seen in Amy Carmichael's *Things as They Are*, which she had to publish herself in 1898 because it exploded the myth of success in Tinnevelly.
2   Founded in 1875 in the Punjab by Dayananda Sarasvati, the Arya Samaj began as a conservative reaction to Christian missions and is strictly theistic and renounces idolatry. The Vedas are the only sacred book acknowledged, and there is a ceremony for accepting Christian converts back into Hinduism, which other sects do not have. Its founder did renounce caste, but this was not maintained.
3   Bengali assistants could have been obtained from the Free Church of Scotland Mission. They supplied CMS missions across the Punjab, as well as running their own clinics, and there is nothing in the archives of the Free Church of Scotland Mission (Duff correspondence to 1875, etc.) to suggest that they lacked spirituality. It is really a case of unconscious racism. Also, such missions never paid Indian staff an adequate wage, expecting the same degree of sacrifice from them, and failing to understand Indian family obligations.
4   It should be noted that his depression lifted when his amoebic dysentery was diagnosed and cured. Dysentery has a very depressive effect.

4 APPRENTICE THEOLOGIAN

1   'Scheduled castes and scheduled tribes' are those social groups listed in the legislation of 1952 as requiring special protection and help as a result of their degraded condition and the discrimination against them within the Hindu religion.
2   Miss G. I. Mather's comment, as secretary, is that this should

have been January 1936; but the meeting, held triennially, might have been postponed for some reason. Bengt Sundkler, *The Church of South India* (Lutterworth Press, 1954), pp. 262f., gives the year as 1936.

3   This was because, until 1940, the bishops were paid by the government as part of the establishment set up by the East India Company Act of 1812. They were originally Company employees whose job was to supervise the work of chaplains. They did not start ordaining Indian clergy until 1824, and the powers to license and deploy missionaries were worked out gradually during the period 1830–60. Many chaplains treated missionaries like an inferior class. Many of the bishops, however, were missionary-minded and gave full support to missions.

4   There is in fact an Anglican attitude to bishops in the Constitution. It says, in effect: the Church of South India has the historic episcopate, but you can believe what you like about the nature of the ministry.

5 APPRENTICE BISHOP

1   Neill's account of the reasons for his leaving India presents the church historian with grave problems. From village catechists in the most rural parts of Tinnevelly, to present-day professors of theology, the common view is that he had to leave because of instances when he struck his clergy. (Even today, for a European missionary to shout at an Indian is an unforgivable sin, because of the colonial overtones.) Contemporaries believe Westcott flew south to tell Neill to resign, not to ask him to stay, but the truth of this will probably never be known. That Neill was under very great stress, severely depressed, and ill, is clear, and one incident in which he lost control could have been magnified out of all proportion.

Much more serious allegations have also been made; these cannot be discussed here, but they will have to be tackled by any future biographer.

8 PROFESSOR IN EAST AFRICA

1   Neill seems to have provoked this debate. See Elliott Kendall, *The End of An Era: Africa and the Missionary* (London: SPCK,

1978), which contains an objective account of the debate, including an analysis of John Gatu's speech in which he criticised Neill's statement that African Christianity is superficial and therefore a constant flow of foreign missionaries is necessary.

2   Neill originally finished this chapter with the following words:
    I have no intention whatever of retiring in the ordinary sense of the term. In fact I hope to settle down again to serious work, after the constant interruptions attendant on eleven years of university work. There are a number of books which I still hope to write. If I manage to complete in ten years all that I have in mind to do, I may then perhaps sit down to write my autobiography, and that would be a far more difficult and exacting task than the setting down of these somewhat random recollections of grace abounding to the chief of sinners over a period of rather more than seventy years.

                                        Nairobi, August 1973

Select Bibliography
of works by Stephen Neill

Anglicanism (Harmondsworth: Penguin Books, 1958)
Bhakti: Hindu and Christian (Madras: CLS, 1974)
Bible Words and Christian Meanings (London: SPCK, 1970)
Christ, His Church and His World (London: Eyre & Spottiswoode, 1948)
The Christian Character (London: Lutterworth Press, 1955)
Christian Faith and Other Faiths: The Christian Dialogue with Other Religions (London: Oxford University Press, 1961)
Christian Faith Today (Harmondsworth: Penguin Books, 1955)
Christian Holiness (London: Lutterworth Press, 1960)
Christian Missions: A History (Harmondsworth: Penguin Books, 1964)
Christian Partnership (London: SCM Press, 1952)
The Christian Society (London: Nisbet & Co., 1952)
The Christian's God (London: Lutterworth Press, 1954)
The Church and the Christian Union (Oxford: Oxford University Press, 1968)
Colonialism and Christian Missions (London: Lutterworth Press, 1966)
Creative Tension (London: Edinburgh House Press, 1959)
Crises of Belief: The Christian Dialogue with Faith and No Faith (London: Hodder & Stoughton, 1984)
The Cross Over Asia (London: Canterbury Press, 1948)
The Eternal Dimension (London: Epworth Press, 1963)
A Genuinely Human Existence: Towards a Christian Psychology (London: Constable & Co., 1959)
A History of Christianity in India: The Beginnings to AD 1707 (Cambridge: Cambridge University Press, 1984)
The Interpretation of the New Testament 1861–1961 (Oxford: Oxford University Press, 1964)
Jesus Through Many Eyes: An Introduction to the Theology of the New Testament (London: Lutterworth Press, 1976)
On the Ministry (London: SCM Press, 1952)
One Increasing Purpose (London: Bible Reading Fellowship, 1969)
Salvation Tomorrow (London: Lutterworth Press, 1976)
The Story of the Christian Church in India and Pakistan (Grand Rapids, MI: Eerdmans, 1970)
The Supremacy of Jesus (London: Hodder & Stoughton, 1984)
Towards Church Union 1937–52: A Survey of Approaches to Closer Union Among the Churches (London: SCM Press, 1952)

The Unfinished Task (London: Lutterworth Press, 1957)
What is Man? (London: Lutterworth Press, 1960)
What We Know About Jesus (London: Lutterworth Press, 1970)

As a Contributing Editor

Stephen Neill, John Goodwin, Arthur Dowle (eds), *Concise Dictionary of the Bible* (London: Lutterworth Press, 1967)

Stephen Neill, Gerald H. Anderson, John Goodwin, (eds), *Concise Dictionary of the Christian World Mission* (London: Lutterworth Press, 1970)

Ruth Rouse and Stephen C. Neill (eds), *A History of the Ecumenical Movement 1517–1948* (London: SPCK, 1954)

Stephen Neill and H.-R. Weber (eds), *The Layman in Church History, A project of the Department of the Laity of the World Council of Churches* (London: SCM Press, 1963)

Stephen Neill (ed.), *The Ministry of the Church: A review by various authors of a book entitled* The Apostolic Ministry (London: Canterbury Press, 1947)

Stephen Neill, (ed.), *Twentieth Century Christianity: A Survey of Modern Religious Trends by Leading Churchmen* (London: Collins, 1961)

As a Contributor

Michael Green (ed.), *The Truth of God Incarnate* (London: Hodder & Stoughton, 1977)

David Martin and Peter Mullen (eds), *No Alternative: The Prayer Book Controversy* (Oxford: Basil Blackwell, 1981)

Index

Note: Stephen Neill is abbreviated to SN